Primer on Structured Programming
Using PL/I, PL/C, and PL/CT

WINTHROP COMPUTER SYSTEMS SERIES
Gerald M. Weinberg, *editor*

CONWAY AND GRIES
  An Introduction to Programming: A Structured Approach Using PL/1 and PL/C-7, Second Edition

CONWAY AND GRIES
  Primer on Structured Programming Using PL/I, PL/C, and PL/CT ·

CONWAY, GRIES, AND ZIMMERMAN
  A Primer on PASCAL

GELLER AND FREEDMAN
  Structured Programming in APL

Future Titles

CONWAY, GRIES, AND WORTMAN
  Introduction to Structured Programming Using PL/1 and SP/k

ECKHOUSE AND SPIER
  Guide to Programming

FINKENAUR
  COBOL for Students: A Functional Approach

GELLER
  Structured Programming in FORTRAN

GILB
  Software Metrics

GREENFIELD
  The Architecture of Microcomputers

WEINBERG AND GILB
  Humanized Input: Techniques for Reliable Keyed Input

WEINBERG, GOETZ, WRIGHT, AND KAUFFMAN
  High-Level COBOL Programming

WILCOX
  Compiler Writing

PRIMER ON STRUCTURED PROGRAMMING
Using PL/I, PL/C, and PL/CT

Richard Conway
David Gries
Cornell University

contributions by
Charles G. Moore III

Winthrop Publishers, Inc.
Cambridge, Massachusetts

Library of Congress Cataloging in Publication Data

Conway, Richard Walter
  Primer on structured programming using PL/I, PL/C,
and PL/CT.

    (Winthrop computer systems series)
    Includes index.
    1. PL/I (Computer program language) I. Gries,
David, joint author. II. Title.
QA76.73.P25C66   001.6'424   75-40276
ISBN 0-87626-688-X

CONTENTS

Preface xi

Part I. Fundamental Concepts 1

1. The Computing Process   1
    1.1 Examples of Programs   2
    1.2 Analysis of a Problem and Design of a Program   8
    1.3 Translation to a Programming Language   11
    1.4 Confirmation of Program Correctness   13
    1.5 Loading, Translation and Execution of Programs 14
    Exercises   16

2. Variables   17
    2.1 Identifiers   19
    2.2 Values   21
    2.3 Type Attributes   22
    Summary   23
    Exercises   24

3. Assignment of Value   25
    3.1 The Assignment Statement   26
    3.2 Arithmetic Expressions   28
    3.3 Built-in Functions   31
    3.4 Assignment from External Data   33
    Summary   37
    Exercises   38

4. Flow of Control   40
    4.1 General Program Structure; Executing Programs   40
    4.2 Repetitive Execution   44
    4.3 Conditional Execution   53
    4.4 Tracing Execution   64
    4.5 Initialization and Exit Problems   66
    Summary   71
    Exercises   72

5. Multiple-Valued Variables   76
    5.1 Arrays of Subscripted Variables   76
    5.2 Variables with Multiple Subscripts   80
    5.3 Declarations of Arrays   82
    5.4 Program for the Example of 1.2.1   84
    Summary   88
    Exercises   89

6. Display of Results   93
    6.1 Display of Values of Variables   93
    6.2 Titling and labeling Results   95
    Summary   99
    Exercises   100

7. The Execution of Programs   101
    7.1 Loading, Translation and Execution   105
    7.2 Analysis of Printed Output   105

8. The Declaration of Variables   111
    8.1 The Form of a Declaration   111
    8.2 Implicit Declaration and Default Attributes   114
    8.3 Initial Values   115
    Summary   117
    Exercises   118

9. Character-Valued Variables   119
    9.1 Declaration of Character Variables   120
    9.2 String Assignments and Expressions   121
    9.3 String Assignment from External Data   127
    9.4 Display of Character Values   128
    9.5 An Example   128
    Summary   130
    Exercises   131

Part II. Program Structure   133

1. Basic Program Units   137
    1.1 The Compound Statement   138
    1.2 The Repetition Unit   139
    1.3 The Alternative Selection Unit   141
    1.4 Units and Levels   148
    1.5 Termination of a Unit   149
    1.6 The Well-Structured Program   152
    Summary   161
    Examples   162

2. Program Schemata   164
    2.1 A Classification of Very Simple Programs   169
    Examples   172

Part III.   Program Development   175

    1.   The Phases of Development   175
         1.1 Clarification of the Problem   176
         1.2 Design of a Solution Strategy   179
         1.3 Choice of Data Structures   182
         1.4 Writing the Program   183

    2.   Examples of Program Development   185
         2.1 Printing a Sublist   185
         2.2 Searching a List   186
         2.3 Ordering a List   191
         2.4 An Accounting Problem   195
         2.5 Scanning for Symbols   207
         2.6 Interactive Computing Systems   210
         Exercises   219

    3.   General Design Considerations   224
         3.1 Top-Down Development   224
         3.2 Sources of Ideas for Refinement   233
         3.3 Handling Data Errors   242

    Part II and III References   246

Part IV.   Independent Subprograms   249

    1.   External Procedures   249
         1.1 A Procedure to Interchange Values   252
         1.2 Definition of a Procedure   256
         1.3 Procedure Calls   262
         1.4 Nested Procedure Calls   271
         1.5 STATIC Variables   275
         Summary   278
         Exercises   279

    2.   The Uses of Procedures   285
         2.1 Subroutines   285
         2.2 Control Sections   286
         2.3 Sectional Independence   289
         Examples   294
         Exercises   296

Part V.   Program Testing   297

    1.   Errors, Testing and Correctness   297
         1.1 The Meaning of Correctness   298
         1.2 Types of Errors   300

    2.   The Design of Test Cases   302
         2.1 Testing I.1.1e   303
         2.2 Multiple Test Cases   304
         Examples   306
         Exercises   308

x

3. Automatic Diagnostic Services   309
    3.1 Detection of Errors   309
    3.2 Automatic Repair of Errors   314
    3.3 PL/C Post-Mortem Dump   316
    Examples   318

4. Explicit Diagnostic Facilities   320
    4.1 Flow Tracing   320
    4.2 The Memory Dump   326
    Summary   328
    Examples   329
    Exercises   332

5. Modular Testing   336
    5.1 Bottom-Up Testing   336
    5.2 Independent Test of Procedures   336
    Examples   339
    Exercises   342

6. Testing Habits and Error Patterns   343
    6.1 Complete Development and Testing Process   344

7. Testing with an Interactive System   347
    7.1 Program Entry and Syntax Checking   347
    7.2 Terminal Procedure of PL/CT   348

APPENDICES

A. Summary of PL/C Subset Used in _Primer_   357

B. Operating Procedures for PL/C-7   361
    B.1 Program Deck Structure   361
    B.2 Program Options   362
    B.3 Card Formats   365

C. The PL/CT Interactive System   369

PL/I and PL/C References   382

INDEX   383

PREFACE

Learning to use a computer to help solve problems is a surprising and widely misunderstood task. You actually need learn very little about the computer. You do have to learn to write with reasonable fluency in a language that is intelligible to a computer, and while this is at first somewhat formidable, it actually is not very difficult. What is difficult is to learn to organize solutions to problems so that they can be described in such a "programming" language.

This book explains the rules of a portion of a programming language called PL/C, which is a dialect of another language called PL/I. But well over half of the book is devoted to the technique of analyzing a problem and designing a solution. We strongly feel you should be properly started on these matters, even though it means using time that might otherwise be spent learning more pieces of the language. Nevertheless the language presented here is very substantial and useful in itself, and unless you become seriously interested in programming you probably won't need anything more.

This Primer is based on our "Introduction to Programming (2nd Edition)". The Primer consists of most of the material of Parts I to V of the Introduction, with more detailed explanations and many more examples. The section numbers are (almost) identical in the two books so that users of the Primer can readily turn to the Introduction for expanded reference, and users of the Introduction can turn to the Primer for expanded explanation of elementary topics. Many of the exercises in the Primer have been drawn from the Introduction. When an exercise number is underlined in the Primer it means that essentially the same exercise is in the Introduction. We plan to use the two books as alternative texts in the same introductory course. Students who are encountering computing for the first time would use this Primer; students with some previous contact with computing would probably prefer the deeper coverage of the Introduction.

Both books represent a philosophy and style that has come to be known as "structured programming". This emphasizes concern with the manner in which a program is organized. It implies that some program constructions are more effective than others, just as one English essay could be far more effective than another even though both are grammatically correct.

Since the publication of the <u>Introduction</u>, Cornell University has released a new interactive version of PL/C called PL/CT. This is completely compatible with PL/C, but permits the use of an individual terminal rather than a card reader and line printer. Charles Moore, the designer of PL/CT, has contributed sections to the <u>Primer</u> concerning the use of an interactive computing system.

We are also indebted to Steven Worona, Manager of the PL/C project at Cornell, and Professor David Levine of the Department of Computer Science at Rutgers University, for many helpful suggestions.

The <u>Primer</u> was produced by an editing program run on the IBM 370/168 of Cornell's Office of Computer Services.

Ithaca, N. Y.   R. Conway
                                                 D. Gries

**Primer on Structured Programming
Using PL/I, PL/C, and PL/CT**

PART I   FUNDAMENTAL CONCEPTS

Section 1   The Computing Process

We are concerned with the process by which a digital computer can be used to solve problems -- or at least aid in the solution of problems. This involves learning to:

1. Choose problems that are appropriate to the computer's abilities,   and   describe   the   problem   requirements, conditions, and assumptions clearly and precisely.

2. Design a solution to a problem ·and describe it in a language intelligible to a computer. This description is called a "program", while the process of producing a program is called "programming". Programming is a systematic, level-by-level process in which the original problem description, usually given in a combination of English and mathematics, is translated into a "programming language". This process must also transform a statement of objectives -- what is required -- into a description of an executable procedure -- how the objectives are to be achieved. A third aspect of the transformation is to make explicit and precise those portions of the problem description that are implicit and rely on the intuition, common sense, or technical knowledge of the reader, since the computer is completely lacking in these virtues.

3. Confirm the correctness of the program. This means demonstrating in as convincing a manner as possible that the program precisely satisfies the problem requirements.

The selection of appropriate problems is as difficult and important as the analysis and programming, but it is impossible to discuss this issue until one has some understanding of the nature of computing systems and their special abilities. However, two initial observations might be helpful. Firstly, problems for which computer assistance is sought are generally of substantial magnitude. There is non-trivial effort involved in the mechanics of obtaining computer assistance, and if the problem is simple, not repetitive, and not likely to recur, computer assistance may cost more than it is worth. One must bear this in mind even though the examples that will be used for instruction will necessarily be short and often trivial. They are presumably used to develop a competence which will be useful for subsequent attack on real and substantial problems.

Secondly, the computer can only assist in the solution of problems which can be stated very precisely and for which a detailed and precise method of solution can be given. Roughly speaking, one cannot expect a computer to perform a process that could not be performed by a human--if he lived long enough. The digital computer permits a tremendous increase in the quantity of symbols that may be considered, in the precision and reliability with which they will be manipulated, and above all in the speed with which the process will be carried out. But in principle the computer is only performing operations that could be carried out by a human being. It is true that the orders-of-magnitude differences in volume, speed and reliability combine to produce spectacular capability, but the fundamental process is simple and not unlike what a human could perform.

For example, a computer can "play chess" only because the game of chess has been described to the computer as an elaborate symbol manipulation task. On the other hand, a computer cannot be requested to "solve the vehicle emission problem" because no one has as yet figured out how to describe this problem strictly in terms of symbol manipulation. As another example, a computer is not infrequently asked to "select a date for a person from a set of potential candidates" and sometimes produces rather humorous recommendations. The source of the humor lies not in the computer's execution of the process but in the fact that no one really knows how to precisely describe this complex selection process.

1.1 Examples of Programs

At this point we present a number of simple examples of computer programs. These problems are unrealistically simple but they will give you some idea of what a program looks like. We will give some explanation after each example, but we do not intend these to be complete explanations. This is just to give you a general idea of what the end product of the programming process is going to be. The details will be explained in later sections.

(1.1a)

```
*PL/C ID='T. WILCOX'
/* ADD 2 INTEGERS AND PRINT RESULT */
ADD2: PROCEDURE OPTIONS(MAIN);
    DECLARE SUM FIXED DECIMAL;
    SUM = 245 + 73;
    PUT LIST(SUM);
    END ADD2;
*DATA
```

The meaning of each line in (1.1a) is the following:

Line 1 announces that the program is written in PL/C, which is a special form of a language called PL/I. Most computing systems accept programs in many different languages and the programmer must indicate which of these he is using. Line 1 also gives the name of the programmer.

Line 2 is a "comment" that describes the purpose of the program. It is ignored by the computer and has no effect on the execution of the program. It is provided solely to make the program easier for a human to read. In PL/I any text between the symbol pairs /* and */ is a comment.

Line 3 marks the beginning of the program, and indicates that the name of this particular program is ADD2.

Line 4 causes space to be set aside in the computer to receive integer values (called "FIXED" in PL/I). This space is given the name SUM so it can be referred to elsewhere in the program.

Line 5 causes the two numbers 245 and 73 to be added together and their sum stored in the space named SUM.

Line 6 causes the value in the space named SUM to be printed out. The external result of executing ADD2 would be the printing of a line with the number 318 on it.

Line 7 marks the end of the program ADD2.

Line 8 is a "control card" that separates the program statements preceding from the program data following. ADD2 doesn't happen to need any data so none follows this control card.

The program ADDTWO in (1.1b) is a minor variation and improvement upon (1.1a). ADD2 just adds two specific numbers -- 245 and 73 -- that are given as constants in the program. ADDTWO will add any pair of integers that are given as data following the program. It is shown in (1.1b) with the same two numbers that were used in (1.1a), but ADDTWO could be rerun with some other pair of integers as data. ADDTWO requires three different spaces to be set aside in the computer -- two to store the input data, and one to store the answer.

(1.1b)
```
*PL/C ID='T. WILCOX'
 /* ADD 2 INTEGERS AND PRINT RESULT */
 ADDTWO: PROCEDURE OPTIONS(MAIN);
     DECLARE (VALUE1, VALUE2, SUM) FIXED DECIMAL;
     GET LIST(VALUE1, VALUE2);
     SUM = VALUE1 + VALUE2;
     PUT LIST(SUM);
     END ADDTWO;
*DATA
245, 73
```

    ADDFIVE in (1.1c) adds five integers, and prints the data   as
well as the answer with appropriate titling.

(1.1c)
```
*PL/C ID='T. WILCOX'
 /* ADD 5 INTEGERS AND PRINT VALUES AND SUM */
 ADDFIVE: PROCEDURE OPTIONS(MAIN);
     DECLARE (VALUE1, VALUE2, VALUE3, VALUE4,
         VALUE5, SUM) FIXED DECIMAL;
     PUT LIST('INPUT DATA ARE:');
     GET LIST(VALUE1); PUT SKIP LIST(VALUE1);
     GET LIST(VALUE2); PUT SKIP LIST(VALUE2);
     GET LIST(VALUE3); PUT SKIP LIST(VALUE3);
     GET LIST(VALUE4); PUT SKIP LIST(VALUE4);
     GET LIST(VALUE5); PUT SKIP LIST(VALUE5);
     SUM = 0;
     SUM = SUM + VALUE1;
     SUM = SUM + VALUE2;
     SUM = SUM + VALUE3;
     SUM = SUM + VALUE4;
     SUM = SUM + VALUE5;
     PUT SKIP(2) LIST('SUM IS:');
     PUT SKIP LIST(SUM);
     END ADDFIVE;
*DATA
245, 73, -62, 0, 1094
```

    ADDN in (1.1d) is a more complicated variation of this adding
program, but it is more realistic and more typical of the
programs you will soon be writing. Each of the previous
examples was designed to accommodate a certain fixed number of
input values -- two in (1.1a) and (1.1b), and five in (1.1c).
ADDN is designed to accommodate a <u>variable</u> number of values. In
each use of this program the number of values to be given is
provided as the first item of data.

(1.1d)

```
*PL/C ID='T. WILCOX'
/* ADD N INTEGERS, LISTING VALUES AND SUM */
ADDN: PROCEDURE OPTIONS(MAIN);
    DECLARE (QTY,      /* QTY OF VALUES */
             VALUE,    /* INDIVIDUAL DATUM */
             SUM)      /* SUM OF VALUES */
                  FIXED DECIMAL;
    PUT LIST('INPUT DATA ARE:');
    SUM = 0;
    GET LIST(QTY);
    SUM_LOOP: DO WHILE(QTY > 0);
        GET LIST(VALUE);
        PUT SKIP LIST(VALUE);
        SUM = SUM + VALUE;
        QTY = QTY - 1;
        END SUM_LOOP;
    PUT SKIP(2) LIST('SUM IS:');
    PUT SKIP LIST(SUM);
    END ADDN;
*DATA
5, 245, 73, -62, 0, 1094
```

With the data given (1.1c) and (1.1d) produce exactly the same results. The difference that makes (1.1d) enormously more useful is that it could be run with the data shown above replaced by the following:

```
*DATA
7, 21, 56, 4, -1, 3, 106, 5
```

(1.1d) could also be run with data that began:

```
*DATA
2500, 23, 705, -301, 0, 521, ...
```

While a program like (1.1c) could be written to compute the sum of 2500 numbers it would be a very tedious process. On the other hand, (1.1d) is already capable of performing this task with no change at all.

ADDN illustrates the concept of a "loop" -- a sequence of instructions that are repeated on different items of data. This idea is central to the computing process. This is what makes it possible for you to write a program of several dozen or several hundred instructions -- and have the computer execute several thousand or several million instructions in accomplishing the desired task. Stripped to the barest essentials what we are going to try to do is teach you to think of <u>problems in terms of loops</u>, and to <u>describe these loops in a language intelligible to computers</u>.

We will give one further example of the loop concept before proceeding with details. Suppose one has to determine the <u>maximum</u> of a list of <u>non-negative numbers</u>. The program to do this uses a process that is repeated for each of the numbers. It will get the next number on the list and compare it to the greatest number encountered "so far". If the new number is greater than the previous maximum it will be retained as a new maximum. The number of numbers is also counted.

This process is straightforward, once it gets started, but some provision is required to make it work properly on the first repetition. Secondly, so that the end of the list can be recognized we will append a dummy number (in this case a -1, which cannot occur in the actual data). The program will check each value as it is read to see if it is this dummy value.

The names of locations in which values are to be stored by this program are:

    NUMBER -- the current number being processed
    MAXNBR -- the maximum number encountered "so far"
    COUNT -- the number of times the central process has been
              repeated "so far"

The complete program for this problem, written in PL/C, is given in (1.1e). The numbers at the beginning of each line of (1.1e) are not part of the program but have been added so we can readily identify each line for discussion.

The printed "output" produced by executing this program with the data on line 27 is:

    NUMBER OF VALUES = 5
    MAXIMUM VALUE =   12

This example will often be referred to in later sections. In particular, Section 1.4 discusses its "correctness".

(1.1e)

```
1)    *PL/C ID='ROBERT CONSTABLE'
2)      /* FIND MAXIMUM OF NON-NEGATIVE INPUT NUMBERS */
3)      /* DUMMY -1 ADDED AT END OF INPUT FOR STOPPING TEST */
4)      FINDMAX: PROCEDURE OPTIONS(MAIN);
5)
6)        DECLARE (NUMBER,        /* THE CURRENT NUMBER */
7)                 MAXNBR,        /* MAXIMUM VALUE SO FAR */
8)                 COUNT)         /* NBR OF NUMBERS SO FAR */
9)                  FIXED DECIMAL;
10)
11)       MAXNBR = -10;    /* INITIAL VALUE LESS THAN ALL */
12)                        /* POSSIBLE DATA VALUES */
13)       COUNT = 0;
14)       GET LIST(NUMBER);
15)
16)       MAX_LOOP: DO WHILE(NUMBER ¬= -1);
17)           COUNT = COUNT + 1;
18)           IF NUMBER > MAXNBR THEN MAXNBR = NUMBER;
19)           GET LIST(NUMBER);
20)           END MAX_LOOP;
21)
22)       PUT LIST('NUMBER OF VALUES =', COUNT);
23)       PUT SKIP LIST('MAXIMUM VALUE =', MAXNBR);
24)       END FINDMAX;
25)
26)    *DATA
27)     3, 7, 12, 2, 6, -1
```

The loop that represents the heart of (1.1e) is given in lines 16 through 20. Line 16 describes the conditions under which the loop is to be repeated -- that is, while the value of NUMBER is not equal to -1. Lines 11 through 14 are called "initialization" -- instructions intended to set up the loop so it operates properly on its first repetition. Lines 5, 10, 15, 21 and 25 are blank and are inserted to visually indicate the separate sections of the program. They have no effect on its execution.

1.2 Analysis of a Problem and Design of a Program

The starting point of the analysis process is a problem statement. For example:

Find the mode and median of a list of numbers.

Solve the annular heat transfer equation for various different coefficients.

Find the roots of the displacement equation for various given coefficients.

Determine the frequency with which each different word appears in a list of words.

Encrypt the following text using a given letter-substitution table.

Problem statements are usually given in English or in a hybrid combination of English and the symbols used in that problem area (mathematical symbols, for example). They generally deal with things -- temperatures, automobiles, colors, voters, dollars, etc. -- that cannot themselves be stored and manipulated by a computer. They are also usually stated in terms of commands that are not intelligible to a computer -- words like "solve", "find", "choose", etc. Typically a problem statement is at least initially somewhat vague and imprecise. This is partly because of a tacit reliance on the knowledge and common sense of the human reader, but also partly because the originator has often not completely formulated the exact requirements.

The end point of the process is a program -- a procedure that can be executed on a computer and that represents a solution to the initial problem. This process of transforming a problem description into a program has several different aspects:

1. A translation of language -- from English/mathematics to a programming language (PL/I, FORTRAN, COBOL, etc.)

2. A conversion from a statement of objectives -- <u>what</u> is to be done -- to an executable procedure -- <u>how</u> the task is to be accomplished.

3. The definition of symbols (variables) in a program to represent the real-world objects of the problem. For example, a variable in one problem might represent the status of one of the squares of a chess board; in another problem, the number of dollars in a bank account; in another, the temperature at a particular point on a rocket nozzle.

4. The elimination of all vagueness, imprecision and ambiguity in the description. There is never any vagueness in a computer program -- every program always tells the

computer _precisely_ what to do. The trick is to construct a program whose execution _exactly_ solves the particular problem in question.

Only on very simple problems (such as those found in programming textbooks) is there much chance of success if one starts immediately to write the program -- no matter how experienced one might be at programming. On problems of any size and complexity a systematic analysis of requirements, and design of the overall structure of the program, should precede any attempt to write program statements. It is convenient to view this process as a "top down" or "level by level" analysis of the problem. The top level is the initial problem statement; the bottom level is a complete program; the number of intervening levels depends on the complexity of the problem.

Generally the second level is just an elaboration of the problem statement -- an attempt to make complete and precise exactly what is required. This is often achieved by a dialog between the programmer and the "customer" -- the owner of the problem. This dialog can involve questions like the following:

1. In what form will the data be supplied?

2. Are there reasonable limits on the values of data that may be expected?

3. How will the end of the data be recognized?

4. What errors in the data should be anticipated? What action should be taken?

5. What form should the output take? What labelling and titling should be provided?

6. What precision (number of significant figures) of results is required?

7. What changes in problem statement are likely to occur during the lifetime of the program?

There may also be questions and discussion of alternative strategies of solution. There might be two approaches -- one more costly to design and program, and the other more costly to execute. The customer must provide information to guide such a choice.

While the objective of this dialog is ostensibly to convey information to the programmer, to help him to understand exactly what has to be done, very often the customer discovers that the problem is not yet well-formulated, and that he himself is not sure, in detail, what he wants done.

The levels occurring after this refinement of the problem statement are generally designed to accomplish two tasks:

1. To <u>break</u> <u>up</u> big problems into little problems -- which in turn are attacked by this same approach.

2. To <u>reduce</u> the <u>commands</u> from English to programming terms. That is, "find", "solve", etc. must be reduced to "read", "print", "assign", "repeat", and then eventually to GET, PUT, DO -- the <u>statements</u> of a programming language.

1.2.1 <u>An Example of Initial Problem Analysis</u>

Suppose a problem statement (level 1) is given in the following way:

1. Given a list of numbers, print the first, second, third numbers, etc., but stop printing when the largest number in the list has been printed.

After some discussion this statement of the problem might be refined to something like the following (level 2):

2. A set of not more than 100 integers, each greater than zero, is given on punched cards. A dummy value of zero will be added to denote the end. The ordering with respect to value is unknown. Print a column of numbers corresponding to these numbers in the order given. Begin printing with the first and terminate when the last number printed is the maximum of the entire set. For example, if 1, 7, 3, 9, 5, 0 are given, the output should be:

```
1
7
3
9
```

It should be evident that it is not known how much printing is to be done until the position of the maximum value is determined, and this cannot be done until the last number of the input data has been examined (since the last could be the maximum). Therefore either the numbers will have to be read twice (once to determine the position of the maximum, and a second time to print the values) or the numbers will have to be read once and stored in the computer memory for later use. Card reading is a relatively slow and expensive operation for a computer, so the second strategy is preferable. This could lead to a third level of description:

3.1 Read a sequence of 100 or fewer positive integers from cards until a zero value is encountered; store these integers in memory, preserving order.

3.2 Find the position of the integer with maximum value in this sequence.

3.3 Print the early values of the sequence, from the first
to the maximum value, one per line.

One would then attack each of these subproblems to reduce the
commands -- "read from cards" and "store in memory" in the first
subproblem -- to the corresponding statements in the target
programming language. We have carried this analysis far enough
here to give the general idea -- the program is completed in
Section 5.4.

1.3 Translation to a Programming Language

The level-by-level transformation of the problem description
is complete when the entire description is in a language that is
intelligible to a computer. However, there is no single,
universal programming language into which all problem
descriptions are translated; there are literally hundreds of
programming languages in use today. The choice of language will
have some influence on the manner in which a problem is solved,
and   may   have   considerable   influence on the difficulty
experienced in obtaining a solution. Some programming languages
have been designed to facilitate solution of certain classes of
problems; they exchange generality for convenience for   a
particular type of problem. For example, some languages are
designed to favor problems in business data processing; some are
oriented toward mathematical computations. Some exist to serve
different makes and models of computers, and many exist just
because there are wide differences of opinion as to what a
programming language should look like. Opinions on the subject
are strongly held, and debated with a fervor normally reserved
for politics or religion.

Although there are hundreds of languages in use, a relative
handful dominate the field. The most widely used programming
language today is COBOL, which was designed for business data
processing problems. (The name comes from the first letters of
the words: COmmon Business-Oriented Language.) The most widely
used language for engineering and scientific computation is
called FORTRAN (from FORmula TRANslation).   Both of these
languages were developed in the 1950s -- a long time ago in this
field. Other important languages are ALGOL, APL, BASIC, LISP,
PASCAL, PL/I, and SNOBOL.

PL/I, the language on which this book is based, was developed
in the mid-60s in an attempt to serve both the scientific and
data processing areas with a single language. The price of this
generality is complexity, and PL/I is a very complicated
programming language. It was also designed in something of a
hurry, and in some respects the design is not as nice as it
could be. Nevertheless, PL/I is the most "modern" of the
programming language in general use. However, it has not come
close to displacing either FORTRAN or COBOL from widespread use.

In many places in this book we are critical of PL/I (or at least apologetic). It is far from an ideal language and we hope that someday it will be replaced by a better language. But the other possible choices for introductory instruction seem to us to have even more serious flaws. (The only reasonable alternative is a language called PASCAL, but this is not yet widely used.) You should try to keep an open mind on the matter and realize that PL/I represents just one compromise solution to the problem of devising a programming language. Not until you have significant experience in several different languages will you be able to appreciate the relative strengths and weaknesses of PL/I.

For most students, the first programming language learned will be only the first of several. This is true both because there are many specialized languages available for various different areas of application, and because progress in the field of computer science should eventually lead to languages that will replace all those in use today. There is a distinct advantage in learning to program in a language like PL/I or PASCAL, rather than FORTRAN or COBOL, even though you might sometime have to use one of the latter. PL/I and PASCAL are more recent designs, and as such are more representative of current thinking on the subject. Future languages will certainly bear more resemblance to PL/I than to FORTRAN. Secondly, PL/I and PASCAL are more general in their capability. All of the programming concepts present in FORTRAN and COBOL are present in PL/I and PASCAL -- but not conversely. It is easier for a student who initially learned PL/I to later learn FORTRAN or COBOL on his own than it would be to proceed in the opposite order.

We will not attempt to present all of PL/I in the Primer, and fortunately you do not have to learn all of the language in order to use part of it. One can learn a subset of the language initially, and then add topics as required to meet new and more challenging tasks. Unfortunately this partitioning of the language is not at all clean, and the unused and unseen portions sometimes intrude upon the initial subset, causing surprising results and forcing one to do things in ways that are not easily explained. One critic compared PL/I to a Swiss Army knife with 100 blades -- there is unquestionably a blade for whatever one might want to do, but there is some risk that in using one blade you will cut yourself with another.

PL/C is a special dialect of PL/I, developed at Cornell University. Some features have been deleted from PL/I and others added in order to facilitate introductory instruction. PL/C is also provided with a translation program which is much more efficient for short programs than its PL/I counterpart, and which provides considerably more help to a neophyte programmer. For the most part PL/C and PL/I are identical, and the student can ignore the differences.

It may seem that teaching PL/I is the major goal of this book, but this is not really the case. Our primary goal is to teach programming principles; to teach problem solving and programming methodologies which can be used no matter what programming language is being used.

1.4 Confirmation of Program Correctness

Confirming correctness of a program requires a convincing demonstration that the program actually satisfies the precise requirements of the problem. This phase of the computing process is typically so badly neglected by writers and teachers that it seems as if they regard the possibility of mistakes as somewhat remote and distinctly embarrassing. In any but the most trivial task many errors will be made in each phase. Anyone who intends to use a computer might as well accept this unfortunate fact and make plans to systematically track down the inevitable errors. Very typically more than half of the total time, effort, and cost of the computing process is devoted to testing and "debugging" the program -- and yet in spite of this effort the process is not often completely successful. An embarrassingly large fraction of programs that are declared to be complete and correct by their authors still contain latent flaws. This situation is so prevalent and serious that a large proportion of society today has diminishing confidence in the computing process. Computers are increasingly thought to be somehow inherently unreliable, but in almost all cases the true fault lies in a program that was ill-designed and/or inadequately tested.

The program given in (1.1e) was deliberately constructed to illustrate this point. It works perfectly for the data given, and also for many other sets of data, but line 9 restricts this program so that it can only successfully handle integer values. However, there is nothing in the problem statement that suggests that the program will only be used for integer values. As a consequence any time this program is used for data that are not all integers (that is, values like 17.3), it is likely to produce incorrect results without even warning the user that he is in trouble. The program "works" for some sets of data but it is not a correct program for the given problem.

Many people seem to regard testing in a negative sense -- as an extra phase of the computing process that must be performed only if there appear to be errors. In fact, it is an essential part of programming. One must take positive action to try and force latent errors into revealing themselves -- so that one can reasonably infer correctness if no errors are exposed by determined and persistent testing. This must be done not just for a few simple test cases, but for maliciously contrived test cases that exercise a program more strenuously than is likely to occur in actual use. Contriving sufficiently difficult test cases is something of an art in itself. While testing is listed

as   a   separate   phase   of   the   programming process it actually
pervades   the   entire   process,   and   if   all   consideration   of
determining   correctness   is   postponed   to the final phase it will
almost   surely   be   unsuccessful.   It   is   essential   that   the
necessity of demonstrating correctness be considered at the time
that the overall structure of the program is chosen and that
provision for testing be incorporated in the program as it is
written, rather than as an afterthought.

1.5 Loading, Translation and Execution of a Program

When the program is complete and data have been prepared,
both must be transmitted to the computer. The usual means of
communication is the "punched card" or "IBM card".   A machine
called   a   "keypunch" is used to encode information in a card by
punching holes in it. Each different character has a different
pattern of holes; each character in the program and data is
represented by the pattern in one vertical column of the card.

An alternative method of introducing information into a
computing system is by means of a "terminal" directly connected
to the computer. The keyboard of such a terminal is like that
of the keypunch -- but instead of punching holes in a card which
will later be detected by the computer, the terminal transmits
its information directly to the computer, essentially as the key
is struck. This has the virtue of immediate response -- the
user is notified of errors after each line of the program, and
sees results as the program is being executed. Although the use
of such terminals is increasing rapidly it is still more
expensive than using punched cards, and the majority   of
introductory instruction still uses cards. For our purposes it
makes little difference which type of access is used and we will
speak of program lines, input lines, and cards almost
interchangeably.

The key point in understanding the loading and execution of a
program is the timing of the reading of the cards. The card
deck consists of two parts -- the program (lines 1 to 25 of
(1.1e)) and the data (lines 26 and 27). The cards for the
entire program are read initially -- before any execution of the
program begins; the cards for the data are not read until
specifically called for during execution of the program.   The
computer does not read a card and execute the statement on it,
read the next card and execute, etc.   Instead it reads the
entire program, creates a copy of the program in "memory", and
then begins execution with the first statement of the program.
In the course of execution the "card read" statements (such as
lines 14 and 19 of (1.1e)) will cause the data cards to be read.

The initial loading of the cards of the user's program is
controlled by execution of another program called a "compiler"
(or sometimes a "translator" or "interpreter").   As   the   user-
program cards are read a translation is performed by the

compiler with the result that the "copy" of the program in memory, while functionally equivalent to the initial program, is very different in appearance. During this translation the compiler checks the program statements for "syntactical" (grammatical) errors and reports these to the user. If any errors are discovered during this loading-translation process most compilers will halt after loading and refuse to initiate execution of the user-program; a few compilers will effect some repair of minor errors and permit execution to begin. Most users will become aware of the existence of a compiler only through this error checking and will never have occasion to see the strange form their program has assumed in memory.

The printed output for a program can also be divided into two parts, corresponding to the loading and execution phases described above. During loading, a copy of the user-program is printed, including announcement of any errors discovered. This much of the printing is automatic -- a service performed by the compiler. Further printing will be done only as called for by the "output" statements (such as lines 22 and 23 of (1.1e)) of the program. If the user fails to include any such statements there will be no output during execution and the results of the computation will never be known.

Section 1 <u>Exercises</u>

   The following all refer to the program example given in (1.1e). You cannot be expected to answer all of these questions at this point, but attempting to do so should be interesting and educational.

<u>1</u>. What would have to be done to cause this program to obtain the maximum of the following eight numbers:
      2, 4, 6, 15, 3, 9, 7, 9

<u>2</u>. What would happen if the program were used to find the maximum of the following nine numbers:
      6, 45, -3, 14, 0, 2, -1, 52, 143

<u>3</u>. What would happen if line 27 looked like the following:
      5, 5, 5, -1, -1, -1

<u>4</u>. What would happen if the order of lines 17 and 18 were reversed? Lines 13 and 14? Lines 18 and 19?

<u>5</u>. Suppose the problem definition were broadened to require the program to work for negative as well as positive numbers. What changes would have to be made?

<u>6</u>. How could the program be changed to obtain the <u>minimum</u> rather than the maximum of the numbers?

<u>7</u>. How could the program be changed to produce both the <u>maximum</u> and the <u>minimum</u> of the numbers?

<u>8</u>. What would happen if line 17 were accidentally left out (say the card was dropped) before the program was submitted to the computer? Line 19? Line 23?

<u>9</u>. What would happen if line 22 were replaced by the following line?

      /* PUT LIST('NUMBER OF VALUES =', COUNT); */

<u>10</u>. How could the program be changed to produce the sum of the numbers in addition to the maximum?

<u>11</u>. What would happen if line 2 were replaced by the following line:

      /* COMPUTE THE PRETTIEST OF THE GREEN NUMBERS */

and no other change were made in the program?

<u>12</u>. Construct a set of test data (a replacement for line 27) that would cause the program to produce incorrect results.

Section 2   Variables

A program describes how a set of values is to be manipulated. However, the description deals not directly with these values, but with entities called "variables". For example, instead of writing

      2 + 3   one could write   X + Y

and make arrangements so that "X had the value 2" and "Y had the value 3". The difference is essentially the same as that between arithmetic and algebra, and yields roughly the same advantage. One gains the ability to specify a procedure which may be applied, without change in the written form, to many different sets of values.

A variable is a place or location in the memory of a computer which can hold a value, and to which a name may be attached. The following line pictorially represents three variables:

    A ——> 20   TOTAL ——> 456.003   ACCOUNT ——> -20.7

The first variable is named A and has the value 20 in its location (on its line). The second variable is named TOTAL and has the value 456.003. Variable ACCOUNT has the value -20.7.

We often omit the arrow in the pictorial representation, if the name and location are close enough so that no misunderstanding can take place:

    A 20   TOTAL 456.003   ACCOUNT -20.7

A variable is relatively permanent -- it is created when execution of a program begins and lasts until execution is completed. The value is generally more transient, and may change often during execution. At any given instant, a variable contains a single, specific value, which is referred to as the current value of the variable. The current value of the variable named A above is 20. The phrase "current value of the variable named A" is long, and is often shortened to "value of A". A's value changes whenever a different value is placed in the location named A.

It is important to clearly distinguish between creating a variable and assigning a value to a variable. A variable is created only once -- when a physical location in the memory of

the computer is set aside to hold its value. The creation
process is also referred to as "declaring" or "defining" a
variable.   Once a variable has been created it may have a value
assigned to it, and that value may be frequently changed.   This
"assignment process" is the topic of Section 3.

In PL/I, "declarations" give the name to be attached to each
variable and describe the kinds of values each variable can
contain. The actual assignment of memory locations is performed
automatically by the computing system and the programmer need
not be concerned with it. He must only give a declaration for
each variable. For example,

DECLARE (MINVALUE, CUM_SUM) FIXED DECIMAL;

defines two different variables named MINVALUE and CUM_SUM, each
of which can contain a decimal integer between -99999 and
$+99999$.   The declaration does not automatically assign an
initial value to the newly created variables; hence they exist,
they have a location ready to receive a value, but have not as
yet received one.

Variables play an important role in programs. Each variable
contains a value with a specific meaning -- for example, the
minimum value of a list of numbers, or the cumulative sum of a
list of numbers. Knowledge of the variables and their meaning
is essential for any person trying to understand a program.   In
order to help the reader, declarations for all variables are
placed at the beginning of the program, before any statement
which uses the variables.

It is a good practice to describe the use of each variable
with a "comment".   In PL/I, "/*" marks the beginning of a
comment and "*/" marks the end. The comment may contain any
characters on the keypunch -- except the sequence "*/" which
would be interpreted as the end of the comment. For example:

```
DECLARE (MINVALUE,    /* MIN VALUE OF X'S SO FAR;  >= 0 */
         CUM_SUM)     /* SUM OF X'S PROCESSED SO FAR */
        FIXED DECIMAL;
```

Clarity and precision in defining the role of each variable
in a program is of vital importance in producing a correct and
understandable program. Many programming difficulties can be
traced to fuzziness in the meaning of key variables. We find it
useful, when asked to help "debug" (find the mistakes in) a
program, to start by asking such questions as:

"What does this variable represent?"
"Does it have the same meaning everywhere in the program?"
"What are the extreme limits on the values it may contain?"

This approach is aided by following a consistent practice of
supplementing the declaration of each variable with comments.

2.1 Identifiers

The sequence of characters that forms the name of a variable is called an "identifier". Each programming language has a set of rules that control the choice or construction of identifiers. These rules sometimes seem arbitrary, and at this stage it is best just to accept and learn them. Among the most widely used programming languages -- FORTRAN, COBOL, PL/I and ALGOL -- the rules are quite similar, but just enough different to be a nuisance to the unwary programmer. In almost any language, however, an identifier can consist of a letter, followed by a sequence of other letters and digits, and this is the kind of identifier you will use most often. PL/I also allows the underscore "_" to be used anywhere after the first letter. For example, the following are all valid PL/I identifiers:

I	SUM	MAXIMUM
X	VALUE	TEMP_VALUE
X2	FEB3_DATUM	TEMPERATURE
LOCATION	X_PTR	JUNE_5_1975

You should choose variable names that suggest the role the variables play in the program. While it may seem clever to name variables after girls or flowers, it doesn't help to make a program understandable. For example, although SUSAN is a legal identifier, using SUSAN as the name of a variable which holds the average of 10 numbers is not helpful. AVERAGE or AVG would be better since it would help to indicate the role of the variable.

The "keywords" of PL/I should not also be used as identifiers. Using these words for the names of variables makes a program hopelessly hard to understand. PL/I will actually permit this dubious practice, but PL/C is more restrictive. In PL/C the keywords that begin the various different statements have been "reserved" and are not allowed to be used as identifiers. These words are:

ALLOCATE	EXIT	OPEN
BEGIN	FLOW	PROC
CALL	FORMAT	PROCEDURE
CHECK	FREE	PUT
CLOSE	GET	READ
DCL	GO	RETURN
DECLARE	GOTO	REVERT
DELETE	IF	REWRITE
DO	NOCHECK	SIGNAL
END	NOFLOW	STOP
ENTRY	ON	WRITE
THEN	TO	WHILE
ELSE	BY	NO

The first part of the list consists of "statement keywords" -- words that begin a PL/C statement. For the statements that you will be using -- DO, IF, GET, PUT, etc. -- it is easy to remember that these words are reserved. However, a problem will arise when you happen to choose an identifier that coincides with some statement you have never been told about. For example, there is an EXIT statement in PL/C, but we do not use it in this Primer. Nevertheless, the word EXIT is reserved and you cannot use it as an identifier. We do not expect you to memorize this list -- just remember that such a list exists. Then when PL/C objects to one of your identifiers with an error message about "misuse of a reserved word", check back here to see if you happen to have stumbled onto part of the PL/C language that you were never told about. (remember the "Swiss Army Knife" of Section 1.3!)

The second part of the reserved word list -- THEN, ELSE, etc. -- are "auxiliary keywords". They do not begin a statement, but are used in the body of some statement. There are well over one hundred such auxiliary keywords in the full PL/C language, but it was not considered practical to reserve them all. Hence only the six listed above absolutely cannot be used as identifiers. This means that the other auxiliary words used in the Primer, which are listed below, could be used as identifiers as far as PL/C is concerned, but should never be used as identifiers as a matter of good practice.

CHAR	FIXED	OPTIONS
CHARACTER	FLOAT	PROCESS
DATA	INIT	SKIP
DEC	INITIAL	STATIC
DECIMAL	LIST	VARYING
EDIT	MAIN	

To use any keyword as an identifier would just make statements harder to understand. For example, the following are legal, but unnecessarily confusing:

```
DECLARE (LIST, SKIP) FLOAT DECIMAL;
PUT SKIP LIST(LIST, SKIP);

DECLARE (FIXED, DECIMAL) FLOAT DECIMAL;
```

It is not as if there were a shortage of potential identifiers -- the loss of these few words should not seriously inhibit your creativity.

2.2 Values

Programming languages allow a variety of different types of values to be stored in variables. The most important types for ordinary numeric computation are signed "integers" (..., -2, -1, 0, 1, 2, ...) and "real numbers" -- such as 20.3, -463.2, .000043, and 4.3×10^{-5}. (Note that the last two real numbers look different but represent the same quantity.) Since each value is placed in a physical location in the computer's memory, there must obviously be a limit on the number of digits allowed. Eventually one must become aware of such limits, but they are not necessary for our present purposes. We assume here that all numerical values will be represented in the computer in conventional decimal notation, and that a reasonably adequate number of digits is permitted in each value.

Constant values are often written in a program. In general, they can be written in their usual form:

   -20   10365   .4   0.15   -.0043   49.65

Alternatively, constants can be written in "scientific" or "exponential" form:

   -20E0   1.0365E+4   4E-1   0.15E0   -4.3E-4

The exponent "E0" following the number specifies that the fractional number is to be multiplied by 10^{0}, which is 1. In general, one can put any integer after the "E" to represent a power of 10. Thus 125 could be alternatively written as 12.5E1, 1.25E2 or .125E3. As another example, the following are all equivalent values:

   4.3E-5   .43E-4   .000043E0   .00000043E+2

This is often called "floating point format", since the position of the decimal point "floats" depending on the exponent following "E".

A value may also be a string (or sequence) of characters, such as 'ITHACA'. Variables with such "character" values are discussed in Section 9. The values "true" and "false" are important in certain contexts and we will discuss them in Section 4. But for the moment we will consider only values that are integers and real numbers.

2.3 Type Attributes

In PL/I each variable is restricted to one particular type of value. The value may change, but the type of value (like the name) is permanent for the life of the variable. For example, if variable COUNT is defined to hold only integer values it might at different times have values such as 2, 1501, -3 and 0, but it could never have values such as 20.3 or 'JONES'.

The properties that determine the type of value that can be stored in a variable are called "attributes" of the variable. We represent attributes by putting them in brackets [and] after the variable. The following examples illustrate how the names, values and attributes of variables will be indicated in the text:

> MAX   20 [fixed decimal]   MAX may only contain integers
>   (e.g. -3, 0, 1, +5)
>
> TB42 -.002 [float decimal]   TB42 may contain real numbers
>   (e.g. 20.3, 20, -.82)
>
> Z4   -20.0 [float decimal]   Z4 may contain real numbers

"FIXED" and "FLOAT" are PL/I's way of saying "integer" and "real", respectively. The term DECIMAL means that the value of MAX will be represented in the computer memory in the decimal number system. (The reader may have assumed that this would be the case, but in fact, the "binary number system" is extensively used in computing.)

A variable always has some particular set of type attributes. When we neglect to mention them it is only because the type of value is not relevant to the point under discussion -- not because attributes do not exist for that variable.

In PL/I type attributes are specified by listing them in the declaration of the variable. For example:

> DECLARE MAX FIXED DECIMAL;
>
> DECLARE TB42 FLOAT DECIMAL, Z4 FLOAT DECIMAL;

When several variables have the same set of attributes, the names may be given in parentheses, and the attributes given only once. For example, the following declarations are equivalent:

> DECLARE (TB42, Z4) FLOAT DECIMAL;
>
> DECLARE TB42 FLOAT DECIMAL, Z4 FLOAT DECIMAL;

Section 2 <u>Summary</u>

1. A variable is a named location in computer memory into which
a value may be placed.

2. All variables to be used in a procedure should be defined
(created) by specifying their names and type attributes in
declarations placed at the beginning of the program.   The name
should be chosen to reflect the role the variable plays in the
program, and the declaration should be supplemented by a comment
that describes the role exactly and clearly. The keywords of
the language -- GET, DECLARE, LIST, etc. -- should not be used
as names of variables.

3. We will use the type attributes FIXED DECIMAL for integer
values and FLOAT DECIMAL for real values.

4. Numeric constants may be written in a program in either
conventional form: 32, -61, 4.3, 0.198, or in exponential form:
3.2E1, -61E0, 4.3E0, 198E-3.

Section 2 Exercises

Exercises 1 to 4 concern the following variables:

        LAST_ONE   -20 [fixed decimal]

        ANSWER   -30.2 [float decimal]

        BAD20   0 [fixed decimal]

        COSINE   -30.2 [float decimal]

        TEXT   30.0 [float decimal]

        MINIMUM +30.2 [float decimal]

1.   a) What is the current value of variable ANSWER?
     b) What is the current value of variable COSINE?
     c) What is the current value of variable TEXT?
     d) Which variables have the value -30.2?
     e) Which variables have the value 20?

2.   Which of the following values:

          -30, -30.1, 0, .0050, 43891, 43891.5, 4.3891E4

     can be stored in variable:

          a) LAST_ONE ?
          b) BAD20 ?
          c) MINIMUM ?

3.   Define the term "variable".

4.   Write a PL/I declaration for the variables given above.

5.   Consider the following declaration:

     DECLARE POSTOT FLOAT DECIMAL, /* TOTAL OF X'S > 0 */
        (SUM, COUNT) FIXED DECIMAL; /* SUM OF Y'S, NO. OF PTS*/

     a) Write a declaration that is exactly equivalent but does
     not use parentheses.

     b) Write three separate declarations (one for each
     variable) that are exactly equivalent to the single
     declaration given.

Section 3   Assignment of Value

The computing process involves the assignment of values to
variables.   The basic assignment process, in any programming
language, has two distinct stages:

1.   The production of a new value.

2.   The assignment of that new value to a variable.

The construction for specifying a new value is called an
"expression". Examples are:

26   X   Y+1   (X3+ABC)/ZZZ

where X, Y, X3, ABC, and ZZZ are variable names.   In the
evaluation of an expression the current value of each variable
referenced is used, but this does not change the values of those
variables.   Regardless of the length and complexity of an
expression the result of its evaluation is a single value.

The second stage of the assignment process is the assignment
of the new value. A logical form for describing this would be:

X + Y —> Z

A precise description of the execution of this process is:

Evaluate the expression X + Y, by adding a copy of the
current value of the variable named X to a copy of the
current value of the variable named Y. Store this sum as
the new value of variable Z (replacing and destroying
whatever previous value Z may have had).

Note that the values of X and Y are only copied and are not
changed in the process. Typical values of X, Y and Z before and
after such an assignment are:

before: X 1   Y 3   Z 2

after: X 1   Y 3   Z 4

3.1 The PL/I Assignment Statement

The syntax for an "assignment statement" in PL/I is:

variable name = expression;

The expression on the right gives the formula to obtain a new
value; the variable on the left receives this new value. The
"=" denotes the assignment process (instead of the arrow used on
the previous page) and the ";" denotes the end of the statement.
The following are examples of PL/I assignment statements:

```
A = 4.3;
Z = X + 1;
I = I + 1;
LOW = CTR - 1.43E-1;
SUM = 0;
SUM = A1 + A2 + A3;
SUM = SUM + NUMBER;
TEMP = (A3 + B4)/BASE;
RATIO = (A+B) / (C+D);
SUP = Z3 + P / (A + B/4E0);
```

Unfortunately, the form of the assignment statement tempts
you to read it in the usual left-to-right manner, and the
similarity to an algebraic equation is also deceptive.   (This
difficulty is not peculiar to PL/I, since most programming
languages use a similar form.)   For example, consider the
assignment of a value to the variable X:

X = Y;

This should be read "get a copy of the value of Y, and store it
in X".   It might seem that this is equivalent to saying "let X
take on the value of Y", but consider the following statement:

X = X + Y;

It is clearer to read this as "add together the current values
of X and Y, and store the result in X", than it would be to say
"let X take on the value of X plus the value of Y".

As mentioned above, the use of "=" improperly suggests a
similarity to an algebraic equation. The assignment statement
is a command to perform a sequence of actions, whereas an
equation is a statement of fact. If equality between the left
and right sides already existed, there would be no point in
writing the statement at all, since no action would be required.
One might try to salvage this "equation interpretation" by
suggesting that it is a command to "make the equation become
true".   However, this interpretation just cannot explain
examples such as:

X = X + Y;   and   W = W + 2;

The assignment statement <u>must</u> be considered a command to perform <u>two distinct actions</u>: first, <u>produce</u> a value from the expression on the right; second, <u>assign</u> this value to the variable on the left.

   Note that the two sides of an assignment statement are not symmetric in role. The following two statements have different meanings, although as equations they would be equivalent:

        X = Y;   and   Y = X;

   Assignment statements are executed in the order in which they appear (reading from left to right, and top to bottom). Consider the two statements

        X = Y + Z;   and   Z = X + Y;

   Assuming a set of initial values, the effect of executing these statements in one order would be:

        before   X 3   Y 5   Z 2
        after   X = Y + Z;   X 7   Y 5   Z 2
        after   Z = X + Y;   X 7   Y 5   Z 12

With the same initial values the effect of executing these same statements in the opposite order would be:

        before   X 3   Y 5   Z 2
        after Z = X + Y;   X 3   Y 5   Z 8
        after X = Y + Z;   X 13   Y 5   Z 8

   As a further example, consider the task of interchanging, or "swapping", the values of two variables. Suppose we want to

change   A 3   B 5

to   A 5   B 3

Since there is no single statement in PL/I to perform this, it must be done with a sequence of assignment statements. Let T be a variable not used in the program so far. The following uses T as a "temporary" variable to accomplish the swap:

        /* SWAP VALUES OF A AND B */
          T = A;
          A = B;
          B = T;

Given the initial values of the variables as shown below, we show the contents of the variables after execution of each statement. Question marks ??? are used as the value of a variable that has not yet been assigned a value.

before		A	3	B	5	T	???
after T = A;		A	3	B	5	T	3
after A = B;		A	5	B	5	T	3
after B = T;		A	5	B	3	T	3

The comment /* SWAP VALUES OF A AND B */ summarizes the actions of the group of statements that follow it (and are indented with respect to it). When reading a program that includes this segment, to find out <u>what</u> is being performed we read the comment <u>instead</u> of the statements indented underneath it. The detailed statements under the comment need be read only to find out <u>how</u> the swap is being performed. Comments are entirely for the benefit of human readers; they have no effect on the execution of the program by the computer. When used properly, comments make it significantly easier for us to read and understand a program, but when badly used they obscure rather than clarify.

3.2 <u>Arithmetic Expressions</u>

Expressions are used in many different contexts in programs. Wherever they occur they always have the same basic purpose -- to provide a <u>formula by</u> which a value can be obtained. The simplest expressions are constants, like 3 or 20.6E0, or variables, like I or TOTAL. In general, an expression can include a number of terms or "operands", and "operations" by which the operand values are to be combined to yield a single value. Examples of expressions are shown in the right side of the assignment statements of Section 3.1. (The semi-colon ends the assignment statement and is not part of the expression.)

3.2.1 <u>Symbols for Operations</u>

The PL/I symbols for arithmetic operations are:

    +   for addition
    -        for subtraction, or to indicate negation
    /   for division
    *   for multiplication
    **   for exponentiation   (X^2 is written as X**2)

The symbol for an operation is often called an "operator". The * operator is used for multiplication in most programming languages, because all the familiar means of indicating multiplication lead to confusion and ambiguity. (For example, a period could get confused with a decimal point -- would 2.34.5 mean 2.34 times 5 or 2 times 34.5?) Similarly, a double asterisk (with <u>no</u> intervening blank) is used to denote exponentiation because there is no way to indicate on a punched card that one symbol is to be elevated.

Other operations operate on non-numeric values. For example, the operations performed on string-valued variables are described in Section 9.

3.2.2 Precedence of Operations

Some concern must be given to the order in which arithmetic operations are performed. For example, should the expression

        A + B * C

be evaluated as A+(B*C) or (A+B)*C? The difference is obviously important.   For example, if A, B and C have values 2, 3 and 4, respectively A+(B*C) evaluates to 14 while (A+B)*C evalutes to 20.

In any expression, however complicated, a lavish enough use of parentheses will remove any possible ambiguity. However, to avoid too many parentheses, PL/I has conventions corresponding to normal algebra to determine the order in which operations are to be performed. For example, in algebra:

$$a + bc, \qquad a - b + c, \qquad -a^2$$

mean $a + (bc), \quad (a - b) + c, \quad -(a^2)$

and not $(a + b)c, \quad a - (b + c), \quad (-a)^2.$

The PL/I rules for evaluation of an expression are:

1.   Expressions in parentheses are evaluated first, from the innermost set of parentheses to the outer.

2.   Subject to rule 1, the order of operations is:
            first: exponentiation (**) and negation (-)
            next: multiplication (*) and division (/)
            last: addition (+) and subtraction (-)

3.   Sequences of operations in the same category under rule 2 are evaluated:
            exponentiations and negations - right to left
            multiplications and divisions - left to right
            additions and subtractions - left to right

    For example:

        X**Y**Z is equivalent to X**(Y**Z)

        -X**Y   is equivalent to -(X**Y)

        X/Y*Z   is equivalent to (X/Y)*Z

        X-Y+Z   is equivalent to (X-Y)+Z

<u>PL/I will always follow these rules</u>, whether you want it to or not! If you give an expression

        X + Y * Z

PL/I will multiply the values of Y and Z first, and then add the value of X to the product. If you want the addition to be performed first you must override this inherent precedence with parentheses by writing

        (X + Y) * Z.

If you prefer not to learn these rules you can get along by always using enough parentheses to make the required order explicit -- but this sometimes takes a lot of parentheses.

3.2.3 <u>Conversion of Values</u>

PL/I is <u>usually</u> quite accommodating with regard to the conversion of values between FIXED and FLOAT forms. FIXED and FLOAT variables, and conventional and exponential constants can all be used in the same expression. When the operands of an arithmetic operator are of different type (one FIXED and the other FLOAT) the non-FLOAT operand will be converted to FLOAT form. (Actually, a <u>copy</u> of the value is converted.) For this purpose, a conventional constant (even one with a decimal point) is considered to be in FIXED form and an exponential constant is in FLOAT form.

However, there are some surprises. One that causes trouble is the fact that a FIXED variable will only accept an integer value no matter what kind of value is produced by the expression on the right side of the assignment statement. For example, if variable INDEX is FIXED, the statement

        INDEX = -17.3;

is legal (no error warning) but upon execution INDEX becomes -17. The value -17.3 has been "truncated" to -17 by dropping the digits to the right of the decimal point. This truncation <u>may</u> be intended by the programmer, but if not, it is a particularly insidious kind of error. The program could be tested on data which are all integers, and work satisfactorily. Then later, if it is used for data that are not all integers, this supposedly correct program could give incorrect results.

Surprises may occur with multiplication and division when constants alone appear as operands. For example, the expression 25 + 1/3 yields the value 5.333333 in PL/I, and .333334 in PL/C (and an "overflow" error in either). The reasons for this are complicated, and we will not go into them here; they have to do with PL/I's unconventional way of dealing with precision of arithmetic values. Avoid the problem by making sure that <u>at least one operand of a division is a variable in FLOAT form</u>.

3.3 Built-in Functions

Some common "functions" are used so often in programming that
they have been included in the language. (This is only a
convenience since the task of each of these functions could be
accomplished by explicitly writing all the statements needed to
evaluate the function.) For example, to obtain the square root
of the value of variable X or of an expression X+Y/Z, write

     SQRT(X)   or   SQRT(X+Y/Z)

The expression whose square root is sought is called the
"argument" of the function.

This functional form can be used as an operand in an
expression, just as one would use a variable:

```
X + SQRT(Y)
SQRT(TEMP - SQRT(T4K/PRESSURE))
B4 * (SQRT(SQRT(J3) + R2PEAK) + SIDE4)
```

Another function gives the maximum of a set of values:

```
MAX(A,B)
```

yields a value equal to the greater of the values of A and B.
The MAX function may have a long list of arguments, and these
may be expressions as well as variables:

```
MAX(A,B,C)
MAX(X+Y, 0, QLOW/4.5E0)
MAX(A, MAX(B,C))   is equivalent to   MAX(A,B,C)
MAX(A**B, SQRT(ZTOP), MEAN)
```

Similarly the MIN function obtains the minimum of its arguments.

The built-in functions included in a language depend heavily
on the problem area for which the language is designed.
FORTRAN, designed primarily for scientific and engineering
computation, has a different set of built-in functions from
COBOL, which was designed for business data processing problems.
PL/I, which was intended to be used in both of these areas, has
a particularly large collection of built-in functions. A
partial list of PL/I built-in functions is given below. This
includes most of the functions commonly needed in introductory
programming examples. For a complete list, consult a PL/I
reference manual, or Appendix A in our Introduction.

ABS(x) -- The result is the absolute value of x.

ATAN(x) -- The result (FLOAT) is the arctangent, in radians,
      of x.

COS(x) -- The result (FLOAT) is the cosine of x, where x is
      expressed in radians.

COSD(x) -- The result (FLOAT) is the cosine of x, where x is expressed in degrees.

EXP(x) -- The result (FLOAT) is e**x, where e is the base of the natural logarithm system.

FLOOR(x) -- The result is the largest integer not greater than x.   FLOOR(3.5) is 3; FLOOR(-3.5) is -4.

LOG(x) -- The result (FLOAT) is the natural logarithm of x. x must be greater than 0.

LOG10(x) -- The result (FLOAT) is the common logarithm of x (base 10).   x must be greater than 0.

LENGTH(s) -- See Section 9.2.2.

MAX(x1,x2,...,xn) -- The result is the maximum value of the arguments x1, x2,..., xn. The result will be FLOAT if at least one argument is FLOAT; otherwise the result is FIXED.

MIN(x1,x2,...,xn) -- The result is the minimum value of the arguments x1, x2,..., xn. The result will be FLOAT if at least one argument is FLOAT; otherwise the result is FIXED.

MOD(x,y) -- The result (FLOAT if either x or y is FLOAT) is the remainder when dividing x by y. If x and y have different signs, the operation is performed on their absolute values, and the result is then ABS(y)-remainder. For example, MOD(29,6) is 5, while MOD(-29,6) is 1.

SIN(x) -- The result (FLOAT) is the sine of x, where x is expressed in radians.

SIND(x) -- The result (FLOAT) is the sine of x, where x is expressed in degreees.

SQRT(x) -- The result (FLOAT) is the square root of x.   x must be greater than or equal to 0.

SUBSTR(s,f,l) -- See Section 9.2.2.

TAN(x) -- The result (FLOAT) is the tangent of x, where x is expressed in radians.

TAND(x) -- The result (FLOAT) is the tangent of x, where x is expressed in degrees.

Problems can arise in distinguishing between a function name and a variable name. One could prohibit the use of the function names as variable names, but this would force the programmer to memorize a list of about 90 names he could not use for variables, including such useful ones as HIGH, INDEX, LOW, LENGTH, ALL, SUM, MAX, MIN, COUNT, DATE, and TIME. To avoid this, PL/I requires only that the same name not be used as a variable and a function in the same part of the program. That is, if you are using the SQRT built-in function you cannot use SQRT as a variable name, but if you are not using the COUNT function (and perhaps didn't know that there was such a function) you can use COUNT as a variable name. The declaration of such a name as a variable indicates that it will not be used as a built-in function.

3.4 Assignment from External Data

Evaluation of an expression generates a new value in terms of values that are already in the computer memory. One also needs a mechanism to enter values from outside the computer. Execution of an "input" statement causes an auxiliary device -- such as a punched card reader, a magnetic tape reader, or a typewriter terminal -- to deliver one or more values to the memory of the computer. The form of the simplest input statement is

> GET LIST(variable-names, separated by commas);

An example is:

> GET LIST(AMOUNT);

Its execution causes the next value to be read from the data list which is given on cards after the program, and assigned to variable AMOUNT. The value is assigned using the same rules as in an assignment statement; if AMOUNT is a FIXED variable the value is truncated to an integer. Execution of the statement

> GET LIST(X, Y);

would cause the next two values to be read (from the data list) and assigned to X and Y, respectively.

Recall (from Section 1.5) that the cards bearing data at the end of the program are not read automatically into memory as the program is being loaded. Loading ends with the last card of the program body, and the cards bearing data wait in the card reader, to be read if and when the program calls for them by executing GET statements. The cards supply a list of values; the reading process moves through this list from left-to-right, one card to the next, as demanded by the execution of GET statements. Each value is read only once from this list. Suppose there are three GET statements in a program, where all variables are FLOAT DECIMAL:

```
...
GET LIST(BASE, HEIGHT);
...
GET LIST(WIDTH, TEMP, TIME);
...
GET LIST(LIMIT);
...
```

and the data list for this program is:

```
          *DATA
          17.5
          83.72
(3.4a)    23.05
          76
          2314
          964.122
```

When the first GET statement is executed the first two values are read from the data list (two values because there are two variables listed in the statement) and 17.5 becomes the value of BASE and 83.72 becomes the value of HEIGHT. When the next GET statement is executed the next three values are read; 23.05 is assigned to WIDTH, 76 to TEMP and 2314 to TIME. When the third GET is executed 964.122 is read and assigned to LIMIT.

A total of six values are read in by the three GET statements and exactly six values are provided in the data list. If more than six had been provided, the extra values would simply have been ignored since the program never calls for them to be read. This could be intentional -- the amount of data processed might depend upon some test the program performs upon the early values. This could also happen by accident if the programmer did not properly coordinate his input statements and data list.

The opposite condition is more common; a GET statement is executed and an inadequate number of data values remain on the list to satisfy all of the variables in the GET. Different languages react to this situation in different ways. It is essentially an error, but is often considered a legitimate way to stop execution. (The PL/I "ENDFILE condition" is a neat way of handling this situation, but we have elected not to use it in the Primer.) In order to detect the end of the data from within the program, we often add some marker value at the end of the actual data. This should be a value that is clearly recognizable -- it cannot be a possible data value -- so that the program can test for it after each GET statement. This technique was used in the example of (1.1e).

An alternative way of recognizing the end of a data list is to provide an initial control value that specifies the length of the list. This technique was illustrated in (1.1d).

The variables listed in the GET statement and the values on the data list must be <u>synchronized with respect to order</u> as well as quantity. The variable to which each value is assigned is entirely determined by the order in which the variable names appear in the GET statements. (For this purpose the order of the GET statements is the order in which they are <u>executed</u>, and not the order in which they are <u>written</u>. This distinction is the topic of Section 4.) Hence the programmer must know exactly what the order of the variables in the "GET lists" will be and arrange the data values accordingly. This is not always easy and is a common source of errors. For example, in the data list above there is nothing in the list that suggests that 17.5 is intended to be assigned to BASE and 83.72 to HEIGHT. If the position of these two values had been reversed the computer would have uncomplainingly assigned 83.72 to BASE and 17.5 to HEIGHT.

3.4.1 Data Format

The data associated with the GET LIST statement is a list of values. No blanks may separate adjacent characters of a value, while adjacent values must be separated by a comma, by one or more blanks, or by both. The entire card may be used, with column 1 considered to come immediately after column 80 of the previous card. (It is generally a good idea to avoid splitting a single value onto two cards -- for example, avoid punching the value 23 with the 2 in column 80 of one card and the 3 in column 1 of the next. PL/I doesn't mind, but it is hard for humans to follow.) Values can be given in either conventional or exponential form.

In example (3.4a) the values were given on six different cards. Each of the following forms is equivalent to (3.4a), although (3.4.1d) is best for humans since the arrangement suggests which values will be read by each GET statement. (3.4.1a) is the least attractive because of the inconsistent (although legal) means of separating values.

```
(3.4.1a)    *DATA
            17.5, 83.72,23.05,        76 2314 ,964.122

(3.4.1b)    *DATA
              17.5, 83.72, 23.05, 76, 2314, 964.122

(3.4.1c)    *DATA
            1.75E1,  8.372E1, 2.305E1, 7.6E1, 2.314E3, 9.64122E2

(3.4.1d)    *DATA
            17.5, 83.72
            23.05, 76, 2314
            964.122
```

Only values can be given as data. It would not make sense to give a variable as a datum -- each datum will be assigned as the value of a variable, and variables of the kind we are using cannot have another variable as value. Arithmetic operations are not allowed in the data -- for example, .5 cannot be given as 1/2.

Section 3 <u>Summary</u>

1. The form of an assignment statement is:

        variable = expression;

To execute an assignment statement, evaluate the expression and
assign the result to the variable on the left of the =.

2. +, -, / denote addition, subtraction and division.   *
denotes multiplication; ** denotes exponentiation. In every
division at   least one of the operands should be in FLOAT form.

3. Parenthesized subexpressions are evaluated from inside out.

4. When not overruled by parentheses the   order   of   operations
is:
        a.   Exponentiation and negation
        b.   Multiplication and division
        c.   Addition and subtraction

Within these categories a sequence of exponentiations and
negations proceeds from right to left; the others from left to
right.

5. When a value is assigned to an integer variable any
fractional part of the value is dropped.

6. A library of built-in functions such as SQRT(...)   is
provided.

7. The form of the simplest input statement is:

        GET LIST(variable-names, separated by commas);

8. The <u>order</u> of data values on cards is crucial, but the <u>format</u>
is quite flexible. The entire card may be used; adjacent values
should be separated by a comma and/or one or more blanks.

Section 3 <u>Exercises</u>

<u>1</u>. In each of the following assignment statements delete all
"redundant" parentheses -- that is, parentheses whose deletion
does not change the result of the statement:

    a) ALT = ALT + (BASE + COL4) + DIV;

    b) PRESSURE = (TEMP + ENTROPY) * SPEC22;

    c) GRADIENT = (GRADIENT - (HGT-SLOPE));

    d) EFF = (EFF + (FULL * (LOSS**H3)));

    e) X = -B + SQRT((B*B -(4*(A*C))));

<u>2</u>. Suppose the following were the values of four variables at a
certain point in a program:

             BASE 4   [float decimal]
             HGT 3   [float decimal]
             SIDE 0   [float decimal]
             TOP 14.2 [float decimal]

Starting at that point, the following four assignment statements
are executed in the order shown below:

             SIDE = SIDE + BASE/HGT;
             SIDE = SIDE + BASE/HGT;
             TOP = BASE + HGT + SIDE + TOP;
             TOP = TOP/HGT;

What are the resulting values of the four variables?

<u>3</u>. The following are all intended to be assignment statements.
Which ones contain at least one syntax error?

    a) A = B + C

    b) A = B, C;

    c) A = (B + C);

    d) A + B = C;

    e) (A = B + C);

    f) A = (B) + C;

    g) A = B (+) C;

    h) A = (B + C;)

<u>4</u>. Write a GET statement and a data list that will assign the
same values as the following pair of assignment statements:

        XPLUS = 93.17;
        XMINUS = -45.93;

<u>5</u>. Suppose the data given with a program are the following:

        *DATA
        2, 4, 6, 8, 10, 12, 14

What would be the values of the variables T4, LOW and VAL after
execution of the following statement (assuming that it is the
first GET statement to be executed in the program):

        GET LIST(VAL, LOW, LOW, T4, LOW, VAL);

Give a different data list and GET statement that will produce
exactly the same result (but are shorter and more reasonable
than the example shown).

Section 4   Flow of Control

Section 4 introduces constructions whose purpose is to control the <u>order</u> in which the statements of a program are <u>executed</u> -- they are generally not executed in the exact order in which they are written. In preparation for this, Section 4.1 examines the execution of a simple program in careful detail.

4.1 <u>General Program Structure; Executing Programs</u>

A complete "job" to be processed by a computer consists of a <u>program</u> and <u>data</u>, in that order. In PL/C, the form of a job is:

```
*PL/C ID='name of programmer'                                 ┐
    /* Comment summarizing program function */                | main
    procedure-name:  PROCEDURE OPTIONS(MAIN);                 |proc-
        Declarations                                          |edure
        Body of procedure                                     ┘
        END procedure-name;
*DATA
        Data cards
```

The program consists of a "main procedure". The "procedure-name" that appears before PROCEDURE and after END is also called an "entry-name" of the procedure, and can be used to refer to the program as a whole. Procedure-names are chosen subject to the same rules as variable identifiers (see Section 2.1) and should be chosen to suggest the action the procedure performs.

A procedure consists of <u>declarations</u> and a <u>body</u>. The declarations describe the variables (giving their names and attributes) to be created before execution of the procedure body begins. They should be written immediately after the procedure heading and are considered part of the heading or preface of the procedure.

The body of the procedure consists of imperative statements that direct the computer to perform certain actions -- such as assign a new value to a variable, read new data values from cards, and print results. Normal execution order of the statements is like the normal order of reading English text -- from left to right, top to bottom, from the beginning to the end of a procedure.

4.1.1 <u>Writing Simple Programs</u>

At this point you have seen almost enough of PL/I to be able
to write simple programs; we need only explain how to get
"output" -- how to cause the computer to write numbers out in a
readable form.

The simplest form of output statement is

          PUT SKIP LIST(variable-names, separated by commas);

Thus, execution of a statement

          PUT SKIP LIST(X, Y, Z);

causes the values of variables X, Y and Z to be printed in a
readable form, on one line. The output resulting from execution
of such PUT LIST statements will accompany the "listing" of the
program you receive after your program has been executed on the
computer.   A more detailed discussion of the control and
interpretation of output is given in Sections 6 and 7.

We now show two examples of complete programs -- the kind you
should be able to write, keypunch and submit for execution.

```
          *PL/C ID='DAVID KIRKPATRICK'
           /* READ TWO VALUES AND PRINT THEM, AND THEIR SUM */
           ADDER: PROCEDURE OPTIONS(MAIN);
                  DECLARE (X, Y,              /* INPUT NUMBERS */
                           Z) FLOAT DECIMAL;/* SUM OF X AND Y */
(4.1.1a)          GET LIST(X, Y);
                  Z = X + Y;
                  PUT SKIP LIST('INPUTS AND ANSWER:');
                  PUT SKIP LIST(X, Y, Z);
                  END ADDER;
          *DATA
           15.5, 10.2
```

The second example is:

```
          *PL/C ID='JOHN HOPCROFT'
           /* PRINT INPUT VALUE AND ITS SQUARE ROOT */
           SROOT: PROCEDURE OPTIONS(MAIN);
                  DECLARE ARG FLOAT DECIMAL;   /* INPUT NUMBER*/
                  DECLARE SRARG FLOAT DECIMAL;/* SQUARE ROOT OF ARG*/
                  GET LIST(ARG);
                  SRARG = SQRT(ARG);
                  PUT SKIP LIST('INPUT AND ANSWER:');
                  PUT SKIP LIST(ARG, SRARG);
                  END SROOT;
          *DATA
           25.01
```

The complete output resulting from computer processing of (4.1.1a) is shown below. It will be explained in detail in Section 7, but you should be able to recognize the listing of the source program and the answer printed as a result of executing the two PUT statements.

```
*PL/C ID='DAVID KIRKPATRICK'

*OPTIONS IN EFFECT*    TIME=(0,15),PAGES=30,LINES=2000,NOATR,NOXREF,FLAGW,BNDRY,NOCMNTS,SORMGIN=(2,72,1),
*CPTICNS IN EFFECT*    ERRORS=(50,50),TABSIZE=2532,UDEF,SOURCE,OPLIST,NOCMPRS,HDRPG,AUXIO=10000,LINECT=60,NOALIST,
*CPTICNS IN EFFECT*    MCALL,MTEXT,DUMP=(S,F,L,E,U,R),DUMPE=(S,F,L,E,U,R),DUMPT=(S,F,L,E,U,R)

    /* READ TWO VALUES AND PRINT THEM, AND THEIR SUM */                      PL/C-R7.1--66 10/20/75 10:58 PAGE    1

    STMT LEVEL NEST BLOCK MLVL  SOURCE TEXT

                                      /* READ TWO VALUES AND PRINT THEM, AND THEIR SUM */
                                      ADDER: PROCEDURE OPTIONS(MAIN);
      2    1            1                 DECLARE (X, Y,              /* INPUT NUMBERS */
                                                  Z) FLOAT DECIMAL;/* SUM OF X AND Y */
      3    1            1                 GET LIST(X, Y);
      4    1            1                 Z = X + Y;
      5    1            1                 PUT SKIP LIST('INPUTS AND ANSWER:');
      6    1            1                 PUT SKIP LIST(X, Y, Z);
      7    1            1                 END ADDER;
    ERRORS/WARNINGS DETECTED DURING CODE GENERATION:

        WARNING: NO FILE SPECIFIED. SYSIN/SYSPRINT ASSUMED. (CGOC)




    INPUTS AND ANSWER:
      1.55000E+01          1.01999E+01           2.56999E+01


    IN STMT    7  PROGRAM RETURNS FROM MAIN PROCEDURE.
```

4.1.2 Tracing Execution

You should understand both the meaning of each PL/I statement and the manner in which they are executed, well enough to be able to follow the execution of a program on a statement-by-statement basis. In fact, you should be able to simulate the action of the computer and "trace" the execution of a program on paper. Your action should differ from the computer's only in speed (by a factor of 10^6 or more).

For example, a detailed trace of the loading and execution of (4.1.1a) is given below:

1. The cards, from *PL/C through *DATA are read; a copy of the program (in translated form) is created in memory.

2. Execution begins by entering the main procedure ADDER.

3. As ADDER is entered three variables are created (recall that ??? is used to indicate that no value yet exists):

    X ??? [float decimal]
    Y ??? [float decimal]
    Z ??? [float decimal]

4. The first statement in the body of ADDER is GET LIST(X, Y);. Execution of this statement reads the two numbers on the first (and only) data card and assigns them to variables X and Y. At this point, the variables are:

    X 15.5 [float decimal]
    Y 10.2 [float decimal]
    Z ??? [float decimal]

5. Execution of the next statement, Z = X + Y;, changes the value of Z. The variables now are:

    X 15.5 [float decimal]
    Y 10.2 [float decimal]
    Z 25.7 [float decimal]

6. Execution of the next statement, PUT LIST(Z);, causes an output line to be printed:

    2.57000E+01

(The actual number printed is 2.56999E+01. The discrepancy is explained in Section IX.1 of our Introduction.)

7. The end of ADDER is reached; execution of the program is finished.

Having completed ADDER, the computer begins execution of some other program. The next program "overwrites" and destroys the ADDER program, and its variables X, Y and Z.

4.2 <u>Repetitive Execution</u>

Example (4.1.1a) is simple to follow because the statements
are executed in the same order as they are written. Execution
begins with the first statement, proceeds to the second, then
the third, etc. Execution is completed when the last statement
has been executed. This is a reasonable way to begin our
explanation, but no useful computer program is really like this.
The execution of real programs is more complicated in the sense
that the execution of an individual statement may be repeated
many times, or it may be skipped and not executed at all.

The "flow-of-control" is the process by which the computer
decides <u>which statement to execute next</u>. The programmer must
precisely specify this path with special "control statements".
Previously we have been concerned with what could be called
"action statements" -- statements that assign a new value to a
variable, or read an item of data, or print a result. Now we
introduce statements whose sole action is to control the course
of execution -- the order in which the statements of the program
are to be executed.

For example, suppose you want to compute the sum of a set of
numbers given on data cards. You could use the following type
of program:

```
/* SET SUM TO SUM OF DATA */
     SUM = 0;
     GET LIST(ITEM);
     SUM = SUM + ITEM;
     GET LIST(ITEM);
     SUM = SUM + ITEM;
          . . .
     GET LIST(ITEM);
     SUM = SUM + ITEM;
```

After the initial statement setting SUM to zero, there is a <u>pair</u>
of statements to read and accumulate <u>for each item of data</u>.
Obviously, if there were many data this type of program would be
painfully long. This type of program would also have to be
changed every time the quantity of data changed. It would be
nice to be able to write something like the following:

```
/* SET SUM TO SUM OF DATA */
     SUM = 0;
     Repeat for each item of data:
          GET LIST(ITEM);
          SUM = SUM + ITEM;
```

Unfortunately, PL/I won't let you express it quite this simply,
but it does provide the means by which you can achieve just this
type of repetition. To control repetition you need to specify
exactly <u>what statements</u> are to be repeated, and <u>how many times</u>
they are to be repeated.

The statements to be repeated are made the "body" of a "loop".   The beginning and end of the body are denoted with the keywords "DO" and "END":

```
loop-name: DO control-phrase;
     Statements to be repeated;
     END loop-name;
```

The "loop-name" helps to identify an END with a particular DO, since we will soon have programs with many ENDs and many DOs. The loop-name is actually optional and may be omitted, but it is good practice to put it in. We give a name to each loop in our examples and suggest you also develop this habit.   Similarly, the indentation shown here is optional, and is entirely for the benefit of a human reader of the program.   But it makes the extent of the body of the loop much more obvious to a reader and we strongly recommend that you adopt the practice of indentation as we show in our examples. The "control-phrase" specifies how many times the body of the loop is to be repeated.   For the summing example above, we could specify "how many repetitions" by preceding the data by another value, indicating the number of items that follow. The program could then be written:

```
/* SET SUM TO SUM OF DATA */
     SUM = 0;
     GET LIST(COUNT);
     SUM_LOOP: DO WHILE (COUNT > 0);
          GET LIST(ITEM);
          SUM = SUM + ITEM;
          COUNT = COUNT - 1;
          END SUM_LOOP;
```

This program segment could be used, without change, for <u>any quantity of data</u> -- from no values at all (COUNT of 0) to thousands of values. Although only a half-dozen statements are written,   the computer may execute thousands of statements as it executes the body of the loop once for each item of data.

This is an example of a "WHILE loop", which is described in more detail in Section 4.2.1. There is a second form of loop (or rather, a second form of control-phrase) described in Section 4.2.2.

4.2.1 Conditional Repetition

The basic PL/I loop has the form

```
loop-name: DO WHILE(condition);
     Body of loop
     END loop-name;
```

The "WHILE loop" is executed as follows:

1. Evaluate the "condition". If the result of evaluation
   is "false", execution of the loop is completed; if
   "true", proceed to step 2.

2. Execute the body of the loop. Upon completion, return
   to step 1.

The action is suggested by the English meaning of the keywords
-- the body is iterated <u>while</u> the condition remains true. The
action can be shown graphically by a "flow-diagram":

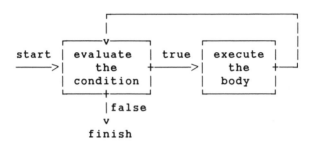

Figure 1. Execution of the WHILE loop

As an example of a WHILE loop, suppose you wanted to sum the
integers from 14 through 728. (There is a simple formula to sum
consecutive integers so this program would not actually be used,
but it provides a simple and clear example of the control of
repetition.) The following program segment could be used:

```
            /* SUM INTEGERS FROM 14 THRU 728 */
            I = 14;
            SUM = 14;
(4.2.1a)    SUM_LOOP: DO WHILE(I < 728);
                 I = I + 1;
                 SUM = SUM + I;
                 END SUM_LOOP;
```

The first two assignment statements establish initial values for
the variables I and SUM. Then the WHILE loop is executed.
Since the condition I < 728 is true (I=14) the loop body is
executed. This changes I to 15 and SUM to 14+15=29. Then the
condition is re-evaluated. It is still true (since the value of
I is now 15) so the body is again executed. This repetition
continues until finally the value of I becomes 728. At this
point the condition is found to be false, and the execution of
the WHILE loop is finished. The required task has been
accomplished -- the variable SUM contains the sum of the
integers from 14 to 728.

As another example, a WHILE loop could be used to scan through the data list to find the first negative number:

```
/* DISCARD DATA UP TO FIRST NEGATIVE VALUE */
      GET LIST(DATUM);
      DISCARD_LOOP: DO WHILE(DATUM >= 0);
            GET LIST(DATUM);
      END DISCARD_LOOP;
```

Execution of the body of a WHILE loop must provide some action that affects the condition, so that it eventually becomes false. For example, in (4.2.1a) an assignment statement increases the value of I to serve this role. If the body never affects the condition, then if it is initially true it will remain true and the body of the WHILE loop will be iterated indefinitely. This is a classic program error called an "infinite iterative loop" and every programmer produces one once in a while. In practice, of course, each program is subject to a time limit so that repetition does not continue forever.

The condition may be false when the WHILE loop is first encountered. In this case the body is not executed -- not even once -- so the statements of the body have no effect upon the condition or upon anything else.

It is important to understanding the action of a WHILE loop to know when the condition is evaluated. This is done before the body itself is executed. If the condition is true then the entire body is executed. Even if statements within the body change the values of variables to make the condition false, the condition is not under continuous review during execution of the body. The condition is not re-evaluated until after execution of the body is completed. For this reason the following program is not correct since it will print the value of the negative number as well as those of the discards.

```
/* DISCARD AND LIST DATA UP TO FIRST NEG VALUE */
      GET LIST(DATUM);
      PUT SKIP LIST(DATUM);
      DISCARD_LOOP: DO WHILE(DATUM >= 0);
            GET LIST(DATUM);
            PUT SKIP LIST(DATUM);
      END DISCARD_LOOP;
```

We leave it as an exercise for you to figure out how to change this program segment to make it correct.

4.2.1.1 Simple Conditions

A simple "condition" or "relational expression" is a special type of expression that involves a "relation". The symbols for the PL/I relations are the following:

symbol	meaning
=	is equal to
¬=	is not equal to
>	is greater than
¬>	is not greater than
>=	is greater than or equal to
<	is less than
¬<	is not less than
<=	is less than or equal to

(The double-character symbols cannot have a blank between characters.) A condition consists of two arithmetic expressions (as described in Section 3.2) separated by a relation:

arith-expr   relation   arith-expr

A condition describes a relationship that is either <u>true</u> or <u>false</u>. For example, 2<3 is a condition that is always true; 2=3, a condition that is always false; J=K, a condition that may be either true or false depending upon the values of the variables J and K at the instant the condition is evaluated.

Other examples are:

```
TEST = 0
J+2 < K
TEMP*(PRESSURE - 4*PI) <= BASE_PRESSURE
```

4.2.1.2 Compound Conditions

Conditions can be made more complex by the use of "Boolean operators". These are "and", "or" and "not". "And" and "or" are used to combine two conditions to form a "compound condition". "Not" is used to reverse the truth of a condition. Letting A and B represent conditions which are true or false, we describe the symbols and meanings of the three operations:

English	symbol	meaning
"and"	&	A & B is true if <u>both</u> A and B are true
"or"	|	A | B is true if <u>either</u> A or B is true
"not"	¬	¬ A is true only if A is <u>not</u> true

The following table gives the values of these compound

conditions for different values of the conditions A, B, C and D.

A	B	A & B	A | B	¬ A
true	true	true	true	false
true	false	false	true	false
false	true	false	true	true
false	false	false	false	true

WHILE loop conditions can be simple or compound:

```
DO WHILE((I > 56) & (I < 729));
DO WHILE((PRESSURE > PRESSMIN) & (TEMP < TEMPMAX));
DO WHILE((REG_GAP <= 15.2 * GAP) | (FLAG = 2));
```

Precedence rules for these operators are analogous to those for arithmetic operations given in Section 3.2.2. "And" is considered before "or", so that

```
A=B & C=D | E=F     is equivalent to     (A=B & C=D) | E=F
```

It is a good idea to use parentheses in compound conditions to be certain that the order of consideration is what you intended.

"Not" should be used sparingly, since it tends to make programs harder to understand. When "¬" must be used, parentheses should always be given to enclose the condition to which it applies. In simple cases, "¬" can often be avoided by choosing the opposite relation:

```
¬(A = B)  is equivalent to A ¬= B
¬(A <= B) is equivalent to A > B
```

4.2.2 Repetition with Different Values

An alternative form of DO group is used to specify that execution of the body is to be repeated with different values of a key variable, called the "index" variable. Example (4.2.1a) could be rewritten in this form as

```
          /* SUM INTEGERS FROM 14 THRU 728 */
          SUM = 0;
(4.2.2a)  SUM_LOOP: DO I = 14 TO 728 BY 1;
              SUM = SUM + I;
              END SUM_LOOP;
```

The index variable I is set equal to 14 and the body is executed; then 1 is added to I, making I equal to 15 and the body is executed again. 1 is again added to I, giving 16, and the body is executed again. This repetition continues until I becomes 728 and the body is executed for the final time. Then 1 is added to I, giving 729, which is greater than the specified "upper-limit", so execution of the loop is finished.

In effect, (4.2.2a) is executed as if it had been written:

```
/* SUM INTEGERS FROM 14 THRU 728 */
    SUM = 0;
    I = 14;
    SUM = SUM + I;
    I = I + 1;
    SUM = SUM + I;
        ...
    I = I + 1;
    SUM = SUM + I;
```

The general form of this type of DO group is:

loop-name: DO index-var = exp^1 TO exp^2 BY exp^3;

(4.2.2b)   Body of group
            END loop-name;

where "exp^1", "exp^2", and "exp^3" are arithmetic expressions. "exp^1" gives the value of the index variable for the first repetition; "exp^3" gives the "increment" to be added to the index variable after each iteration; and "exp^2" gives the termination test value. Iteration continues until the value of the index variable "passes" this test value. If the increment is positive iteration continues until the index variable is greater than the test value; if the increment is negative, until the index variable is less than the test value.

Execution of such a DO group can be explained in terms of an equivalent WHILE loop. Let INCR and TERM be two new variables that are not used in the body of (4.2.2b). If the initial value of exp^3 is positive, then (4.2.2b) is exactly equivalent to:

```
    index-var = exp¹;
    TERM = exp²;
    INCR = exp³;
    loop-name: DO WHILE(index-var <= TERM);
(4.2.2c)      Body of (4.2.2b)
            index-var = index-var + INCR;
            END loop-name;
```

If the initial value of exp^3 is negative then the equivalent WHILE loop would begin with the line

loop-name: DO WHILE(index-var >= TERM);

Studied carefully, the equivalent WHILE loop reveals some interesting properties of the new form of DO group:

1. A form of assignment is embedded in the control phrase; the index variable is changed just as if it were the left-side variable of an ordinary assignment statement.

2. Since the index variable is incremented and tested
<u>after</u> the last execution of the body, the final value of
the index variable is <u>not</u> the same as the value during the
last execution of the body.

3. It is not necessary to use the index variable in the
body. Frequently it serves only as a "counter" to
determine the number of iterations of the body.

4. Alteration of the index variable within the body
affects the control of iteration. This dangerous practice
usually leads to confusion.

5. Assignment within the body to a variable that appears
in a control expression exp^1, exp^2 or exp^3 has no effect on
the control of iteration; these expressions are only
evaluated <u>before the first iteration of the body</u>.

This second form of repetition can be quite useful. However,
you should recognize that it is just a special case of the more
general WHILE loop. When iteration is of this special form it
is certainly easier to write "I = 14 TO 728 BY 1" than to write
the statements necessary to initialize and increment the index
variable in a WHILE loop. However, not all iteration has this
form and one should not try to force it to do work for which it
was not intended. <u>The WHILE loop is the general form -- always</u>
<u>to be used except when this special form of iteration is</u>
<u>required</u>.

To illustrate the use of a negative increment, (4.2.2a) could
be rewritten:

```
              /* SUM INTEGERS FROM 728 DOWN THRU 14 */
                 SUM = 0;
(4.2.2d)         SUM_LOOP: DO I = 728 TO 14 BY -1;
                    SUM = SUM + I;
                    END SUM_LOOP;
```

The DO groups in (4.2.2a) and (4.2.2d) produce the same final
value of SUM, but different final values of I. After executing
(4.2.2a) the value of I is 729; after (4.2.2d) it is 13.

4.2.3 <u>Nesting of Loops</u>

Since the body of a loop is a sequence of statements, and
since an entire loop is itself effectively a statement, one loop
can be included in the body of another. Suppose the input data
consists of a list of pairs of numbers, and for each pair (LOW,
HIGH) we want to print the sum of the integers from LOW to HIGH.
We always have LOW <= HIGH, and the last pair is followed by the
pair (1,0). For example, for the input "1,2, 2,3, 1,0" we
should print "3, 5". The program segment given in (4.2.3a) is
designed to perform this task, but the segment has not been

completed.   Part of the action is given as a comment -- which
describes <u>what</u> has to be done, but not <u>how</u>.

```
      /* READ INPUT PAIRS (LOW,HIGH) UNTIL LOW > HIGH */
      /* FOR EACH PAIR PRINT LOW + (LOW+1) + ... + HIGH */
          GET LIST(LOW, HIGH);
          PAIR_LOOP: DO WHILE(LOW <= HIGH);
(4.2.3a)      /* SET SUM TO SUM FROM LOW TO HIGH */
          PUT LIST(SUM);
          GET LIST(LOW, HIGH);
          END PAIR_LOOP;
```

Now using the integer summing segment of (4.2.2a), we can
expand, or refine, the comment into PL/I statements that specify
<u>how</u> the summing is to be done:

```
          /* SET SUM TO SUM FROM LOW TO HIGH */
          SUM = 0;
          SUM_LOOP: DO I = LOW TO HIGH BY 1;
              SUM = SUM + I;
              END SUM_LOOP;
```

The segment given in (4.2.3a) can be completed by adding this
refinement:

```
      /* READ INPUT PAIRS (LOW,HIGH) UNTIL LOW > HIGH */
      /* FOR EACH PAIR PRINT LOW + (LOW+1) + ... + HIGH */
          GET LIST (LOW, HIGH);
          PAIR_LOOP: DO WHILE(LOW <= HIGH);
              /* SET SUM TO SUM FROM LOW TO HIGH */
              SUM = 0;
              SUM_LOOP: DO I = LOW TO HIGH BY 1;
                  SUM = SUM + I;
                  END SUM_LOOP;
          PUT LIST(SUM);
          GET LIST(LOW, HIGH);
          END PAIR_LOOP;
```

As a final example, consider the program segment

```
          OUTSUM = 0;
          INNERSUM = 0;
          OUT_LOOP: DO OUTINDEX = 1 TO 5 BY 1;
              OUTSUM = OUTSUM + 1;
              IN_LOOP: DO ININDEX = 1 TO 4 BY 1;
                  INNERSUM = INNERSUM + 1;
                  END IN_LOOP;
              END OUT_LOOP;
```

Both index variables OUTINDEX and ININDEX are counters that
control the number of iterations but are not used within the
body. The segment does nothing useful, but study it until you
understand very clearly why after its execution the values of
the variables are:

OUTSUM <u>5</u>   INNERSUM <u>20</u>   OUTINDEX <u>6</u>   ININDEX <u>5</u>

Note that each segment in these examples could be presented
and discussed out of context -- it was not necessary to specify
whether it was part of some larger, unseen loop.   Each segment
could in fact be buried in the interior of a nest of loops
several layers deep, so that its execution would be repeated
many times.

Once you start to write loops which are nested within other
loops it should be obvious why the optional loop-names are
useful in matching ENDs with the proper DO. If you give these
names, as shown in the examples, PL/I will help you by checking
to make sure that you are ENDing the innermost loop first --
that is, checking to make sure that your loops are properly
nested, and are not overlapped.   But if you don't give the
names, PL/I will not object, but neither can it help you match
ENDs with DOs. Similarly, the indentation convention becomes
very helpful in making the structure of the nested loops
apparent to the reader.   But remember that indentation is
irrelevant to PL/I.   If your indentation does not accurately
reflect the program structure it will only confuse the reader --
it will have no effect whatever on PL/I.

4.3 <u>Conditional Execution</u>

It is often useful to be able to include a statement in a
program in such a way that it <u>may</u> or <u>may not be executed</u>. We
would like the decision as to whether or not the statement is to
be executed to be made when that statement is reached in
execution of the program, and to depend upon some result of
computation prior to that point. We say that the execution of
the statement is "conditional" -- the statement is to be
executed <u>if</u> some specified <u>condition is satisfied</u>. For example,
suppose we wanted to read an item of data and print a warning
message if the value is negative:

```
GET LIST(ITEM);
IF ITEM < 0
    THEN PUT SKIP LIST('NEGATIVE DATUM', ITEM);
```

The PUT statement to print the message is executed only if the
value of ITEM is less than zero; if ITEM is equal to, or greater
than zero, the PUT is skipped and execution continues with the
next statement.

Another example was given in the sample program in (1.1e) to
find the maximum of a set of values:

```
IF NUMBER > MAXNBR THEN MAXNBR = NUMBER;
```

The candidate number in NUMBER was compared to the largest that
had been encountered up to that point. <u>If</u> the new candidate was

larger, <u>then</u> execution of the assignment statement recorded it as the largest encountered. If the new number was not larger, then that assignment statement had to be skipped.

In PL/I the conditional statement has two forms. The simpler one, used in the examples above, is

IF condition THEN statement[1]

The interpretation is suggested by the English meaning of the keywords "IF" and "THEN":

<u>If</u> the condition is true <u>then</u> execute statement[1]. If the condition is false, do not execute statement[1].

This flow-of-control is as follows:

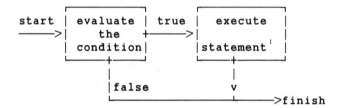

Figure 2. Conditional Execution

The second form of the IF statement is very similar:

IF condition
    THEN statement[1]
    ELSE statement[2]

The interpretation is:

<u>If</u> the condition is true <u>then</u> execute statement[1]. <u>Else</u> (that is, if the condition is false) execute statement[2].

<u>One or the other</u> of statement[1] and statement[2], but <u>not both</u>, will be executed, depending upon the truth or falsity of the condition. The flow-of-control is:

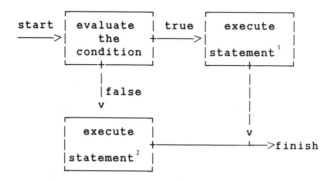

Figure 3.   Alternative Execution

Either simple or compound conditions can be used, as
described   in   Sections   4.2.1.1   and 4.2.1.2. Note that the IF
construction does not require the condition to be enclosed in
parentheses, unlike the WHILE loop where the condition must be
in parentheses. (A programming language should not have such
inconsistencies, but PL/I does, and you will just have to learn
to live with them.)

Examples of conditional statements are given below. None of
the parentheses in the conditions in these examples is required;
they have been added only to make the meaning clearer to a human
reader.

        IF (NEWVALUE > MAXVALUE) THEN MAXVALUE = NEWVALUE;

        IF QTY < 0
            THEN NEGCOUNT = NEGCOUNT + 1;
            ELSE POSCOUNT = POSCOUNT + 1;

        IF (B**2 - 4*A*C) < 0 THEN PUT SKIP LIST('IMAGINARY ROOT');

        IF (CONTROL = J+1) | (VALUE = 0) THEN GET LIST(VALUE);

The "THEN statement" following the condition is mandatory;
the "ELSE statement" is optional, since it is only present in
the second form. Situations arise where it seems useful to have
only an "ELSE statement" -- that is, a statement to be executed
only if a condition is false. This could be done by giving a
"dummy THEN statement":

            IF condition
                THEN;
                ELSE statement^{1}

However, this seems artificial and confusing to the reader and
it is generally preferable to avoid this by reversing the sense
of the condition. For example, instead of writing

```
IF A > B
    THEN;
    ELSE statement
```

you should write

```
IF A <= B THEN statement
```

Instead of writing

```
IF (A = B) | (C < D)
    THEN;
    ELSE statement
```

you should write

```
IF ¬((A = B) | (C < D)) THEN statement
```

or

```
IF ((A ¬= B) & (C >= D)) THEN statement
```

4.3.1 Compound Statements

Any single statement may follow the THEN or ELSE in a conditional statement. Thus an assignment statement, a GET statement, a loop, or another conditional statement may appear in this position. (Also see Section 4.3.4.) Sometimes one wants to execute more than one statement conditionally. To do this, a "compound statement" of the following form is used:

```
DO;    Body    END;
```

This form of DO group (without a "control-phrase") is not repetitive -- the body is executed only once. The "delimiters" DO and END serve only to indicate that the enclosed statements are to be considered as a single unit. Examples are:

```
/* TEST  FOR NEGATIVE VALUE, RECORD ERROR, CORRECT TO +1 */
    IF VALUE < 0
        THEN DO; ERRORCOUNT = ERRORCOUNT + 1;
                 PUT SKIP LIST('IMPROPER VALUE', VALUE);
                 VALUE = 1; END;

/* SUM AND COUNT NEGATIVE AND NON-NEGATIVE VALUES */
    IF NEWVAL < 0
        THEN DO; NEGCOUNT = NEGCOUNT + 1;
                 NEGSUM = NEGSUM + NEWVAL; END;
        ELSE DO; POSCOUNT = POSCOUNT + 1;
                 POSSUM = POSSUM + NEWVAL; END;
```

A compound statement can be given a name:

```
statement-name: DO;
    Body
    END statement-name;
```

If the body is long this would help to identify the END with the
proper DO.   However, in most of our examples we feel that this
is not necessary.   This means that in our examples if you
encounter an END without a name following, you can assume it is
the END of a compound statement.   The END of a procedure or a
loop will always be followed by a name.

   Note that there are _three different uses_ for END:

   1.   terminate a compound statement,

   2.   terminate a DO loop, and

   3.   terminate a procedure.

PL/I always assumes that any END goes with the _closest_ DO or
PROCEDURE _unless_ there is a name after the END.   If there is a
name after END, PL/I will match the END with the DO or PROCEDURE
with the same name.   _If necessary, PL/I will supply ENDs for_
closer DOs and PROCEDUREs in order to accomplish the match.
This can be confusing -- so don't give PL/I the opportunity to
supply any missing ENDs.   Always give an END for each DO or
PROCEDURE, and give matching names for ENDs of loops and
procedures as we show in our examples.

4.3.2 _Exit from a Program Segment_

   Greater flexibility in choosing program structures is
possible if one can "exit" from a program segment "prematurely";
that is, if one can terminate execution of a program segment
before its normal completion.   In the case of a loop this means
terminating execution of the body, or terminating execution of
the entire loop.   In PL/I this type of exit must be accomplished
by a "conditional branch".   In addition to the conditional
statement, this involves the "GO TO statement" and the concept
of a "statement label".

   A _statement label_ is an identifier that assigns a name to a
statement.   Label identifiers are chosen subject to the same
rules as identifiers for variables (see Section 2.1) and should
be chosen to suggest the role of the statement being named.   A
label identifier should be different from the other identifiers
in the program.   The label is given as a "prefix" and punctuated
with a colon.   The GO TO statement refers to such a label:

```
GO TO label;
...
label: statement
```

Execution of the GO TO statement causes control to "branch" or "jump" to the statement whose label is specified. That is, the next statement to be executed is the one whose label is referenced in the GO TO, rather than the statement immediately following the GO TO.

As an example, the program below uses a GO TO to terminate execution of the loop body (not the whole loop). Here, label SKIP_SUM is a prefix on an "empty" or "null" statement (just the semicolon). This null statement has no effect on execution, since its execution does nothing; its sole purpose is to provide a statement on which to hang the label. (This example uses the MOD function; MOD(I,J) yields the remainder of I/J.)

```
           /* SUM AND COUNT THE INTEGERS FROM BASE TO TOP */
           /* WHICH ARE DIVISIBLE BY 3 OR 5 */
               KSUM = 0;
               KCOUNT = 0;
               SUM_LOOP: DO K = BASE TO TOP BY 1;
                   IF (MOD(K,3) ¬= 0) & (MOD(K,5) ¬= 0)
                       THEN GO TO SKIP_SUM;
(4.3.2a)           KSUM = KSUM + K;
                   KCOUNT = KCOUNT + 1;
                   SKIP_SUM:;
               END SUM_LOOP;
```

The GO TO exit is not really necessary in this example, since the same result could be achieved much more clearly with a compound statement:

```
           /* SUM AND COUNT THE INTEGERS FROM BASE TO TOP */
           /* WHICH ARE DIVISIBLE BY 3 OR 5 */
               KSUM = 0;
               KCOUNT = 0;
               SUM_LOOP: DO K = BASE TO TOP BY 1;
(4.3.2b)           IF (MOD(K,3) = 0) | (MOD(K,5) = 0)
                       THEN DO; KSUM = KSUM + K;
                               KCOUNT = KCOUNT + 1; END;
               END SUM_LOOP;
```

The style of (4.3.2b) is certainly preferable in this case, and should be employed whenever practical. However, as loops become larger and more complex, situations arise in which the structure is made clearer if one can branch directly to the END and thus terminate (or skip) a particular iteration of the body.

In general, branches make it harder to understand execution of a program, and make it harder to show that it is correct. Consequently, the GO TO should be used sparingly and only when necessary.

It is also useful to be able to escape from a loop earlier than provided by the control phrase, by branching to a null statement following the loop. For example:

```
                /* SUM INTEGERS FROM BASE TO TOP, SUBJECT TO KLIMIT */
                   KSUM = 0;
                   SUM_LOOP: DO K = BASE TO TOP BY 1;
                      IF KSUM + K > KLIMIT THEN GO TO TERM_SUM;
(4.3.2c)              KSUM = KSUM + K;
                      END SUM_LOOP;
                   TERM_SUM:;
```

The same result would be achieved by assigning the label to the
first statement of the next section of the program, but the
logical role of the exit would be less clear. The GO TO is
being used to <u>exit</u> from this program segment, and <u>not to enter</u>
the next segment. Hence the target label should be positioned
as the <u>last</u> statement of this segment, rather than as the <u>first</u>
statement of the next. The label-name should be chosen to
suggest that a segment is being <u>terminated</u>, rather than that a
new segment is being <u>entered</u>.

We have adopted the convention of having all exit labels used
in this way begin with the characters "TERM_" so that the role
of the GO TO in terminating the loop is unmistakable. This is
just an arbitrary convention -- not a rule of the programming
language -- but this type of consistency makes a program more
predictable and easier for a human reader to understand.

Notice the different indentation of the SKIP_SUM and TERM_SUM
labels in examples (4.3.2a) and (4.3.2c). In (4.3.2a) the label
is indented to show that it is part of the body of the loop. In
(4.3.2c) it is lined up under the DO to show that it <u>follows</u> the
loop.

As in the case of (4.3.2a), the GO TO exit is not necessary
in (4.3.2c). It would be better to use a WHILE loop and include
the exit condition in the main control phrase. (4.3.2d) is
equivalent to (4.3.2c) in function and preferable in style:

```
                /* SUM INTEGERS FROM BASE TO TOP, SUBJECT TO KLIMIT */
                   KSUM = 0;
                   K = BASE;
                   SUM_LOOP: DO WHILE((K <= TOP) &
                                      (KSUM + K <= KLIMIT));
(4.3.2d)              KSUM = KSUM + K;
                   K = K + 1;
                   END SUM_LOOP;
```

As another example, suppose we are given integer variables A,
B, C, and Y, and we desire a program segment which will print Y
if the following is true:

(4.3.2e) There is <u>no</u> integer n such that
         $1 \leq n \leq Y$ and $Y = A + B \cdot n + C \cdot n^2$

This can be detected by examining values of $A+B \cdot n+C \cdot n^2$ for
n = 1,2,...,Y. The following segment uses a GO TO to end
execution of the segment when it has attained its goal:

```
           TEST_LOOP: DO I = 1 TO Y BY 1;
(4.3.2f)    IF A + B*I + C*I*I = Y THEN GO TO TERM_YPRINT;
           END TEST_LOOP;
         PUT LIST(Y);
         TERM_YPRINT:;
```

We now write a segment which prints up to 5 values of Y, for Y = 1, 2, ..., 50, which satisfy property (4.3.2e). The following segment illustrates the use of a GO TO to end execution of a program segment, in performing this function.

```
    /* PRINT UP TO 5 VALUES OF Y (FOR Y=1,2,...,50) WHICH */
    /* SATISFY PROPERTY (4.3.2E) */
      Y = 0;
      COUNT = 0;
      Y_LOOP: DO WHILE((Y < 50) & (COUNT < 5));
        Y = Y + 1;
        /* PRINT Y IF IT SATISFIES PROPERTY (4.3.2E) */
            TEST_LOOP: DO I = 1 TO Y BY 1;
                IF A + B*I + C*I*I = Y THEN GO TO TERM_YPRINT;
                END TEST_LOOP;
            PUT LIST(Y);
            COUNT = COUNT + 1;
            TERM_YPRINT:;
        END Y_LOOP;
```

The GO TO should be used sparingly. It <u>can</u> be used much more widely, and many programming texts consider it to be the principal control mechanism. With ingenious use of labels, IFs and GO TOs one can "handcraft" control structures equivalent to all the others described in Section 4, but it does not follow that this is desirable. Such programs are not necessarily more efficient and seldom exhibit their logical structure as clearly as programs using the more complex control statements. One philosophy of programming -- called "structured programming" -- considers the GO TO to be both inelegant and dangerous. We agree wholeheartedly, and use the GO TO only when PL/I does not offer a more natural alternative. The principal example of such use is as an exit, as has been described in the preceding paragraphs. (Further discussion of this "exit problem" is given in Section 4.5.)

As a general rule, never resort to the use of a GO TO until you have tried to design the program in another way that would avoid it. <u>Use a GO TO only when the alternative is even more awkward.</u>

4.3.3 Indefinite Repetition

In some cases, a program is clearer and more logical if the control of iteration is performed entirely within the body of the DO group. The exit technique described in 4.3.2 can be used, but some mechanism must be provided to continue the iteration until the exit takes effect. PL/I offers no way of doing this directly, so one must choose the least unattractive way of contriving a mechanism.

We prefer the use of a WHILE loop, with a condition that is always true. Any simple condition, such as 0=0, would suffice, but the best solution is to write

            DO WHILE('1'B);

'1'B is PL/I's way of saying "true", while '0'B is used for "false". By giving '1'B as an always-true condition, the programmer's intention is unmistakable.

For example, consider the following problem:

The input consists of integers which are to be read and printed until one is read which satisfies one of the following three conditions:
a) the number is negative
b) the number ends in "3"
c) the number is a power of two (1,2,4,8,16,...)

The requirement is not complicated or difficult, but the termination test cannot be conveniently written as the condition of a WHILE loop. The following is a reasonable solution (using the MOD built-in function):

```
        /* PRINT NON-NEGATIVE INTEGERS WHICH DO NOT END IN 3 AND */
        /* WHICH ARE NOT POWERS OF TWO.  */
            P32_LOOP: DO WHILE('1'B);
                GET LIST(A);
(4.3.3a)    IF (MOD(A,10) = 3) | (A < 0) THEN GO TO TERM_P32;
            /* TEST A FOR POWER OF 2 */
                POWER_OF_TWO = 1;
                POWER_LOOP: DO WHILE(POWER_OF_TWO < A);
                    POWER_OF_TWO = POWER_OF_TWO * 2;
                    END POWER_LOOP;
                IF POWER_OF_TWO = A THEN GO TO TERM_P32;
            PUT SKIP LIST(A);
            END P32_LOOP;
        TERM_P32:;
```

4.3.4 <u>Nesting of Conditional Statements</u>

The statement following THEN or ELSE in a conditional statement <u>can be another conditional statement</u>. When this occurs they are said to be "nested". For example, the form of a complete, symmetric nest of three conditional statements, each with both THEN and ELSE statements, is:

```
            IF condition₁
               THEN IF condition₂
                       THEN statement₁
(4.3.4a)               ELSE statement₂
               ELSE IF condition₃
                       THEN statement₃
                       ELSE statement₄
```

The flow-of-control in this nest is:

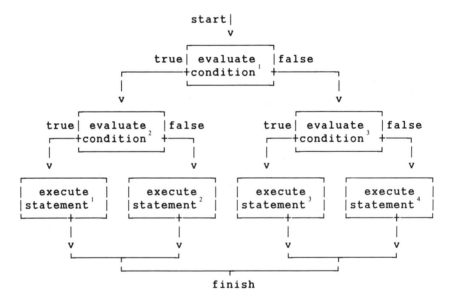

Figure 4. Nested Conditional Statements

Great care is required in using nested conditional statements since it is very easy to write nests that are syntactically correct (hence do not receive any warning messages) but do not do exactly what was intended. For example, suppose in (4.3.4a) the second conditional statement did not have an ELSE statement. If the fourth line were simply removed from (4.3.4a) the program would look like:

$\quad$ IF condition^1
$\quad\quad$ THEN IF condition^2
(4.3.4b) $\quad\quad\quad\quad$ THEN statement^1
$\quad\quad\quad$ ELSE IF condition^3
$\quad\quad\quad\quad\quad$ THEN statement^3
$\quad\quad\quad\quad\quad$ ELSE statement^4

The indenting in (4.3.4b) is deceptive and does not accurately show the program structure. (Remember that the computer _ignores_ indentation.) The lines should be indented as:

$\quad$ IF condition^1
$\quad\quad$ THEN IF condition^2
$\quad\quad\quad\quad$ THEN statement^1
$\quad\quad\quad\quad$ ELSE IF condition^3
$\quad\quad\quad\quad\quad\quad$ THEN statement^3
$\quad\quad\quad\quad\quad\quad$ ELSE statement^4

This is because _an ELSE belongs with the last preceding conditional statement that lacks an ELSE._ To achieve the intended flow-of-control a null ELSE statement could be provided for the second conditional statement:

$\quad$ IF condition^1
$\quad\quad$ THEN IF condition^2
$\quad\quad\quad\quad$ THEN statement^1
$\quad\quad\quad\quad$ ELSE ;
$\quad\quad\quad$ ELSE IF condition^3
$\quad\quad\quad\quad\quad$ THEN statement^3
$\quad\quad\quad\quad\quad$ ELSE statement^4

A preferable way of writing this to avoid the clumsiness of the null statement is:

$\quad$ IF condition^1
$\quad\quad$ THEN DO;IF condition^2
$\quad\quad\quad\quad$ THEN statement^1 END;
$\quad\quad\quad$ ELSE IF condition^3
$\quad\quad\quad\quad\quad$ THEN statement^3
$\quad\quad\quad\quad\quad$ ELSE statement^4

If you find these schematic nests hard to follow you may well believe that when written with actual conditions and statements (including compound statements), and even deeper nesting, this construction becomes very difficult to understand.

Fortunately the most obvious and common type of nested conditional statements can usually be replaced by a single conditional statement with a compound condition. The following examples are effectively equivalent:

$\quad$ IF condition^1 $\qquad\qquad\qquad\qquad$ IF condition^1 & condition^2
$\quad\quad$ THEN IF condition^2 $\qquad\qquad\qquad$ THEN statement^1
$\quad\quad\quad\quad$ THEN statement^1

4.4 <u>Tracing Execution</u>

    Tracing was introduced in Section 4.1.2, before our examples
had loops.   Now we would like to consider tracing of programs
with loops.   To trace execution of a loop, construct a table
with a row for each variable, and a column for the execution of
each statement that changes the value of at least one variable.
For   example, consider the following program, which is a
variation of (1.1d):

```
        *PL/C ID='JOHN WILLIAMS'
         /* SUMMING PROGRAM */
         WILL_SUM: PROCEDURE OPTIONS(MAIN);
            DECLARE N FIXED DECIMAL; /* NUMBER OF DATA */
            DECLARE I FIXED DECIMAL; /* LOOP COUNTER */
            DECLARE X FLOAT DECIMAL; /* NEW DATUM */
            DECLARE SUM FLOAT DECIMAL; /* SUM OF DATA */

            GET LIST(N);
            SUM = 0;
            SUM_LOOP: DO I = 1 TO N BY 1;
                GET LIST(X);
                SUM = SUM + X;
                END SUM_LOOP;
            PUT SKIP LIST('SUM IS:', SUM);
            END WILL_SUM;
        *DATA
            3, 5.6, 42.1, 31.7
```

The first part of the trace table for this program is:

Vari-able	Values as execution proceeds ->									
N	???	3	3	3	3	3	3	3	3	3	3
I	???	???	???	1	1	1	2	2	2	3	3
X	???	???	???	???	5.6	5.6	5.6	42.1	42.1	42.1	31.7
SUM	???	???	0	0	0	5.6	5.6	5.6	47.7	47.7	47.7

    Tracing execution is for the programmer's benefit -- to help
him understand a program or to help him detect an error in it.
Thus, tracing occurs mainly when he is in difficulty of one sort
or another.   It must be done with care, one step at a time.
While tracing, the programmer must execute the program the way
the   machine does, without thinking about the task being
performed. Too often, a programmer executes what he <u>thinks</u> is
there, and not what really <u>is</u> there, which of course doesn't
help at all.

It is not necessary to write down each value in each column,
but only that value that is being changed. The trace table
shown above would then be

Variable	Values as execution proceeds ->							
N	???	3						
I	???		1		2		3	
X	???		5.6		42.1		31.7
SUM	???	0		5.6		47.7		

Often, the trace table becomes complicated and messy, and it
is difficult to go back and analyze it. To aid in studying it,
one often uses an extra row to indicate which statement is being
executed, or to indicate the result of evaluating a condition.
For example, consider the program segment

```
START: SUM = 0;
       GET LIST(X);
       SUM_LOOP: DO WHILE(X ¬= 0);
         L: IF X < 0
                THEN SUM = SUM - X;
                ELSE SUM = SUM + X;
           GET LIST(X);
           END SUM_LOOP;
         SUM = SUM + 1;
         ...
   *DATA
      8, -5, 0
```

In the trace table below, the top row indicates either the
statement executed (by giving its label) or the result of
evaluating a condition of a loop or conditional statement.

Variable	STA-RT:	loop true	L: X>0		loop true	L: X<0		
SUM	???	0	0	0	0	8	8	8	8	13	13
X	???	???	8	8	8	8	-5	-5	-5	-5	0

The amount of information needed in the trace table varies
from program to program, depending on how difficult it is and
how much trouble the programmer is having. But get in the habit
of putting in as much information as possible.

4.5 Initialization and Exit Problems

Most problems with iteration involve <u>starting</u> and <u>stopping</u> the iteration, or equivalently, <u>entering</u> and <u>exiting</u> the program segment that performs the iteration. If one can get the first and last iterations to work properly, the iterations in between generally pose much less of a problem. Developing correct loops is one of the hardest parts of programming. We give some direction in this matter here; the subject is discussed again in Section II.1.5.

4.5.1 Exit Problems in Loops

Exit problems seem to have two principal sources:

1. Design of the stopping condition -- in particular, treatment of the "=" case.

2. Position of the "increment step" relative to the rest of the body.

These problems are more often associated with the DO WHILE form since these tasks are handled more or less automatically in the DO index-var form. However, since the DO WHILE is the more general and important form these questions can neither be ignored nor avoided.

We use an integer summing example, similar to (4.2.1a):

```
            /* SET SUM TO SUM OF INTEGERS 14-728 */
            I = 14;
            SUM = 0;
(4.5.1a)    SUM_LOOP: DO WHILE(I < 729);
                    SUM = SUM + I;
                    I = I + 1;
                    END SUM_LOOP;
```

The condition in this segment could just as well have been written (I <= 728). That is, it could be written to include the case of equality, and with a test value that is to be used in the body. Either form is equally correct -- they result in exactly the same execution -- and there are no general grounds for preferring one form to the other. However, there are two other possibilities that are likely to occur:

condition	result in (4.5.1a)
(I< 728)	one iteration too few
(I<=728)	correct number
(I< 729)	correct number
(I<=729)	one iteration too many

As indicated, the improper matching of the stopping value and the condition will cause improper timing of the exit. This is

an _exceedingly common type of error_, even among experienced
programmers.

Similarly, the position of the increment step can   be
critical.   Changing its position, (4.5.1a) could be written as
below. The comment notwithstanding, (4.5.1b) sums the   integers
from _15_ through _729_.

```
          /* SET SUM TO SUM INTEGERS 14-728 */
          I = 14;
          SUM = 0;
(4.5.1b)  SUM_LOOP: DO WHILE(I < 729);
              I = I + 1;
              SUM = SUM + I;
              END SUM_LOOP;
```

If it is important to have the increment step in the position
used in (4.5.1b) other parts of the segment could be changed.
For example, (4.5.1c) is a corrected version of (4.5.1b):

```
          /* SET SUM TO SUM INTEGERS 14-728 */
          I = 13;
          SUM = 0;
(4.5.1c)  SUM_LOOP: DO WHILE(I < 728);
              I = I + 1;
              SUM = SUM + I;
              END SUM_LOOP;
```


4.5.2 Initialization and Entry Problems

Typically, one or more variables must be "initialized" prior
to entry of a loop, as for example, SUM in (4.5.1a). This is
obvious, and logically straightforward, but nevertheless it is
overlooked surprisingly often.

The benign form of error, in this regard, is to accidentally
place the initialization within the body of the loop, as in
(4.5.2a). This form of error is annoying but is usually
revealed during testing, since it makes the loop ineffective.

```
          /* SET SUM TO SUM INTEGERS 14-728 */
          I = 14;
(4.5.2a)  SUM_LOOP: DO WHILE(I < 729);
              SUM = 0;
              SUM = SUM + I;
              I = I + 1;
              END SUM_LOOP;
```

The malignant form of error is to omit initialization
altogether. For example, if the SUM = 0; statement were omitted
from (4.5.1a), the result of execution would depend upon what
value SUM happened to have when this segment was encountered.
If this happened to be zero throughout testing the   error   would

not be detected and this faulty program would be proclaimed
"correct". Later, in production use, different initial values
for SUM might arise, and this latent error would affect the
results of the program. If the user is fortunate, the effect
will be so dramatic that it is obvious that something is wrong.
If he is less fortunate the error will remain hidden, and it
will intermittently injure the results by varying amounts.

Initialization problems can be much more subtle than the
previous example might suggest. For example, consider the
following task:

Read data from cards and sum the values, until a value of
-1 is encountered. Do not include the -1 in the sum.

Execution of a program for this task will involve the following
sequence of actions:

                    Read a value
                    Add the value just read to a running sum
                    Read a value
                    Add the value just read to a running sum
                    ...
                    Read a value and discover it is -1

Obviously this will involve a loop whose body includes a GET
and an assignment statement, but the entry and exit from the
loop are not as obvious. Note that the sequence must both begin
and end with a read. That is, at least one value must be read,
and when the last value (the -1) is read, it must not be
followed by an addition.

If you think of this program in terms of iteration of a pair
of actions
                    Read a value
                    Add the value just read to a running sum

then the simple DO WHILE loop cannot be used, since it is unable
to prevent the addition from following the last read. You could
use the techniques described in Sections 4.3.2 and 4.3.3:

```
              /* READ AND SUM DATA UNTIL FIRST -1 */
                 SUM = 0;
(4.5.2b)         SUM_LOOP: DO WHILE('1'B);
                        GET LIST(VAL);
                        IF VAL = -1 THEN GO TO TERM_SUM;
                        SUM = SUM + VAL;
                        END SUM_LOOP;
                 TERM_SUM:;
```

Alternatively, you could think of the program in terms of
iteration of the pair

                    Add the value just read to a running sum
                    Read another value

This simplifies the exit problem considerably, and a normal WHILE loop can be used:

```
SUM_LOOP: DO WHILE(VAL ¬= -1);
    SUM = SUM + VAL;
    GET LIST(VAL);
    END SUM_LOOP;
```

However, now the problem is to get the loop started properly. One method would be to read the first value as an initialization action, outside of the DO group:

```
          /* READ AND SUM DATA UNTIL FIRST -1 */
          SUM = 0;
          GET LIST(VAL);
(4.5.2c)  SUM_LOOP: DO WHILE(VAL ¬= -1);
              SUM = SUM + VAL;
              GET LIST(VAL);
              END SUM_LOOP;
```

It is not very clean to have to rewrite a portion of the body of the loop as initialization, but all things considered, for most simple tasks the style of (4.5.2c) is preferable to that of (4.5.2b). Since at least one number must be read, having the first number read outside of the loop makes sense.

The style of (4.5.2c) begins to become burdensome as the size and complexity of the initialization action grows. If an appreciable number of statements in the body must be rewritten outside, the risk increases that they will not be exactly the same. They might start out identical, but subsequent changes in one location might not be faithfully repeated in the other. In such cases, one sometimes contrives a way to get the iteration started, with minimal initialization. For example:

```
          /* READ AND SUM DATA UNTIL FIRST -1 */
          SUM = 0;
          VAL = 0;
(4.5.2d)  SUM_LOOP: DO WHILE(VAL ¬= -1);
              SUM = SUM + VAL;
              GET LIST(VAL);
              END SUM_LOOP;
```

(4.5.2d) differs from (4.5.2c) only in the replacement of GET LIST(VAL); with VAL = 0; but the difference in philosophy is quite significant. A dummy value has been contrived to force execution of the loop body; and the first statement in the body is executed pointlessly but harmlessly. This was done just to avoid having to write a duplicate of a portion of the body outside the loop. It should be obvious that this is a tricky and dangerous practice.

The previous examples illustrate three unattractive ways of performing a very common kind of task: (4.5.2b) requires a GO TO exit; (4.5.2c) requires rewriting a portion of the body outside the loop; and (4.5.2d) requires a devious contrivance to get the loop started. The least unattractive of these will vary, depending upon context and other circumstances. Basically, the problem is that PL/I (as well as most other programming languages) does not offer a natural and convenient way to perform this task.

Section 4 <u>Summary</u>

1. A PL/I job consists of a "main procedure", optionally
followed by data.   The execution of a program consists of a
single execution of the main procedure.

2. The normal order of statement execution is the order in
which the statements are written.

3. A loop is a control mechanism to provide iteration of a
group of consecutive statements.   The two basic forms of a loop
are:

```
        loop-name: DO WHILE(condition);
             Body of loop;
             END loop-name;

        loop-name: DO index-variable = expr¹ TO expr² BY expr³;
             Body of loop;
             END loop-name;
```

4. A condition is an expression involving a relational
operator, and possibly Boolean operators.   Its evaluation yields
either "true" or "false".   In PL/I, "true" and "false" are
represented by the constants '1'B and '0'B, respectively.

5. There are two forms of conditional execution of a statement:

```
        IF condition THEN statement¹

        IF condition THEN statement¹ ELSE statement²
```

Statement¹ and statement² can be either simple or compound
statements.

6. A conditional branch may be used to terminate execution of a
program segment.   This is the primary use of the GO TO in PL/I:

```
        /* comment describing segment action */
           ...
           IF condition THEN GO TO TERM_segment-name;
           ...
           TERM_segment-name:;
```

Section 4 <u>Exercises</u>

<u>1</u>. Write a separate, complete program (similar to the examples in Section 4.1.1) to perform each of the following tasks:

 a) Read five data values, compute their sum and print the sum.

 b) Read three data values, compute the first times the sum of
    the second and third, and print the result.

 c) Without reading any data (no GET statements) compute the sum
    of the integers from 1 to 8 and print the result.

 d) Read four data values, print the maximum of the four values.

<u>2</u>. Write a single program that will perform all four of the tasks listed in Exercise 1, one after another.

<u>3</u>. Trace the execution of the programs in Exercise 1.

<u>4</u>. Keypunch and run the programs in Exercise 1.

<u>5</u>. Trace the execution of the following program segments:

```
a) TOTAL = 0;
   TOTAL_LOOP: DO WHILE(TOTAL < 5);
        TOTAL = TOTAL + 1;
        END TOTAL_LOOP;

b) R1 = 0;
   R2 = 0;
   R3 = 0;
   R1_LOOP: DO I = 1 TO 3 BY 1;
        R1 = R1 + 1;
        R2_LOOP: DO J = 3 TO -1 BY -1;
             R2 = R2 + 1;
             R3_LOOP: DO K = 3 TO 5 BY 2;
                  R3 = R3 + 1;
                  END R3_LOOP;
             END R2_LOOP;
        END R1_LOOP;
```

```
c) A = 2;
   B = 5;
      /* COMPUTE Z=A**B, ASSUMING A > 0 AND B > 0 ARE */
      /* INTEGERS */
         Z = 1;
         X = A;
         Y = B;
         NONZERO_LOOP: DO WHILE(Y ¬= 0);
            EVEN_LOOP: DO WHILE(FLOOR(Y/2E0) * 2 = Y);
               Y = Y/2E0;
               X = X * X;
               END EVEN_LOOP;
            Y = Y - 1;
            Z = Z * X;
            END NONZERO_LOOP;
```

d) Same as c), but with "A=2; B=5;" replaced by "A=1; B=1;".

e)
```
   /* PRINT THE FIRST 7 FIBONACCI NUMBERS */
         N = 7;
         FIRST = 0;
         PUT LIST(FIRST);
         SECOND = 1;
         PUT LIST(SECOND);
         FIB_LOOP: DO I = 3 TO N BY 1;
            NEXT = FIRST + SECOND;
            PUT LIST(NEXT);
            FIRST = SECOND;
            SECOND = NEXT;
            END FIB_LOOP;
```

f)
```
      GET LIST(N);
       PRINT_LOOP: DO I = 1 TO N BY 1;
       GET LIST(X);
       IF X < 0 THEN DO;
            Y = X + 1;
            PUT SKIP LIST(Y); END;
       END PRINT_LOOP;
       ...
    *DATA
       0, 8 , 8, 9, 8 3
```

g) Same as f), but with the data

```
    *DATA
       5, -30, 40, 50, -60, -70, -80
```

<u>6</u>. The following exercises are to be written using only
conditional statements, assignment statements, and GET and PUT.

a) Write a single conditional statement with only an
   assignment statement as a substatement, for the following:

```
IF X < 0 THEN
  IF Y < 0 THEN
    IF Z = 5 THEN A = X + Y + Z;
```

b) Rewrite the following using a single conditional statement:

```
IF X < 0
  THEN DO; IF Y < 0 THEN A = X + Y + Z; END;
  ELSE IF X = 5 THEN A = X + Y + Z;
```

c) Given three variables A, B and C, write a program segment
   to interchange the values of A, B and C so that the largest
   is in A and the smallest is in C.

d) Given three variables X, Y, and Z, write a program to
   determine if they are the sides of a triangle. (X, Y, and
   Z are the lengths of the sides of a triangle if all are
   greater than 0 and if X+Y>Z, X+Z>Y, and Y+Z>X.)

e) Write a program segment to print '1' if X, Y, and Z are the
   lengths of the sides of an equilateral triangle, and '2' if
   they are the sides of a non-equilateral triangle.   A
   triangle is equilateral if all its sides are the same.

f) A, B and C are three variables with different values.   One
   of these variables has the "middle value" -- one other is
   greater, one smaller. Write a program segment that will
   set variable D to this middle value. Compare this to the
   program for c).

<u>7</u>. Exercises with loops.

a) Write a WHILE loop with initialization that is equivalent
   to:

```
FACT = 1;
FACT_LOOP: DO I = 2 TO N BY 1;
     FACT = FACT * I;
     END FACT_LOOP;
```

b) Write a program segment to read in a sequence of 50 numbers
   and print out those numbers that are > 0.

c) Given a variable N with a value greater than 0, write a
   program segment to print N, N**2, ..., N**N.

d) Given variables N and M, both with values > 0, write a
segment to print all powers of N that are less than M.
That is, print the value N**i for all i such that N**i < M.

e) The <u>Fibonacci</u> <u>numbers</u> are the numbers 0, 1, 1, 2, 3, 5, 8,
13, 21, ... The first one is 0, the second is 1, and each
succesive one is the sum of the two preceding ones.   The
segment of Exercise 1 e) calculates the first 7 Fibonacci
numbers and prints them out. Given a variable N≥2, write a
program segment to print out all Fibonacci numbers which
are less than N (<u>not</u> the first N Fibonacci numbers).

<u>8</u>. Write complete programs for the following problems. Most of
these use the program segments written in earlier exercises.

a) The input consists of groups of three numbers.   The last
group is an end-of-list signal consisting of three zero
values. Write a program to read each group in, print it
out, and print an indication of whether the three numbers
represent the sides of a triangle. (See Exercise 6d.)

b) The input consists of an integer N ≥ 0, followed by N
groups of three numbers. Write a program to read the
groups of numbers in, print them out, and then print the
middle value of the three. Each group and its middle value
should appear on a separate line.

c) The input consists of a single integer N. Write a program
to read in N and print the first N Fibonacci numbers. (If
N < 1, don't print any out.)

d) The input consists of two positive integers M and N, with M
≥ N. Write a program to print all Fibonacci numbers which
lie between M and N.

e) The input consists of a positive integer N.   Write a
program to read N and to print out the first, second, third
and fourth powers of the integers 2, 3, ..., N.   The
beginning of your output should look like

```
        2            4            8           16
        3            9           27           81
```

Section 5 Multiple-Valued Variables

5.1 Arrays of Subscripted Variables

Suppose it is necessary to store and process a large amount of data at the same time. For example, we might want to calculate a set of numbers, then sort them into increasing order, and finally print them in sorted order. If there were 50 different numbers, using 50 different variables with different names would be cumbersome. In order to handle such situations, most programming languages use a "data structure" called an array.

An array is a set of variables, each having a separate value just like an ordinary simple variable, but with all the variables of the set sharing a common identifier. A "subscript" is added to this common identifier to produce a unique name for each individual element of the set. For this reason these are often called subscripted variables. For example, an identifier X could refer to a set of five variables:

(5.1a)
$$\begin{array}{ll} X(1) & \underline{20} \\ X(2) & \underline{-2} \\ X(3) & \underline{6} \\ X(4) & 2\underline{17} \\ X(5) & \underline{8} \end{array}$$

Programming languages are unable to use conventional subscripts because the keypunch (and most other input devices) lack the capability of depressing a character below the normal printing line. As a consequence subscripts are generally identified by being enclosed in parentheses.

In the example above, X is called an "array of subscripted variables". Each of the variables named X(1), X(2), X(3), X(4) and X(5) is itself called a "subscripted variable". (Unsubscripted variables -- those discussed before this section, whose names are just simple identifiers -- will now be called "simple variables".) The "name" of a subscripted variable has the form:

identifier(integer)

Thus X(1), X(0), X(+1), and X(-1) are all valid subscripted

variable names.   X(1) and X(+1) refer to the same variable.
Note that the parentheses are necessary: X(2) is a subscripted
variable, while X2 is just a simple variable with no relation
whatever to the array X of subscripted variables.

Subscripted variables usually have positive subscripts, but
zero and negative subscripts can also be used when convenient.

For example, suppose we need a table whose values represent
the number of minutes in a day that the temperature is between i
and i+1 degrees Fahrenheit. For each integer i, we can store
the number of minutes that the temperature is between i and i+1
in the appropriate element of an array named MINUTES. Thus, the
value of MINUTES(2) represents the number of minutes the
temperature is between 2 and 3 degrees; MINUTES(47) represents
the number of minutes between 47 and 48 degrees, MINUTES(-3) the
number of minutes between -3 and -2, etc.

The name of a subscripted variable can be used exactly as the
name of a simple variable is used. For example, execution of

        A = X(3) * X(1);

causes the current value of X(3) (which is given as 6 in (5.1a))
to be multiplied by X(1) (which is 20), and the result 120 to be
stored in simple variable A. Similarly, a subscripted variable
can be given as the target of. an assignment process:

        X(2) = X(4) * 5;

The value of X(4) (which is 217) is multiplied by 5 and the
result (1085) is stored in X(2). At this point, then, there
seems to be little difference between a simple and subscripted
variable, except that the name of the latter has a somewhat more
complicated form. The real power of subscripted variables is
shown in the next section.

5.1.1 Referencing Subscripted Variables

Suppose we wish to write a program to obtain the sum of the
values of 50 different variables. We could use 50 simple
variables named V1, V2, V3, ..., V50, and obtain their sum using
a single, long assignment statement:

```
        /* SET SUM TO SUM OF V1 THROUGH V50 */
        SUM = V1 + V2 + V3 + V4 + V5 + V6 + V7 + V8 +
            V9 + V10 + V11 + V12 + V13 + V14 + V15 +
            V16 + V17 + V18 + V19 + V20 + V21 + V22 +
            V23 + V24 + V25 + V26 + V27 + V28 + V29 +
            V30 + V31 + V32 + V33 + V34 + V35 + V36 +
            V37 + V38 + V39 + V40 + V41 + V42 + V43 +
            V44 + V45 + V46 + V47 + V48 + V49 + V50;
```

Alternatively the sum could be obtained using a sequence of   51
assignment statements:

```
         /* SET SUM TO SUM OF V1 THROUGH V50 */
            SUM = 0;
            SUM = SUM + V1;
            SUM = SUM + V2;
            SUM = SUM + V3;
               . . .
            SUM = SUM + V50;
```

   A slight modification of this second method would be to use
an array U of subscripted variables:

```
         /* SET SUM TO SUM OF U(1:50) */
            SUM = 0;
            SUM = SUM + U(1);
(5.1.1a)    SUM = SUM + U(2);
            SUM = SUM + U(3);
               . . .
            SUM = SUM + U(50);
```

The term U(1:50) in the comment is a convenient way of saying
"all of the variables U(1) through U(50)".

   Now suppose there is a simple variable I with value 2:

```
      I    2
```

and suppose we execute the following assignment statement:

```
      SUM = SUM + U(I);
```

This is interpreted as follows:

      Add a copy of the current value of variable SUM to a copy
      of the current value of one of the subscripted variables of
      the array U. The subscripted variable to be used is
      determined by the value of the variable I. Since I's value
      is currently 2, the term U(I) refers to U(2). Hence a copy
      of the value of U(2) is added to the value of SUM. The
      result is stored as a new value for SUM.

Note that the assignment process remains the same except that a
preliminary evaluation of variable I is required to determine
which of the subscripted variables of U is to be used. This may
not seem significant on first encounter, but it is, in fact,
exceedingly powerful. Using this method of referencing
subscripted variables and the means of controlling repetition
introduced in Section 4.2, (5.1.1a) can be written as

```
            /* SET SUM TO SUM OF U(1:50) */
                 I = 0;
                 SUM = 0;
                 SUM_LOOP: DO WHILE(I < 50);
(5.1.1b)             I = I + 1;
                     SUM = SUM + U(I);
                 END SUM_LOOP;
```

Assuming a set of values for the array U, after execution of the first two assignment statements of this program the values might be the following:

U(1)	$\underline{5}$	I	$\underline{0}$
U(2)	$\underline{7}$	SUM	$\underline{0}$
U(3)	$\underline{1}$		

Execution of the WHILE loop starts with the evaluation of the condition. The condition is true, since the current value of I, 0, is less than 50, and the body of the loop is executed. First I is increased to 1. The second assignment statement in the body involves a subscripted variable. The current value of I, which appears as the subscript, is 1 so the current value of U(1), which is 5, is added to the value of SUM. Thus 5 is stored as the new value of SUM. At this point the values of the variables are:

U(1)	$\underline{5}$	I	$\underline{1}$
U(2)	$\underline{7}$	SUM	$\underline{5}$
U(3)	$\underline{1}$		

The condition is then evaluated. I is still less than 50 so the body is again executed. The first assignment statement increases I to 2. Since I is now 2, the value of the subscripted variable U(2) is added to SUM to give 12. This is stored as the new value of SUM.

You should continue this exercise until convinced that the result is the same as that obtained by (5.1.1a). Of particular interest is the last execution of the loop body, when I is 49. At this time I is increased to 50, and the value of U(50) is added to SUM (which by then contains the sum of the first 49 elements of the array U). Evaluation of the condition now yields false and execution of the loop is finished.

(5.1.1b) could also be written using the second loop form:

```
            /* SET SUM TO SUM OF U(1:50) */
                 SUM = 0;
                 SUM_LOOP: DO I = 1 TO 50 BY 1;
                     SUM = SUM + U(I);
                 END SUM_LOOP;
```

As a further example, suppose the problem required the sum of the variables U(1), U(2), ..., up to the first variable with zero value. The two alternative DO group forms would be:

```
/* SET SUM TO SUM OF U(1:50) THRU FIRST 0 */
I = 1;
SUM = U(I);
SUMFZ_LOOP: DO WHILE((U(I) ¬= 0) & (I < 50));
    I = I + 1;
    SUM = SUM + U(I);
    END SUMFZ_LOOP;

/* SET SUM TO SUM OF U(1:50) THRU FIRST 0 */
SUM = 0;
SUM_LOOP: DO I = 1 TO 50 BY 1;
    IF U(I) = 0 THEN GO TO TERM_SUM;
    SUM = SUM + U(I);
    END SUM_LOOP;
TERM_SUM: ;
```

An expression may be given for a subscript -- the constants
and variables in the examples so far are just special cases of
expressions. The only restriction is that when evaluated the
expression must yield an appropriate integer value. Expression
subscripts can be very useful. For example, suppose there were
two arrays, LEFT and RIGHT, each consisting of 15 variables.
The following segment of program would copy the values of LEFT
into RIGHT in inverted order:

```
/* SET RIGHT(1:15) TO REVERSE-ORDER OF LEFT(1:15) */
REVERSE_LOOP: DO I = 1 TO 15 BY 1;
    RIGHT(I) = LEFT(16-I);
    END REVERSE_LOOP;
```

5.2 Variables with Multiple Subscripts

It is sometimes convenient to use more than one subscript to
designate a particular variable from an array. This is done
when there is more than one natural pattern for referencing
variables from the array. For example, suppose one had grades
for up to fifty students in as many as nine courses apiece.
Assume variables NUMCRS and NUMSTUD give the number of courses
and number of students, respectively. We store these grades in
an array GRADE of doubly-subscripted variables so that
GRADE(I,J) represents the grade of the jth student in the ith
course. That is, GRADE(3,17) is the grade of the 17th student
in the 3rd course. Then to obtain the average grade in a
certain course you could write:

```
/* SET AVGGRADE TO AVERAGE GRADE IN ITH COURSE */
TOTGRADE = 0;
STUD_LOOP: DO J = 1 TO NUMSTUD BY 1;
    TOTGRADE = TOTGRADE + GRADE(I,J);
    END STUD_LOOP;
AVGGRADE = TOTGRADE/NUMSTUD;
```

To obtain the average for a particular student for all of his courses you could write:

```
     /* SET STUDAVG TO AVERAGE GRADE FOR JTH STUDENT */
        SUMGRADE = 0;
        CRS_LOOP: DO I = 1 TO NUMCRS BY 1;
            SUMGRADE = SUMGRADE + GRADE(I,J);
            END CRS_LOOP;
        STUDAVG = SUMGRADE/NUMCRS;
```

Note that this assumes that each student has exactly the same number of grades -- the number given by NUMCRS. If a student had fewer grades than NUMCRS and the omitted grades were represented by zeros in GRADE this program segment will produce incorrect averages. To remedy this we would need another array NBRCOURSES(1:50) to give the number of courses for each student. The program to produce an average for an individual student would be:

```
     /* SET STUDAVG TO AVERAGE GRADE FOR JTH STUDENT */
        SUMGRADE = 0;
        CRS_LOOP: DO I = 1 TO NBRCOURSES(J) BY 1;
            SUMGRADE = SUMGRADE + GRADE(I,J);
            END CRS_LOOP;
        STUDAVG = SUMGRADE/NBRCOURSES(J);
```

   The overall average (all students in all courses) could be obtained by executing

```
     /* SET OVAVG TO OVERALL AVERAGE GRADE */
        GSUM = 0;
        STUD_LOOP: DO J = 1 TO NUMSTUD BY 1;
            /* SET STUDAVG TO AVG GRADE FOR JTH STUD */
            SUMGRADE = 0;
            CRS_LOOP: DO I = 1 TO NBRCOURSES(J) BY 1;
                SUMGRADE = SUMGRADE + GRADE(I,J);
                END CRS_LOOP;
            STUDAVG = SUMGRADE/NBRCOURSES(J);
            GSUM = GSUM + STUDAVG;
            END STUD_LOOP;
        OVAVG = GSUM/NUMSTUD;
```

However, note that the following might be an equally plausible interpretation of the same problem:

```
     /* SET OVAVG TO OVERALL AVERAGE GRADE */
        GSUM = 0;
        TOTAL_COURSES = 0;
        STUD_LOOP: DO J = 1 TO NUMSTUD BY 1;
            TOTAL_COURSES = TOTAL_COURSES +
                     NBRCOURSES(J);
            CRS_LOOP: DO I = 1 TO NBRCOURSES(J) BY 1;
                GSUM = GSUM + GRADE(I,J);
                END CRS_LOOP;
            END STUD_LOOP;
        OVAVG = GSUM/TOTAL_COURSES;
```

Only under certain circumstances would these two interpretations give the same answer -- can you see why? In general, one or the other of these program segments is not interpreting "overall average" in the way intended by the person asking the question. This may begin to suggest why it is so easy to come up with programs that are not quite right.

An array of singly-subscripted variables is a "list" of variables -- with the subscript specifying the position on the list. The analogous interpretation of an array of doubly-subscripted variables is a "table" or "matrix". The first subscript specifies the <u>row</u> position and the second specifies the <u>column</u>:

$$GRADE(1,1) \quad GRADE(1,2) \quad GRADE(1,3) \quad GRADE(1,4) \quad ...$$

$$GRADE(2,1) \quad GRADE(2,2) \quad GRADE(2,3) \quad GRADE(2,4)$$

$$GRADE(3,1) \quad GRADE(3,2) \quad GRADE(3,3) \quad GRADE(3,4)$$

. . .

It is also common to visualize the variables of an array as being distributed in a geometric space. An array of singly-subscripted variables is said to be a "one-dimensional array" or "vector". The values are considered to be positioned along a line, with the subscript giving the position on the line. An array of doubly-subscripted variables is called a "two-dimensional array" or "matrix" and the pair of subscripts specifies a position in the plane of values. Although singly- and doubly-subscripted variables are the most common, three or more subscripts can be used if required.

5.3 <u>Declaration of Arrays</u>

An array declaration specifies the number of subscripted variables to be created and the number of subscripts to be used for referencing each variable, as well as the type of value each variable   can   contain.   The   most   common   form   for   a   one-dimensional array is

DECLARE identifier(bound) attributes;

An example is:

DECLARE TEMP(50) FLOAT DECIMAL;

This defines an array of 50 variables named TEMP(1), TEMP(2), ..., TEMP(50), each capable of holding one FLOAT DECIMAL number.

If subscript values are to start anywhere except 1, then a lower bound must also be given. For example, to define an array of 22 variables named POP(-1), POP(0), ..., POP(20), use

```
DECLARE POP(-1:20) FLOAT DECIMAL;
```

Multiple subscripts are indicated by two or more bounds, separated by commas. For example, to define an array of 450 doubly-subscripted variables with the values of the first subscript ranging from 1 to 9, and the second from 1 to 50, use

```
DECLARE GRADE(9,50) FLOAT DECIMAL;
```

Don't confuse the role of the comma and the colon in the bounds declaration. The comma separates bounds, indicating how many dimensions the array has and how many subscripts each reference to an element in the array must have. The colon separates lower and upper bounds of a <u>single</u> dimension. The comma must be present if there is more than one dimension; the colon is necessary only in particular dimensions where the lower bound is different from one. For example

```
DECLARE (TABLE1(3:4), TABLE2(3,4)) FLOAT DECIMAL;
```

creates two arrays: TABLE1 with one dimension and only two elements, and TABLE2 with two dimensions and twelve elements.

As a final example, the following declaration defines a three-dimensional array of 60 integer variables, each with three subscripts. The values of the first subscript range from -5 to -2; the second from 1 to 3; and the third from 0 to 4.

```
DECLARE POINT(-5:-2,3,0:4) FIXED DECIMAL;
```

In referring to arrays in the text we will generally use the same form as the declaration. That is, MAT(1:5,1:9) refers to the array defined by the declaration

```
DECLARE MAT(1:5,1:9) FLOAT DECIMAL;
```

We use the complete form of the declaration in these references -- MAT(1:5,1:9) rather than MAT(5,9) -- since this distinguishes between a reference to the complete array and a reference to the particular subscripted variable with maximum subscript values. We also use the notation to refer to an array segment -- a part of the array. For example, if A(1:100) is an array, we might discuss the segment A(1:50), or A(1:N) where N contains the subscript value. A(1:1) refers to the single element A(1), while A(1:0) refers to the array segment containing <u>no</u> elements, the <u>empty</u> segment.

5.4 Program for the Example of 1.2.1

In Section 1.2.1 the analysis of a problem description was
carried   through   several   levels,   but   the   programming   was
postponed until subscripted variables could be employed.   The
analysis in Section 1.2.1 had reached the following stage:

> 3.1 Read a sequence of 100 or fewer positive integers from
> cards until a zero value is encountered; store these
> integers in memory, preserving order.
>
> 3.2 Find the position of the integer with maximum value in
> this sequence.
>
> 3.3 Print the early values of the sequence, from the first
> to the maximum value, one per line.

Each of these subtasks is well defined and detailed program
design can begin.   The next step is to specify the data
structures that will be used.

The principal data structure will have to be an array since
there are many values to be stored at once. Call it INTEGER to
remind us that only integer values are allowed.   It needs at
least 100 elements since there may be that many data values, and
should be FIXED DECIMAL.   There should be a variable TOP (say)
to indicate the number of values currently in the array, and a
variable MAXP (say) to mark the position of the maximum value.
Later, as we design the different subtasks, we may find that
other variables will be needed.

Now the problem statement can be rewritten in terms of the
variables that will be used:

> 4.1 Read data into INTEGER(1:TOP) until a zero value is
> encountered (keeping the value of TOP as defined above).
>
> 4.2 Set MAXP to mark the position of the maximum value in
> INTEGER(1:TOP).
>
> 4.3 Print the values in INTEGER(1:MAXP), one per line.

This description is now very close to programming language
terms.   Although it may not seem so to one who is just learning
the language, the hardest part of the programming process is
bringing the problem description to this level. The analysis
and design have been completed -- from here on it is just a
matter of translating into the proper form.

We will program the sub-tasks one at a time, taking them in
reverse order just to demonstrate their relative independence.
The program for 4.3 is obviously a loop:

```
PRINT_LOOP: DO I = 1 TO MAXP BY 1;
    PUT SKIP LIST(INTEGER(I));
    END PRINT_LOOP;
```

Problems concerning extreme values of MAXP might arise in this subtask. If MAXP<1 no values will be printed. This makes sense since MAXP<1 means that <u>no</u> values appeared in the input -- only the end signal 0. If MAXP>100 an invalid subscript will be used, so prior statements must ensure that MAXP<=100.

The program for 4.2 must take into account that no values may be supplied in the data -- only the end-of-list signal may appear. We set MAXP to zero initially, to indicate that no maximum has been found yet. We also find it advantageous to introduce a variable MAXVAL to contain the maximum value encountered so far; we initialize it to -1, which is less than any possible value. If there is actually no list then the body of the loop labeled FINDMAX will never be executed and MAX will remain at zero.

```
MAXVAL = -1;
MAXP = 0;
FINDMAX_LOOP: DO I = 1 TO TOP BY 1;
    IF INTEGER(I) > MAXVAL THEN DO;
        MAXVAL = INTEGER(I);
        MAXP = I; END;
    END FINDMAX_LOOP;
```

This routine has potential problems if TOP>100.   However, note that if 0≤TOP≤100, this segment automatically guarantees a value for MAXP that will be acceptable to the routine for 4.3.

The program for 4.1 is less obvious and could be done in several different ways. It must make provision for a number of extreme conditions with respect to the input data:

1. It must work properly for every valid quantity of data -- as little as none, to as much as 100 values.

2. It must provide adequate warning when it encounters improper data -- no data at all, too much data, data without the proper end signal, or improper values as described in 3 below.

3. The problem statement specifies that the data will be positive integers. A fundamental decision must be made as to whether the program will <u>trust</u> that it will only be presented with such proper data, or whether it will <u>test</u> to make sure that this is the case. As a general philosophy, programs should be <u>suspicious and trust no one</u>.

Reading each value directly into a FIXED DECIMAL variable would cause it to be truncated without warning. So that we can test for non-integers, each value will instead be read into a temporary variable TFLOAT which is FLOAT DECIMAL. The following

segment (which still includes English statements) contains a
loop which reads and processes the data until the endmarker 0 is
read or until 100 values have been processed. The last
statement prints an error if the endmarker has not been read.
The segment also relies on PL/I to provide a warning if it runs
out of data unexpectedly; this would occur if the endmarker was
missing and there were 100 or fewer proper values. By "process
TFLOAT" we mean to check for errors in TFLOAT and store it in
the array. Remember, TOP always indicates the number of values
in the array.

```
TOP = 0;
GET LIST (TFLOAT);
LOAD_LOOP: DO WHILE((TOP < 100) & (TFLOAT ¬= 0));
    Process TFLOAT;
    GET LIST(TFLOAT);
    END LOAD_LOOP;
IF TFLOAT ¬= 0 THEN Print error;
```

The complete program, after further refinement, is

```
*PL/C ID='EVAN CONWAY'
 /* LIST POSITIVE INTEGERS FROM FIRST TO MAXIMUM */
 LISTTOMAX: PROCEDURE OPTIONS(MAIN);
      DECLARE (INTEGER(1:100), /* THE POSITIVE VALUES READ*/
               TOP,            /* ARE IN INTEGER(1:TOP).  */
               MAXVAL,         /* IF NO VALUES, MAXP=0; ELSE*/
               MAXP,           /* MAXP MARKS MAXVAL POSITION*/
               I)              /* MAXVAL=MAX(INTEGER(1:TOP))*/
                  FIXED DECIMAL;
      DECLARE TFLOAT FLOAT DECIMAL; /* LAST VALUE READ IN */

      /* READ DATA, CHECK, AND STORE IN INTEGER(1:100) */
      /* UNTIL 0 IS FOUND.  */
        TOP = 0;
        GET LIST(TFLOAT);
        LOAD_LOOP: DO WHILE((TOP < 100) & (TFLOAT ¬= 0));
           IF (TFLOAT > 0) & (FLOOR(TFLOAT) = TFLOAT)
              THEN DO; TOP = TOP + 1;
                   INTEGER(TOP) = TFLOAT; END;
              ELSE PUT SKIP LIST('IMPROPER DATA:', TFLOAT);
           GET LIST(TFLOAT);
           END LOAD_LOOP;
        IF TFLOAT ¬= 0 THEN
              PUT SKIP LIST('MORE THAN 100 VALUES');

      /* SET MAXP TO MARK POSITION OF MAX IN INTEGER(1:TOP) */
        MAXVAL = -1;
        MAXP = 0;
        FINDMAX_LOOP: DO I = 1 TO TOP BY 1;
              IF INTEGER(I) > MAXVAL THEN DO;
                   MAXVAL = INTEGER(I);
                   MAXP = I; END;
              END FINDMAX_LOOP;

      /* PRINT NUMBERS IN INTEGER(1:MAXP) */
        PRINT_LOOP: DO I = 1 TO MAXP BY 1;
              PUT SKIP LIST(INTEGER(I));
              END PRINT_LOOP;

      END LISTTOMAX;
*DATA
```

Section 5 <u>Summary</u>

1. An array is a set of subscripted variables. These are distinct variables but all have the same identifier and contain the same type of value.

2. A subscripted variable reference consists of an identifier with a subscript -- an expression enclosed in parentheses. Upon evaluation the subscript expression must yield an appropriate integer value. Multiple subscripts are expressions separated by commas.

3. An identifier is declared to be an array by giving the upper bound on the subscript:

DECLARE identifier(bound) attributes;

If a lower bound is other than 1, it must be explicitly specified:

DECLARE ident(lower-bound:upper-bound) attributes;

For multiple subscripts the bounds are separated by commas.

4. References to an array in the text will generally be in the same form as a declaration, including explicit lower bounds on subscript values. For example, MATRIX(1:5,1:10), SET(0:4).

Section 5 Exercises

<u>1</u>. The following are values of certain arrays and simple variables: (??? means no value has been assigned yet.)

```
        B(-3)   20        AGE(1)   1        I  1
        B(-2)   25        AGE(2)  13        J  2
        B(-1)   42        AGE(3)  21        K  3
        B(0)     9        AGE(4)   6        M  4
        B(1)     8        AGE(5)   7      SUM  ???
        B(2)    13        AGE(6)  12        C  ???
        B(3)   -20        AGE(7)   8      MAX  ???
        B(4)   -40        AGE(8)   0      MIN  ???
        B(5)    50
```

a) Give the values of B(-2), AGE(5), B(I), AGE(I+J).

b) Give the name of the variable containing the largest value in array B(-3:5); in array AGE(1:8).

c) Evaluate the following expressions:

```
        B(1) + AGE(4)
        B(3) * AGE(1)
        5 + B(5) + AGE(5)
        AGE(6)/6
```

d) Give the value of B(1), B(I+1), B(I+J).

e) Which of the following refer to existing variables?

```
        AGE(I-M)      B(I-M)      AGE(I+M)      B(I+M)
```

f) Give the values of:

```
        B(AGE(1))    B(AGE(M)-1)    AGE(AGE(4))    AGE(AGE(M+I)-2)
```

g) Evaluate the following expressions:

```
        M + AGE(M)
        M + AGE(K)
        B(3)*3 - AGE(3)
        AGE(J+J)/AGE(J)
        B(M-I)
```

h) Give declarations for all of the arrays and variables shown. (Assume FIXED DECIMAL values for I, J, K and M; FLOAT DECIMAL for the others.)

i) Write assignment statements to assign the values to the variables as shown.

j) Write GET statements and a data list to assign the values to the variables as shown.

2. Assuming variables with initial values as in Exercise 1, trace the execution of the following program segments and show the values that result from their execution.

```
a) /* SET SUM TO SUM OF AGE(J:M) */
        C = J;
        SUM = 0;
        SUM_LOOP: DO WHILE(C <= M);
            SUM = SUM + AGE(C);
            C = C + 1;
            END SUM_LOOP;

b) /* SET MAX TO MAX OF AGE(I:M) */
        MAX = AGE(I);
        C = I + 1;
        MAX_LOOP: DO WHILE(C <= M);
            IF MAX < AGE(C) THEN MAX = AGE(C);
            C = C + 1;
            END MAX_LOOP;

c)  /* ADD THE SUBSCRIPT VALUE I TO EACH VARIABLE B(I) */
        C = -3;
        SUBSCRIPT_LOOP: DO WHILE(C <= 5);
            B(C) = B(C) + C;
            C = C + 1;
            END SUBSCRIPT_LOOP;

d)  /* SET AGE(1:8) TO "FIBONACCI SEQUENCE" */
        /* THAT IS, AGE(1) = 0; AGE(2) = 1; */
        /* AGE(I) = AGE(I-2) + AGE(I-1) FOR I > 2 */
        AGE(1) = 0;
        AGE(2) = 1;
        C = 3;
        FIB_LOOP: DO WHILE(C <= 8);
            AGE(C) = AGE(C-1) + AGE(C-2);
            C = C + 1;
            END FIB_LOOP;

e)  /* SET B(5:-3) TO ABS(B(5:-3)) WITHOUT ABS FUNCTION */
        C = 5;
        ABS_LOOP: DO WHILE(C >= -3);
            IF B(C) < 0 THEN B(C) = -B(C);
            C = C - 1;
            END ABS_LOOP;

f)  /* MOVE EACH VALUE IN B(-3:5) UP 1 POSITION */
    /* STORE 0 IN B(-3), DISCARD B(5) */
        C = 5;
        MOVE_LOOP: DO WHILE(C > -3);
            B(C) = B(C-1);
            C = C - 1;
            END MOVE_LOOP;
        B(-3) = 0;
```

3. Draw lines (locations) as shown in Exercise 1 for variables declared as follows:

a) DECLARE (A, B) FIXED DECIMAL;

b) DECLARE AGE(3,4) FIXED DECIMAL;

c) DECLARE COST(-3:0) FLOAT DECIMAL;

d) DECLARE (PAY(0:10),AMOUNT(0:10),I) FLOAT DECIMAL;

4. Write program segments to accomplish each of the following tasks, using the variables declared in Exercise 3:

a) Set all of the variables in the array AGE(1:3,1:4) to zero.

b) Set each variable in the array AGE(1:3,1:4) equal to the sum of its own subscripts -- that is, AGE(I,J) equal to I + J.

c) Set each variable in the array COST(-3:0) equal to whatever is the minimum of the initial values of the variables in COST.

d) Subtract the value of each variable in the array AMOUNT(0:10) from the variable in the corresponding position in the array PAY(0:10).

e) Compute the sum of the values of all of the variables in the array PAY(0:10).

f) Swap the values of PAY(1:10) to put the largest in PAY(10). Thus if initially PAY is

        PAY $\underline{10}$ $\underline{9}$ $\underline{8}$ $\underline{7}$ $\underline{6}$ $\underline{5}$ $\underline{4}$ $\underline{3}$ $\underline{2}$ $\underline{1}$

then after execution, the array might be

        PAY $\underline{9}$ $\underline{8}$ $\underline{7}$ $\underline{6}$ $\underline{5}$ $\underline{4}$ $\underline{3}$ $\underline{2}$ $\underline{1}$ $\underline{10}$
    or PAY $\underline{1}$ $\underline{9}$ $\underline{8}$ $\underline{7}$ $\underline{6}$ $\underline{5}$ $\underline{4}$ $\underline{3}$ $\underline{2}$ $\underline{10}$

5. Suppose array B(1:N) contains a sequence of values, some of which appear more than once. Write a program segment to "delete" duplicates, moving the unique values towards the beginning of the array. Assign to variable M the number of unique values. The order of the values should be preserved. For example, if we have

        N $\underline{7}$ B $\underline{1}$ $\underline{6}$ $\underline{1}$ $\underline{8}$ $\underline{3}$ $\underline{7}$ $\underline{6}$

after execution the variables should be as follows (where "-" indicates that the value is immaterial):

        N $\underline{7}$ M $\underline{5}$ B $\underline{1}$ $\underline{6}$ $\underline{8}$ $\underline{3}$ $\underline{7}$ $\underline{-}$ $\underline{-}$

6. The following segment searches array segment B(1:N) for a
value equal to X. When it finds it, it sets J to the index of X
in B so that B(J) = X.   (This is called a "linear" search
algorithm since execution time is proportional to the length of
the segment.)

```
        J = 1;
        SEARCH_LOOP: DO WHILE(B(J) ¬= X);
             J = J + 1;
             END SEARCH_LOOP;
```

a) What value is in J after execution if X is not in the array?

b) Change the program to set 0 in J if X is not in the array.

c) What happens if N = 0? Change the program segment to store
   0 in J if this is the case. (Such a case actually arises
   in programming, and is not always a mistake.)

7. The following questions refer to the program in Section 5.4.

a) Suppose there is a tie for maximum -- several input numbers
   are the same and are greater than all others. What should
   the program do in this case; what does the program do?

b) What does the program do if several improper data values are
   included?

c) Precisely what happens if 110 data values followed by the
   end-of-input signal appear in the input?

d) What would the output look like if the following data were
   presented?

```
        *DATA
         14, 13, -3, 15, 2, 7, 15, 12, 0, 23
```

Section 6   Display of Results

Printed output from a PL/I program is produced by execution
of "output" statements.   The detailed discussion of these
statements is prefaced by two general comments on output.

First, <u>output during execution</u> of a program is entirely the
<u>programmer's responsibility</u>.   A copy of the program, called a
"source listing", is produced automatically, but once execution
begins, the only further printing is the result of executing
output statements of the program. All values produced during
execution are lost unless specifically printed. Unless you
specifically ask to have results displayed you will not know
what happened during execution of the program.

Second, the statements that control output are typically the
most complex statements in a programming language. If not the
most difficult in concept they are at least the richest in
detail and the most tedious to learn to use. This seems to be
required in order to give the programmer flexible control over
what information is to be displayed and the format in which it
is to appear. PL/I is certainly not an exception in this
regard, and the following paragraphs offer a brief introduction
to only the simplest type of PL/I output statement.

6.1 Display of Values of Variables

The simplest output statement in PL/I has the form

        PUT LIST(variable-names, separated by commas);

The variables may be simple or subscripted. For example:

(6.1a)   PUT LIST(TOTAL, I, PLACE(I), MAXPLACE);

The standard output format divides the printed page
horizontally into five "fields" of 24 columns each. (The number
of fields is a local installation option and may differ from
five at some installations.)   The field origins are somewhat
analogous to the "tab stops" on a typewriter.   Each column is
one "print position" and will contain one character. Each field
is used to display the value of one variable from the list given
in the PUT statement. In example (6.1a) the value of TOTAL will
be printed in the first (leftmost) field; I in the second;

PLACE(I) in the third; and MAXPLACE in the fourth. (The particular variable from the array PLACE to appear in the third field will of course depend upon the value of the subscript I at the time the statement is executed.) Each value begins at the left of the field and uses as many columns as required. Any unused columns of the field are left blank and the next value begins in the leftmost column of the next field.

    FIXED variables are printed in integer form, FLOAT variables in exponential form. The decimal point is always given after the first digit and the power of ten required to properly position the point is given after the digits of the number. For example, if the variables contain:

TOTAL	-.0036	[float decimal]
I	2	[fixed decimal]
PLACE(1)	-124.3	[float decimal]
PLACE(2)	63.7	[float decimal]
MAXPLACE	806	[float decimal]

the values displayed by PUT statement (6.1a) would be as below (the full number of blanks between values is not shown here since the print line in this book is not a full 120 positions):

        -3.60000E-03   2   6.37000E+01   8.06000E+02

    A PUT LIST statement does not automatically begin a new line. It begins with the next unused field, wherever that may be. For example, if PUT LIST(J); places J's value in the third field of a line, then the next executed PUT statement will place its first value in the fourth field on that same line. Thus, (6.1a) is exactly equivalent to the sequence

        PUT LIST(TOTAL, I);
        PUT LIST(PLACE(I), MAXPLACE);

In other words, the variables in consecutively executed PUT statements form one continuous list -- to be assigned to the continuous sequence of fields on the printed page. After the fifth field of one line comes the first field of the next line.

    The programmer can control the placement of values on a line by using the "SKIP option". The keyword SKIP causes the statement to begin placement with the first field of a new line, regardless of where the last PUT statement left off. Hence

        PUT SKIP LIST(TOTAL, I);
        PUT SKIP LIST(PLACE(I), MAXPLACE);

will cause two new lines to be printed, with values in the first two fields of each line. Note, however, that unless the next PUT statement also specifies SKIP it will begin placing values in the third field of this second line.

A number of lines may be skipped by giving an integer in parentheses after the keyword SKIP. For example:

          PUT SKIP(3) LIST(TOTAL);

will leave two lines blank and place the value of TOTAL in the first field of the third line. SKIP is equivalent to SKIP(1).

As a further example

          /* TABULATE I, HEIGHT(1:10) AND WIDTH(1:10) */
             TAB_LOOP: DO I = 1 TO 10 BY 1;
                  PUT SKIP(2) LIST(I, HEIGHT(I), WIDTH(I));
                  END TAB_LOOP;

will produce ten double-spaced lines with values in the first three fields of each print line.

The PUT statement can be used with the SKIP option alone to terminate a logical section of printed output. For example, the PUT SKIP(4); below ensures that this section of output will be separated by at least three blank lines from what follows, regardless of the form of the next PUT:

          ...
          PUT SKIP LIST(X, Y, Z);
          PUT SKIP LIST(R, S, T);
          PUT SKIP(4);
          ...

6.2 Titling and Labeling Results

The appearance of printed results can be improved by adding appropriate titles and labels. To a limited extent this can be done with LIST format output by placing a "literal" instead of a variable in the list of the PUT statement. A literal is a string of characters enclosed in single quotes. For example:

          'TOTAL'
          'TEMPERATURE ='
          'RESULTS FOR 9/23/72 ARE:'
          '*-*-*-*-*-*-*'
          ' '   (blank is a valid character)

The character string is printed exactly as given -- without the quotes. The printing begins in the leftmost column of the "next" field. For example, if TOTAL and SUM have values

          TOTAL 642.17 [float decimal]
          SUM   -1043.7 [float decimal]

then execution of the statements

```
PUT SKIP LIST('TOTAL =', TOTAL);
PUT SKIP LIST('SUM =', SUM);
```

would produce the output

```
TOTAL =                    6.42170E+02
SUM =                     -1.04370E+03
```

The appearance of these lines can be improved by including blanks in the literals to displace the words toward the right in the 24 position print field:

```
PUT SKIP LIST('                    TOTAL =', TOTAL);
PUT SKIP LIST('                     SUM =',SUM);
```

These statements will produce:

```
TOTAL = 6.42170E+02
SUM = -1.04370E+03
```

Literals are often used to identify different values, using their variable names. For example,

```
PUT SKIP LIST('X', X);
```

will print the name X, in the first field of a line, and the value of X in the second field. Whatever is included in the literal is printed; the content of the literal has no significance to PL/I. For example, execution of the following would cause the deceptive label to be printed, without complaint:

```
PUT SKIP LIST('THE VALUE OF Y IS:', X);
```

Blank literals can be used to control the placement of other values on the printed line. For example, the following PUT statement causes the value of X to be printed in the second field of a new line, and the value of Y in the fourth field.

```
PUT SKIP LIST(' ', X, ' ', Y);
```

PUT statements whose list consists of a single literal are frequently used. For example:

```
PUT SKIP LIST('IMPROPER DATA ENCOUNTERED');
PUT SKIP LIST('UNEXPECTED NEGATIVE VALUE');
```

Another example is shown in the sample program in Section 5.4. Such statements announce to the programmer that the flow-of-control has reached a certain point in the program or that an exceptional condition has occurred. One often includes such statements to help test a new program; they are removed after the correctness of the program has been established. This technique is discussed in Section V.4.

If a literal of more than 24 characters is given it will simply continue into the next field on the line. (A literal of exactly 24 characters completely fills one field and causes the next to be skipped.) If a literal reaches the end of a line it will continue in the first field of the next line. This applies to the printed output line -- a different rule applies to the cards on which the PUT statement itself is punched.

PL/C normally forbids a "symbol" to be split between two cards -- to be started on one card and continued on the next. Keywords, variables and constants are all symbols. A literal or a comment, however long, is also considered a single symbol. A statement may be continued onto as many cards as necessary, but an individual symbol cannot be split over a card boundary. (This can be permitted under the NOBNDRY option for comments and literals; see Appendix B.2.) Hence, the following would not be valid in PL/C:

```
PUT SKIP LIST(TOTAL,SUM,AVERAGE,MEDIAN,'THESE STATISTICS
ARE OBTAINED FROM 9/23/72 DATA');
```

This same statement would be valid if it were divided between symbols instead of in the middle of the literal:

```
PUT SKIP LIST(TOTAL, SUM, AVERAGE, MEDIAN,
    'THESE STATISTICS ARE OBTAINED FROM 9/23/72 DATA');
```

Although the statement is now acceptable, the format of the printed output is likely to be disappointing since the long literal will begin in the fifth field of the line and spill over into the first field of the following line. The following sequence would produce more attractive and readable output:

```
PUT SKIP LIST('STATISTICS FROM 9/23/72 DATA:');
    PUT SKIP LIST('          TOTAL =', TOTAL);
    PUT SKIP LIST('          SUM =', SUM);
    PUT SKIP LIST('          AVERAGE =', AVERAGE);
    PUT SKIP LIST('          MEDIAN =', MEDIAN);
```

Since a quote ends a literal it is not obvious how you can get a quote to appear in a literal. PL/I's solution to this dilemma is to require two consecutive quotes when you want one quote to appear in the literal. That is, a quote does not end a literal if it is immediately followed by another quote. For example, the execution of

```
PUT SKIP LIST('SOLUTION BY CRAMER''S RULE');
```

would cause the printing of

```
SOLUTION BY CRAMER'S RULE
```

As another example, the execution of

```
PUT SKIP LIST('''','''');
```

would cause the printing of

```
','
```

6.2.1 Automatic Identification of Variables

An alternate form of the PUT statement will automatically label the values of variables. DATA format output will display the name as well as the value of the variables listed. For example, assuming variables TOTAL and SUM have the values indicated earlier,

```
PUT SKIP DATA(TOTAL, SUM);
```

will display a line

```
TOTAL= 6.42170E+02        SUM=-1.04370E+03;
```

Section 6 <u>Summary</u>

1. The form of the simplest PL/I output statement is:

     PUT LIST(variables and literals, separated by commas);

2. The "LIST format" print line consists of five fields of 24
characters each.   Fields are filled from left to right, top to
bottom, starting wherever the last PUT statement left off.   Each
element on the PUT list starts a new field, and continues
through as many fields as are required to display its value.

3. The SKIP(i) option will cause a PUT statement to skip down i
lines.   SKIP(1), or SKIP, will skip to the beginning of the next
line; SKIP(2) will skip to the second line, etc.

4. A <u>literal</u> is a quoted string of characters that will be
printed exactly as given.   Literals can be used to title and
label results, and to print messages.

5. The names as well as the values of variables will be printed
by the "DATA format" output statement:

     PUT DATA(variable-names, separated by commas);

Section 6 Exercises

1. Write a single PUT statement to produce the same printed output as the following sequence:

```
PUT SKIP LIST(TOTAL);
PUT LIST(MAX);
PUT LIST(MINIMUM, AVG);
```

2. What would the output from the following segment look like?

```
PRINT_LOOP: DO I = 1 TO 5 BY 1;
    PUT SKIP LIST(I,I,I,I,I);
    END PRINT_LOOP;
```

3. What is the result of executing the following statement?

```
PUT LIST(' ',' ');
```

4. What is printed by execution of the following statement?

```
PUT SKIP LIST('PUT SKIP LIST(X);');
```

5. What is printed by execution of the following statement?

```
PUT SKIP LIST(' ' /* CHECKPOINT 19 */);
```

6. What is printed by execution of the following statement?

```
PUT SKIP LIST('5',',',/*4*/'3','/*2*/');
```

7. What is printed by execution of the following statement?

```
PUT SKIP LIST(',',',',',',',',',');
```

8. Write a PUT LIST statement that will produce output equivalent to the following statement:

```
PUT SKIP DATA(X, Y, Z(4));
```

Section 7   The Execution of Programs

After a program has been written, and painstakingly checked
for errors in logic and syntax, it must be transmitted to a
computer for execution. This is usually done by "punching" both
the program statements and suitable test data onto cards. Each
card generally contains one line of the program as it was
written on paper, and columns should be skipped at the left of
the card to reflect the indentation of the program lines.

"Keypunching" is a major source of errors. Many programs,
correct on paper, reach the computer in garbled form simply
because the lines are not exactly represented by the information
actually punched in the cards. Much time and effort is saved if
the cards are checked against the written form, with great care,
before the deck is submitted for processing. If at all
possible, you should get a "listing" of the cards and check this
listing, rather than attempt to read the cards directly.

When cards containing keypunch errors have been replaced, the
deck is arranged as follows for presentation to the computer:

```
        *PL/C ID='name of programmer'    options
         /* Comment summarizing program function */
         procedure-name: PROCEDURE OPTIONS(MAIN);
             Cards containing declarations
             Cards containing program statements
             END procedure-name;
        *DATA
             Cards containing data
```

The *PL/C and *DATA cards must begin in column 1. Program and
comment cards must not begin in column 1. Data cards may begin
in column 1. (See Appendix B.3 for further information on card
formats.)

The following pages show the output resulting from processing
of the program given in Section 5.4. The program was run with
XREF and ATR options (see Section 7.2.2). The following data
were supplied to the program:

```
        *DATA
         15, 23, 46.9, -5, 29, 17, 5.5, 6, 0, 52
```

```
*PL/C ID='EVAN CONWAY', XREF, ATR, CMPRS


*OPTIONS IN EFFECT*    TIME=(0,15),PAGES=30,LINES=2000,ATR,XREF,FLAGW,BNDRY,NOCMNTS,SORMGIN=(2,72,1),ERRORS=(50,50),
*OPTICNS IN EFFECT*    TABSIZE=2532,UDEF,SOURCE,OPLIST,CMPRS,HDRPG,AUXIO=10000,LINECT=60,NOALIST,MCALL,MTEXT,DUMP=(S,
*OPTICNS IN EFFECT*    F,L,E,U,R),DUMPE=(S,F,L,E,U,R),DUMPT=(S,F,L,E,U,R)
```

```
/* LIST POSITIVE INTEGERS FROM FIRST TO MAXIMUM */                              PL/C-R7.1--66 10/20/75 10:58 PAGE   1

   STMT LEVEL NEST BLOCK MLVL  SOURCE TEXT


                                    /* LIST POSITIVE INTEGERS FROM FIRST TO MAXIMUM */
       1                            LISTTOMAX: PROCEDURE OPTIONS(MAIN);
     WARNING: STMT     1  EXTERNAL NAME TOO LONG (SY2F)
       2    1            1          DECLARE (INTEGER(1:100), /* THE POSITIVE VALUES READ*/
                                             TOP,            /* ARE IN INTEGER(1:TOP).  */
                                             MAXVAL,         /* IF NO VALUES, MAXP=0; ELSE*/
                                             MAXP,           /* MAXP MARKS MAXVAL POSITION*/
                                             I)              /* MAXVAL=MAX(INTEGER(1:TOP))*/
                                            FIXED DECIMAL;
       3    1            1          DECLARE TFLOAT FLOAT DECIMAL; /* LAST VALUE READ IN */

                                    /* READ DATA, CHECK, AND STORE IN INTEGER(1:100) */
                                    /* UNTIL 0 IS FOUND.  */
       4    1            1          TOP = 0;
       5    1            1          GET LIST(TFLOAT);
       6    1            1          LOAD_LOOP: DO WHILE((TOP < 100) & (TFLOAT ¬= 0));
       7    1    1       1              IF (TFLOAT > 0) & (FLOOR(TFLOAT) = TFLOAT)
       8    1    1       1              THEN DO; TOP = TOP + 1;
      10    1    2       1                  INTEGER(TOP) = TFLOAT; END;
      12    1    1       1              ELSE PUT SKIP LIST('IMPROPER DATA:', TFLOAT);
      13    1    1       1              GET LIST(TFLOAT);
      14    1    1       1              END LOAD_LOOP;
      15    1            1          IF TFLOAT ¬= 0 THEN
      16    1            1              PUT SKIP LIST('MORE THAN 100 VALUES');

                                    /* SET MAXP TO MARK POSITION OF MAX IN INTEGER(1:TOP) */
      17    1            1          MAXVAL = -1;
      18    1            1          MAXP = 0;
      19    1            1          FINDMAX_LOOP: DO I = 1 TO TOP BY 1;
      20    1    1       1              IF INTEGER(I) > MAXVAL THEN DO;
      22    1    2       1                  MAXVAL = INTEGER(I);
      23    1    2       1                  MAXP = I; END;
      25    1    1       1              END FINDMAX_LOOP;

                                    /* PRINT NUMBERS IN INTEGER(1:MAXP) */
      26    1            1          PRINT_LOOP: DO I = 1 TO MAXP BY 1;
      27    1    1       1              PUT SKIP LIST(INTEGER(I));
      28    1    1       1              END PRINT_LOOP;

      29    1            1          END LISTTOMAX;

 DCL NC.      IDENTIFIER                            ATTRIBUTES AND REFERENCES


      19       FINDMAX_LOOP                         STATEMENT LABEL CONSTANT

       2       I                                    AUTOMATIC,ALIGNED,DECIMAL,FIXED(5,0)
```

DCL NO.	IDENTIFIER	ATTRIBUTES AND REFERENCES
		19,20,22,23,26,27
2	INTEGER	(*)AUTOMATIC,ALIGNED,DECIMAL,FIXED(5,0)
		10,20,22,27
1	LISTTGMAX	ENTRY,BINARY,FIXED(15,0)
6	LOAD_LOOP	STATEMENT LABEL CONSTANT
2	MAXP	AUTOMATIC,ALIGNED,DECIMAL,FIXED(5,0)
		18,23,26
2	MAXVAL	AUTOMATIC,ALIGNED,DECIMAL,FIXED(5,0)
		17,20,22
26	PRINT_LOOP	STATEMENT LABEL CONSTANT
3	TFLOAT	AUTOMATIC,ALIGNED,DECIMAL,FLOAT(6)
		5,6,7,7,7,10,12,13,15
2	TOP	AUTOMATIC,ALIGNED,DECIMAL,FIXED(5,0)
		4,6,9,9,10,19

ERRORS/WARNINGS DETECTED DURING CODE GENERATION:

    WARNING: NO FILE SPECIFIED. SYSIN/SYSPRINT ASSUMED. (CGOC)

```
IMPROPER DATA:          4.68999E+01
IMPROPER DATA:         -5.00000E+00
IMPROPER DATA:          5.50000E+00
        15
        23
        29
```

IN STMT   29 PROGRAM RETURNS FROM MAIN PROCEDURE.

IN STMT   29 SCALARS AND BLOCK-TRACE:

***** MAIN PROCEDURE LISTTOMAX

TFLOAT= 0.00000E+00   I =   4   MAXP=   3   MAXVAL=   29   TOP=   5

NON-0 PROCEDURE EXECUTION COUNTS:
NAME   STMT COUNT NAME   STMT COUNT NAME   STMT COUNT NAME   STMT COUNT NAME   STMT COUNT
LISTTCMAX   0001 00001

LABEL EXECUTION COUNTS:
NAME   STMT COUNT NAME   STMT COUNT NAME   STMT COUNT NAME   STMT COUNT NAME   STMT COUNT
PRINT_LOOP 0026 00001 FINDMAX_LOO 0019 00001 LOAD_LOOP   0006 00001

         COMPILATION STATISTICS (0029 STATEMENTS) | EXECUTION STATISTICS
SECONDS ERRORS WARNINGS PAGES LINES CARDS INCL'S | SECONDS ERRORS WARNINGS PAGES LINES CARDS INCL'S AUX I/O
 .11   0   2   2   93   40   0 | .02   0   0   1   11   1   0   0
---+--
BYTES   SYMBOL TABLE   INTERMEDIATE CODE   OBJECT CODE | STATIC CORE   AUTOMATIC CORE   DYNAMIC CORE   TOTAL STORAGE
USED   1168(2K)   740(1K)   1128(2K) | 346(1K)   1087(2K)   0(0K)   3511(4K)
UNUSED   8960(8K)   9292(9K)   18394(17K) | 16973(16K)   16973(16K)   9292(9K)   16973(16K)
```

THIS PROGRAM MAY BE RERUN WITHOUT CHANGE IN A REGION  16K BYTES SMALLER USING TABLESIZE=    292
```

7.1 Loading, Translation and Execution

Processing a program takes place in two distinct stages. First, the program is "loaded" into the memory of the computer; second, it is executed. In order to load a program, the deck of cards is placed in a device called a "card reader". The card reader examines the cards one at a time, in the order presented, detects the position of holes in the cards, and transmits this information to the computer. The card-reading operation appears to proceed very rapidly (500 to 1000 cards per minute) but it is in fact very slow compared to the speed with which statements are executed once the program is loaded.

The loading of a program for processing is actually performed by another program, called a "compiler", which is already in the computer. During loading, the compiler scans the program for errors and translates the PL/I statements into an internal form that the computer can understand and execute.

A crucial point is that the program is not executed as it is loaded. Only after the complete program has been loaded, does the second stage -- execution -- begin. Execution of a PL/I program consists of one execution of the "main procedure".

At the moment that execution begins only the cards containing the program statements have been read. Cards containing data remain in the card reader -- ready to be read when called for by the execution of GET statements in the program.

7.2 Analysis of Printed Output

The amount and type of printed output produced during the processing of a program can vary considerably. Certain portions are always provided, some portions depend upon the choice of "options" for the particular program, and some depend upon the execution of output statements in the program.

Each computing facility has predetermined a set of standard or "default" choices for the various options. These are presumably chosen to be the most appropriate for the greatest number of users of the computer. The default options are automatically assigned to each program -- but you can override the defaults by specifying your own choice of options. In PL/C, options are specified on the *PL/C card -- the first card of the program. Many of the important options are described in the following sections; a complete list is given in Appendix B.2.

The complete printed output produced during loading, translation and execution of a PL/C program can be divided into the following sections, to be described in more detail subsequently:

Header Pages: Several pages produced by a general supervisory program (called the "operating system") to identify the beginning of a new program, report its cost, the language used -- and scores of other statistics that are of little importance to the neophyte programmer. (These pages are not included in the previous sample output.)

Source Listing: A copy of the program, with additional information such as statement numbers and error messages.

Cross-Reference and Attribute Listing: A listing of all identifiers, where they are declared, their type attributes, and where they are used. This is not typically a standard option -- it will only appear if the programmer requests the ATR and XREF options.

Execution Output: The result of executing PUT statements (with error messages, if necessary).

PL/C Post-Mortem Dump: A listing of the final values of variables (values after the end of execution), and various PL/C summary statistics.

Trailer Pages: Additional more-or-less incomprehensible pages supplied by the operating system. (These pages are not included in the previous sample output.)

7.2.1 Source Listing

   The source listing is a copy of the program, to which certain other information has been added.

1) At the top of the first page are three lines titled

    OPTIONS IN EFFECT

Any question about what options are standard, or whether the programmer's requests for special options were successful, should be answered by studying these lines.

2) The card following the *PL/C card is used to automatically title the pages of the source listing. The contents of this card are printed as a title at the top of each page. Page numbers are also printed.

3) At the left of the program statements in the main body of the source listing are five columns headed STMT, LEVEL, NEST, BLOCK, and MLVL. The LEVEL and BLOCK columns describe the "block structure" of the program. Programs written using only the portion of PL/C covered in this book will always have a LEVEL of 1. BLOCK gives the number of the procedure in which the statement appears. At this point our programs consist of a

single procedure -- so this will always be 1 -- but in Part IV
we will introduce programs with more than one procedure.   MLVL
specifies the "macro level" -- referring to a feature of PL/C
that is not included in this book.

   The column headed NEST shows the nesting level of DO groups.
Statements in the body of an "outer" DO group have "1" in this
column; statements in the body of the next inner DO group will
have a "2", etc.

   The column headed STMT gives "statement numbers" that are
assigned by PL/I. Statements are numbered in the order that
they are loaded. One minor difficulty is that PL/I is very
generous in what it considers a "statement". Declarations are
numbered as if they were statements, as are PROCEDURE, DO and
END. This STMT numbering is quite obvious, as long as there is
exactly one statement per line. When there is more than one
statement per line or more than one line per statement, the
numbering is still straightforward, but the printing of the
numbers is not. The number of the first statement on the line
will be printed. When a single statement takes more than one
line, the statement number will be printed only once.

   Give careful attention to these numbers. They are generated
in a very systematic way, so that if they do not run as you
would expect them to, there is a misunderstanding about the
structure of the program. Discouraging as it may seem at first,
it is never the computer that misunderstands the program. It is
always you, misunderstanding what you wrote.

   These STMT numbers are used throughout the printed output to
refer to individual statements -- in error messages, in the
cross-reference listing, and in the post-mortem dump.

4) When errors are detected during the initial scanning of a
program, an error message is printed directly following the
offending statement. Usually, PL/C attempts to repair the error
so that the program can be executed; this correction is printed
below the error message. For example:

                . . .
    8   1   1   X=Y*(X+Z;
      ERROR IN STMT   8 MISSING) IN COLUMN 10 (SY04)
             FOR STMT 8 PL/C USES   X=Y*(X+Z);
                . . .

Unfortunately, the repair is not always successful.   Sometimes,
in its efforts to construct a syntactically correct program,
PL/C constructs statements that are very unlike what the
programmer intended. The proper attitude is to be appreciative
when the correction is helpful; amused when it is not; and try
to give PL/C as few opportunities to make corrections as
possible. Note that even though a particular correction does

not recreate what you intended, it still permits execution of the program. This execution will often yield information that will help expose other faults in the program.

5) Certain errors are easily detected only after the complete program has been scanned. Since the listing of the program statements is printed as the program is loaded and scanned, these additional error messages cannot be printed immediately after the offending statement. Instead they are collected, and printed in a group after the end of the program statement listing.

These messages are especially confusing when they describe an improper meaning that is a direct consequence of an earlier PL/C "correction". When one of these errors is completely mystifying, see if there has been a previous error message and correction for the same statement.

Using the GET and PUT statements described in this book your program output will always include the warning:

WARNING: NO FILE SPECIFIED. SYSIN/SYSPRINT ASSUMED. (CGOC)

Actually the full form of the GET and PUT statements includes a "file phrase":

        PUT FILE(SYSPRINT) SKIP LIST(...);

        GET FILE(SYSIN) LIST(...);

Since these phrases are automatically supplied by PL/C if omitted by the programmer we have elected to omit them. The warning simply reminds you that the phrases have been supplied.

7.2.2 Cross-Reference and Attribute Listing

Typical default options do not include the production of this section of output, so the ATR and XREF options must be given on the *PL/C card in order to obtain it. These are two distinct options which produce two different types of information, but they are almost always used together.

The attribute listing describes all identifiers used in the program. Each identifier is listed by name, in alphabetical order, with the STMT number where it was declared and the attributes that were assigned to it. The numbers given after the FIXED and FLOAT attributes specify their "precision" -- the number of digits in their value. DECIMAL FLOAT(6) means a decimal number with six significant figures. DECIMAL FIXED(5,0) means a decimal integer of five digits, with no digits to the right of the decimal point. The attribute list will include several attributes that we have not discussed. "AUTOMATIC" is discussed in Section IV.1.5; "ALIGNED" and "UNALIGNED" are irrelevant for our purposes.

The cross-reference (XREF) option adds to the entry for each identifier a list of the statement numbers of all statements that refer to that particular identifier.

If the attribute and cross-reference list is studied carefully it will reveal two important kinds of errors:

1. Misspellings of identifiers that accidentally create new identifiers.

2. Missing or faulty declarations of variables, resulting in surprising assignments of attributes.

7.2.3 Execution Output

The output generated by the actual execution of a program is completely dependent upon execution of PUT statements in the program. If no PUT statements are executed, there is no execution output. PL/I intrudes in this output only if an error is committed during execution. For example, suppose

        BASE_VALUE = SQRT(LEFT_PT);

is executed at a point where LEFT_PT $<$ 0. Since the SQRT built-in function requires a non-negative value as argument, an error message is inserted at that point in the execution output.

This section of output is not automatically titled in any way, nor are the pages numbered. It normally begins at the top of a new page. The end of execution output is denoted by a line that announces the completion of execution of the program:

        IN STMT nn PROGRAM RETURNS FROM MAIN PROCEDURE

7.2.4 PL/C Post-Mortem Dump

The automatic "post-mortem dump" is a feature of PL/C that is not provided by PL/I. This dump supplies information on the final values of variables, and certain other statistics that summarize execution. This information can be very useful in program testing. The content of the dump is controlled by various "DUMP" options specified on the *PL/C card (see Appendix B.2). The different sections of the dump are:

1) The final values of simple (or "scalar") variables. Optionally, array values will also be included (see Appendix B.2). When a value ??? is displayed for a variable, this means that nowhere in the program was a value assigned to this

variable. All such instances should be investigated, for they often reveal a misspelling of a variable name, or a logical error.

2) The number of times that each label and procedure-name (entry-name) was encountered during execution. This can be exploited to provide a complete history of how many times each section of a program is executed. If, during testing of a program, you temporarily insert labelled null statements (for example, CHECKPOINT_1:;, CHECKPOINT_2:;, etc.) at key points in the program, PL/C will automatically count the number of times each such point is reached in execution, and report these statistics in the dump.

3) Optionally, the history of the last 18 situations where flow-of-control departed from normal, sequential execution. Consider the following program, with STMT numbers shown as assigned by PL/C:

```
STMT 1     INTSUM: PROCEDURE OPTIONS(MAIN);
STMT 2         DECLARE (I, SUM) FIXED DECIMAL;
STMT 3         SUM = 0;
STMT 4         SUM_LOOP: DO I = 1 TO 50 BY 1;
STMT 5             SUM = SUM + I;
STMT 6             END SUM_LOOP;
STMT 7         PUT LIST(SUM);
STMT 8         END INTSUM;
```

After execution of this program, PL/C would report the flow-of-control history in the following form:

```
IN STMT     8 DYNAMIC FLOW TRACE:
      50*(0006->0004)        0004->0007
```

The flow-of-control is read left-to-right, as follows:

a) The report is issued after execution of STMT 8.

b) Progress from 1->2->3->4->5->6 is not reported, since this is the normal, sequential execution.

c) The next 50 departures from sequential order all involved the end of an iteration of the loop.

d) The last transfer was from 4 to 7 (the completion of the loop).

Since this program is very short the complete flow-of-control history is reported. On larger programs only the final 18 transfers are reported.

4) Statistics concerning the amount of memory used.

5) The amount of computer time required to translate and to execute the program.

Section 8   The Declaration of Variables

Declarations have been mentioned in several earlier sections. These are so crucial that their consideration could not be entirely postponed to this point, but the previous fragmented presentation is not sufficient. Section 8 provides a general discussion of declarations, repeating much of what has been mentioned previously. The following is a summary of the previous references to the declaration of variables:

1. Variables are defined by listing their names in a declaration. Section 2.

2. Declarations are part of the heading of a procedure, and are placed at the beginning. Creation of the variables takes place as the procedure is entered -- before execution of any statement in the procedure.

3. The type of value that a variable can contain is determined by the type attributes given in the declaration of that variable. Section 2.3.

4. A variable can be declared to be an array by specifying the bounds on its subscript values in its declaration. Section 5.3.

8.1 The Form of a Declaration

The declaration of an unsubscripted variable has the form

        DECLARE identifier attributes;

Examples are:

        DECLARE POLYPHASE FLOAT DECIMAL;

        DECLARE K_BOUND DECIMAL FIXED;

Note the following:

1. The attributes follow the identifier.

2. Order within a list of attributes is immaterial -- FIXED DECIMAL and DECIMAL FIXED are equivalent.

3. <u>No comma is given after the identifier or between the attributes</u>.

Several variables may be included in the same declaration, separated by commas. For example, the following are equivalent:

    DECLARE J FIXED DECIMAL, SUM FLOAT DECIMAL;

    DECLARE J FIXED DECIMAL; DECLARE SUM FLOAT DECIMAL;

Two or more variables having exactly the same attributes can be grouped in parentheses, so that the attribute list need not be repeated. The attributes are said to be "factored". For example, the following declarations are equivalent:

    DECLARE I FIXED DECIMAL, J FIXED DECIMAL,
                K FIXED DECIMAL;

    DECLARE (I, J, K) FIXED DECIMAL;

Two keywords may be abbreviated:

    DCL is equivalent to DECLARE

    DEC is equivalent to DECIMAL

Using these abbreviations, and factoring the attribute lists, the following are equivalent:

    DCL MAX FIXED DEC, (ZB42, Z4) FLOAT DEC;

    DECLARE MAX FIXED DECIMAL, ZB42 FLOAT DECIMAL,
                Z4 FLOAT DECIMAL;

Any list of popular PL/I errors would have several entries concerning these abbreviations. The use of DEC as an abbreviation for DECLARE is an all-time favorite error. Similarly, <u>neither FIXED nor FLOAT has a valid abbreviation</u>, and any attempt to invent one just creates a new variable named FIX, or FLT, or whatever is used -- and the effect on execution is usually surprising and disastrous.

These shortcuts are convenient -- but are often overdone. It should not become a matter of pride to see how brief you can make your declarations. <u>Clarity</u> is much more important than <u>brevity</u>.

In general, declarations are a major source of student errors. Declarations are exceedingly <u>sensitive to the placement of each comma and parenthesis</u>. For example, consider the effect of changing the position of commas and parentheses in the following declaration:

    DECLARE (NUMBER, QTY) FLOAT DECIMAL;
            two variables, NUMBER and QTY, each float decimal

```
DECLARE NUMBER, QTY FLOAT DECIMAL;
     two variables
          NUMBER default attributes (see Section 8.2)
          QTY float decimal

DECLARE NUMBER, QTY, FLOAT DECIMAL;
     three variables
          NUMBER default attributes
          QTY default attributes
          FLOAT decimal (and default float)

DECLARE NUMBER, QTY, FLOAT, DECIMAL;
     four variables
          NUMBER default attributes
          QTY default attributes
          FLOAT default attributes
          DECIMAL default attributes
```

Each of these declarations is syntactically correct, but each has a distinctly different meaning. Only one of these forms could actually create the proper variables; the others would create variables different from what was intended. Sometimes the effects of such differences are catastrophic; it is obvious that something is wrong and you will eventually find the mistake. Unfortunately, the effects are sometimes latent and subtle. If the effects do not happen to appear during testing, a faulty program can be pronounced "correct".

The best protection against such problems is to request the optional listing of the variables that have been created, along with the attributes that have been assigned to them. (See Section 7.2.2.) Careful examination of this list will indicate whether the variables actually created were those intended.

8.1.1 Declaration of Arrays

An array is declared by specifying bounds on its subscript values immediately after the identifier. The general form is:

        DECLARE   identifier(lb1:ub1, lb2:ub2,...) attributes;

where lb1, ub1, lb2, ub2, ... are expressions giving the lower bound and upper bound for the first subscript; the lower bound and upper bound for the second subscript, etc. If only an upper-bound-expression is given, a lower bound of 1 is assumed. For example:

        DCL (X(5), MAT(0:6,5)) FLOAT DECIMAL;

creates two arrays of FLOAT DECIMAL variables. X consists of five singly-subscripted variables. MAT is doubly-subscripted -- the first subscript ranging from 0 to 6; the second from 1 to 5.

8.2 Implicit Declaration and Default Attributes

You will soon discover that PL/I does not demand the explicit declaration of every variable. This discovery will probably occur the first time you make a keypunch mistake, misspelling the name of a variable. Rather than recognize the error, in most contexts PL/I accepts the misspelling as a new identifier, and considers it the "implicit declaration" of a different variable. No announcement is made and unless the ATR or XREF options are in effect, such an error may be difficult to detect.

Since type attributes are not specified in such an implicit declaration they must be assumed by PL/I. These "default attributes" depend upon the <u>first letter of the identifier</u>, and not upon the context in which the implicit declaration occurs. The rules are:

> If the identifier begins with one of the letters I, J, K, L, M or N the type attributes are FIXED BINARY, and the value is of type "integer".

> Otherwise the type attributes are FLOAT DECIMAL, and the value is of type "real".

These rules are an unfortunate carryover from the FORTRAN language of 20 years ago. The BINARY attribute specifies that the value should be represented in the computer memory in the binary (rather than decimal) number system. The choice of internal representation is of no significance for our purposes, and we mention it here only because you will probably see BINARY on an ATR listing, and wonder what it means.

These same rules for default attributes apply if a variable is declared explicitly, but no type attributes are given. For example, the following are equivalent:

DECLARE TOTAL;

DECLARE TOTAL FLOAT DECIMAL;

The rules that apply when a variable is explicitly declared, but with only partial specification of type attributes, are more complex (and not very reasonable).

This whole business of implicit declarations and spelling-dependent default type attributes is an unfortunate characteristic of PL/I. The best way to protect yourself is to:

1. Explicitly declare all variables at the beginning of the procedure.

2. Specify the type attributes FIXED DECIMAL or FLOAT DECIMAL for each variable. (In Section 9 we will introduce a third type of variable which is an alternative to these two.)

3. Specify XREF and ATR options as a check against the
    possibility that you failed to do either 1 or 2, or
    simply made a keypunch mistake.

8.3 Initial Values

    The creation of a variable and the assignment of value are
distinctly   different   actions   and   initial   values are not
automatically supplied when a variable is created.   It is such a
common mistake to assume that an initial value of zero is
automatically supplied that a few languages, including PL/C,
supply a zero value for numeric variables.   But this is a
correction of an error and a warning message is printed.

    PL/I does permit the programmer to specify both _creation_ and
assignment of initial value in a declaration, using the optional
"initial" attribute. The form is:

        INITIAL(constant)   or   INIT(constant)

During creation, the specified constant is assigned to the
variable. An example of use would be:

        DECLARE SUM FLOAT DECIMAL INITIAL(0);

The variable SUM would be created and _immediately_ assigned a
value of 0. This is _almost_ equivalent to writing:

        DECLARE SUM FLOAT DECIMAL;
        SUM = 0;

The difference lies only in the timing. When an initial value
is assigned by the declaration, it takes place with creation --
that is, before the execution of any statement in the procedure.

    The INITIAL attribute is especially convenient for arrays.
In this case a list of initial values is specified -- usually
one value for each element of the array. The form is:

        INITIAL(c1, c2, c3, ...)

where c1, c2, c3, ... are constants. These values are assigned
to the elements in row-major order. For example:

        DECLARE X(4) FIXED DECIMAL INITIAL(5,6,7,8);

causes creation and assignment of initial values as follows:

        X(1) 5   X(2) 6   X(3) 7   X(4) 8

A "repetition factor", which is an expression in parentheses, may be given to indicate that the same value is to appear in several consecutive positions:

DECLARE XP(5) FIXED DECIMAL INITIAL(6,(3)7,8);

This would create the following:

XP(1) <u>6</u>   XP(2) <u>7</u>   XP(3) <u>7</u>   XP(4) <u>7</u>   XP(5) <u>8</u>

The repetition factor can be applied to a list of constants, which for this purpose is enclosed in parentheses. For example

DECLARE X(4) FIXED DECIMAL INITIAL((2)(8, 5));

would create   X(1) <u>8</u>   X(2) <u>5</u>   X(3) <u>8</u>   X(4) <u>5</u>

The length of the INITIAL list need not coincide exactly with the number of elements in the array. Fewer values on the list causes the final elements of the array to remain uninitialized; excess values are ignored.

The INITIAL attribute may be factored:

DCL (AA, BB) FIXED DECIMAL INIT(5);

DCL (X(2),Y(2)) FIXED DECIMAL INIT(5,6);

would create the following:

AA <u>5</u>   X(1) <u>5</u>   Y(1) <u>5</u>

BB <u>5</u>   X(2) <u>6</u>   Y(2) <u>6</u>

However, the following declaration illustrates a common error; it will <u>not</u> assign 7 to CC and 8 to DD.

DCL (CC, DD) FLOAT DECIMAL INITIAL(7,8);

The INITIAL list is applied to each of the factored identifiers -- so PL/I attempts to assign <u>both</u> 7 and 8 to CC, which can only hold a single value, and <u>both</u> 7 and 8 to DD, which is also single-valued. To assign 7 as initial value to CC and 8 to DD you would have to write

DCL CC FLOAT DEC INIT(7), DD FLOAT DEC INIT(8);

This could be factored in the following way:

DCL (CC INIT(7), DD INIT(8)) FLOAT DECIMAL;

Section 8 <u>Summary</u>

1. Variables are created, and have their type attributes
assigned by a declaration:

     DECLARE identifier attributes;

2. Declarations are placed at the beginning of a procedure.
Variables are created immediately upon entry to the procedure --
before the execution of any statement in that procedure.

3. Several variables can be be given in the same declaration:

     DECLARE ident attributes, ident attributes, ... ;

4. Variables with identical attributes can be grouped in
parentheses:

     DECLARE (ident, ident, ...) attributes;

5. The <u>only</u> allowable abbreviations are:

     DCL   for   DECLARE
     DEC   for   DECIMAL
     INIT for   INITIAL

6. The form for declaration of an array is:

     DECLARE identifier(lb1:ub1, lb2:ub2, ...) attributes;

If only an upper-bound-expression is given, a lower bound of 1
is assumed.

7. Initial values are not automatically assigned to a variable
when it is created. A value must be assigned before the
variable can be used.

8. An initial value <u>can</u> be assigned at the time of creation by
specifying the INITIAL attribute in the declaration. The form
for a simple variable is:

     INITIAL(constant)

The form for an array is

     INITIAL(c1, c2, ...)

Constants on the list may be repeated by specifying a repetition
factor:

     INITIAL(c1, (r1)c2, (r2)(c3, c4), c5, ...)

Section 8 <u>Exercises</u>

<u>1</u>. Write a declaration to create a variable named TOTAL that will hold values such as -123.79 and .00062.

<u>2</u>. Write a declaration equivalent to the following, that does not use parentheses:

        DECLARE X FIXED DECIMAL, (Y, Z) FLOAT DECIMAL,
                  (I, J) FIXED DECIMAL;

<u>3</u>. What types of variables are created by each of the following declarations:
    a) DECLARE ITEM;
    b) DECLARE Z_COORDINATE;
    c) DCL A;
    d) DCL TOTAL, FLOAT, DECIMAL;

<u>4</u>. What type of variables are created by the declaration

        DCL (COL(0:1), TABLE(4:10,14)) FLOAT DEC;

<u>5</u>. Write a declaration that will create variables with the following names, attributes and initial values:

        TOP(1) 5   [float decimal]
        TOP(2) 6.5 [float decimal]
        BOT(1) 5   [float decimal]
        BOT(2) 6.5 [float decimal]
        SIDE   5   [float decimal]
        WIDE   5   [fixed decimal]

6. Write a declaration that will create two four by four integer arrays named T1 and T2, and assign initial values of 3 to all of their elements.

Section 9   Character-Valued Variables

Up to this point we have considered numeric-valued variables. We have used non-numeric "strings" of characters as literals in a PUT statement (Section 6.2), but not as values to assign to variables. Some languages are only capable of processing numeric values, and are considered useful primarily for scientific and engineering applications. However, in many types of applications it is useful to be able to store, manipulate, and display values that include characters that are not digits. Values that include letters and special symbols as well as digits are called "character data", or "strings".

For example, programs called "text editors" take a sequence of words, punctuation marks, and format commands, and format the words and punctuation marks into lines, paragraphs, and pages. This book was produced by such a program.

Many important applications involve both numeric and character data. Consider a program to maintain a customer charge account system for a retail store. Each account includes numeric information on charges, payments, balance due, arrears, finance charges, etc. It also contains character information giving the name of the customer, his address, credit references, etc. A majority of the world's computers are used primarily for file processing, and computers, in the aggregate, process more character data than numeric data.

Since PL/I was designed to serve both scientific and file processing applications it includes facilities for processing strings.

The characters that may appear in a string are those that occur on the keypunch. They are the following, with "ƀ" representing the <u>blank</u> character:

ƀ.<(+|&$*);¬-/,%_>?:#= ABCDEFGHIJKLMNOPQRSTUVWXYZ0123456789

String processing is in a sense more fun than numeric processing. After learning a few details, you will find it easy to format output nicely, to write programs to print out graphs and pictures, and to perform other interesting tasks.

9.1 Declaration of Character Variables

The declaration of a character-valued variable has the form:

        DECLARE identifier CHARACTER(length);

"Length" specifies the number of characters in the value. As indicated in the examples below, CHAR is a valid abbreviation for CHARACTER, and this attribute can be factored.

        DECLARE TITLE CHARACTER(30);
        DCL (NAME, ADDRESS) CHARACTER(40);
        DCL WORD CHAR(10), LINE CHAR(60);

The CHARACTER attribute is incompatible with the numeric attributes FIXED, FLOAT and DECIMAL; they cannot be given to the same variable. They can appear in the same declaration:

        DCL LINE CHAR(50), LINE_COUNT FIXED DECIMAL;

An array can consist of string-valued subscripted variables. The following declaration describes an array of fifty, singly-subscripted variables, each of whose values is a string of 20 characters:

        DCL WORD(50) CHAR(20);

Multiple subscripts and lower bounds other than 1, are declared in the same way as for numeric-valued arrays.

An optional attribute for a character-valued variable is VARYING (abbreviated as VAR):

        DECLARE PHRASE CHARACTER(50) VARYING;
        DCL SYMBOL CHAR(10) VAR;

Here, the length in the declaration is the _maximum_ length. The _actual_ length of a VARYING string variable varies between 0 and the maximum during processing. A VARYING variable may contain the "empty string" -- the string of length zero, consisting of no characters at all. Without the VARYING attribute, the length of the variable is always exactly equal to the declared length.

9.1.1 Initial Character Values

   Non-VARYING strings are not initialized upon creation.
VARYING strings are assigned the null string (a string of length
0) when they are created. These defaults can be overridden by
using an INITIAL attribute in the declaration. For example:

```
          DCL KEYWORD CHAR(4) INIT('FOR ');
          DCL PAGE CHAR(4) INITIAL('PAGE');
          DCL LETTER(1:5) CHAR(1) INIT('A','B','C','D','E');
```

The assignment of the literals to the variables is done under
the normal rules of assignment as discussed in the next section.

   Repetition factors are treated slightly differently with
initial strings. (5)'2' means a single string of five twos, and
(5)('2') means five separate strings of a single two each. The
difference is very important in initializing an array. For
example

```
          DECLARE WORD(5) CHAR(10) INIT((5)'A');
```

```
          DECLARE WORD(5) CHAR(10) INIT((5)('A'));
```

The first example initializes WORD(1) to a string of five A's;
WORD(2:5) is uninitialized. The second example initializes each
of the five elements of WORD to a string consisting of a single
A.

9.2 String Assignments and Expressions

9.2.1 String Assignment

   The string assignment statement has the same form as a
numeric assignment:

```
          variable = expression;
```

The string variable denoted by the left side is first
determined, the expression is evaluated to yield a string value,
and this value is assigned to the variable.

   The simplest form of string expression is a literal -- a
quoted string of characters. Literals, discussed in Section
6.2, are used as string constants, in the same way that numeric
constants are used. For example, if WORD has been declared
CHARACTER(5), then

```
          WORD = 'ABCDE';
```

would assign the value ABCDE to variable WORD. The quotes
around ABCDE are crucial -- without them, ABCDE would be

interpreted as the name of a variable, rather than as a value:

        WORD = ABCDE;

This means get the value of variable ABCDE and assign it to variable WORD. (If there is no variable ABCDE this usage constitutes an "implicit declaration" of such a variable.) To further illustrate the point, consider

        WORD = 'A + B';

Like the previous example, the right side of this assignment statement is just a five-character literal. Without the quotes the right side would be interpreted as an arithmetic expression consisting of two variables and an addition. Note that the quotes enclose the value, but are not part of the value. The value consists of the five characters between the quotes:

        WORD A⁊+⁊B [char(5)]

A string variable not declared to be VARYING always has the same fixed length. A shorter value assigned to a string variable is automatically extended on the right with blanks until the required length is achieved. For example, if WORD is declared CHAR(5), then all of the following are equivalent:

        WORD = 'A';
        WORD = 'A ';
        WORD = 'A ';
        WORD = 'A   ';
        WORD = 'A   ';

If the value to be assigned is longer than the target variable, the value is truncated on the right to the same length as the target variable. This means that

        WORD = 'A⁊⁊⁊⁊B';

is equivalent to the assignments above, since only the first five characters of the right-side value are used. This same adjustment takes place even if the value is the result of the evaluation of a complex string expression.

A VARYING string variable always has the length of the last value assigned to it, up to its declared maximum. For example, consider the following:

        DCL A CHAR(3) VARYING, B CHAR(3);
        ...
        A = '';
        B = '';

The literal on the right side of both assignment statements is the empty (or null) string (since no characters are given between the quotes). Since A has the attribute VARYING and B does not, after execution of these statements the values are:

A   [char(3) var]   (length is 0)
B ƀƀƀ [char(3)]   (length is 3)

9.2.2 Expressions

A string expression yields a string of characters as a result. The only string operator is concatenation. Operands may be literals, string variables, and functions which return strings as values.

Concatenation

Strings are built by combining two smaller strings end to end. The operation is called "concatenation"; the PL/I symbol for it is "||". (These two adjacent vertical strokes have no intervening blanks; the vertical stroke is the character above the Y on the keypunch.) For example, suppose that the following variables exist:

STR(1) ABCƀ [char(4)]
STR(2) DEFƀ [char(4)]
CHR(1) ƀƀƀƀƀƀƀƀƀƀ [char(10)]
CHR(2) 1234567890 [char(10)]
SVAR   1234567890 [char(10) var]

After execution of the assignment statements

CHR(1) = STR(1) || STR(2);
CHR(2) = STR(1) || ' ' || STR(2);
SVAR = ' ' || STR(1) || STR(2);

the values would be

STR(1) ABCƀ [char(4)]
STR(2) DEFƀ [char(4)]
CHR(1) ABCƀDEFƀƀƀ [char(10)]
CHR(2) ABCƀƀDEFƀƀ [char(10)]
SVAR   ƀABCƀDEFƀ [char(10) var]

SUBSTR Built-in Function

The substring function is used to refer to a portion of a string. The form of the function is

SUBSTR(char-expr, start-pos, length)

where char-expr is an expression which yields a string value, start-pos is the position number (counting from 1, left to right) of the leftmost position of the desired substring, and

length is the number of positions in the substring. Start-pos
and length are expressions that evaluate to integers. Their
values must be reasonable; they must specify a substring that
really exists in the string referred to. For example:

```
SUBSTR('ABCDEF',2,3) is 'BCD'
SUBSTR('ABCDEF',1,1) is 'A'
SUBSTR('ABCDEF',1,6) is 'ABCDEF'
SUBSTR('ABC'||'DEF',2,5) is 'BCDEF'
```

As further examples, if variables and values are

```
SA  ABC  [char(3)]
SB  DEF  [char(3)]
J   2       [fixed decimal]
K   3       [fixed decimal]
```

then

```
SUBSTR(SA,1,2) is 'AB'
SUBSTR(SA||'ABC',2,4) is 'BCAB'
SUBSTR(SA||' '||SB,J,K+2) is 'BCⱮDE'
SA||SUBSTR(SB,3,1) is 'ABCF'
SUBSTR(SUBSTR(SB,1,2),2,1) is 'E'
```

   The SUBSTR function can be given without specifying "length".
In this case, the value of the function is the right portion of
the string, starting with the position specified. For example,

```
SUBSTR(SA,2) is 'BC'
SUBSTR(SA||SB,3) is 'CDEF'
```

LENGTH Built-in Function

   The LENGTH built-in function has the form

```
LENGTH(char-expr)
```

Its value is the actual length of the string expression given as
argument. It is generally used to determine the length of a
VARYING string. For example, if the value of WORD is:

```
WORD  HOPE  [char(10) var]
```

then

```
LENGTH(WORD) is 4
LENGTH(WORD||'XY') is 6
LENGTH(SUBSTR(WORD,2)) is 3
```

String Values in Conditions

String expressions can be used in conditions. The form is:

          char-expr   relation   char-expr

The relations are the same as those used for arithmetic-expression conditions (listed in Section 4.2.1.1.) Compound conditions can be used as described in Section 4.2.1.2.

The relationship between two string values depends upon an ordering that has been defined over all of the valid characters that might be included in such a value. This ordering is called the "collating sequence". In PL/I it is defined to be:

   ␢.<(+|&$*);¬-/,%_>?:#= ABCDEFGHIJKLMNOPQRSTUVWXYZ0123456789

This is an extension of "alphabetical order" with the digits higher than Z, and the special characters lower than A. The blank is lowest of all. Any character in this sequence is said to be "less than" a character to its right in the sequence.

If two strings being compared have different lengths, the shorter one is extended on the right with blanks until it is the same length as the longer. Both this length equalization, and the effect of the collating sequence are illustrated by the following conditions -- all of which are true:

                'A' = 'A'
                'A' = 'A␢'
                'A' ¬= '␢A'
                'A' ¬= 'AB'
                'A' < 'B'
                '/' < 'A'
                'Z' < '3'
                'AA' < 'AB'
                'A' < 'AB'
                '␢B' < 'AB'
                'ZZ' < '1.'
                'ANDREWS GREGORY' < 'ANDREWS, GREGORY'

9.2.3 The SUBSTR Pseudo-Variable

It is often necessary to assign to a part of a string variable. For example, we might like to change the variable

        S A SECOND ONE   to   S A FIRST ONE

This can be done using the SUBSTR "pseudo-variable", which has the same form as the SUBSTR function except that the first argument must reference a variable:

        SUBSTR(string-variable, start-pos, length)

The arguments have the same meaning as in the SUBSTR function;
the length can be left out (in which case the longest length
possible is assumed). For example, to effect the change shown
above, execute the statement

        SUBSTR(S, 3, 6) = 'FIRST ';

The SUBSTR pseudo-variable always refers to a fixed length part
of the string variable. One cannot delete part of the variable
by assigning it the null string; all this does is store blanks
in that part. For example, if we have

        X <u>A SECOND ONE</u>

then executing

        SUBSTR(X,1,1) = 'THE';   changes X to   X <u>T SECOND ONE</u>
and SUBSTR(X,1,4) = 'THE';   changes X to   X <u>THE COND ONE</u>

   As another illustration, the segment below changes all
occurrences of ';' to 'b' in string variable CARD:

        /* CHANGE ALL ;S IN CARD TO BLANK */
           I = 0;
           SEMI_LOOP: DO WHILE(I < LENGTH(CARD));
              I = I + 1;
              IF SUBSTR(CARD, I, 1) = ';'
                 THEN SUBSTR(CARD, I, 1) = ' ';
           END SEMI_LOOP;

The following segment reverses the characters in string S.   T is
a CHARACTER(1) variable used to temporarily hold a character:

        /* REVERSE CHARACTERS IN STRING S */
           FIRST = 1;
           LAST = LENGTH(S);
           REVERSE_LOOP: DO WHILE(FIRST < LAST);
              T = SUBSTR(S, FIRST, 1);
(9.2.3a)   SUBSTR(S, FIRST, 1) = SUBSTR(S, LAST, 1);
              SUBSTR(S, LAST, 1) = T;
              FIRST = FIRST + 1;
              LAST = LAST - 1;
              END REVERSE_LOOP;

9.3 String Assignment from External Data

String variables may appear in the list of a GET statement. The value assigned from the data will be truncated or extended with blanks, exactly as discussed under "String Assignment".

The data format is similar to that described in Section 3.4.1, except that any value on a data card to be assigned to a string variable must be enclosed in quotes. For example, if X and Y are FIXED DECIMAL, and SA and SB are CHAR(1), then values could be read from data cards as follows:

```
          GET LIST(X, SA, Y, SB);
          ...
     *DATA
          ...
          5, 'P', 7, '9'
```

Note that even though the final datum happens to be a number it must be quoted in the data list because it is destined for assignment to a string variable.

9.3.1 EDIT Format Character Data

Placing quotes around each string on a data card is a nuisance. If only string values are to appear on a card, the use of quotes can be avoided by reading the entire card as a single string value. For example, if CARD is CHAR(80) values can be assigned to CARD from data with the statement

```
          GET EDIT(CARD)(COL(1),A(80));
```

The COL(1) phrase causes reading to start at column 1 of the card, no matter where reading for the previous GET left off. The character positions in CARD correspond to the columns of the card, so the SUBSTR function can be used to extract individual strings from CARD. For example, SUBSTR(CARD,1,8) gives the first eight columns of the card.

The two alternative methods of reading string values from data cards are illustrated in the program segments below. In (9.3.1a), using LIST format, the preparation of the data is more difficult. In (9.3.1b), using EDIT format, preparation of the data is simplified but the program must use the SUBSTR function to break up the card into individual strings. The use of SUBSTR could be avoided by using a more complicated form of EDIT format control, but we have elected not to include that in the Primer.

(9.3.1a)
```
          DCL (W1, W2, W3) CHAR(20);
          ...
          GET LIST(W1, W2, W3);
          ...
    *DATA
    'HOOD', 'YAWL', 'SEA FEVER'
```

(9.3.1b)
```
          DCL CARD_IMAGE CHAR(80);
          DCL (W1, W2, W3) CHAR(20);
          ...
          GET EDIT(CARD_IMAGE)(COL(1),A(80));
          W1 = SUBSTR(CARD_IMAGE, 2, 4);
          W2 = SUBSTR(CARD_IMAGE, 7, 4);
          W3 = SUBSTR(CARD_IMAGE, 12, 9);
          ...
    *DATA
    HOOD YAWL SEA FEVER
```

9.4 Display of Character Values

String variables may be included in a PUT LIST statement.
Values are displayed in the standard format, as described in
Section 6.1. The value begins in the left-most print position
of the "next" field. If the length of the value is greater than
24, it simply continues into the following field.

9.5 An Example

Consider the following problem. The input contains the names
of 50 people, each consisting of a first name followed by a last
name, all enclosed in quotes. A name may be at most 20
characters long. One blank separates the last from the first
name. For example, the first two names in the list might be

       'BOB CONSTABLE'   'TIM TEITELBAUM'

The program should read in these 50 names, and print out all the
last names which begin with 'T'. For the two names shown above,
the program should select and print only TEITELBAUM.

Our program first reads all the names into an array, then
selects and prints. In this case, the array is not necessary,
since the names could be examined as they are read. Note that
the selection criterion is a search for the sequence 'ᑳT', which
signifies the beginning of a last name starting with T. This
program illustrates the topics of Section 9, but is highly
vulnerable to errors in the data. For example, both of the
following names would be selected for printing:

' TOM BROWN'   'ROBERT T JONES'

```
*PL/C ID='CAROL HILTON'
 /* PRINT LAST NAMES BEGINNING WITH T */
 PRINT_NAMES: PROCEDURE OPTIONS(MAIN);
     DECLARE (NAME(50),  /* LIST OF NAMES */
               NM)          /* NAME CURRENTLY BEING PROCESSED*/
                 CHAR(20) VARYING;
     DECLARE (I, J) FIXED DECIMAL;
     /* LOAD NAME(1:50) */
          LOAD_LOOP: DO I = 1 TO 50 BY 1;
               GET LIST(NAME(I));
               END LOAD_LOOP;
     /* PRINT EACH NAME FROM NAME(1:50) CONTAINING ' T' */
          NAME_LOOP: DO I = 1 TO 50 BY 1;
               NM = NAME(I);
               SCAN_LOOP: DO J = 1 TO LENGTH(NM)-1 BY 1;
                    IF SUBSTR(NM,J,2) = ' T' THEN DO;
                       TNAME = SUBSTR(NM,J);
                       PUT SKIP LIST(TNAME);
                       GO TO TERM_SCAN; END;
                    END SCAN_LOOP;
               TERM_SCAN:;
               END NAME_LOOP;
     END PRINT_NAMES;
*DATA
```

Section 9 <u>Summary</u>

1. A string variable is declared in the following way:

        DECLARE identifier CHARACTER(length);

CHARACTER may be abbreviated CHAR.

2. The length of a string variable is fixed, at the length
given in the declaration, unless the optional VARYING (or VAR)
attribute is given. With this attribute, the length of the
variable is the same as the length of the value most recently
assigned to it (but not more than the declared maximum length).

3. Fixed-length string variables <u>do not</u> have an automatic
initial value. VARYING string variables are automatically
initialized to the null string if no INITIAL attribute is given.

4. An initial value may be assigned at the time of creation, by
the use of the optional INITIAL attribute.

5. A string constant is a literal -- a sequence of characters
enclosed in single quotes.

6. In PL/C string variables cannot be subject to arithmetic
operations, even if their values happen to be numbers.

7. The only operation that can be performed on string values is
"concatenation". The symbol is "||"; the action is to join two
string values, end to end.

8. The SUBSTR built-in function extracts a portion of the value
of a string expression. The form is:

        SUBSTR(char-expr, start-pos, length)

If the length is not specified, the entire right portion of the
value is assumed.

9. The LENGTH built-in function gives the length of a string
expression. The form is:

        LENGTH(char-expr)

10. The SUBSTR pseudo-variable has the same form as the SUBSTR
function, except that the first argument must refer to a
variable. The SUBSTR pseudo-variable may be used on the left
side of an assignment to change part of the string variable.

Section 9 <u>Exercises</u>

Write programs for the following problems.

<u>1</u>. Read a string of up to 40 characters, reverse the order of
the characters, and print it out. For example, 'EVIL' becomes
'LIVE'. You may determine the input form.

<u>2</u>. Read a string of up to 40 characters, using GET LIST.
Delete all blanks up to the first non-blank; print the result.

<u>3</u>. Read a string of up to 40 characters, delete all characters
'A', and print the result. You may determine the input form.

<u>4</u>. Read in three strings, call them A, PATTERN, and REPLACEBY.
Replace every occurrence of PATTERN in A by the string
REPLACEBY. Print the result. For example, if we have

        A <u>BIG, BIGGER, BIGGEST</u>   PATTERN <u>BIG</u>   REPLACEBY <u>SMALL</u>

the program should print the string

        'SMALL, SMALLGER, SMALLGEST'.

Be careful. If we have

        A <u>LAST</u>   PATTERN <u>A</u>   REPLACEBY <u>EA</u>

A should not be changed to 'LEAST', then to 'LEEAST', and then
to 'LEEEAST', etc. Stop with 'LEAST'.

5. Read a string of up to 40 characters and determine whether
or not it is a "palindrome". (A palindrome is a string whose
characters are the same whether read from left-to-right or
right-to-left. For example: AHA, NOON, I, LEVEL, LON NOL.)

<u>6</u>. Read a three-digit integer and print it in English.   For
example, print 182 as ONE HUNDRED AND EIGHTY TWO. You will need
string arrays to hold the English equivalents of the digits.

<u>7</u>. The input consists of three two-digit numbers representing a
date. The first is the day, the second the month, and the third
the last two digits of the year. For example: 25, 12, 75. Read
the date in this numeric form and print it in the usual text
form. For example, DECEMBER 25, 1975. Use an array for the
names of the months.

<u>8</u>. Read in a list of words and print out (1) the number of
words made up of 1 to 6 characters, (2) the number with 6 to 12
characters, and (3) the number of times the word 'THE' appears.
The words appear on one card each, left-justified in columns 1
through 12, with no surrounding quotes.

PART II   PROGRAM STRUCTURE

Part II introduces no new PL/I features. It is entirely concerned with ways in which the statements presented in Part I should be used to enhance the clarity, readability and understandability of programs. We assume not only that you can now write PL/I statements to perform simple tasks, but also that you realize that there are various different ways of performing the same task. Once you pass the first threshold of being happy to find any way at all of programming a given task, you should become concerned with which of several possible ways is better.

A program to solve a particular problem is not unique -- many different programs could solve the same problem. But although different programs may produce the same final answers, there may still be significant differences between them and hence strong reasons to prefer one form of program over another. Some of the possible reasons for prefering one program over another are:

1. One is easier to write than the other.

2. One is easier to test and show correctness than the other.

3. One is easier to change, if problem requirements are later altered.

4. One takes less computer time to execute than the other.

5. One is shorter and requires fewer variables -- hence requires less computer memory space during execution.

In Part II we are concerned with the first three of these reasons, which are generally involved with a form of programming that is easy to read and understand. This form does not necessarily produce programs that are efficient as far as the computer is concerned (reasons 4 and 5), but neither are they obviously inefficient. At this point human efficiency is more important to us than computer efficiency and we will concentrate on a type of programming that is oriented to human understanding.

Programs are <u>not</u> <u>only</u> meant to convey information to a computer; programs are written by people <u>to</u> <u>be</u> <u>read</u> by people, and for many reasons:

1. Except for trivial problems, programs are rarely completed at a single sitting. Programs take several days to over a year to complete, and you must often review what you have done before.

2. Programs are rarely entirely correct on the first try, and the testing process requires that the program be read.

3. A programming task is often divided among several people who must read and understand portions of each other's work, so that their sections communicate properly.

4. Program segments are often reused in contexts other than the one for which originally written. To do so it is necessary to understand exactly what the segment does.

5. Programs often need to be modified to meet changes in problem requirements.

Most people read programs not for enjoyment, but in order to <u>understand</u> <u>what</u> <u>the</u> <u>program</u> <u>does</u> <u>when</u> <u>executed</u> <u>by</u> <u>a</u> <u>computer</u>. This does not just mean what it will do in one particular execution with one particular set of input data, but what it will do in general, for any possible set of data, any choice of execution options, and any other conditions of context or environment. This is a difficult task at best, and the reader needs all the help he can get.

We must of course understand the precise meaning of each statement type in the programming language so that we can, if necessary, trace or simulate the action of the computer. In theory, we can simulate the entire execution and thereby understand the meaning of any program. In practice this just isn't reasonable. Even for programs of modest size we lack the time or patience to read them as if we were a computer. So we are forced to try to read programs in a way that is quite different from a computer. For example, consider the simple program segment:

```
TOTAL = 0;
TOTAL_LOOP: DO I = 1 TO N BY 1;
    TOTAL = TOTAL + ARR(I);
    END TOTAL_LOOP;
```

Depending upon the value of N, the computer may execute hundreds or even thousands of statements from this segment. Regardless of the value of N, the human reader should regard this as a single task: <u>compute the sum of the values of ARR(1:N)</u>. Instead of making the reader figure this out for himself, the writer can help by describing the task just this way in a heading comment:

```
/* SET TOTAL TO SUM OF VALUES OF ARR(1:N) */
   TOTAL = 0;
   TOTAL_LOOP: DO I = 1 TO N BY 1;
       TOTAL = TOTAL + ARR(I);
       END TOTAL_LOOP;
```

As far as the computer is concerned the program is unchanged --
the presence or absence of comments, and the contents of
comments are immaterial. But the human reader now has a choice
as to what to read: either the heading comment or the program
indented under the comment. He can read the comment to find out
what the segment does, or the program statements to find out how
the task is performed.

   Being able to understand substantial programs depends on our
being able to understand them at a level higher than that of the
individual PL/I statement. To facilitate reading a program in
this way the programmer must structure the program in terms of
higher-level units, and organize and present the program so that
its structure is clear and obvious. If this is carefully done
it is much easier to view the program in terms of larger units
and to understand its action without a statement-by-statement
trace of execution.

   For example, consider the two program segments given below.
These segments give identical results; they include exactly the
same PL/I statements. They differ only in that in (IIb) the
statements have been slightly reordered into a more logical
grouping, indentation has been used to show the relationship
between various statements, and comments have been added to
summarize the purpose of various subsections.   These   two
segments are equivalent as far as the computer is concerned, but
the second is much clearer and easier for us to understand.
This particular task is simple enough that either form of the
program can be figured out, but it is easier to understand
(IIb).   If the program required several hundred statements the
form illustrated by (IIa) would be very difficult to understand
-- and yet several hundred statements is not really a large
program. The larger the program, the more important it is to
use an understandable style.

```
(IIa)     TOTAL = 0; NREAD = 0;
          DO I = 1 TO T BY 1;
          M(I) = 0; END;
          I = 0;
          DO WHILE(NREAD<N); GET LIST(A);
          IF A = 0 THEN GO TO EXITLOOP;
          IF A > 0 THEN DO; TOTAL = TOTAL + A;
          I = I + 1;
          M(I) = A;
          NREAD = NREAD+1; END; END;
          EXITLOOP:;
```

```
(IIb)
    /* SET M(1:T) TO ZEROES */
        ZERO_LOOP: DO I = 1 TO T BY 1;
            M(I) = 0;
            END ZERO_LOOP;
    /* READ VALUES UNTIL N HAVE BEEN READ OR UNTIL 0 IS READ */
    /* STORE POSITIVE VALUES IN M(1:I) AND THEIR TOTAL IN SUM*/
        I = 0; TOTAL = 0; NREAD = 0;
        READ_LOOP: DO WHILE (NREAD < N);
            GET LIST(A);
            IF A = 0 THEN GO TO TERM_READ_VALUES;
            IF A > 0 THEN DO;
                TOTAL = TOTAL + A;
                I = I + 1;
                M(I) = A;
                NREAD = NREAD + 1;   END;
            END READ_LOOP;
        TERM_READ_VALUES:;
```

Consider the ways in which the writer of (IIb) has undertaken
to help the reader. Most importantly, he shows with comments
and indentation that the program consists of two subtasks that
are relatively independent. The first clears M to zeroes; the
second loads and sums. The same two subtasks are present in
(IIa), but the reader must discover this for himself. Not only
does he not have comments and indentation to aid him; the
statement order does not suggest this logical division. (IIa)
starts with two statements that are part of the initialization
of the second subtask. As far as the computer is concerned
these can just as well be first, but it diverts the human reader
to find these statements that are not related to or needed by
their immediate successors. The point is that (IIa) must be
studied as a single entity, while (IIb) can be studied as a
sequence of smaller, simpler subtasks.

Even the task of understanding the individual statements is
easier in (IIb). To understand the extent of a DO loop in (IIa)
the reader must scan the entire program and count ENDs very
carefully. In (IIb) the extent of each loop is indicated by
indentation, and confirmed by the loop-name given as a prefix to
the DO and a suffix to the END of each loop.

The style of (IIb) is recommended, not as a matter of
consideration for some hypothetical reader of your program, but
simply as a matter of self-interest. You will repeatedly have
to read and understand your own programs. The process of
completing later parts requires re-reading earlier parts; the
process of testing requires frequent re-reading. The time spent
in carefully organizing and presenting a program is handsomely
repaid before you have finished with the program.

Section 1   Basic Program Units

The previous section stated our objective of making programs more readily <u>understandable to a human reader</u>. Now we propose a systematic method by which this can be done.

The easiest program construction to understand is a <u>sequence</u> of actions that has <u>no loops or branches</u>. That is, given a sequence

        S1
        S2
        S3

we know that S1 will be executed first, then S2, and finally S3. However, it must be obvious from the examples of Part I, and even from the statement types of PL/I, that programs must have loops and branches. In a sense, what we are going to do is try to hide that fact. We will try to write programs that actually contain loops and branches in such a way that they can be read and understood as if they were a simple sequence of actions. In effect, we will say that it is useful to be able to regard the execution of a program as "first S1, then S2, and finally S3", even though we know that internally S2 involves a loop.

We are interested in identifying patterns of statements that can be usefully regarded as a single unit for purposes of reading and understanding the action of a program. The three patterns that dominate are called "the compound statement", "the repetition unit" and "the alternate selection unit". Each of these basic units behaves as if it were a single "statement" in some language that is at a higher level than PL/I. The key point is that, as a statement, each of these units has a <u>single entry point</u> and a <u>single exit point</u>. The only control of flow between such units is the normal sequential order -- the order in which they are written.

1.1 The Compound Statement

Any simple sequence of statements that follow one after another can be considered a "compound statement". For example, a sequence of three assignment statements could be considered a compound statement, or unit, to interchange the values of two variables:

```
/* INTERCHANGE VALUES OF A AND B */
     T = A;
     A = B;
     B = T;
```

We require only that the statements perform some logically related task and that the statements follow one another in normal sequential order. Other examples are:

```
/* PRINT TITLE AND HEADING FOR TABLE */
     PUT SKIP(3) LIST
          (' ', 'TEMPERATURE-PRESSURE EQUIVALENTS');
     PUT SKIP(2) LIST
          ('STANDARD CONCENTRATION WITHOUT CATALYST');
     PUT SKIP(3) LIST
          ('TEMPERATURE', 'PRESSURE', 'REACTION TIME');

/* INITIALIZE TABLE LINE GENERATION */
     LINE_COUNT = 0;    COLUMN_SUM = 0;
     TIME_BASE = TEMP_BASE/EQUIL_CONST;
```

We want to be able to regard an entire sequence of PL/I statements as if they were a single statement in some even-higher-level language than PL/I. A single statement has a single entry point and a single exit point:

enter⟶| Si |⟶exit

So if a sequence is to behave as a single statement we require that the <u>entire sequence has a single entry point and a single exit point</u>:

enter⟶| ⟶| S1 |⟶| S2 |⟶...⟶| Sn |⟶ |⟶exit

Figure 1.   A Compound Statement

The heading comment of a compound statement summarizes the action of the entire statement; the individual PL/I statements indented beneath the heading comment specify <u>how</u> this action is performed.

We used the concept of a compound statement in Section
I.4.3.1 in order to conditionally execute more than one
statement:

     IF condition THEN DO; S1; S2; ... Sn; END;

In that context the compound statement is significant to PL/I
and we must indicate that the entire sequence S1;...Sn is to be
treated as a single unit by marking the beginning and end of the
sequence with DO and END. A heading comment and indentation
would not suffice since neither of these is recognized by PL/I.
Now we are talking about structuring a program for the benefit
of a human reader -- to whom comments and indentation are
significant, but to whom the DO-END delimiters are irrelevant.
The general rules for format of a compound statement are:

     Write a comment to summarize the purpose (or action) of the
     compound statement and indent the comment so it is left-
     aligned with the heading of the preceding unit.   The
     individual components of the unit are left-aligned with
     respect to each other and indented with respect to the
     heading comment.

1.2 The Repetition Unit

     Repetition is a common task in programs, and it is relatively
difficult for a human reader to comprehend. With the other
types of units the execution sequence is at least similar to the
sequence that appears on the program listing; with repetition it
is very different. Hence it is crucial that sections involving
repetition be carefully organized and clearly presented.

     Repetition is always accomplished with some type of DO loop.
The loop may be preceded by initialization statements and it may
be followed by termination statements.   The idea of the
"repetition unit" is to regard this entire sequence as a single
entity:

(1.2a)   /* Description of what the unit does */
               Sequence of statements to initialize for loop;
               loop-name: DO ...
                    Body of loop
                    END loop-name;
               Sequence of statements to terminate the unit;

     The general form of a loop is shown in Figure 2. The "cond"
represents the condition of a DO WHILE loop and indicates by
becoming false when the loop should terminate.   The statements
S1 through Sn form the body of the loop. This loop was
discussed in Section I.4.2.

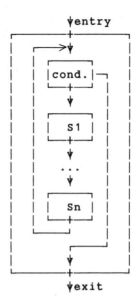

Figure 2. DO WHILE Loop

    Although the individual statements in a loop may be repeated,
and the condition causes a branch, <u>taken as a whole, the loop
has a single entry point and a single exit point</u>. It can be
regarded as a single statement, so that with the initializing
and terminating statements (1.2a) is a single-entry, single-exit
compound statement. But because of the presence of the loop we
recognize it as a special type of compound statement and call it
a "repetition unit". Examples are given below.

```
/* SET SUM TO SUM OF INTEGERS FROM 14 THRU 728 */
    INT = 14;   SUM = 14;
    SUM_LOOP: DO WHILE (INT < 728);
        INT = INT + 1;
        SUM = SUM + INT;
        END SUM_LOOP;

/* MOVE A(J:K) TO B(J:K) */
    MOVE_LOOP: DO I = J TO K BY 1;
        B(I) = A(I);
        END MOVE_LOOP;

/* SET AVG TO AVERAGE OF X(1:N) */
    SUM = 0;
    SUM_LOOP: DO I = 1 TO N BY 1;
        SUM = SUM + X(I);
        END SUM_LOOP;
    AVG = SUM/N;
```

```
/* TITLE AND PRINT A(1:M) */
   PUT SKIP(3) LIST('VALUES OF A(1:M)');
   PUT SKIP;
   PRINT_LOOP: DO J = 1 TO M BY 1;
       PUT SKIP LIST(A(J));
       END PRINT_LOOP;
   PUT SKIP(2) LIST('END OF A(1:M)');
```

The general rules for the format of a repetition unit are:

1. Write a heading comment that summarizes <u>what</u> the <u>entire</u>
unit does. Indent this comment so it is left-aligned with
the heading of the preceding unit.

2. The individual components of the unit --
initialization, loop and termination -- are left-aligned
with respect to each other, and indented with respect to
the heading comment.

3. The statements that constitute the body of the loop
should be indented with respect to the DO statement that
controls the loop (which means two levels of indentation
with respect to the heading comment of the unit). The END
is left-aligned with the statements of the body of the
loop.

4. If the loop body is long or complex it should be
treated as a compound statement (or as several compound
statements), with a heading comment that describes what the
body does <u>on each repetition</u>.

5. The DO statement controlling the loop should be given a
label prefix that suggests the role of the loop. (We have
adopted the convention that a loop-name always ends in the
characters "_LOOP" to help make these labels immediately
recognizable.) The loop-name should also be given as a
suffix after the END of the loop.

1.3 <u>The Alternate Selection Unit</u>

1.3.1 <u>The Single-Alternative Unit</u>

The third basic type of unit occurs when one of several
alternative tasks is to be selected for execution. The simplest
and most common case is when there are two alternatives, but one
of the two is null. That is, there is one statement that may or
may not be executed. This is of course the "conditional
execution" described in Section I.4.3 and programmed with the IF
construction. However, now we want to make the IF construction
(Figure 2 of I.4.3) conform to our single-entry, single-exit
requirement. We do this simply by regarding the entire
construction as a single unit, as shown in Figure 3.

entry

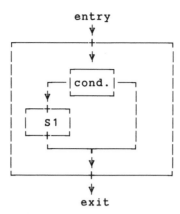

exit

Figure 3. The Single-Alternative Unit

There is a single entry-point and a common exit-point <u>whether or</u>
<u>not the conditional statement is executed</u>. The following are
examples of single-alternative or conditional units:

(1.3.1a) /* REPLACE NEGATIVE X BY 0 */
            IF X(I) < 0
                THEN X(I) = 0;

(1.3.1b) /* REPLACE NEGATIVE DATUM */
            IF DATUM < 0
                THEN GET LIST(DATUM);

(1.3.1c) /* DISCARD AND REPORT NEGATIVE DATUM */
            IF DATUM < 0
                THEN DO; ERRORCOUNT = ERRORCOUNT + 1;
                    PUT SKIP(2) LIST('ERROR NUMBER',
                        ERRORCOUNT);
                    PUT SKIP LIST('NEGATIVE DATUM', DATUM);
                    GET LIST(DATUM); END;

(1.3.1d) /* SAVE NEW MAXIMUM VAL */
            IF VAL > MAXVAL
                THEN MAXVAL = VAL;

(1.3.1e) /* SAVE VAL AND POINTER IF NEW MAXIMUM */
            IF VAL(I) > MAXVAL
                THEN DO; MAXVAL = VAL(I);
                    MAXLOC = I; END;

Since single-alternative units are often short and obvious, as
in these examples, we often shortcut the full-blown unit format
shown above. The criteria, as always, are readability and
clarity.   If the actual PL/I statements are clear and obvious
then a summary comment is not needed. In fact, being redundant,
the comment then tends to clutter and obscure the program rather
than clarify it. Some judgement is required. In the examples

above (1.3.1a), (1.3.1b) and (1.3.1d) probably do not need a
heading comment and perhaps are clearer without it. The
indentation is also not necessary in these cases. They would be
better written as:

        IF X(I) < 0 THEN X(I) = 0;

        IF DATUM < 0 THEN GET LIST(DATUM);

        IF VAL > MAXVAL THEN MAXVAL = VAL;

On the other hand, (1.3.1c) is probably large enough that the
heading comment is useful, and (1.3.1e) could be written either
way.

    Note that if the conditional statement is itself a compound
statement the DO and END delimiters must be used. The extent of
the conditional statement must be conveyed to PL/I as well as
the human reader, and PL/I does not consider comments and
indentation.

    The general rules for the format of a single-alternative unit
are:

    1. If the unit is long or complex it should be treated
    formally as a distinct unit, with a heading comment left-
    aligned with the heading of the preceding unit. The IF
    should be indented with respect to the heading, and the
    alternative should be indented with respect to the IF. (It
    doesn't matter whether the THEN and the DO are on the line
    with the IF or are considered part of the body. The
    structure is quite clear either way.)

    2. If the unit is short and obvious it should just be
    written as a simple statement. That is, there should be no
    heading comment and the IF should be left-aligned with the
    preceding statement. If the alternative does not entirely
    fit on the line beginning with IF, its continuation should
    be indented with respect to the IF (just like any other
    continuation line).

1.3.2 The Two-Alternative Unit

    The case with two non-null alternatives is obviously
programmed with the IF-THEN-ELSE construction (see Section
I.4.3). It can still be viewed as a unit with a single exit
point, as shown in Figure 4.

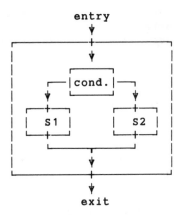

entry

exit

Figure 4.   The Two-Alternative Unit

Examples of two-alternative units are the following:

```
IF A < B
   THEN X = B;
   ELSE X = A;
```

```
/* SET VAL FROM A OR DATA LIST */
   IF A(I) ¬= 0
        THEN VAL = A(I);
        ELSE GET LIST(VAL);
```

```
IF NEWVAL >= 0
   THEN POSCOUNT = POSCOUNT + 1;
   ELSE NEGCOUNT = NEGCOUNT + 1;
```

```
/* READ NEXT VALUE INTO NUMBER OR LETTER */
   IF TYPEFLAG = 1
        THEN DO; GET LIST(NUMBER(I));
              I = I + 1; END;
        ELSE DO; GET LIST(LETTER(J));
              J = J + 1; END;
```

The two-alternative unit should <u>not be used   to   combine   two unrelated tasks</u>. The following is an example of <u>poor usage</u>:

```
/* PRINT TITLE OR ERROR MESSAGE */
   IF N > 50
        THEN DO; PUT SKIP(3) LIST('EXCESSIVE DATA');
              GO TO TERM_READ_LOOP; END;
        ELSE DO; PUT SKIP(2) LIST('LIST OF INPUT DATA:');
              PUT SKIP; END;
```

The title in this example should not be viewed as an alternative to the error message. It would be clearer when presented in the following way:

```
/* TEST FOR EXCESSIVE DATA */
   IF N > 50 THEN DO;
        PUT SKIP(3) LIST('EXCESSIVE DATA');
        GO TO TERM_READ_LOOP; END;
PUT SKIP(2) LIST('LIST OF INPUT DATA:');
PUT SKIP;
```

The general rules for the format of a two-alternative unit are:

1. If the unit is long or complex it should be treated formally as a distinct unit, with a heading comment left-aligned with the heading of the preceding unit. The IF should be indented with respect to the heading, and the two alternatives should be indented with respect to the IF.

2. The THEN and ELSE lines should be indented with respect to the IF and left-aligned with respect to each other. If the body of the alternative cannot be completed on the same line as the THEN or ELSE its continuation lines should be indented with respect to the THEN or ELSE. The critical aspect is that the parallel relationship between the THEN and ELSE alternatives be made.clear.

1.3.3 The Multiple-Alternative Unit

The general case, with more than two alternatives, is shown in Figure 5. S1 to Sn are the alternatives, one of which is to be executed; "cond" is the condition by which selection of one alternative is made.

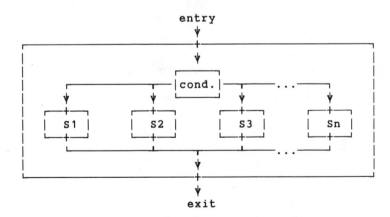

Figure 5.   An Alternate Selection Unit

The entire construction has a single entry-point and a single exit and can be treated as a single unit. Unfortunately, there

is no really clear way of programming this unit in PL/I.   Some
programming languages have a "case statement" for this purpose,
but PL/I does not, and we must make do with a combination of IF
statements.

   There are two possible constructions using only the IF
statement.   Suppose we have four alternatives, one of which is
to be executed depending upon the value of a variable CLASS.
(1.3.3a) and (1.3.3b) show possible constructions. Both are
functionally equivalent and have the desirable single entry and
single exit.   We prefer (1.3.3a) since it is simpler and seems
to exhibit more clearly the parallel relationship between the
alternatives. Deeply nested IF constructions, such as (1.3.3b),
are difficult to write correctly, difficult to test and to
change, and very difficult to read and understand. (1.3.3a)
does require the use of GO TOs, but only in a restricted way
that is entirely internal to the unit. They do not add any exit
points to the unit. This is an example of a situation in which
the GO TO is less unattractive than the available alternatives.
The GO TO is just being used to simulate the natural higher
level control structure (the "case statement"), which happens to
be missing from the language we are using.

```
(1.3.3a)  /* COMPUTE TOLL, DEPENDING UPON CLASS */
            IF CLASS = 1 THEN DO;
                TOLL = .25;
                GO TO TOLL_EXIT; END;
            IF CLASS = 2 THEN DO;
                TOLL = .25 + WEIGHT_FACTOR;
                GO TO TOLL_EXIT; END;
            IF CLASS = 3 THEN DO;
                TOLL = .10 * NBR_PASSENGERS;
                GO TO TOLL_EXIT; END;
            /* COMPUTATION FOR CLASS ¬= 1, 2 OR 3 */
                TOLL = .0125 * MILES_DRIVEN;
            TOLL_EXIT:;


(1.3.3b)  /* COMPUTE TOLL, DEPENDING UPON CLASS */
            IF CLASS = 1
                THEN DO;
                    TOLL = .25;
                    END;
            ELSE IF CLASS = 2
                THEN DO;
                    TOLL = .25 + WEIGHT_FACTOR;
                    END;
            ELSE IF CLASS = 3
                THEN DO;
                    TOLL = .10 * NBR_PASSENGERS;
                    END;
            ELSE DO; /* COMPUTATION FOR CLASS ¬= 1, 2 OR 3 */
                TOLL = .0125 * MILES_DRIVEN;
                END;
```

(1.3.3c) shows a third construction that looks like a minor
variation of (1.3.3a) but in fact is dangerous and should be
avoided:

```
(1.3.3c)  /* COMPUTE TOLL, DEPENDING UPON CLASS */
             IF CLASS = 1
                 THEN DO; TOLL = .25; END;
             IF CLASS = 2
                 THEN DO; TOLL = .25 + WEIGHT_FACTOR; END;
             IF CLASS = 3
                 THEN DO; TOLL = .10 * NBR_PASSENGERS; END;
             IF (CLASS¬=1) & (CLASS¬=2) & (CLASS¬=3)
                 THEN DO; /* COMPUTE FOR CLASS ¬= 1, 2 OR 3 */
                     TOLL = .0125 * MILES_DRIVEN; END;
```

(1.3.3c) avoids the use of GO TOs but it is no longer a strictly
alternate construction. The possibility now exists that more
than one of the alternatives could be executed (if, for example,
the value of CLASS is changed in the body of one of the
alternatives). The construction illustrated in (1.3.3a)
executes at most one of the alternatives, regardless of the
action performed by that alternative. (1.3.3c) executes exactly
one alternative only if the alternatives refrain from doing
certain things (such as changing the value of CLASS).

The general rules for the format of an alternate selection
unit with more than two alternatives are:

1. Write a heading comment that summarizes what the entire
unit does, emphasizing that one of many alternatives is to
be executed. Indent this comment so it is left-aligned
with the heading of the preceding unit.

2. The individual alternatives are indented with respect
to the heading comment and left-aligned with respect to
each other. Their alignment should show their parallel
role. If the strategy shown in (1.3.3a) is used, the IF
statements should be left-aligned. If the strategy of
(1.3.3b) is used the ELSEs should be left-aligned. In
either event the body of the alternatives should be
indented with respect to the IF or ELSE so that the
beginning of each alternative is emphasized.

3. If an individual alternative is long or complex it
should be treated as a compound statement with its own
heading comment, etc.

1.4 Units and Levels

In the preceding sections the basic units were generally described as if their components were simple PL/I statements. Actually the components can just as well be units, since units have a single entry and exit point and in that regard behave as if they were single statements. An entire compound statement (Figure 1), a repetition unit (Figure 2) or an alternate unit (Figures 3, 4 and 5) could be inserted in the position of any one of the Si blocks in any of these figures. The properties of the units, and the rules for their presentation, remain the same whether their components are simple statements, or program units -- which in turn can have units as their components.

This means that in general there is a hierarchy of these units. At the highest level there will be a compound statement -- a simple sequence of units. Each of these can be a unit of any type, whose components are in turn also units, etc. At some lowest level the components will be single PL/I statements. Since there is no limit either to the size of an individual unit or to the number of levels in the structure, there is no limit to the size or complexity of program that can be organized and presented in this manner.

For example, consider a program to read 100 numbers, sort them into ascending order, and print the sorted list:

```
*PL/C ID='MIKE MEEHAN'
 /* READ, SORT AND PRINT A LIST OF 100 NUMBERS */
 RSP: PROCEDURE OPTIONS(MAIN);
     DECLARE (A(100), T) FLOAT DECIMAL;
     DECLARE (I, J) FIXED DECIMAL;
     /* LOAD A(1:100) FROM DATA */
         READ_LOOP: DO I = 1 TO 100 BY 1;
             GET LIST(A(I));
             END READ_LOOP;
     /* SORT A(1:100) */
         SORT_LOOP: DO J = 1 TO 100 BY 1;
             /* PUT MIN OF A(J:100) IN A(J) */
                 MIN_LOOP: DO I = 100 TO J+1 BY -1;
                     IF A(I) < A(J) THEN DO;
                         T = A(I);
                         A(I) = A(J);
                         A(J) = T; END;
                     END MIN_LOOP;
             END SORT_LOOP;
     /* PRINT A(1:100) */
         PRINT_LOOP: DO I = 1 TO 100 BY 1;
             PUT SKIP LIST(A(I));
             END PRINT_LOOP;
     END RSP;
 *DATA
     98, 96, 95, 98.1, etc.
```

The overall program RSP is a compound statement. This "statement" has three components, each of which is itself a unit. The unit actions are described by their heading comments:

```
/* LOAD A(1:100) FROM DATA */
/* SORT A(1:100) */
/* PRINT A(1:100) */
```

The load and print units are simple repetition units, such as the examples given in Section 1.2. The sort unit is more complex. It is a repetition unit, with the body of the loop performing the task:

```
/* PUT MIN OF A(J:100) IN A(J) */
```

This body is itself a repetition unit containing a loop named MIN_LOOP. The body of MIN_LOOP is a single-alternative unit (although it is not formally presented as such).

In summary, <u>every level of a program is just a compound statement</u> -- a simple sequence of tasks to be performed in order. At the higher levels the components of this compound statement are themselves units. At the lowest level the components are individual PL/I statements.

1.5 <u>Termination of a Unit</u>

A unit normally terminates by reaching its exit. It is then followed in execution by the unit appearing next on the listing (if any). However, it is often convenient (and sometimes necessary) to permit a unit the option of terminating not only itself, but also <u>some unit at a higher level</u>.

For example, suppose that in some compound statement such as shown in Figure 1, you would like the unit represented by S2 to have the option of terminating the entire compound statement as shown in Figure 6.

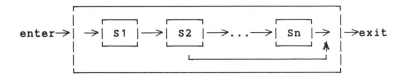

Figure 6. Compound Statement with Termination Exit

This could be implemented with a conditional GO TO and a target label at the end of the compound statement:

```
      /* Purpose of compound statement */
         /* S1 */
            ...
         /* S2 */
            ...
(1.5a)         IF cond THEN GO TO TERM_statement-name;
            ...

      ...
      /* Sn */
         ...
      TERM_statement-name:;
```

In Figure 6 and example (1.5a) unit S2 has been given a
conditional second exit, whose purpose is to terminate the
entire compound statement -- the unit at the next higher level.
The compound statement itself still has a single exit point.

It is generally possible to avoid a termination exit such as
the one shown in Figure 6 and example (1.5a). For example,
(1.5b) uses a termination exit and (1.5c) is a revision of
(1.5b) that avoids the need for the exit.

```
         /* LOAD AND OPTIONALLY PRINT A(1:N) */
            /* LOAD A(1:N) */
               LOAD_LOOP: DO I = 1 TO N BY 1;
                  GET LIST(A(I));
(1.5b)            END LOAD_LOOP;
            IF PRINTFLAG = 0 THEN GO TO TERM_LOADPRINT;
            /* PRINT A(1:N) */
               PRINT_LOOP: DO I = 1 TO N BY 1;
                  PUT SKIP LIST(A(I));
                  END PRINT_LOOP;
            TERM_LOADPRINT:;
```

```
         /* LOAD AND OPTIONALLY PRINT A(1:N) */
            /* LOAD A(1:N) */
               LOAD_LOOP: DO I = 1 TO N BY 1;
                  GET LIST(A(I));
(1.5c)            END LOAD_LOOP;
            /* PRINT A(1:N) IF PRINTFLAG IS ON */
               IF PRINTFLAG ¬= 0 THEN
                  PRINT_LOOP: DO I = 1 TO N BY 1;
                     PUT SKIP LIST(A(I));
                     END PRINT_LOOP;
```

Even though the strategy used in (1.5c) is always possible, it
is not always preferable. If the portion of the unit to be
skipped is large and complex it may be clearer to use a
termination exit as in (1.5b) rather than have to make a large
section of program conditional, as in (1.5c). Particularly when
the "normal", or "most frequently followed" path of the
execution is to continue through the remainder of the compound
statement, it can be less clear to make this portion conditional
and indent it further than the initial portion. This is another

situation in which the use of a GO TO is sometimes less
unattractive than the alternative. However, this use of the
GO TO and provision of a second exit point to a unit should
always be subject to these restrictions:

1. It should be used only to terminate a unit at a higher
level.

2. The target label must be positioned below the GO TO.
That is, always go forward; never go back.

3. The target label must always be positioned at the end
of a unit; never at the beginning of the "next" unit. The
name should be chosen to suggest the end of something
rather than the beginning of whatever comes next.

The body of a loop (S1 to Sn in Figure 2) can be considered a
compound statement. Then the termination shown in Figure 6 is
the means of terminating one particular execution of the body.
The target label would be attached to a null statement preceding
the END that denotes the end of the body. This technique was
introduced in Section I.4.3.2 and is illustrated in (I.4.3.2a).

Termination arises sometimes when one of the repeated
components (say S2 in Figure 2) of a repetition unit needs to
terminate the entire loop, or some outer unit, rather than just
one particular repetition of the loop. This can be accomplished
by a GO TO with a target label at the end of that unit. (1.5d)
illustrates both kinds of termination exits.

```
          /* SET SUM TO SUM OF POS ELMTS OF A(1:N), STOP ON 0 */
              SUM = 0;
              SUM_LOOP: DO I = 1 TO N BY 1;
                  IF A(I) = 0 THEN GO TO TERM_SET_SUM;
(1.5d)            IF A(I) < 0 THEN GO TO SKIP_SUM;
                  SUM = SUM + A(I);
                  SKIP_SUM:;
                  END SUM_LOOP;
              TERM_SET_SUM:;
```

(1.5d) could easily be written without requiring the SKIP_SUM
exit, in the manner of (1.5c), but it is presented this way to
contrast the two types of exit. Note the indentation of the
TERM_SET_SUM label showing that it is not part of the body of
SUM_LOOP.

In effect, a unit can have three different kinds of exits, as
shown in Figure 7. Allowing more than one exit from a unit
obviously makes a program more difficult to understand, but it
is sometimes just unavoidable. The contortions required to
preserve the strict single-exit property sometimes do more harm
than good. Good judgement is required to decide what is the
best and clearest structure in each situation.

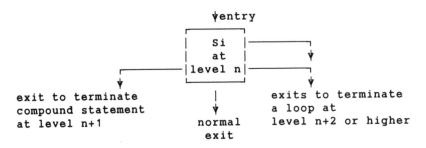

Figure 7.   Termination Exits of a Unit

1.6 The Well-Structured Program

A program is said to be "well-structured" if it is organized so that the entire program is itself a unit of one of the types described above. The components of this unit are themselves units, etc., to however many levels are required. This means that the program consists of segments that are readily understandable at a level higher than individual PL/I statements, and that the control paths between segments are few in number and simple in form.

Structure and format are actually two different issues, although the preceding sections have treated both together. A program is well-presented if its structure is clearly and quickly apparent to the reader. This means grouping statements in a logical way, and providing heading comments so the purpose of each group is apparent without having to figure it out from the individual PL/I statements. It also means using indentation in a clear and consistent way to emphasize the grouping, and to indicate the flow-of-control during execution.

A program that is both well-structured and well-presented has a high degree of predictability, and this is useful to the reader. For example, suppose you encounter the following line in reading a program:

/* SET MINPN TO MIN OF PN FUNCTION */

If, at the moment, you are looking for something else in the program and don't need to know how the program actually finds that minimum, you can confidently skip over the lines indented with respect to that heading comment. The next line below that is left-aligned with this comment will be the next line to consider. Note that it is the commenting and indenting convention that helps you find this next line quickly, but it is the unit structure convention that allows you to go directly to that line without worrying that the program might have executed a random GO TO somewhere in the SET MINPN unit. Knowing that the SET MINPN unit has a single exit point you know that it will reach that next line, without having to trace through the detail of SET MINPN to make sure.

In a well-structured program the different PL/I statements will always be used in a consistent manner. For example, repetition is always controlled by a DO loop, and never with some construction handcrafted from IF, GO TO and a label. This means that when you encounter an IF or a GO TO you do not have to wonder whether it might be part of a homemade DO loop.

You can read and understand a well-structured program more quickly, simply because you actually have <u>less to learn about the program</u>. You know in advance how the program will be organized, how it will be presented, and how each PL/I statement type will be used. If a program <u>doesn't</u> use these conventions, then you must approach it with much less of a headstart. All you have is your knowledge of the meaning of each individual PL/I statement. For example, when you encounter a GO TO in a well-structured program, you know that some unit is being terminated early. The label given as a target of the GO TO helps suggest what unit is being terminated. You know that that label is assigned to some statement further down the page, and when you locate it, its indentation will confirm the level of the unit being terminated. You do not have to figure out what the role of the GO TO is -- you know that in advance. All that has to be determined is which unit is being terminated.

<u>Variation in program style is not desirable</u>. A given programmer, when confronted with similar tasks at different points in a program, should solve those tasks in a similar way. From the point of view of the reader, when he encounters apparently similar tasks that are handled in different ways, he should take this as a warning that he does not fully understand the tasks -- and not just that the programmer got bored with one approach and decided to try another. For example, suppose that in the process of reading a program you encounter the following three segments at three different points:

```
/* MOVE A(1:N) TO B(1:N) */
    MOVE_LOOP: DO I = 1 TO N BY 1;
        B(I) = A(I);
        END MOVE_LOOP;

/* REPLACE X(1:N) WITH Y(1:N) */
    REP_LOOP: DO I = N TO 1 BY -1;
        X(I) = Y(I);
        END REP_LOOP;

/* COPY R(1:N) INTO S(1:N) */
    I = 0;
    COPY_LOOP: DO WHILE (I < N);
        I = I + 1;
        S(I) = R(I);
        END COPY_LOOP;
```

First you might wonder whether "move", "replace", and "copy" mean exactly the same thing to the writer, or whether there are subtle differences in objective. You should certainly wonder if there is something peculiar about X and Y that makes it necessary to index backward (that is, from N to 1) over their elements. Finally, you should be concerned with why the writer chose to use a WHILE loop for R and S when he has used a DO-index loop in other cases. If it turns out that these are in fact exactly comparable tasks, and the writer simply amused himself by seeing how many different ways he could find to write the same task, you will have wasted time looking for differences that don't exist and are entitled to be annoyed -- especially if you were the writer at some earlier time.

Effectively, you are asked to yield some of your freedom of choice in writing a program. But this compromise is for your own benefit. It is in your best interest to do this, since you the programmer are the most frequent reader of the program. You must find the errors in it; you must be sure of its correctness.

Another major virtue of the structure recommended above is the limitation of context. This structure makes it possible to understand a particular unit with relatively little knowledge about surrounding units. Without this type of discipline it may be necessary to examine and understand an entire program before one can understand much about a particular small segment. This same characteristic allows units of a program to be written, and later modified or replaced, while only considering a carefully circumscribed local environment of that unit. This makes it possible to produce relatively large programs and achieve the same confidence in their correctness as is possible for small programs.

The harmful effect of the unrestricted use of the GO TO statement should be obvious from this discussion. If a unit is allowed to branch arbitrarily to other sections of the program its successor is no longer unique or apparent. The sequence of statements executed is very different from the sequence as written. Similarly, if other units have the privilege of unrestricted branching then the entry point and entry conditions of the unit under consideration are not easily determined.

This structure is not always the most obvious or natural for a problem. But it is the most desirable structure for a program, and it is worth trying to organize a problem so that it takes this form. It is not always easy to do so and it takes a good deal of practice. For non-trivial programs the effort is clearly worthwhile. The additional time spent in initial planning is more than recovered by a reduction in testing time, and the overall result is a significant improvement in clarity and reliability.

For very small programs a less structured organization may suffice, and a well-structured program does require some extra work in the initial writing. While an experienced programmer who knows how to produce a good program might be permitted to "shortcut" under special circumstances, a beginner trying to learn the art of programming should practice using the proper style at every opportunity. Even for the professional a casual approach is risky since very often little programs reappear later as pieces of big programs.

If there is a "break-even point" with regard to these practices it occurs at a surprisingly small size of program. The extra effort pays off for programs as small as 20 statements just in a reduction in the time required to adequately test the program. This means it will be valuable even for exercises that are encountered in a first programming course.

1.6.1 The Art of Writing Comments

It is comparatively difficult to learn to write good, useful comments in a program, and many programmers never deign to learn. The difficulty lies in the complete freedom that is allowed. A programming language specifies precisely the form of the statements that are allowed, and the translator <u>enforces</u> those rules, but for comments the language and translator require only that they be properly identified. Thus the programmer must develop his own rules, and there is no mechanism to remind him when he departs from his rules. We have tried to use comments in a consistent manner throughout the book, but there are undoubtedly lapses where we should have done better. Ours is admittedly an extreme position among programmers with regard to comments and you will encounter much skepticism among knowledgeable programmers. Ultimately, you will have to decide for yourself whether our comments help you to understand our examples, and more importantly, whether your comments help you to write and test your own programs.

The rules that we are trying to observe, and that we recommend to you, are the following:

1. In many contexts and for many purposes <u>comments should be read as an alternative to a group of program statements</u>. To be able to read comments in this way the reader must have complete confidence that a comment is a valid alternative -- that it says the same thing as the program statements, but in a different form. To maintain this confidence, comments must be precise and accurate. For example, compare the following possible heading comments for a segment to read data:

```
/* LOAD AR(1:50) FROM DATA.  STOP ON FIRST -1 */

/* READ DATA */

/* LOAD AR */
```

The first example specifies fairly precisely what is going to be done, and for many purposes it would be unnecessary to read the corresponding program statements. The second and third possibilities just generally describe the purpose of the statements, but with these comments you would be more likely to have to read the statements to understand the action of that part of the program.

Use specific variable names in comments. For example, compare the following alternatives:

```
/* SET MINA TO MIN OF A(J:K) */

/* FIND MINIMUM */
```

Keep your comments up-to-date. When you change program statements, adjust the comments accordingly. No matter how well-written the comments were initially, unless they are kept current the reader can have no confidence in them. This confidence is a fragile thing -- once the reader has discovered one inaccurate or obsolete comment in a program he must be suspicious of all other comments.

There must be some convention (usually indentation) to indicate the precise scope of each comment -- that is, the program statements to which it is an alternative. Our convention is that program statements are indented with respect to the corresponding comment. The next line that is left-aligned with a comment (whether that next line is itself a comment or a statement) is the beginning of the next unit of the program. For example

```
/* LOAD X(1:N) FROM DATA */
    GET LIST(N);
    LOADX_LOOP: DO I = 1 TO N BY 1;
        GET LIST(X(I));
        END LOADX_LOOP;
SUM = 0;
COUNT = 0;
/* WRITE TITLE AND COLUMN HEADINGS */
    PUT SKIP(3) LIST(' ', ' ', 'DEMOGRAPHIC PROFILE');
    PUT SKIP LIST('TOMPKINS COUNTY, 1970 CENSUS');
    PUT SKIP(2) LIST
        ('SIZE','NUMBER','SOURCE','INCOME','LOCN');
    PUT SKIP(2);
```

2. The reason for having comments as an alternative description for a human reader is to provide a form that is more efficient for him -- that is, a form that is both more concise and more comprehensible. The comments should be written in a semi-formal higher-level language. They should never simply duplicate the program statements. For example, the following are examples of poor comments -- in each case the program would be at least as clear without them so there is no reward for the effort of writing them.

```
      SUM = 0; /* INITIALIZE SUM TO 0 */

      /* GET NEW VALUE OF N */
         GET LIST(N);

      /* EXIT IF ITEM IS NEGATIVE */
         IF ITEM < 0 THEN GO TO TERM_READ;

      /* PUT TWO WORDS TOGETHER */
         LONGWORD = LEFT || RIGHT;
```

The purpose of a comment is <u>not</u> to explain the action of a program statement to a reader who does not understand the programming language. Start with the assumption that the reader <u>could</u> read and understand the program statements, if necessary, but your job is to make it unnecessary for him to do so in many cases. Remember that you are going to be the most frequent reader, hence the principal beneficiary of this kindness.

In summary, comments can be useful, but only <u>if you take them seriously</u>. Time spent in writing comments that are precise, concise alternatives to program segments is generously repaid later in the programming and testing process. Comments that are casually written -- and inserted more because of compulsion than conviction -- are probably not worth the bother. Evaluate our examples critically in this regard and decide what your own "comment conventions" should be.

1.6.2 <u>A Comparative Example</u>

With this discussion as background we now give another example, presenting the same program in both "well-structured" and "conventional" form, as we did in (IIa) and (IIb). Consider a program which is to read in a 2-dimensional array of integers A(N,N), and then determine the following three values:

  1. The largest element on the principal diagonal -- the maximum A(I,I) for I=1,2,...,N. Call this maximum DMAX.

  2. The largest element in row I, the row in which DMAX occurs. Calls this RMAX.

  3. The largest element in column I, the column in which DMAX occurs. Call this CMAX.

The input consists of a number N, less than 25, followed by the N^2 numbers of the array in row-major order -- that is, the numbers of the top row, left to right, followed by the numbers of the second row, left to right, etc. The required output is a display of the array and the values of DMAX, RMAX and CMAX.

(1.6.2a) and (1.6.2b) are alternative programs which are correct and solve the problem. (1.6.2a) is typical of conventional programming style and format. (Although we are obviously trying to persuade you that (1.6.2b) is preferable we have tried not to make (1.6.2a) deliberately obscure.) (1.6.2b) is written following the recommendations of the preceding sections. As you consider these two programs, realize that they are <u>identical, as far as the computer is concerned</u>. They differ only in the manner in which they are <u>organized and presented for a human reader</u>.

(1.6.2a)

```
    *PL/C ID='JOHN WILLIAMS'
    MAXELMT: PROCEDURE OPTIONS(MAIN);
    DCL (A(24,24),N,LD,LR,LC,I,J) FIXED DECIMAL;
    GET LIST(N); LD=1; LR=1; LC=1;
    IF (N<1)|(N>24) THEN DO; PUT SKIP LIST('WRONG SIZE',N);
    GO TO FIN; END;
    DO I = 1 TO N BY 1; PUT SKIP;
    DO J = 1 TO N BY 1;
    GET LIST(A(I,J)); PUT LIST(A(I,J));
    END; END;
    DO I = 2 TO N BY 1;
    IF A(I,I) > A(LD,LD) THEN LD = I; END;
    PUT SKIP LIST('DMAX IS:',A(LD,LD),'IN ROW,COL',LD);
    DO I = 2 TO N BY 1;
    IF A(LD,I) > A(LD,LR) THEN LR=I;
    IF A(I,LD) > A(LC,LD) THEN LC=I; END;
    PUT SKIP LIST('RMAX IS:',A(LD,LR),'IN COL',LR);
    PUT SKIP LIST('CMAX IS:',A(LC,LD),'IN ROW',LC);
    FIN: END MAXELMT;
```

```
(1.6.2b)
   *PL/C ID='JOHN WILLIAMS'
   /* FIND DMAX, RMAX AND CMAX IN A(N,N).  */
   MAXELMT: PROCEDURE OPTIONS(MAIN);
       DCL (A(24,24),N,
            LD,        /* ROW, COL OF DMAX */
            LR,        /* COL OF RMAX */
            LC,        /* ROW OF CMAX */
            I,J) FIXED DECIMAL;
       /* READ IN ARRAY A, STOP IF IMPROPER SIZE */
            GET LIST(N);
            IF (N < 1) | (N > 24) THEN DO;
                PUT SKIP LIST('SIZE OF ARRAY WRONG:',N);
                GO TO TERM_MAXELMT; END;
            READ_ROW_LOOP: DO I = 1 TO N BY 1;
                READ_COL_LOOP: DO J = 1 TO N BY 1;
                    GET LIST(A(I,J));
                    END READ_COL_LOOP;
                END READ_ROW_LOOP;
       /* PRINT ARRAY A */
            PRINT_ROW_LOOP: DO I = 1 TO N BY 1;
                PUT SKIP;
                PRINT_COL_LOOP: DO J = 1 TO N BY 1;
                    PUT LIST(A(I,J));
                    END PRINT_COL_LOOP;
                END PRINT_ROW_LOOP;
       /* FIND INDEX LD OF DMAX */
            LD = 1;
            LD_LOOP: DO I = 2 TO N BY 1;
                IF A(I,I) > A(LD,LD) THEN LD = I;
                END LD_LOOP;
       /* FIND INDEX LR OF RMAX, LC OF CMAX */
            LR = 1; LC = 1;
            LRLC_LOOP: DO I = 2 TO N BY 1;
                IF A(LD,I) > A(LD,LR) THEN LR = I;
                IF A(I,LD) > A(LC,LD) THEN LC = I;
                END LRLC_LOOP;
       /* PRINT RESULTS */
            PUT SKIP LIST('DMAX IS:',A(LD,LD),
                    'IN ROW,COL',LD);
            PUT SKIP LIST('RMAX IS:',A(LD,LR),'IN COL',LR);
            PUT SKIP LIST('CMAX IS:',A(LC,LD),'IN ROW',LC);
       TERM_MAXELMT:;
       END MAXELMT;
```

(1.6.2b) is more readily understandable than (1.6.2a) even though it has more lines to read. (1.6.2b) makes it obvious that the program is a compound statement -- a simple sequence of five subtasks:

```
Read in array A
Print array A
Find index LD of DMAX
Find index LR of RMAX and LC of CMAX
Print results.
```

Each of these subtasks is itself a compound statement, and four of them involve looping, but that does not obscure the fact that there are essentially five steps in executing the program. Within each of the subtasks the extent and purpose of each loop are made clear by labelling and indentation.

It is probably not obvious at this stage of your programming development, but real programs are often modified. That is, after a program is completed and tested, and has been used for awhile, it is not unusual for problem requirements to be slightly changed. Then someone -- not always the original author -- must go back and re-read the program and find the appropriate points at which to make changes. Consider (1.6.1b) from the point of view of making changes. It is easier to find the place to make the change, easier to write the new statements, and we have greater confidence that the change is correct and does not disturb other sections of the program. In effect, we really have to study (1.6.2a) in order to find out information that is readily apparent in (1.6.2b). For example, consider the relative ease and confidence with which (1.6.2a) and (1.6.2b) could be modified to make one or more of the following changes:

1. The program is to be run only on "sparse" arrays -- arrays where most of the elements are 0. To make it easier to keypunch the input data, change the program to accept input of the following form, where the user need only specify the non-zero elements:
   a) card 1 contains the integer N
   b) each successive card describes one non-zero array element by giving its row number, its column number and its value
   c) the last card contains three zero values.

2. Change the program so that DMAX is the largest value on the lower-left-to-upper-right diagonal.

3. Change the output format so the array is printed with 2 stars "**" on either side of the values DMAX, RMAX and CMAX.

Section 1 <u>Summary</u>

1. A well-structured program is a hierarchy of program units.
The highest level is a unit, whose components are also units,
etc. The lowest level consists of simple PL/I statements.

2. A program unit is a group of statements that are logically
related to each other in that they perform some well-defined
task. There are three principal kinds of units: "compound
statement", "repetition" and "alternate selection".

3. A unit should begin with a comment that is left-aligned with
the heading of the preceding unit. The components of the unit
should be left-aligned with each other and indented with respect
to the heading comment.

4. A unit has a single entry point and a single normal exit
point.   It may also have a termination exit that terminates
execution of either the body or the entire containing unit at a
higher level.

5.   Comments are principally used as a "higher-level"
description of the action of a program segment. If well-
written, they can often be read <u>instead of</u> the corresponding
program statements.

Section 1 __Examples__

```
*PL/C ID='T. BISHOP'

*OPTICNS IN EFFECT*     TIME=(0,15),PAGES=30,LINES=2000,NOATR,NOXREF,FLAGW,BNDRY,NOCMNTS,SORMGIN=(2,72,1),
*OPTIONS IN EFFECT*     ERRORS=(50,50),TABSIZE=2532,UDEF,SOURCE,OPLIST,NOCMPRS,HDRPG,AUXIO=10000,LINECT=60,NOALIST,
*CPTICNS IN EFFECT*     MCALL,MTEXT,DUMP=(S,F,L,E,U,R),DUMPE=(S,F,L,E,U,R),DUMPT=(S,F,L,E,U,R)

    /* PRINT LIST OF WORDS WITHOUT DUPLICATES */                           PL/C-R7.1--66 10/20/75 10:58 PAGE   1

    STMT LEVEL NEST BLOCK MLVL   SOURCE TEXT


                                /* PRINT LIST OF WORDS WITHOUT DUPLICATES */
        1                       NODUP: PROCEDURE OPTIONS(MAIN);
        2    1           1          DCL DIFWORD(1:100) CHAR(20) INIT((100)' '); /* LIST OF WORDS */
        3    1           1          DCL NEWWORD CHAR(20);
        4    1           1          DCL (WCOUNT, DWCOUNT) FIXED DEC INIT(0);
                                    /* TITLE OUTPUT LIST */
        5    1           1          PUT LIST('LIST OF WORDS WITH DUPLICATES DELETED');
        6    1           1          PUT SKIP(2);
                                    /* PROCESS DATA TO 'ENDDATA' */
        7    1           1          GET LIST(NEWWORD);
        8    1           1          DATA_LOOP: DO WHILE(NEWWORD ¬= 'ENDDATA');
        9    1    1      1              WCOUNT = WCOUNT + 1;
                                        /* TEST FOR PREVIOUS OCCURRENCE */
       10    1    1      1              IF WCOUNT ¬= 1 THEN
       11    1    1      1                  TP_LOOP: DO WD = 1 TO DWCOUNT BY 1;
       12    1    2      1                      IF DIFWORD(WD) = NEWWORD
       13    1    2      1                          THEN GO TO SKIPPRT;
       14    1    2      1                  END TP_LOOP;
                                        /* ENTER INTO WORD LIST, AND PRINT */
       15    1    1      1              DWCOUNT = DWCOUNT + 1;
       16    1    1      1              DIFWORD(DWCOUNT) = NEWWORD;
       17    1    1      1              PUT SKIP LIST(NEWWORD);
       18    1    1      1          SKIPPRT:;
       19    1    1      1              GET LIST(NEWWORD);
       20    1    1      1          END DATA_LOOP;
                                    /* PRINT SUMMARY LINE */
       21    1           1          PUT SKIP(2) LIST('AMONG', WCOUNT, 'WORDS THERE WERE');
       22    1           1          PUT SKIP LIST(DWCOUNT, 'DIFFERENT WORDS');
       23    1           1      END NODUP;

ERRORS/WARNINGS DETECTED DURING CODE GENERATION:

        WARNING: NO FILE SPECIFIED. SYSIN/SYSPRINT ASSUMED. (CGOC)


LIST CF WORDS WITH DUPLICATES DELETED


AB
BA
AA
AMONG                            5              WORDS THERE WERE
        3                DIFFERENT WORDS


IN STMT   23  PROGRAM RETURNS FROM MAIN PROCEDURE.
```

```
*PL/C ID='EDYTHE DAVIES', XREF, ATR, NOOPLIST
 /* PRODUCE FREQUENCY TABLE, FIND MODE; READ DATA TO 1ST ZERO */                        PL/C-R7.1--66 10/20/75 10:58 PAGE   1

STMT LEVEL NEST BLOCK MLVL  SOURCE TEXT

                                    /* PRODUCE FREQUENCY TABLE, FIND MODE; READ DATA TO 1ST ZERO */
    1                               FTM: PROCEDURE OPTIONS(MAIN);
    2    1            1                 DECLARE ITEM FLOAT DEC;  /* DATA ITEM JUST READ */
    3    1            1                 DECLARE COUNT FIXED DEC INIT(0); /* NUMBER OF ITEMS SO FAR */
    4    1            1                 DECLARE VALUE(1:100) FLOAT DEC INIT((100)0),
                                            FREQ(1:100) FIXED DEC INIT((100)0);
    5    1            1                 DECLARE TL FIXED DEC; /* INDEX OF LINE IN FREQ-TABLE */
    6    1       .    1                 DECLARE MAXFREQ FIXED DEC INIT(0);
    7    1            1                 DECLARE TLMAXFREQ FIXED DEC; /* LINE IN WHICH MAX OCCURS */
                                        /* PRODUCE FREQ-TABLE FROM DATA */
    8    1            1                    GET LIST(ITEM);
    9    1            1                    DATA_LOOP: DO WHILE(ITEM ¬= 0);
   10    1    1       1                       COUNT = COUNT + 1;
                                              /* RECORD VALUE IN FREQ-TABLE */
   11    1    1       1                       TL_LOOP: DO TL = 1 TO 100 BY 1;
   12    1    2       1                          IF VALUE(TL) = 0 THEN DO;
                                                    /* ENTER NEW VALUE */
   14    1    3       1                               VALUE(TL) = ITEM;
   15    1    3       1                               FREQ(TL) = 1;
   16    1    3       1                               GO TO TERM_TL_LOOP; END;
   18    1    2       1                          IF VALUE(TL) = ITEM THEN DO;
                                                    /* RECORD REPEATED VALUE */
   20    1    3       1                               FREQ(TL) = FREQ(TL) + 1;
   21    1    3       1                               GO TO TERM_TL_LOOP; END;
   23    1    2       1                          IF TL = 100 THEN DO;
                                                    /* ANNOUNCE TABLE FULL */
   25    1    3       1                               PUT SKIP LIST('FREQ-TABLE IS FULL');
   26    1    3       1                               PUT LIST('NO MORE NEW VALUES',
   27    1    3       1                                    'WILL BE CONSIDERED'); END;
   28    1    2       1                          END TL_LOOP;
   29    1    1       1                       TERM_TL_LOOP:;
   30    1    1       1                       GET LIST(ITEM);
   31    1    1       1                       END DATA_LOOP;
   32    1            1                    IF COUNT = 0 THEN DO;
   34    1    1       1                       PUT SKIP(2) LIST('NO DATA RECEIVED');
   35    1    1       1                       GO TO TERM_FTM; END;
                                        /* DISPLAY FREQ-TABLE */
   37    1            1                    PUT SKIP(2) LIST('FREQUENCY TABLE');
   38    1            1                    PUT SKIP(2) LIST('VALUE', 'FREQUENCY');
   39    1            1                    PUT SKIP;
   40    1            1                    LN_LOOP: DO TL = 1 TO 100 BY 1;
   41    1    1       1                       IF FREQ(TL) ¬= 0  THEN
   42    1    1       1                          PUT SKIP LIST(VALUE(TL), FREQ(TL));
   43    1    1       1                       END LN_LOOP;
                                        /* COMPUTE MODE (VALUE WITH MAX FREQ) */
   44    1            1                    TL = 1;
   45    1            1                    MODE_LOOP: DO WHILE((FREQ(TL) ¬= 0) & (TL <= 100));
   46    1    1       1                       IF FREQ(TL) > MAXFREQ THEN DO;
   48    1    2       1                          MAXFREQ = FREQ(TL);
   49    1    2       1                          TLMAXFREQ = TL; END;
   51    1    1       1                       TL = TL + 1;
   52    1    1       1                       END MODE_LOOP;

   53    1            1                    PUT SKIP(2) LIST('MODE IS', VALUE(TLMAXFREQ));
   54    1            1                    PUT SKIP LIST('WHICH OCCURS', MAXFREQ, 'TIMES');
   55    1            1                 TERM_FTM:;
   56    1            1                 END FTM;
```

Section 2   Program Schemata

When we introduced the IF construction in Section I.4.3 we
gave the model of the construction as

> IF condition THEN statement.

This gave the form or "schema" of that conditional statement in
PL/I.   The symbol "statement" in the schema stands for any
simple or compound PL/I statement.   The symbol "condition"
stands for any simple or compound condition.   Written in this
form, before some particular statement and particular condition
is specified, the schema is said to be "uninterpreted". We
defined the action of the IF construction in terms of an
uninterpreted   schema;   that   is,   we described its action
independent of what particular statement and particular
condition might be given in a specific example.

This seems like a complicated way of explaining something
that was fairly obvious on first encounter, but we would like to
extend this argument to larger program constructions.   For
example, (2a) is a schema for a particular kind of repetition
unit, one in which the body is to be repeated a definite number
of times:

```
          /* Comment describing action of the unit */
             i = 0;
             loop-name: DO WHILE ( i < n );
                i = i + 1;
(2a)         Body
             END loop-name;
```

This is a schema uninterpreted with respect to the body, the
index variable i, the stopping value n, the loop-name and the
heading comment -- the elements given in lower-case letters.   A
particular example or interpretation of this schema would have
these lower-case elements replaced by specific PL/I elements.
For example, the following are specific interpretations of (2a):

```
          /* MOVE A(1:K) TO B(1:K) */
             J = 0;
             MOVE_LOOP: DO WHILE ( J < K );
                J = J + 1;
                B(J) = A(J);
                END MOVE_LOOP;
```

```
/* PRINT 12 LINES OF 10 *'S EACH */
   I = 0;
   PRINT_LOOP: DO WHILE ( I < 12 );
      I = I + 1;
      PUT SKIP LIST('**********');
      END PRINT_LOOP;


/* CLEAR X(1:K) TO ZERO */
   M = 0;
   CLEAR_LOOP: DO WHILE ( M < K );
      M = M + 1;
      X(M) = 0;
      END CLEAR_LOOP;


/* CLEAR A(1:K,2:M) IF < A(1:K,1) */
   I = 0;
   CLRK_LOOP: DO WHILE ( I < K );
      I = I + 1;
      /* CLEAR ITH ROW */
         CLR_ROW_LOOP: DO J = 2 TO M BY 1;
            IF A(I,J) < A(I,1)
               THEN A(I,J) = 0;
            END CLR_ROW_LOOP;
      END CLRK_LOOP;
```

Although these examples perform very different tasks, in each case the basic structure is the same -- some task is repeated a definite number of times. That subtask may be a single statement or a substantial program segment, but the statements that control its repetition are the same (except for the particular names used). Each of these examples follows the pattern shown in (2a) with the lower-case elements of (2a) replaced by particular PL/I elements. These different interpretations of (2a) differ from each other only in the choices of specific elements to replace the lower-case elements of (2a).

Definite repetition is a common task, and (2a) can be regarded as a schema for a "statement" to accomplish this task. You can learn this schema and use it more-or-less automatically each time that you need to repeat some action a definite number of times. It means that you will not have to "re-invent" a mechanism for definite repetition each time it is required.

There are many other common tasks and corresponding schemata. For example, suppose some action is to be performed on each item of a data list, where the end of the list is recognized by the presence of some distinctive value. (2b) gives an appropriate schema.

```
        /* Comment describing task and stopping flag */
            Initialize
            GET LIST(item);
            loop-name: DO WHILE(item ¬= stopping flag);
(2b)            Perform action on item
            GET LIST(item);
            END loop-name;
```

Each of the following is an example (or interpretation) of (2b):

```
        /* FIND MAX X, STOPPING AT FIRST 0 */
            XMAX = 0;
            GET LIST(X);
            MAX_LOOP: DO WHILE( X ¬= 0 );
                IF X > XMAX THEN XMAX = X;
                GET LIST(X);
                END MAX_LOOP;
```

```
        /* PRINT, SUM AND COUNT DATA UNTIL -999 */
            PUT SKIP(2) LIST('LIST OF INPUT DATA:');
            PUT SKIP;
            SUM = 0;
            COUNT = 0;
            GET LIST(ITEM);
            PSC_LOOP: DO WHILE(ITEM ¬= -999);
                PUT SKIP LIST(ITEM);
                SUM = SUM + ITEM;
                COUNT = COUNT + 1;
                GET LIST(ITEM);
                END PSC_LOOP;
```

An especially common task in programs is to perform some
action on each element of an array, or on some portion of an
array. (2c) gives a schema for this task.

```
        /* Perform action on each element of a(j:k) */
            Initialize
            loop-name: DO i = j TO k BY 1;
(2c)            Perform action on a(i)
            END loop-name;
```

The following are examples of interpretations of (2c):

```
        /* DISPLAY VALUES OF AR(A:B) */
            PUT SKIP(3) LIST('VALUES OF AR(A:B)');
            PUT SKIP LIST('A =', A, 'B =', B);
            PUT SKIP;
            AB_LOOP: DO I = A TO B BY 1;
                PUT SKIP LIST(AR(I));
                END AB_LOOP;
```

```
/* LOAD X(1:N) FROM DATA */
   GET_LOOP: DO I = 1 TO N BY 1;
            GET LIST(X(I));
            END GET_LOOP;


/* MOVE X(1:N) TO Y(1:N) */
   MOVE_LOOP: DO J = 1 TO N BY 1;
            Y(J) = X(J);
            END MOVE_LOOP;
```

Sometimes a task can be viewed in several different ways. For example, suppose you are required to read data values into an array X(1:N), but not past the first -1 in the data list. That is, the reading process will read N values, or up to the first -1, whichever occurs first. This could be written as an interpretation of (2c):

```
/* LOAD X(1:N), UP TO FIRST -1 */
   GET_LOOP: DO I = 1 TO N BY 1;
            GET LIST(X(I));
            IF X(I) = -1 THEN GO TO TERM_LOAD_X;
            END GET_LOOP;
   TERM_LOAD_X:;
```

Alternatively, the same task could be written as an interpretation of (2b):

```
/* LOAD X(1:N), UP TO FIRST -1 */
   I = 1;
   GET LIST(X(I));
   GET_LOOP: DO WHILE( X(I) ¬= -1 );
            I = I + 1;
            IF I > N THEN GO TO TERM_LOAD_X;
            GET LIST(X(I));
            END GET_LOOP;
   TERM_LOAD_X:;
```

These segments are quite comparable and there is no strong reason to prefer one over the other. However, you might note that it is <u>possible that neither is correct</u>, depending upon the precise requirements of the problem. Both will include the stopping flag value (-1) as an element of X, if it occurs within the first N items on the data list. This may well not be a valid element for X and probably should not be included. Also note that for either example the only way of knowing how many items were actually loaded is the value of I after finishing the loop, and this value is <u>1 too large</u>. That is, the final value is I is either N+1 or the subscript of the element containing -1. Either version could be written to avoid this flaw. For example:

```
/* LOAD X(1:N), UP TO FIRST -1 */
    I = 0;
    GET LIST(Y);
    GET_LOOP: DO WHILE( Y ¬= -1 );
        IF I = N THEN GO TO TERM_LOAD_X;
        I = I + 1;
        X(I) = Y;
        GET LIST(Y);
        END GET_LOOP;
    TERM_LOAD_X:;
```

As a final example of a schema, another common task is to perform some action on each element of a data list, when the list is preceded by an integer specifying the number of items on the list. An appropriate schema is given in (2d).

```
       /* Read n, and perform action on n following items */
       Initialize
       GET LIST(n);
       loop-name: DO WHILE( n > 0 );
           GET LIST(item);
(2d)       Perform action on item
           n = n - 1;
           END loop-name;
```

An interpretation of (2d) is the following:

```
       /* LOAD M ELEMENTS INTO A(1:N) */
       I = 0;
       GET LIST(M);
       LOAD_LOOP: DO WHILE( M > 0 );
           IF I = N THEN DO;
               PUT SKIP(2) LIST('EXCESS DATA');
               GO TO TERM_LOAD_M; END;
           I = I + 1;
           GET LIST(A(I));
           M = M - 1;
           END LOAD_LOOP;
       TERM_LOAD_M:;
```

We cannot catalog all common program tasks for you and give schemata for them. We are just trying to make you aware that there are certain patterns that recur frequently, and that you should learn to recognize them. You should develop your own repertoire of schemata, and apply them whenever a familiar task appears. This will save you the time and effort of re-inventing solutions to these problems, and make your programs more consistent and predictable.

Notice that it is the control structure of the segment that recurs more often than the specific action. The action will vary from problem to problem, but the manner in which it is repeated is often familiar. There are infinitely many different problems to be solved -- you will rarely meet one that is identical to one you have solved before. But any problem can be

broken down into sections, and many of the sections may be
recognizable as some action to be repeated in some familiar way.
Viewed in this way, even large problems are not quite so
formidable.

2.1 A Classification of Very Simple Programs

For many of the very simple problems used as examples and
exercises in introductory programming courses one can give
schemata for the entire program, rather than just for segments
of it. Many of these simple problems consist of some repetition
of three actions:

1. Read an item of data;
2. Perform some action upon the item;
3. Print some result.

The problem requirements will detail the action to be performed,
and the result to be printed. This will dictate which of two
basic strategies must be used.

The simplest strategy consists of·dealing with the data items
one at a time. There is never any need to have more than one
item available at any point in execution of the program. The
entire program is just an interpretation of schema (2b) or (2d).
For example, (2.1a) gives a schema for the entire program based
upon (2b).

```
            *PL/C ID='programmer name'
            /* read, process and print, one item at a time */
            program-name: PROCEDURE OPTIONS(MAIN);
                 Declarations
                 Initialize
                 GET LIST(item);
                 loop-name: DO WHILE(item ¬= stopping flag);
                      Perform action on item
(2.1a)                PUT SKIP LIST(item result);
                      GET LIST(item);
                      END loop-name;
                 PUT SKIP LIST(final result);
                 END program-name;
            *DATA
                 data list
```

A simple interpretation of (2.1a) is a program to print a copy
of the data list:

```
*PL/C ID='T. WILCOX'
 /* PRINT LIST OF DATA, UP TO FIRST NEGATIVE VALUE */
 PRINTDATA: PROCEDURE OPTIONS(MAIN);
      DECLARE VALUE FLOAT DECIMAL;
      PUT LIST('WILCOX DATA LIST:');
      PUT SKIP;
      GET LIST(VALUE);
      PRINT_LOOP: DO WHILE(VALUE >= 0);
           PUT SKIP LIST(VALUE);
           GET LIST(VALUE);
           END PRINT_LOOP;
      PUT SKIP(2) LIST('END OF LIST');
      END PRINTDATA;
*DATA
      14, 23.56, 23E2, -1
```

Another example of an interpretation of (2.1a) would be to print
running sums of the values on a data list, stopping when -999 is
encountered:

```
*PL/C ID='J. HOPCROFT'
 /* PRINT RUNNING SUMS OF DATA LIST; STOP ON -999 */
 HOPSUM: PROCEDURE OPTIONS(MAIN);
      DECLARE (ITEM, SUM) FLOAT DECIMAL;
      DECLARE COUNT FIXED DECIMAL;
      COUNT = 0;  SUM = 0;
      GET LIST(ITEM);
      SUM_LOOP: DO WHILE(ITEM ¬= -999);
           SUM = SUM + ITEM;
           COUNT = COUNT + 1;
           PUT SKIP LIST(SUM);
           GET LIST(ITEM);
           END SUM_LOOP;
      IF COUNT = 0
           THEN PUT LIST('NO DATA GIVEN');
           ELSE PUT LIST('SUM OF', COUNT, ' ITEMS IS', SUM);
      END HOPSUM;
*DATA
      45, 0, 0, 23, -1, 56.1, -999
```

Now suppose the problem requirements were changed just enough
to make it necessary to retain <u>many data values at the same
time</u>. (2.1a) can no longer be used since it is limited to a
single data value at a time. The program will now require an
array to hold the data list, and will likely involve two
principal steps, each one being a loop over the elements of the
array. A schema such as (2.1b) would be required. The "load-
loop" in (2.1b) could be of the form of either schema (2b) or
(2d). The "process-loop" is likely to be of the form of schema
(2c).

```
          *PL/C ID='programmer name'
           /* Summary of program action */
           program-name: PROCEDURE OPTIONS(MAIN);
               Declaration of array to hold data
               Declarations of other variables
               /* Load array from data-list */
(2.1b)              Load-loop
               /* Process elements of array */
                    Process-loop
               END program-name;
          *DATA
               data-list
```

A simple example of an interpretation of (2.1b) would be a
problem requiring printing some summary result before printing a
copy of the data list. For example:

```
    *PL/C ID='ROBERT CONSTABLE'
     /* COUNT, TITLE, AND PRINT DATA, UP TO 1ST NEG VALUE */
    CTPDATA: PROCEDURE OPTIONS(MAIN);
         DECLARE DLIST(50) FLOAT DECIMAL;
         DECLARE DTEMP FLOAT DECIMAL;
         DECLARE (I, J) FIXED DECIMAL;
         PUT LIST('CONSTABLE DATA LIST');
         /* LOAD DLIST(50) FROM DATA, UP TO 1ST NEG VAL */
         /* AND SET I TO INDEX OF LAST ELEMENT */
             I = 0;
             GET LIST(DTEMP);
             LOAD_LOOP: DO WHILE( DTEMP >= 0 );
                 IF I = 50 THEN DO;
                     PUT SKIP LIST('EXCESS DATA');
                     GO TO TERM_LOAD_DLIST; END;
                 I = I + 1;
                 DLIST(I) = DTEMP;
                 GET LIST(DTEMP);
                 END LOAD_LOOP;
             TERM_LOAD_DLIST:;
         /* COMPLETE TITLE */
             PUT SKIP(2) LIST(I, 'ITEMS READ AS DATA');
             PUT SKIP(2);
         /* PRINT DLIST(1:I) */
             PRINT_LOOP: DO J = 1 TO I BY 1;
                 PUT SKIP LIST(DLIST(J));
                 END PRINT_LOOP;
         END CTPDATA;
      *DATA
           12, 24, 36.48, 29.001, .03, 1.0, -1
```

A good way to get started on your first programming exercise
is to study the problem requirements to see whether it is a "one
at a time" problem or an "all at once" problem. Then view your
program, not as an entirely original creation, but just as an
interpretation of either (2.1a) or (2.1b). This prescription
won't handle all of your assigned problems, but it should help
with many of them.

Section 2 <u>Examples</u>

```
*PL/C ID='ROBERT CONSTABLE'

*OPTIONS IN EFFECT*    TIME=(0,15),PAGES=30,LINES=2000,NOATR,NOXREF,FLAGW,BNDRY,NOCMNTS,SORMGIN=(2,72,1),
*OPTIONS IN EFFECT*    ERRORS=(50,50),TABSIZE=2532,UDEF,SOURCE,OPLIST,NOCMPRS,HDRPG,AUXIO=10000,LINECT=60,NOALIST,
*OPTICNS IN EFFECT*    MCALL,MTEXT,DUMP=(S,F,L,E,U,R),DUMPE=(S,F,L,E,U,R),DUMPT=(S,F,L,E,U,R)
```

```
/* COUNT, TITLE, AND PRINT DATA, UP TO 1ST NEG VALUE */                       PL/C-R7.1--66 10/20/75 10:58 PAGE   1

   STMT LEVEL NEST BLOCK MLVL   SOURCE TEXT

                                      /* COUNT, TITLE, AND PRINT DATA, UP. TO 1ST NEG VALUE */
     1                                CTPDATA: PROCEDURE OPTIONS(MAIN);
     2     1            1                DECLARE DLIST(50) FLOAT DECIMAL;
     3     1            1                DECLARE DTEMP FLOAT DECIMAL;
     4     1            1                DECLARE (I, J) FIXED DECIMAL;
     5     1            1                PUT LIST('CONSTABLE DATA LIST');
                                         /* LOAD DLIST(50) FROM DATA, UP TO 1ST NEG VAL */
                                         /* AND SET I TO INDEX OF LAST ELEMENT */
     6     1            1                I = 0;
     7     1            1                GET LIST(DTEMP);
     8     1            1                LOAD_LOOP: DO WHILE( DTEMP >= 0 );
     9     1     1      1                   IF I = 50 THEN DO;
    11     1     2      1                      PUT SKIP LIST('EXCESS DATA');
    12     1     2      1                      GO TO TERM_LOAD_DLIST; END;
    14     1     1      1                   I = I + 1;
    15     1     1      1                   DLIST(I) = DTEMP;
    16     1     1      1                   GET LIST(DTEMP);
    17     1     1      1                END LOAD_LOOP;
    18     1            1                TERM_LOAD_DLIST:;
                                         /* COMPLETE TITLE */
    19     1            1                PUT SKIP(2) LIST(I, 'ITEMS READ AS DATA');
    20     1            1                PUT SKIP(2);
                                         /* PRINT DLIST(1:I) */
    21     1            1                PRINT_LOOP: DO J = 1 TO I BY 1;
    22     1     1      1                   PUT SKIP LIST(DLIST(J));
    23     1     1      1                END PRINT_LOOP;
    24     1            1             END CTPDATA;

ERRORS/WARNINGS DETECTED DURING CODE GENERATION:

     WARNING: NO FILE SPECIFIED. SYSIN/SYSPRINT ASSUMED. (CGOC)

CONSTABLE DATA LIST

          6              ITEMS READ AS DATA


    1.20000E+01
    2.40000E+01
    3.64799E+01
    2.90C09E+01
    2.99999E-02
    1.00000E+00


IN STMT   24  PROGRAM RETURNS FROM MAIN PROCEDURE.
```

```
*PL/C ID='J. ROGERS'

*OPTIONS IN EFFECT*     TIME=(0,15),PAGES=30,LINES=2000,NOATR,NOXREF,FLAGW,BNDRY,NOCMNTS,SORMGIN=(2,72,1),
*OPTIONS IN EFFECT*     ERRORS=(50,50),TABSIZE=2532,UDEF,SOURCE,OPLIST,NOCMPRS,HDRPG,AUXIO=10000,LINECT=60,NOALIST,
*OPTIONS IN EFFECT*     MCALL,MTEXT,DUMP=(S,F,L,E,U,R),DUMPE=(S,F,L,E,U,R),DUMPT=(S,F,L,E,U,R)
```

```
/* COMPUTE MEAN, MAX AND MIN OF DATA */                          PL/C-R7.1--66 10/20/75 10:58 PAGE   1

STMT LEVEL NEST BLOCK MLVL  SOURCE TEXT

                              /* COMPUTE MEAN, MAX AND MIN OF DATA */
                              /* STOP WHENEVER A VALUE OCCURS TWICE IN SUCCESSION */
    1                         MMM: PROCEDURE OPTIONS(MAIN);
    2    1            1           DCL (LAST, CURRENT) FLOAT DEC;  /* VALUES READ FROM DATA */
    3    1            1           DCL (MAXVAL, MINVAL) FLOAT DEC;
    4    1            1           DCL (SUM, MEAN) FLOAT DEC;
    5    1            1           DCL COUNT FIXED DEC;  /* NUMBER OF VALUES READ */
                                  /* INITIALIZE */
    6    1            1               GET LIST(LAST);
    7    1            1               COUNT = 1;
    8    1            1               MAXVAL = LAST;
    9    1            1               MINVAL = LAST;
   10    1            1               SUM = LAST;
   11    1            1               GET LIST(CURRENT);
   12    1            1           DATA_LOOP: DO WHILE (CURRENT ¬= LAST);
   13    1    1       1               COUNT = COUNT + 1;
   14    1    1       1               SUM = SUM + CURRENT;
   15    1    1       1               MAXVAL = MAX(MAXVAL, CURRENT);
   16    1    1       1               MINVAL = MIN(MINVAL, CURRENT);
   17    1    1       1               LAST = CURRENT;
   18    1    1       1               GET LIST(CURRENT);
   19    1    1       1               END DATA_LOOP;
                                  /* PRINT RESULTS */
   20    1            1               PUT LIST('RESULTS OF MEAN-MAX-MIN PROGRAM');
   21    1            1               PUT SKIP(2) LIST(COUNT, 'VALUES READ');
   22    1            1               MEAN = SUM/COUNT;
   23    1            1               PUT SKIP LIST('MEAN IS', MEAN);
   24    1            1               PUT SKIP LIST('MAXIMUM IS', MAXVAL);
   25    1            1               PUT SKIP LIST('MINIMUM IS', MINVAL);
   26    1            1           END MMM;

ERRORS/WARNINGS DETECTED DURING CODE GENERATION:

      WARNING: NO FILE SPECIFIED. SYSIN/SYSPRINT ASSUMED. (CGOC)



RESULTS OF MEAN-MAX-MIN PROGRAM

        6                 VALUES READ
MEAN IS                   2.93333E+01
MAXIMUM IS                7.50000E+01
MINIMUM IS                1.00000E+00



IN STMT   26  PROGRAM RETURNS FROM MAIN PROCEDURE.
```

```
*PL/C ID='R. PERRY'

*OPTIONS IN EFFECT*    TIME=(0,15),PAGES=30,LINES=2000,NOATR,NOXREF,FLAGW,BNDRY,NOCMNTS,SORMGIN=(2,72,1),
*OPTIONS IN EFFECT*    ERRORS=(50,50),TABSIZE=2532,UDEF,SOURCE,OPLIST,NOCMPRS,HDRPG,AUXIO=10000,LINECT=60,NOALIST,
*OPTIONS IN EFFECT*    MCALL,MTEXT,DUMP=(S,F,L,E,U,R),DUMPE=(S,F,L,E,U,R),DUMPT=(S,F,L,E,U,R)
```

```
/* COUNT A'S IN INPUT WORDS. STOP ON 'ENDDATA' */                         PL/C-R7.1--66 10/20/75 10:58 PAGE    1

  STMT LEVEL NEST BLOCK MLVL  SOURCE TEXT

                                /* COUNT A'S IN INPUT WORDS. STOP ON 'ENDDATA' */
   1                            COUNTA: PROCEDURE OPTIONS(MAIN);
   2    1          1               DCL (WORDCOUNT, ACOUNT) FIXED DEC INIT(0);
   3    1          1               DCL WORD CHAR(80) VARYING;
   4    1          1               DCL POSN FIXED DEC; /* POSITION IN WORD */
   5    1          1               GET LIST(WORD);
   6    1    1     1               WORD_LOOP: DO WHILE(WORD ¬= 'ENDDATA');
   7    1    1     1                   WORDCOUNT = WORDCOUNT + 1;
                                       /* COUNT A'S IN WORD */
   8    1    1     1                   COUNT_LOOP: DO POSN = 1 TO LENGTH(WORD) BY 1;
   9    1    2     1                       IF SUBSTR(WORD,POSN,1) = 'A'
  10    1    2     1                           THEN ACOUNT = ACOUNT + 1;
  11    1    2     1                   END COUNT_LOOP;
  12    1    1     1                   GET LIST(WORD);
  13    1    1     1               END WORD_LOOP;
                                   /* PRINT RESULTS */
  14    1          1               PUT LIST('RESULTS OF "A" COUNTING PROGRAM ');
  15    1          1               PUT SKIP(2) LIST('IN', WORDCOUNT, 'WORDS');
  16    1          1               PUT SKIP LIST('THERE WERE', ACOUNT, 'A''S');
  17    1          1            END COUNTA;

ERRORS/WARNINGS DETECTED DURING CODE GENERATION:

     WARNING: NO FILE SPECIFIED. SYSIN/SYSPRINT ASSUMED. (CGOC)




RESULTS OF "A" COUNTING PROGRAM

IN                              3              WORDS
THERE WERE                      6              A'S


IN STMT   17  PROGRAM RETURNS FROM MAIN PROCEDURE.
```

PART III   PROGRAM DEVELOPMENT

Section 1   Phases of Development

Our task is to write a program to solve some problem.   Given
the problem description in English, we have to figure out a way
in which a computer can be used to solve the problem, and then
describe this plan very precisely in some programming language.
This process has four distinct phases:

1. Clarify the problem requirements.

2. Design a program strategy.

3. Specify critical data structures.

4. Write the program statements.

Although the phases should occur roughly in the order listed,
there   is   a   good deal of overlap and backtracking, and
particularly for small problems they are difficult to separate.
Nevertheless they each represent a distinct function that must
be performed in every programming process. At least initially,
while struggling to learn the details of a programming language,
phase four may look the most formidable.   With practice and
experience you will discover that if the other three phases are
properly done then writing the program statements is quite
straightforward.   It may still be time-consuming and error-
prone, but it will not be the critical phase.

In this section we give a brief introduction to each of these
phases.   In Section 2 we illustrate the complete process for
several simple programs.   In Section 3 we elaborate upon general
problems and considerations that arise in various phases of the
process.

1.1 Clarification of the Problem

Surprisingly, clarification of the problem is a major phase
of the process. It would seem reasonable that a clear and
precise statement of the problem would be given, but in fact
this is rarely the case and more programming disasters can be
blamed on failure in this regard than any other. It is very
easy to misunderstand the precise requirements of a problem and
proceed to write a program that solves the wrong problem. This
phase is hard enough even in an programming course where the
problem is stated by someone who (presumably) understands what
can be programmed, and chooses problems to be only interestingly
difficult. Real problems are usually posed by someone who isn't
sure exactly what he wants done, much less how the computer is
going to contribute to a solution, and the problem definition
often becomes precise only in response to persistent and pointed
questions on the part of the programmer.

A substantial fraction of the clarification dialog is
concentrated on three key issues:

>   1. Input. What is its format and order? What are the
>   limits of volume that may occur and how will the end of the
>   input be recognized? What are the limits on values that
>   will be encountered?

>   2. Output. What is the content, format and order of
>   output? What titling is appropriate? What limits on
>   volume may be expected?

>   3. Errors. What types of errors (both in input and in
>   processing) must the program guard against, and what action
>   should be taken when they are encountered? Which problem
>   specifications can be taken as guaranteed, and which only
>   as good intentions -- to be checked by the program?

For example, suppose you are given the following problem:

(1.1a) Write a program to compute the sum of a list of numbers.

This statement gives only a general idea of the objective of the
program; much more detailed information is required before you
could begin to design the program. For example:

>   1a. Can the data be presented on punched cards in a format
>   acceptable to the PL/I GET LIST statement?

>   b. How many values can there be? How can the end of the
>   list of values be recognized?

>   c. What types and sizes of values might be expected?

>   2a. In what form should the sum be displayed?

>   b. What identifying title should be provided?

3a. What action should be taken for values on the list that
    violate the specifications of 1c?

 b. What action should be taken if the quantity of values
    violates instructions given in 1b?

After obtaining specific answers to these questions you might
have the following refinement of (1.1a):

(1.1b) Write a program to compute the sum of a list of positive
       integers, given in PL/I LIST format. The end of the data
       list will be denoted by two consecutive values of -999.
       Improper values on the list should be rejected (excluded
       from the sum) and printed on a list titled "REJECTED
       VALUES:". Any irregularity in termination should result in
       a warning message. The result should be given in three
       lines, after the list of rejects (if any):

        SUM OF POSITIVE INTEGERS

           n VALUES INCLUDED

           SUM IS s

   As a second example, consider a simple text-processing
problem:

(1.1c) Write a program to delete duplicates from a word list.

Clarification of (1.1c) might result in something like the
following:

(1.1d) Write a program to print a list of words, one per line,
       in the order given, but excluding any word that has
       appeared earlier in the list. The data will be given as an
       integer n (not more than 100), followed by n words, each a
       quoted character string in LIST format. These words may
       vary in length from one to twenty characters. Each word
       should consist of a sequence of letters A-Z; no digits,
       blanks or special characters are allowed. The output
       should be given as follows:

        WORD LIST WITHOUT DUPLICATES:
           m ENTRIES

           first word
           second word
           ...

The value m given in the title indicates the length of the
final list, after duplicates and improper words have been
rejected. Report any difficulties with the length of the
list, but produce some list if at all possible.

(1.1b) and (1.1d) have obviously been written by someone who understands programming, and who is anticipating many of the difficulties the program must face. Given a description in this form and this much detail, the program is well-specified and not very difficult to write. But, in general, (1.1a) and (1.1c) are samples of what you can expect to be given as an initial problem statement. (1.1b) and (1.1d) are the corresponding samples of what _you_ must produce by asking the right questions. In a programming course your assignments may look more like (1.1b) and (1.1d), but someday you will face problems like (1.1a) and (1.1c).

Whenever possible, obtain samples of input and corresponding output. English is a disappointingly ambiguous descriptive tool, and a concrete example often clarifies (or obviates) a voluminous description.

When beginning on a problem don't even think about the _program_ you are to write; concentrate on the _problem_ until it becomes absolutely clear. Make up several sets of input data, and figure out the corresponding output results. This sample data should be designed to test and increase your understanding of the _details_ of the problem, and not just its general nature. It might seem a waste of time to make up input data and perform hand calculations, but in doing so you are actually executing an algorithm to solve the problem. Thus while concentrating on understanding the problem, you are also working toward designing the solution.

While studying the problem you should ask questions like "What is to be done if the input number is incorrect?", "What happens if this particular number is 0? Is it correct or incorrect and what should I do with it?", and "What should I do here -- the problem statement seems to be ambiguous?" It is important that these questions be raised and answered _before_ any programming is done. Proper understanding of the problem before you begin programming is crucial. Without this understanding, the program can never be correct.

The clarification of a significant problem is rarely completed as the first step in development. In general you will discover the omission of some necessary detail in the problem requirements only after you are engaged in the detailed execution of a later phase. For example, you will discover the lack of some detail about the volume of data only when you are attempting to specify the data structures and need a specific value to give as the size of an array. Or you will discover that you don't know how to process a particular error when you are actually writing the conditional unit to check for that error. In either case, you have discovered that the first phase is not quite completed and you must return and work on it further.

1.2 Design of a Solution Strategy

   This is certainly the hardest part of the process for which
to   give   general   advice   as to how to proceed.   Whatever
creativity exists in programming is concentrated in this phase.
We will give some vague suggestions as to where you may get
ideas, and will give some helpful procedures for developing
ideas once you have them -- but we recognize that we are helping
you least just where you need it most. We recommend you read
Polya's classic book How to Solve It.

   A useful device is to initially ignore the computer and its
programming language, and try to figure out how you would solve
the problem by hand, if you were presented with the data on
cards in such a way that you could see each item only once, and
only in the order given. Assume further that the only "scratch
paper" available to you is a number of very small cards (one
number apiece) on which you can write, erase and rewrite
numbers. If you can figure out some way to solve the problem by
hand under these restrictions, then you can generally figure out
how to describe that method in a program.

   The important thing is to separate the process of planning a
solution from the task of describing that solution in a
programming language. Once you learn to make this separation,
the challenging and difficult part of the process will be the
planning. For example, if you are unable to write a program to
"sort" a list of numbers into increasing order, it is likely
because you cannot figure out how to do it by hand in a
systematic   manner, and not because you don't know PL/I.
Conversely, if your sorting program is particularly efficient it
is because you devised a clever plan, and not because a mediocre
plan was cleverly described in PL/I statements.

1.2.1 Algorithms

   An algorithm is a sequence of statements to be executed in
order, to produce some desired result. It may also contain
comments or descriptions to aid us in "executing" or
understanding it. A cooking recipe, instructions to put a
Heathkit tuner together, or instructions to build a model
airplane are all good examples of algorithms.

   Algorithms should be written in whatever language and
notation will make them most understandable to the reader.
Often we assume a certain background and knowledge on the part
of the reader and adopt some technical vocabulary that makes the
algorithm more precise and compact. Algorithms are written for
people to read, rather than for computers and are therefore
generally not written in a programming language.   We adopt or
invent whatever language seems best for the particular problem.
Often this is a combination of English, mathematics and whatever
technical vocabulary is peculiar to the problem area.

A _program is an algorithm that has been translated into a
programming language_. We regard a program as a specific
implementation of an algorithm. The point is that the algorithm
comes first, and it is written in an informal (but still
precise) English-like language. The program comes later, and
its preparation is a process of translation rather than
creation.

An algorithm can be translated into different programming
languages. However, since we often know in advance what
language we will use, we tend to bias the algorithm toward
convenient operations of that language. In our case, knowing
that we are headed for a PL/I program, we start with a mixture
of English and PL/I, using PL/I terms where convenient but
inventing terms whenever that seems more convenient. Generally
the terms we invent are at a "higher level" than PL/I
statements. For example, we say "Swap A and B". PL/I has no
single statement to "Swap" and this will later be translated
into three assignment statements:

```
          T = A;
          A = B;
          B = T;
```

We can use terms like "find", "solve", and "search" that are at
a much higher level and will eventually be expressed as a
substantial segment of program. In our examples, as we
illustrate the gradual and systematic conversion of an algorithm
into a program, we use upper case (capital) letters for phrases
in PL/I and lower case letters for phrases that have not yet
been translated into PL/I. This is the same convention we used
in Section II.2 to present program schemata:

```
          /* Comment describing task and stopping flag */
              Initialize
              GET LIST(item);
              loop-name: DO WHILE(item ¬= stopping flag);
                  Perform action on item
                  GET LIST(item);
                  END loop-name;
```

We will sometimes simply _replace_ the English phrase with its
PL/I equivalent, but usually we will _carry the English phrase
over into the program as a heading comment_, to be followed by
the PL/I implementation of the function described in the
comment.

1.2.2 <u>Top-Down Development</u>

The general plan of attack is called "top-down development" or "successive refinement". We try to decompose a problem into a simple sequence of sub-problems. Given a problem P, try to discover a set of smaller problems P1, P2, P3, ... such that solving P1 first, then P2, etc, will be equivalent to solving the original P. Then apply the same approach to each of these sub-problems in turn -- determine a set of sub-sub-problems P11, P12, P13, ... whose solutions in sequence constitute a solution to P1. This leads quite naturally to a well-structured program as described in Section II.1.6.

Each time we find a sequence of sub-problems that correspond to a given problem we are, in effect, <u>refining</u> the statement of that problem into one with more detail and more indication as to <u>how</u> the problem is to be solved. This process continues until we have refined all of the high-level English phrases into PL/I statements. At this point we have completely specified how the problem is to be solved, and have a program ready for testing.

The top-down analysis of a problem can usefully be guided by constructing a "development tree":

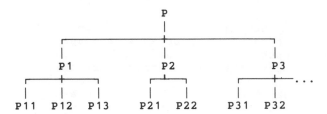

Such a tree is not a "flow-chart". A flow-chart shows alternative paths of flow-of-control; a tree shows the structure of a program. Each horizontal level of the tree is a <u>complete description</u> of the problem; each lower level refines that description to give more detail. All the sub-problems on any horizontal level are to be executed, in left to right order.

1.2.3 <u>A Comment Outline</u>

A convenient way to preserve the information contained in the development tree and at the same time initiate the actual preparation of the program is to transform the tree into a "comment outline". Those phrases in the tree which are not in PL/I become a separate PL/I comment, and the vertical position in the tree is reflected by the indentation in the outline. Left-to-right order in the tree becomes normal sequential order (top-to-bottom) in the outline. These comments serve as headings for program units and describe the function performed by the statements indented beneath them. For example, the tree in 1.2.2 would become:

```
/* P ... */
P: PROCEDURE OPTIONS(MAIN);
      /* P1 ... */
            /* P11 ... */
            /* P12 ... */
            /* P13 ... */
      /* P2 ... */
            /* P21 ... */
            /* P22 ... */
      /* P3 ... */
            /* P31 ... */
            /* P32 ... */
            ...
      END P;
```

1.3 Choice of Data Structures

Key decisions must be made with regard to what elements of
the problem will require storage. Variables have to be
specified to accomplish this storage, including names,
dimensions, type attributes, and the logical relationship
between variables. Much of this information obviously comes
from the clarification of the problem with respect to the volume
and form of the input data, but the choice of data structures
depends equally importantly on the program strategy.

Although we treat them here as separate phases, in general
data structure and program strategy are inextricably related.
For example, consider the programs classified in Section II.2.1.
The strategy represented by (II.2.1a) needs only one datum at a
time, while strategy (II.2.1b) requires an array to hold all the
data at once.

The choice of data structures takes place after the program
strategy has been chosen, and sometimes the final choice can be
delayed until after most of the actual program statements are
written. In general, postpone the final specification of data
structures as long as possible. This will reduce the
backtracking that is required. There are often details that
don't become clear until much of the program has been written.

Relationships between variables are important, and you should
emphasize these relationships to the reader by the order in
which you give declarations. For example, consider two sets of
declarations (1.3a) and (1.3b) which are equivalent to PL/I:

```
(1.3a)      DCL ((PR,TP)(50),MAX,MIN) FLOAT DEC;
                  /* TABLES OF PRESSURE AND TEMPERATURE */
            DCL (N,M,POSMAX) FIXED DEC;
                  /* LENGTHS AND POSITION OF MAX */
```

(1.3b)   DCL PR(50) FLOAT DEC,/* TABLE OF PRESSURES IS */
                PRTOP FIXED DEC, /* PR(1:PRTOP) */
                PRMAX FLOAT DEC, /* MAX VALUE IN PR(1:PRTOP) */
                PRMIN FLOAT DEC; /* MIN VALUE IN PR(1:PRTOP) */

            DCL TP(50) FLOAT DEC,/* TABLE OF TEMPERATURES IS */
                TPTOP FIXED DEC, /* TP(1:TPTOP) */
                TPPOSMAX FIXED DEC;
                    /* POSITION OF MAX VALUE IN TP(1:TPTOP) */

It takes a little longer to write declarations like (1.3b) but
they are much clearer to the reader. Both the names and the
grouping emphasize the relationships between variables.
Grouping variables just to avoid repeating attributes is false
economy. (1.3b) also avoids names such as MAX and MIN which
would prevent the use of the built-in functions with those
names.

1.4 Writing the Actual Program Statements

    Relatively little needs to be said about the detailed
programming phase. If phase two has been adequately done you
have a detailed comment outline describing the action of each
unit of the program. Phase three has defined the objects upon
which those units must act. All that remains is to translate
these detailed English-like specifications into statements of
PL/I (or whatever programming language is being employed).

    However, as suggested earlier, as you write the detailed
program statements you often discover that the data structures
are not quite right, so you have to return to phase three. You
may also find it necessary to return to phase two to alter the
organization of the program. Rarely can you complete the
detailed translation without having to return at least once to
phase one to clarify some aspect of the problem definition,
which in turn may require changes in the program organization or
data structures. Backing up and making changes can be a tricky
business. The difficulty lies in making sure that you have
identified all the implications of the change and have made all
the necessary adjustments. The development tree is particularly
helpful in indicating what program sections are affected.

    Few people compose well at a keypunch. The usual practice is
to write the program statements by hand, and then keypunch (or
enter on a typewriter terminal) from this handwritten copy. The
accuracy of the keypunching depends, to a considerable extent,
upon the legibility of the handwritten copy. We often see
students punching from copy that is at best only semi-legible.
This inevitably introduces errors into the program. I's get
mistaken for 1's; 2's for Z's; O's for zeros; inserts get
inserted in the wrong place; and the indentation is generally
fouled up. Considering how hard it is to detect and remove
errors once they are in a program it is worth spending some time

and effort keeping them out in the first place.

The initial writing of a program can be a pretty messy process. Statements have to be added, or deleted, or changed. They sometimes have to be shifted left or right to reflect changes in the nesting level. (An optimist has been defined as someone who programs in ink.) It is usually worthwhile copying a program over to have a clear, readable copy before attempting to keypunch it. This makes keypunching a simple transcription process, rather than a deciphering problem. The time spent in producing the extra initial copy will be more than offset by a reduction in testing time.

Section 2   Examples of Program Development

The following sections present the development of six different examples in varying degrees of completeness. Although we are primarily concerned with the development process rather than the particular problems, three of these examples -- searching, sorting and scanning for symbols -- are in fact important problems with which you should become familiar.

We try to describe the development process in some detail, identifying each phase and presenting some of the alternatives from which one must choose. For short examples this may seem laborious since one obviously can produce a satisfactory program by a much less studied and formal process. However, the process described here is indispensable for larger and more complicated problems. It is not entirely natural or intuitively obvious, so if you are to use this technique when it is needed, you must learn and practice it in situations where it may not be absolutely necessary.

2.1 The Example of I.1.2.1

In Section I.1.2.1 the following problem is posed:

Given a list of numbers, print the first, second, third numbers, etc., but stop printing when the largest number in the list has been printed.

The development begun in I.1.2.1 is later completed in Section I.5.4. You should now reread these sections and try to identify the various phases of the development.

A development tree was not given for this problem. It would be something like the following:

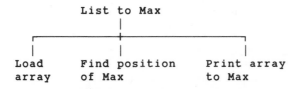

```
                    List to Max
                         |
         ┌───────────────┼───────────────┐
         |               |               |
       Load         Find position    Print array
       array         of Max          to Max
```

The data structures consist of an array INTEGER of sufficient size to hold all the data, and two variables TOP and MAX to point to the last position used in INTEGER and to the position of the maximum.

The development tree can be converted to a comment outline:

```
/* PROGRAM TO LIST VALUES FROM FIRST TO MAXIMUM */
    /* LOAD DATA INTO INTEGER(1:N) UNTIL FIRST ZERO */
    /* SET MAX TO POSITION OF MAXIMUM IN INTEGER(1:Z-1) */
    /* PRINT INTEGER(1:MAX), 1 PER LINE */
```

Now analyzing the subproblems presented by these headings, the first subproblem is an example of the basic program schema (2b) given in Section II.2. A list of data is to be read, with a specified stopping flag. The task to be performed on each datum is a test, with "good" values to be preserved in an array. The second subproblem is a variation of (I.1.1e), differing only in that the data whose maximum is sought is already in an array, rather than in an external data list. The third subproblem is a straightforward printing task such as the examples given in Section I.6.1. Although this problem may have looked formidable when you first read Section I.5.4, it is apparent now that it actually consists of a simple sequence of three subproblems, each of which is some variation of a task that you have seen previously.

Of course, you are entitled to be suspicious of examples in textbooks, where everything works out neatly and the authors obviously had every opportunity to rig things to make their point. Nevertheless this is not an atypical experience. You will discover that each new problem can be broken down into subproblems, most of which are variations of things you have done before. There are a relatively small number of basic tasks -- perhaps several dozen -- that recur very often in problems that seem entirely different.

2.2 The Problem of Searching a List

Consider the following "list-searching" problem:

Given is a "list" of numbers, in a particular order, and a set of "inquiries" -- numbers which may or may not be duplicates of those included in the list. For each inquiry determine whether or not it is on the list. If it is on the list, indicate what position it occupies; if it is not on the list report that fact.

For example, if a list consists of the numbers 9, -4.5, 16 and 5, in that order, then the inquiry "16" should result in the report that this number is in third position on the list; the inquiries "12" and "4.5" should result in a report that they are not on the list.

Clarifying the problem will lead to detail about the quantity and the form of the input. This might result in the following specification:

> The input will consist of: a) an integer specifying the length of the list; b) the list values, in order; c) an integer specifying the number of inquiries; d) the inquiries. The list will have not more than 100 values, which can be positive, negative or zero, and in integer, decimal or exponential form.

This means that the example above would be given in the form:

```
*DATA
4, 9, -4.5, 16, 5,
3, 16, 12, 4.5
```

Detailed specifcation of required output might be the following:

> For each inquiry print a line (double-spaced) that gives the value, and either its position on the list or the fact that it does not appear on the list.

With this specification the exact format and wording of the output line is left to the programmer's discretion. Presumably lines such as the following would be acceptable (but it is worth checking in advance to make sure):

> 16 IS IN POSITION 3
>
> 12 IS NOT ON THE LIST
>
> 4.5 IS NOT ON THE LIST

The only data errors that can occur in this problem are in the control values that specify the length of the list and the number of inquiries. Error processing might be specified as follows:

> The list length may be anything from 0 to 100; if not, terminate execution with an appropriate warning. The number of inquiries is arbitrary.

This method of specifying list length with a control value is not a particularly good idea. It is easy to handle in the program, but the program cannot check for certain obvious and ruinous errors. For example, if the list length is specified as 90, but 91 values are actually given, then the 91st will be interpreted as the number of inquiries. If only 89 values are given then the number of inquiries will become the last item on the list, and the first inquiry will be taken to be the number of inquiries. Such miscounting is a common error, and the program can do little against it. On the other hand, the specification that the program should work for a list of length zero, or for no inquiries is not unreasonable. Posed as a

separate problem, it would be foolish for anyone to run the
program with no list or no inquiries, but such programs are
often later incorporated into a larger program. The ability to
operate properly for extreme values -- in particular, the
ability to do nothing, gracefully -- is very valuable.

Obviously, the entire list must be available for processing
each inquiry. This is the reason the list is placed before the
inquiries in the input data. On the other hand, each inquiry is
processed separately and there is no need to retain an inquiry
value after it is processed. Hence the problem does not quite
fall in any of the simple categories described in Section
II.2.1. But it can be divided into two sub-problems:

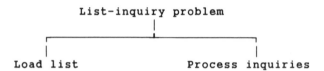

List-inquiry problem

Load list   Process inquiries

"Load list" is an interpretation of program schema (2d) given in
Section II.2. The body of the schema in this case is simply to
insert each datum in an array. "Process inquiries" is another
interpretation of the same schema. The body in this case is
more complex, involving searching the list and reporting
results. The second level of development would be:

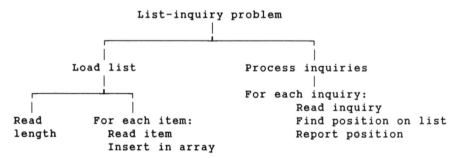

List-inquiry problem

Load list   Process inquiries

Read   For each item: For each inquiry:
length   Read item   Read inquiry
               Insert in array   Find position on list
                                    Report position

The principal data structure is an array to hold the list,
together with a variable to indicate its length. The array must
have at least 100 elements since the given list may be that
long, and must consist of FLOAT DECIMAL variables since no
restriction assures that the values will be integers. We will
call the list "GLIST", for "given list", avoiding the obvious
name "LIST" since this happens to be a keyword in PL/I. To also
use LIST as an array name would result in unnecessarily
confusing statements such as GET LIST(LIST(I)).

No array is necessary to store the inquiries since they can
be processed one at a time. A simple FLOAT DECIMAL variable
"INQ" will suffice to hold the current inquiry value. You could
not elect to read all the inquiries into a second array and then
process them one at a time from that array, because you have no

idea how large an array is required. (PL/I does provide a facility to permit the size of arrays to be specified from data, but we have chosen not to use it in the <u>Primer</u>. See Section VI.3 of our <u>Introduction to Programming</u>.) We also need variables to store the number of inquiries remaining to be processed, and the position of a particular value in the list. The values of these variables will always be integers.

The development tree can be converted into a comment outline as shown below. The declarations of the required data structures are also included.

```
/* LIST-INQUIRY PROGRAM */
LISTINQ: PROCEDURE OPTIONS(MAIN);
     DCL GLIST(100) FLOAT DEC; /* GIVEN LIST IS */
     DCL GLNG FIXED DEC; /* GLIST(1:GLNG) */
     DCL GPOS FIXED DEC; /* A POSITION IN GLIST */
     DCL INQ  FLOAT DEC; /* CURRENT INQUIRY VALUE */
     DCL NINQ FIXED DEC; /* NBR INQUIRIES STILL TO BE */
                                    /* PROCESSED */

     /* LOAD LIST, SKIP IF ERROR */
          /* READ LENGTH */
          /* FOR EACH ITEM, READ AND INSERT IN GLIST */

     /* PROCESS INQUIRIES */
          /* FIND POSITION ON LIST */
          /* REPORT POSITION */

     END LISTINQ;
```

Finally we are ready to write PL/I statements to perform the actions. "Read length" can be programmed:

```
/* READ LENGTH */
     GET LIST(GLNG);
     IF (GLNG<0)|(GLNG>100) THEN DO;
          PUT SKIP LIST('IMPROPER LIST LENGTH',GLNG);
          GO TO TERM_LISTINQ; END;
```

Testing, such as that shown here, should take place any time a control value is read. You should think of such testing as an inherent part of "read". TERM_LISTINQ is a label that must be prefixed to a statement that will terminate execution of the program.

The "insert in GLIST" task could be programmed:

```
/* FOR EACH ITEM, INSERT IN GLIST */
     INSERT_LOOP: DO GPOS = 1 TO GLNG BY 1;
          GET LIST(GLIST(GPOS));
          END INSERT_LOOP;
```

The "process inquiries" task is obviously a repetition unit, modeled after schema (II.2d):

```
/* PROCESS INQUIRIES */
   GET LIST(NINQ);
   INQ_LOOP: DO WHILE (NINQ > 0);
      GET LIST(INQ);
      /* FIND POSITION OF INQ ON LIST */
      /* REPORT POSITION */
      NINQ = NINQ - 1;
      END INQ_LOOP;
```

Two tasks comprise the principal body of this loop. "Find position" is itself a repetition unit:

```
/* FIND POSITION OF INQ ON LIST */
   FIND_LOOP: DO GPOS = 1 TO GLNG BY 1;
      IF INQ = GLIST(GPOS) THEN GO TO TERM_FIND;
      END FIND_LOOP;
   TERM_FIND:;
```

FIND_LOOP terminates either when a value is found -- in which case it reaches TERM_FIND with GPOS pointing to that value -- or when the loop has indexed past GLNG -- in which case it reaches TERM_FIND with GPOS equal to GLNG+1.

"Report position" is a "multiple alternative" unit, with selection depending on the outcome of the list search:

```
/* REPORT POSITION */
   IF GPOS > GLNG
      THEN PUT SKIP(2) LIST(INQ,'IS NOT ON THE LIST');
      ELSE PUT SKIP(2) LIST(INQ,'IS IN POSITION',GPOS);
```

The complete program can now be assembled from these segments:

```
/* LIST-INQUIRY PROGRAM */
LISTINQ: PROCEDURE OPTIONS(MAIN);
   DCL GLIST(100) FLOAT DEC; /* GIVEN LIST IS */
   DCL GLNG FIXED DEC; /* GLIST(1:GLNG) */
   DCL GPOS FIXED DEC; /* A POSITION IN GLIST */
   DCL INQ  FLOAT DEC; /* CURRENT INQUIRY VALUE */
   DCL NINQ FIXED DEC; /* NBR INQUIRIES STILL TO BE */
                       /* PROCESSED */

   /* LOAD LIST, SKIP IF ERROR */
      /* READ LENGTH */
         GET LIST(GLNG);
         IF (GLNG < 0)|(GLNG > 100) THEN DO;
            PUT SKIP LIST
               ('IMPROPER LIST LENGTH',GLNG);
            GO TO TERM_LISTINQ; END;
      /* FOR EACH ITEM, READ AND INSERT IN GLIST */
         INSERT_LOOP: DO GPOS = 1 TO GLNG BY 1;
            GET LIST(GLIST(GPOS));
            END INSERT_LOOP;
```

```
        /* PROCESS INQUIRIES */
            GET LIST(NINQ);
            INQ_LOOP: DO WHILE (NINQ > 0);
                GET LIST(INQ);
                /* FIND POSITION OF INQ ON LIST */
                    FIND_LOOP: DO GPOS = 1 TO GLNG BY 1;
                        IF INQ = GLIST(GPOS)
                            THEN GO TO TERM_FIND;
                        END FIND_LOOP;
                    TERM_FIND:;
                /* REPORT POSITION */
                    IF GPOS > GLNG
                        THEN PUT SKIP(2) LIST
                                (INQ,'IS NOT ON THE LIST');
                        ELSE PUT SKIP(2) LIST
                                (INQ,'IS IN POSITION',GPOS);
                NINQ = NINQ - 1;
                END INQ_LOOP;

    TERM_LISTINQ:;
    END LISTINQ;
```

Some final observations with regard to this program:

1. The program should check the value read for NINQ to make
sure it is reasonable.

2. The program has many comments relative to the number of
statements, but this is because the tasks in this case are
simple. As problems grow larger it requires more substantial
segments to do what each comment heading specifies.

3. The search algorithm used in "find position" is simple, but
not efficient for long lists. Much more efficient algorithms
could be used. (Examples are given in Section VII.2.4 of our
Introduction to Programming.) Note that the program is
structured so the search segment can be easily replaced without
requiring a change anywhere else in the program.

2.3 The Problem of Ordering a List

A common task is to reorder the elements of a list so that
their values are "in order". For numeric variables this is
usually "algebraic order", either increasing or decreasing; for
character variables it is usually according to the collating
sequence given in Section I.9.2.2, which implies both
alphabetical and algebraic order. The process of rearranging
values so they satisfy some order relationship is called
"sorting". A simple form of sorting problem is:

> Given a list of numbers, sort them so they are in order of
> increasing value. Display the list before and after
> sorting.

For example, if the list 5, 0, -7, 6.2, 1 is given, the list
-7, 0, 1, 5, 6.2 is to be produced. One possible clarification
of the problem is:

> Given data consisting of an integer n (not greater than 50)
> followed by a list of n numbers, sort these n numbers into
> increasing order. Display the list in original order in a
> single column, followed by the sorted list in single
> column. Provide appropriate titles.

Obviously we need to have <u>all the data available at once</u>, so we
cannot use a program like (II.2.1a). But excluding the final
printing task the rest of the problem is an interpretation of
(II.2.1b). The first level of development might be:

(2.3a)

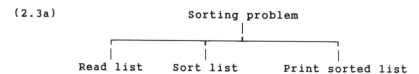

Sorting problem

Read list   Sort list   Print sorted list

(2.3a) does not indicate when the display of the initial list
will take place. There are two possibilities -- either before
or after sorting. The most obvious is to display the initial
order before it is changed. This could be done either as part
of the "read" task or as a separate task:

(2.3b)

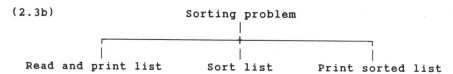

Sorting problem

Read and print list   Sort list   Print sorted list

(2.3c)

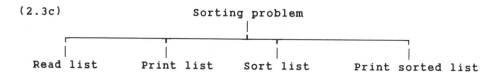

Sorting problem

Read list   Print list   Sort list   Print sorted list

(2.3c) results in two separate DO loops, and (2.3b) in a single
loop with two statements (GET and PUT) in the body. There seems
to be no advantage in separation and we decide, at least
tentatively, in favor of (2.3b). If we wanted to have all
printing done in one section of the program we would have to
make an extra copy of the list, so we could sort one copy and
keep the other in initial order. The development then would be:

(2.3d)

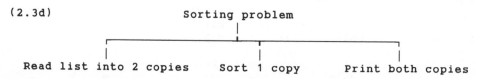

Sorting problem

Read list into 2 copies   Sort 1 copy   Print both copies

(2.3d) is unnecessary in this case and we will use (2.3b), but

note that only a slight variation in the original problem
statement -- to require the display in side-by-side columns --
would make strategy (2.3d) necessary.

So now we have separated off two minor tasks "read and print"
and "print" -- each an interpretation of schema (II.2b) or
schema (II.2.1b). By now the programming of tasks like these
should be familiar and almost automatic. It is also clear that
the principal data structure will be an array to hold the list
and a variable to specify how much of the array is used. The
elements of the array will have to be FLOAT DECIMAL since no
restriction on values is implied by the problem statement. What
remains is the following task:

Given L(1:N), reorder its elements into increasing order.

To figure out a method for reordering, suppose you had n
3 by 5 cards, each bearing a number, laid out in a row. How
would you go about rearranging the cards so the numbers were in
increasing order? There is the additional restriction that you
can only look at and compare two cards at a time (since PL/I has
this restriction). One way would be·to scan over the cards and
find the one with the largest value. This card could be
interchanged with the one at the end of the row. Now, ignoring
that card (which has been properly positioned), you could repeat
the process for the remaining n-1 cards. That is, locate the
card with the second largest value (the largest of the remaining
n-1) and interchange it with the second from last (the last of
the n-1). Now with the last two cards in proper position, work
on the remaining n-2 cards in the same way. If this is
continued until finally the last two cards are put in order, the
entire row will have been sorted. Let us transform this idea
into an algorithm:

        Repeat for lists of diminishing length m=n,n-1,n-2,...,2:
            1. Find the maximum value of L(1:m);
            2. Interchange the maximum with L(m).

Interchanging values is a familiar task by now, and finding the
maximum is similar to a problem you have seen before. This
version differs from (I.1.1e) only in that the numbers are
already in an array (rather than being an external data list)
and in that we need to find the position as well as the value of
the maximum. A program segment to do this is:

```
        /* SET MAXPOS TO POSITION OF MAX IN L(1:M) */
            MAXVAL = L(1);
            MAXPOS = 1;
            MAX_LOOP: DO I = 2 TO M BY 1;
                    IF L(I) > MAXVAL THEN DO;
                        MAXVAL = L(I);
                        MAXPOS = I; END;
                END MAX_LOOP;
```

Given that MAXPOS points to the maximum value in L(1:M) the

interchange is simply:

```
/* INTERCHANGE MAX AND LAST IN L(1:M) */
    TEMP = L(M);
    L(M) = L(MAXPOS);
    L(MAXPOS) = TEMP;
```

These two segments must be repeated for lists whose lengths M vary from N down to 2:

```
/* SORT L(1:N) */
    SUBLIST_LOOP: DO M = N TO 2 BY -1;
        /* SET MAXPOS TO POSITION OF MAX IN L(1:M) */
            MAXVAL = L(1); MAXPOS = 1;
            MAX_LOOP: DO I = 2 TO M BY 1;
                IF L(I) > MAXVAL THEN DO;
                    MAXVAL = L(I);
                    MAXPOS = I; END;
                END MAX_LOOP;
        /* INTERCHANGE MAX AND L(M) IN L(1:M) */
            TEMP = L(M);
            L(M) = L(MAXPOS);
            L(MAXPOS) = TEMP;
        END SUBLIST_LOOP;
```

(2.3e)

The complete program would have (2.3e) inserted in the following:

```
*PL/C ID='PAT MOORE'
/* SORT AND DISPLAY A LIST OF NUMBERS */
SORT: PROCEDURE OPTIONS(MAIN);
    DCL L(50) FLOAT DECIMAL;
    DCL N FIXED DEC; /* ACTUAL LENGTH OF LIST IN L */
    DCL M FIXED DEC; /* LENGTH OF SUB-LIST */
    DCL I FIXED DEC;
    DCL TEMP FLOAT DEC;
    /* READ AND DISPLAY INITIAL LIST */
        GET LIST(N);
        IF (N < 0) | (N > 50) THEN DO;
            PUT SKIP(3) LIST('IMPROPER LENGTH:',N);
            GO TO TERM_SORT; END;
        PUT SKIP LIST('LIST IN INITIAL ORDER'); PUT SKIP;
        RD_LOOP: DO I = 1 TO N BY 1;
            GET LIST(L(I));
            PUT SKIP LIST(L(I));
            END RD_LOOP;
```

```
     /* SORT L(1:N) */
         insert (2.3e)
     /* DISPLAY L(1:N) */
         PUT SKIP(3) LIST('SORTED LIST'); PUT SKIP;
         DISP_LOOP: DO I = 1 TO N BY 1;
             PUT SKIP LIST(L(I));
             END DISP_LOOP;
     TERM_SORT: ;
     END SORT;
  *DATA
```

Sorting is an important problem in practice, and a very
convenient problem to illustrate points in programming. We will
refer back to this often in future sections and it will help if
you understand this simple version very thoroughly.

2.4 An Accounting Problem

A bank would like to produce records of the transactions
during an accounting period in connection with their checking
accounts. For each account the bank wants a list showing the
balance at the beginning of the period, the number of deposits
and withdrawals, and the final balance. (This is a simplified
version of a very common and important type of computer
application.)

The accounts and transactions for an accounting period will
be given on punched cards as follows:

1. First will be a sequence of cards describing the
accounts. Each account is described by two numbers: the
account number (greater than 0), and the account balance at
the beginning of the period, in dollars and cents. The
last account is followed by a "dummy" account consisting of
two zero values to indicate the end of the list. There
will be at most 200 accounts.

2. Following the accounts are the transactions. Each
transaction is given by three numbers: the account number,
a 1 or -1 (indicating a deposit or withdrawal,
respectively), and the transaction amount, in dollars and
cents. The last real transaction is followed by a dummy
transaction consisting of three zero values.

The following sample input has been supplied, where the words
at the right are not part of the input, but explanatory notes.

Input numbers			meaning
1025	61.50		(account 1025 contains $61.50)
1028	103		(account 1028 contains $103)
1026	100		(account 1026 contains $100)
0	0		(end of accounts)
1025	1	500	(deposit $500 in account 1025)
1028	-1	20	(withdraw $20 from account 1028)
1025	-1	400	(withdraw $400 from account 1025)
1025	+1	50	(deposit $50 in account 1025)
0	0	0	(end of transactions)

For this input, the output should be:

ACCOUNT	PREV BAL	WITHDRAWALS	DEPOSITS	FINAL BAL
1025	61.50	1	2	211.50
1028	103	1	0	83
1026	100	0	0	100

Some of the errors that could occur in the data are:

1. An account is listed two or more times.

2. The end-of-account signal is missing or incorrect.

3. A transaction number is not in the list of accounts.

4. The withdrawal-deposit number is not 1 or -1.

5. The transaction amount is negative.

6. The end-of-transaction signal is wrong or missing.

All these errors could be detected by the program. Detecting other situations such as overdrafts (which are not really input errors) would probably make the program more valuable. Of course, not all errors can be detected by the program. For example, a withdrawal keypunched as a deposit or an error in a transaction amount can not be detected. To keep our program development to manageable size we will ignore the question of data errors. In the real world this is clearly unrealistic, and the program would have to detect and process these errors.

The following steps give a reasonable chronological record of the development of a program for this problem.

Step 1. <u>Discovering the overall structure of the algorithm.</u>

Looking at the problem description, note that the account data precedes the transactions. Thus all accounts must be read and stored internally, before the transactions can be read and "processed". Moreover, while processing the transactions we must be able to access any account at any time, since no ordering of the transactions by account number is mentioned in the description of the problem. The sample data confirm this lack of ordering. Also, since the last transaction may apply to

any account, no result may be printed for an account until all
transactions have been processed. This analysis indicates that
the structure of the program will be:

(2.4a)   2a1: Read in and set up the accounts in a "table";
          2a2: Read in and process the transactions;
          2a3: Print the results;

In tree form this would be:

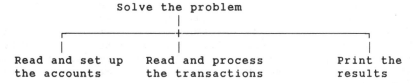

                       Solve the problem

          Read and set up   Read and process   Print the
          the accounts   the transactions   results

     It should already be apparent that the structure of this
problem is somewhat similar to the list-searching problem of
Section 2.2. Task 2a1 is directly comparable to the first task
of 2.2, except that the table of accounts is a more complex data
structure than the list of values in 2.2. Task 2a2 searches for
a particular entry in the table, but instead of reporting the
position of the entry it modifies the entry. Task 2a3 is added;
it has no counterpart in 2.2.

     (2.4a) is an algorithm using the English commands "read",
"set up", "process" and "print".   These are not yet precise
enough to specify the action to be taken, and our task is to
refine them so that they are precise and are expressed in PL/I
terms.

     There are now three separate, smaller problems, but they are
obviously not entirely independent of each other. All three
share the data structures used to contain the accounts and the
information connected with them.   Whenever we split a problem
into several smaller parts, it is important to look at the
"interface"   or   connections between them.   Often, several
strategies exist for implementing each one, but implementing one
in a particular way may reduce the flexibility in designing the
others. We must weigh carefully the benefits and disadvantages,
including effects on other modules, in choosing a strategy for a
given module.

Step 2.   <u>The data structures representing the accounts</u>.

     We must keep the accounts accessible in a table until all
transactions have been processed and the results have been
reported. This can be done using an array ACCT (say) to hold
the ACCounT numbers and an array IBAL to hold the corresponding
Initial BALances. We also need a variable N (say) to hold the
number of accounts. Thus, if i is an integer between 1 and N,
ACCT(i) contains an account number and IBAL(i) contains the
corresponding initial balance.   Other alternatives for storing

the data exist of course, but this is probably the simplest and
easiest.

Now review the problem statement to make sure the accounts
have been described completely and accurately. Certainly this
is all we need initially, but look at the sample output.   After
processing the transactions, in addition to the initial balance
we must report the number of deposits and withdrawals and also
the final balance.   This will require three more arrays; we need
two arrays to contain the number of withdrawals and deposits,
and a third to contain the balances. The arrays holding the
number of withdrawals and deposits will be initially set to 0,
and will be increased to count the number of withdrawals and
deposits that are processed for each account.   Similarly, the
array holding the final balances will be initialized to the
initial balances and will be updated as transactions are
processed.

To summarize, we write down the names of the variables which
describe the accounts and define as precisely as possible how
they will be used:

    1. Variable N contains the number of accounts.

    2. Five arrays describe the accounts: ACCT, IBAL, WITH, DEP
       and   CBAL (meaning Current BALance).   If i is an
       integer between 1 and N, then during execution of the
       program

       ACCT(i)   is an ACCounT number,
       IBAL(i)   is the corresponding Initial BALance,
       WITH(i)   is the number of WITHdrawals processed so far,
       DEP(i)   is the number of DEPosits processed so far,
       CBAL(i)   is the Current BALance in the account.

CBAL(i) depends of course on the withdrawals and deposits
processed so far.   In order to fix these definitions more
clearly in our minds, consider some examples.   Just after
reading in all the accounts in the sample input, the arrays are:

	ACCT	IBAL	WITH	DEP	CBAL
(1)	1025	61.50	0	0	61.50
(2)	1028	103	0	0	103
(3)	1026	100	0	0	100

Note that each CBAL(i) is the same as IBAL(i), since no
transactions have been processed. After processing the first
transaction, the arrays are:

	ACCT	IBAL	WITH	DEP	CBAL
(1)	1025	61.50	0	1	561.50
(2)	1028	103	0	0	103
(3)	1026	100	0	0	100

At this point we could write declarations for these data structures, but it is better to wait. These structures should be considered tentative, and may have to be revised as the detailed design of the program unfolds.

We have looked at the data structures which contain the accounts from the viewpoint of the information that must be available as the program executes. Now consider how this information is accessed and changed -- how the three statements of algorithm (2.4a) use the information. Statement 2a2, "Read in and process the transactions", requires us to locate in the table of accounts the account associated with each transaction. This means a search in the array ACCT of account numbers for each transaction account number. That is, given a transaction like (1028, 1, 100), we have to find an integer i such that ACCT(i) = 1028. Assuming a search algorithm such as the one used in Section 2.2, on the average we must look at half of the accounts in order to find the right one. If there are only a few hundred accounts this may be feasible. But if there are 5000 or more accounts the time to search would be in seconds for each transaction, and we could not afford to structure the table of accounts as we have done.

This search time can be drastically reduced if the accounts are rearranged so that the account numbers are in ascending order: $ACCT(1) \leq ACCT(2) \leq \ldots \leq ACCT(N)$. If we sort the array of accounts as we read them in, we can process the transactions more efficiently. But sorting takes time too, and we must carefully weigh the sorting time against the efficiency gained in processing, before we decide which approach to take. This depends on the number of accounts relative to the number of transactions, and we now realize that we lack such information. The problem description is not complete, and without such information we cannot design the best program.

An even better solution would be for the bank to keep their accounts in ascending order, so that neither sorting nor a slow search would be required.

This discussion should illustrate the need for thinking about the various ways of implementing each succesive statement of an algorithm, and considering the effects of each. For now, assume that the accounts cannot be kept sorted because of other considerations, and that the simple search algorithm of Section 2.2 is adequate.

Step 3. <u>Refining the statement "Read and set up the accounts."</u>

Statement 2a1 is not yet in PL/I, so it must be refined
further. The required action is

        Read and set up the first account;
        Read and set up the second account;
                        . . .
        (until the account just read has account number 0)

Such a sequence of similar statements can be replaced by a loop
which iteratively executes a single statement like "Read and set
up the Kth account", where K is of course increased after each
execution.   There are several ways of writing this loop. One
method recognizes that the first statement "Read and set up the
first account" must always be executed and can therefore be put
outside the loop:

        K = 1;
        Read and set up the Kth account;
        RSET_LOOP: DO WHILE (ACCT(K) ¬= 0);
          K = K + 1;
          Read and set up the Kth account;
          END RSET_LOOP;
        N = K - 1;

The final statement that assigns K-1 instead of K to N is
necessary because the last account read is just a dummy account
serving as a stopping flag.

An alternative technique uses a dummy account ACCT(0) whose
account number is set to 1 so that the loop body is <u>always</u>
executed at least once:

        K = 0;
        ACCT(0) = 1;
        RSET_LOOP: DO WHILE (ACCT(K) ¬= 0);
(2.4b)   K = K + 1;
          Read and set up the Kth account;
          END RSET_LOOP;
        N = K - 1;

Either refinement could be used.   <u>If</u> the refinement of the
statement "Read and set up the Kth account" turned out to be
long and difficult, we would tend to choose (2.4b) because this
difficult statement only appears once. (Recall the discussion
of this issue in Section I.4.5.2.) At this point we arbitrarily
choose (2.4b) and the development tree is:

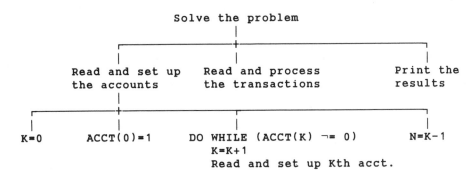

We have introduced a variable K, and should indicate what it means. While executing (2.4b) (and only then), K is the number of accounts read in so far, including the end-of-list signal as an account.

Note that when we declare the array ACCT we must give an upper bound on the number of elements in it. If the input happens to have more than that number of accounts, then (2.4b) will execute incorrectly.

Algorithm (2.4b) still contains an English statement which must be translated into PL/I. To "read and set up account K", we must obtain values from the input data and store the account number and balance in ACCT(K) and IBAL(K), and initialize the other three variables that comprise account K:

```
(2.4c)    GET LIST (ACCT(K), IBAL(K));
          WITH(K) = 0;
          DEP(K) = 0;
          CBAL(K) = IBAL(K);
```

As a final step, we insert this refinement into (2.4b) to yield the following program segment. Note that the original statement 2a1 becomes a comment of the PL/I program which replaces it:

```
          /* READ AND SET UP THE ACCOUNTS.*/
          K = 0;
          ACCT(0) = 1;
(2.4d)    RSET_LOOP: DO WHILE (ACCT(K) ¬= 0);
             K = K+1;
             GET LIST(ACCT(K), IBAL(K));
             WITH(K) = 0;
             DEP(K) = 0;
             CBAL(K) = IBAL(K);
             END RSET_LOOP;
          N = K - 1;
```

Step 4. Refining "Read and process the transactions."

Consider statement 2a2, keeping in mind that the table of
accounts is not ordered by account number. Two actions are
required -- reading and processing the transactions -- and there
may be several ways of performing them. Two possibilities come
to mind:

1. First read and store all the transactions, then process
   all the transactions.

2. Read and process the first transaction, read and process
   the second transaction, etc.

The first possibility requires arrays in which to store all
the transactions. How big should the arrays be? We don't know,
since we have no idea how many transactions there may be. To
use this method, we would have to determine the maximum number
of transactions in any one run. This is essentially the same
question we faced with inquiries in Section 2.2 and the
distinction between the two simple types of program in II.2.1.

The question with the second method is feasibility. Is it
possible to process a single transaction without having access
to the others? The answer in this case is yes.

This is not really such a pointless question to ask as it
might seem. For example, consider the task "Read in a list of
transactions and print them out in order of the account number."
We cannot "Read one and print, read one and print, etc.", so we
must read all of them before we can begin printing.

With the second method, an array is not needed to hold the
transactions, since we need only keep track of one transaction
at a time. This second method seems to have no disadvantages
compared to the first, and should be used.

Note that without a change in the problem definition, we are
forced to use the second method. Since we don't know how many
transactions might appear, we cannot assume any maximum and
hence cannot use the first method. Quite often, a careful
examination of the problem will answer a question for us. We
should be continually asking ourselves questions like: "Have I
used everything that was given to me?" "Could the problem
definition be changed to make the solution easier, clearer, or
more efficient?" "Have I assumed something that is not
explicitly stated to be true?"

A second point is the question of efficiency. For example,
we use the second possibility rather than the first, because it
uses less computer storage space but otherwise is essentially
the same. We may strive for efficiency with respect to
execution time, storage space, or with respect to the time it
takes to write the program. There is always a trade-off when
trying to gain efficiency; usually what executes faster will

take more space, or what is easier to program and understand may
be slower. A programmer must know what the value criterion is
for each program he is to design.

Our choice, then, for reading and processing transactions is

        Read a transaction;
        Process the transaction just read;
                ...
        Read a transaction;
        Process the transaction just read;
        Read a transaction;
            (until transaction acct. number is 0)

This is a sequence of (a pair of) statements which is to be
executed several times, and we can use a loop. Since the first
statement "Read a transaction" must always be executed and the
last transaction is <u>not</u> to be processed, it is easiest to
perform the first "read" outside the loop and to let the loop
body consist of "Process transaction; Read transaction". That
is, we are pairing the statements as indicated by the spacing in
the following algorithm:

        Read a transaction;

        Process the transaction just read;
        Read a transaction;
                ...

        Process the transaction just read;
        Read a transaction
            (until transaction acct. number is 0)

The algorithm using a WHILE loop is:

        Read a transaction;
        TRAN_LOOP: DO WHILE (transaction account number ¬= 0);
(2.4e)   Process the transaction just read;
            Read a transaction;
            END TRAN_LOOP;

    Further refinement requires a decision as to how the
transactions are to be stored. We should question the format of
the input transactions. If we allow a negative amount to
specify a withdrawal, then the withdrawal-deposit code is not
necessary. Let us assume that the bank says the given form is
indeed necessary, and continue with the development.

    Since only one transaction need be accessed at any time, only
three simple variables are needed:

        TACCT   contains the Transaction ACCounT number.
(2.4f) DEPWITH contains the action code:
                    1 means DEPosit, -1 means WITHdrawal.
        AMT   contains the AMounT of the transaction.

This leads to the following refinement of algorithm (2.4e):

```
          GET LIST(TACCT, DEPWITH, AMT);
          TRAN_LOOP: DO WHILE (TACCT ¬= 0);
(2.4g)       Process the transaction just read;
          GET LIST(TACCT, DEPWITH, AMT);
          END TRAN_LOOP;
```

The final task is to reduce the phrase "Process the transaction just read" to PL/I. Processing a transaction requires us to find the corresponding account in the array ACCT. Suppose that while searching ACCT we store in a new variable J an integer so that TACCT = ACCT(J). Then account ACCT(J) is to be changed as follows: If DEPWITH(J) = 1 then add 1 to DEP(J) and add AMT to CBAL(J); if DEPWITH(J) = -1 then add 1 to WITH(J) and subtract AMT from CBAL(J).

   A search algorithm similar to that of Section 2.2 will be used:

```
          /* PROCESS THE TRANSACTION JUST READ */
           /* SEARCH FOR TRANSACTION ACCOUNT */
            J = 1;
            SEARCH_LOOP: DO WHILE (ACCT(J) ¬= TACCT);
(2.4h)         J = J + 1;
              END SEARCH_LOOP;
          IF DEPWITH = 1
            THEN DO; DEP(J) = DEP(J) + 1;
                     CBAL(J) = CBAL(J) + AMT;   END;
            ELSE DO; WITH(J) = WITH(J) + 1;
                     CBAL(J) = CBAL(J) - AMT;   END;
```

Note that we assume that DEPWITH is a 1 or -1, without checking. The program should check for values other than 1 or -1 and print a message if an error has occurred. We also assume that the transaction account number will be valid -- that the account will be found in the table. The program should check for this, as in Section 2.2.

Step 5. Refining "Print the results."

   Statement 2a3 is the easiest to translate into PL/I. Since an order was not specified by the problem description, we will print the accounts in the easiest order possible -- the order in which they were read in.

```
          /* PRINT THE RESULTS */
           PUT SKIP LIST('ACCOUNT', 'PREV BAL', 'WITHDRAWALS',
                         'DEPOSITS', 'FINAL BAL');
(2.4i)     PRINT_LOOP: DO I = 1 TO N BY 1;
             PUT SKIP LIST(ACCT(I), IBAL(I), WITH(I), DEP(I),
                         CBAL(I));
             END PRINT_LOOP;
```

The development tree now has become:

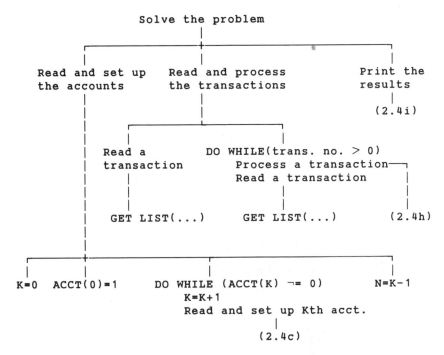

Step 6. <u>Assembling the complete program.</u>

The final task is to gather together the refinements for the three statements of (2.4a) into a PL/I program. These refinements are (2.4d), (2.4g) with (2.4h) replacing the single English statement of (2.4g), and (2.4i). We also produce declarations from the descriptions of variables written in steps 2 and 4. We end up with the program below. It should be pointed out that this is not the only possible program. Just considering the same basic algorithm, there are many minor variations. For example, arrays WITH and DEP could be initialized in the declarations, the array IBAL could be assigned to CBAL using an array assignment statement, and the statement "Read and set up the accounts" could have been written so that the array could be declared ACCT(1:200) instead of ACCT(0:201). Many possibilities exist, and one cannot always say which is better.

```
*PL/C ID='C. CONSTABLE'
 /* SIMPLIFIED BANK ACCOUNTING PROGRAM */
 BANK: PROCEDURE OPTIONS(MAIN);
     DECLARE (                     /* THE ACCOUNTS, IN ORDER READ:*/
         N,                        /* THERE ARE N ACCOUNTS*/
         ACCT(0:201),              /* THE ACCOUNT NUMBERS*/
         WITH(1:201),              /* NUMBER OF WITHDRAWALS*/
         DEP (1:201))              /* NUMBER OF DEPOSITS*/
             FIXED DECIMAL;
     DECLARE (
         IBAL(1:201),              /* THE INITIAL BALANCES */
         CBAL(1:201))              /* THE CURRENT BALANCES*/
             FLOAT DECIMAL;
     DECLARE (                     /* CURRENT TRANSACTION:*/
         TACCT,                    /* TRANSACTION ACCOUNT NUMBER*/
         DEPWITH)                  /* 1=DEPOSIT, -1=WITHDRAWAL*/
             FIXED DECIMAL,
         AMT                       /* TRANSACTION AMOUNT*/
             FLOAT DECIMAL;
     DECLARE (I, J, K) FIXED DECIMAL;

     /* READ AND SET UP THE ACCOUNTS */
       K = 0;
       ACCT(0) = 1;
       RSET_LOOP: DO WHILE (ACCT(K) ¬= 0);
         K = K+1;
         GET LIST(ACCT(K), IBAL(K));
         WITH(K) = 0;
         DEP(K) = 0;
         CBAL(K) = IBAL(K);
         END RSET_LOOP;
       N = K - 1;
     /* READ AND PROCESS THE TRANSACTIONS */
       GET LIST(TACCT, DEPWITH, AMT); /* FIRST TRANSACTION*/
       TRAN_LOOP: DO WHILE (TACCT ¬= 0);
         /* PROCESS THE TRANSACTION JUST READ */
           /* SEARCH FOR TRANSACTION ACCOUNT */
             J = 1;
             SEARCH_LOOP: DO WHILE (ACCT(J) ¬= TACCT);
               J = J + 1;
               END SEARCH_LOOP;
           IF DEPWITH = 1
             THEN DO; DEP(J) = DEP(J) + 1;
                   CBAL(J) = CBAL(J) + AMT;   END;
             ELSE DO; WITH(J) = WITH(J) + 1;
                   CBAL(J) = CBAL(J) - AMT;   END;
         GET LIST(TACCT, DEPWITH, AMT);
         END TRAN_LOOP;
```

```
    /* PRINT THE RESULTS */
      PUT SKIP LIST('ACCOUNT', 'PREV BAL', 'WITHDRAWALS',
                        'DEPOSITS', 'FINAL BAL');
      PRINT_LOOP: DO I = 1 TO N BY 1;
        PUT SKIP LIST(ACCT(I), IBAL(I), WITH(I), DEP(I),
                        CBAL(I));
        END PRINT_LOOP;
    END BANK;
*DATA
```

2.5 Scanning for Symbols

Many programs process "text". The PL/C translator is such a program; this book was produced by a "text-editing program" (see Section 3.2.2). Such programs have the common sub-problem of reading lines of text and dividing them into separate "symbols". This sub-problem may be stated separately as follows:

> The input consists of a sequence of "symbols" on cards. Each symbol consists of 1 to 60 nonblank characters, and each adjacent pair of symbols is separated by one or more blanks. The last symbol is also followed by at least one blank. A symbol may be split onto two cards.

> Write a program segment which, when executed, will store the next symbol which has not yet been processed into variable SYMBOL. SYMBOL has the attributes CHAR(60) VARYING. If a symbol is more than 60 characters long, it may be split into two or more symbols without giving any error message.

Let us assume that a CHAR VARYING variable named CARD will always contain that part of the input that has been read but not yet "processed". Initially, then, we have CARD = ''. The process of getting the next symbol into SYMBOL consists of deleting blanks preceding the next symbol in the input, finding the end of the symbol, moving it to SYMBOL, and finally, deleting the symbol from CARD. Thus we write down the following algorithm:

    S1: Delete blanks preceding the first nonblank in CARD
          and the rest of the input;
    S2: Find the first blank in CARD and the input;
    S3: Put the symbol into SYMBOL;
    S4: Delete the symbol from CARD;

Step 1.   Refinement of S1, Deleting the Blanks

There are two difficulties with S1. First, CARD may contain nothing but blanks, and secondly it might even contain nothing (as it does the first time this segment is executed). Either case should cause us to read in more input. The following program segment serves the purpose:

```
/* DELETE BLANKS BEFORE SYMBOL */
  /* SET I TO POSITION OF FIRST NONBLANK */
     FIND_LOOP: DO WHILE ('1'B);
       /* SEARCH CARD AND TERMINATE IF NONBLANK FOUND */
          SEARCH_LOOP: DO I = 1 TO LENGTH(CARD) BY 1;
             IF SUBSTR(CARD,I,1) ¬= ' ' THEN GO TO TERM_NONB;
             END SEARCH_LOOP;
          GET EDIT(CARD) (A(80));
          END FIND_LOOP;
     TERM_NONB:;

  /* DELETE THE BLANKS IN POSITIONS 1:I-1*/
     CARD = SUBSTR(CARD,I);
```

Step 2.   Refinement of S2, Finding the End of the Symbol

The only difficulty with S2 is that the symbol may be split on two cards. We must also watch out for the length of the symbol. We should stop when the length is 60. The program uses a CHAR(80) variable named CARD1 as a temporary location to hold a card just read.

```
/* SET I TO POINT TO CHAR AFTER SYMBOL */
  SETI_LOOP: DO I = 1 TO 60 BY 1;
    IF I > LENGTH(CARD) THEN DO;
      GET EDIT(CARD1) (A(80));
      CARD = CARD || CARD1; END;
    IF SUBSTR(CARD,I,1) = ' ' THEN GO TO TERM_SETI;
    END SETI_LOOP;
  TERM_SETI:;
```

Step 3. The Final Program

Statements S3 and S4 of the original algorithm are simple statements, so the development is finished. We assemble the various segments below, adding the necessary declarations. This is given not as a complete program, but as a segment to be included in a program that will use the symbols produced by this segment.

```
    ...
    DECLARE CARD CHAR(139) VARYING, /* CONTAINS INPUT READ */
                                    /* BUT NOT YET PROCESSED*/
            CARD1 CHAR(80),          /* USED TO READ IN A CARD*/
            SYMBOL CHAR(60) VARYING,/* HOLDS OUTPUT SYMBOL*/
            I FIXED DECIMAL;
    ...

/* SET SYMBOL TO NEXT SYMBOL OF INPUT */
  SYMSCAN: DO;
    /* DELETE BLANKS BEFORE SYMBOL */
      /* SET I TO POSITION OF FIRST NONBLANK */
        FIND_LOOP: DO WHILE ('1'B);
          /* SEARCH CARD AND TERMINATE IF NONBLANK FOUND */
            SEARCH_LOOP: DO I = 1 TO LENGTH(CARD) BY 1;
              IF SUBSTR(CARD,I,1) ¬= ' ' THEN GO TO TERM_NONB;
              END SEARCH_LOOP;
          GET EDIT(CARD) (A(80));
          END FIND_LOOP;
        TERM_NONB:;
    /* DELETE THE BLANKS IN POSITIONS 1:I-1 */
        CARD = SUBSTR(CARD,I);

    /* SET I TO POINT TO CHAR AFTER SYMBOL */
        SETI_LOOP: DO I = 1 TO 60 BY 1;
          IF I > LENGTH(CARD) THEN DO;
            GET EDIT(CARD1) (A(80));
            CARD = CARD || CARD1; END;
          IF SUBSTR(CARD,I,1) = ' ' THEN GO TO TERM_SETI;
          END SETI_LOOP;
        TERM_SETI:;

    SYMBOL = SUBSTR(CARD,1,I-1);
    CARD = SUBSTR(CARD,I);
    END SYMSCAN;
```

2.6 Interactive Computing Systems

The distinctive characteristic of an "interactive" computing system is, as the name implies, the opportunity for the user to interact with the program during its execution. He does this by supplying data to be read by the GET statements as they are executed in the program. The key point is that he does not have to supply all the data at once and in advance of execution. Up to this point we have been describing computer systems where the data are prepared and submitted as a unit with the program for processing. When processing is completed all of the output is returned in one batch to the user. These are often called "batch" processing systems.

Now we are talking about a system in which the user employs a "terminal" -- usually a device like an electric typewriter, although sometimes equippped with a TV-like screen on which characters are displayed rather than a printing mechanism. The terminal is connected directly to the computer while the program is being executed. Execution output -- the result of executing PUT statements -- appears on the terminal, and the data requested by the execution of GET statements is entered from the terminal. The crucial point is that the input and output are interleaved on this same device, corresponding to the order in which GETs and PUTs are encountered in execution of the program. This means that the data are not entered all at once, but just as needed for each execution of a GET statement. In deciding what data to supply in response to a particular request the user has before him all of the execution output produced up to that point in the program. The user interacts with the program by examining output and deciding on the basis of this information what data to supply in response to the next request. This in turn may influence the next output to appear, which affects future input, etc.

This mode of operation opens up some interesting new possibilities. The user and the program can cooperate or they can compete. For example, a problem could be attacked by a "trial and error" strategy in which the user supplies a trial value and the program obtains a solution based on this estimate and reports it to the terminal. The user then supplies the next trial value based somehow on the results of the previous trials. If the user can precisely describe the algorithm by which new trial values are determined from previous results then it can be incorporated into the program and the entire process can be run in the conventional batch mode. But there are some problems where the selection of new trial values is largely intuitive and the user cannot readily reduce his thought process to an algorithm. An interactive system allows some part of the process to remain intuitive while part is described algorithmically in the program. If done cleverly this makes it possible to combine the best features of human intelligence and computer processing, and allows an attack on problems that are not susceptible to a completely intuitive or completely algorithmic approach.

Another opportunity arises in programs in which the user is the adversary of the program. These are called "game-playing" problems, although the objective may in fact be serious business rather than pure entertainment. In such programs the user makes a "move" and describes it in input data to the program. The program operates on these data to determine its own "move", and reports this to the user. The program is usually performing two roles. It implements the mechanics of operating the game, as well as the implementation of the strategy of the opponent. (The user must trust that these roles are fairly separated and that his automated opponent is not in programmed collusion with the referee.)

In principal, an interactive system could be used for any problem a batch system could execute, in addition to those interactive problems for which it is uniquely qualified. However, interactive execution is generally more costly than batch execution, and the terminal is a relatively slow device for input and output. Hence programs with voluminous input and/or output may be painfully slow on an interactive system, and it may be somewhat extravagant to use an interactive system where its unique capabilities are not required. This issue is the subject of impassioned argument, with the apostles of interaction maintaining that a good, flexible interactive system is uniformly preferable and that eventually all computing will be done in this mode. Their arguments are quite persuasive.

2.6.1 Development of an Interactive Program

The development of a program to be used on an interactive system is not markedly different from that of a batch program. At the initial or highest levels of development one should essentially regard the user as part of the computing system, and his actions as part of the "program". For example, suppose we were developing a program to play a two-person game, such as Checkers. Our intention is to have the program represent one player, and keep track of the progress of the game, while a human user at a terminal represents the other player. The high-level comment outline for such a Checker-playing program might be something like the following:

```
/* PLAY CHECKERS */
    /* INITIALIZATION */
        /* OPTIONAL INSTRUCTIONS */
            /* RULES OF CHECKERS */
            /* CONVENTIONS OF THIS GAME */
        /* INITIALIZE BOARD */
        /* DETERMINE WHO PLAYS FIRST */
    /* PLAY GAME: ALTERNATE MOVES -- USER & PROG */
        /* DETERMINE MOVE */
        /* UPDATE BOARD STATUS */
        /* CHECK FOR TERMINATION */
    /* REPORT OUTCOME */
```

At this level the tasks are described in the same way --
regardless of whether they involve the user, the program or
both. But as these tasks are further refined, the interactive
nature of the process becomes apparent. Some tasks, such as
"INITIALIZE BOARD", for example, are conventional programming
tasks just like our previous examples, and they would be
developed and programmed in the same way. But some tasks, like
"OPTIONAL INSTRUCTIONS", would involve some interaction with the
user at the terminal. This task would probably be refined into
something like the following:

```
/* OPTIONAL INSTRUCTIONS */
    PUT SKIP LIST
        ('DO YOU WANT INSTRUCTIONS?',
         '''YES'' OR ''NO''');
    GET LIST(ANSWER);
    IF ANSWER = 'YES' THEN DO;
        /* RULES OF CHECKERS */
            PUT SKIP LIST(...
```

(Recall that to print a quote two consecutive quotes must be
given in the literal.) The "DETERMINE WHO PLAYS FIRST" task
would similarly be refined to a user-program dialog.

The "DETERMINE MOVE" task would be something like the
following:

```
/* DETERMINE MOVE */
    IF NEXT_MOVE = 'USER'
        THEN DO;
            /* GET USER MOVE */
            NEXT_MOVE = 'PROG'; END;
        ELSE DO;
            /* DETERMINE PROGRAM MOVE */
            NEXT_MOVE = 'USER'; END;
```

The refinement of "GET USER MOVE" would be a dialog with the
user at the terminal; the "DETERMINE PROGRAM MOVE" would be an
exceedingly complex (but non-interactive) program.

2.6.2 Programming for an Interactive System

The principal differences in programming technique
appropriate for an interactive system are concerned with
obtaining input from the terminal. There are two key issues:
prompting and persistence in the face of errors.

Prompting is the process of providing instructions to the
user at each point that input is required. Each GET in an
interactive program will ordinarily be immediately preceded by a
PUT which displays at the terminal sufficient instructions to
tell the user what is expected of him. This is unique to an
interactive system since in a batch system nothing printed by a

particular execution of a program can be seen by the user in
time to be of any help to him in preparing input. Once you
understand the opportunity to prompt, and the need for it, it is
not difficult to compose appropriate messages. However, unless
your system uses a display screen you must remember that these
messages will be printed on a printer that is painfully slow.
It takes practice to develop skill in composing messages that
are concise without being cryptic.

   Long descriptive messages that are initially very helpful to
the user will eventually become unnecessary, and finally become
very annoying. It is often desirable to have several levels of
prompting and to be able to switch to an abbreviated form as
execution continues. For example, our Checker-playing program
might initially prompt the user:

>   ENTER YOUR MOVE ON THE TERMINAL. GIVE RANK AND FILE
>   OF PIECE TO BE MOVED, AND THEN RANK AND FILE WHERE IT
>   IS TO BE MOVED. THAT IS, GIVE MOVE AS 4 INTEGERS.

After the first move this could be reduced to:

>   YOUR MOVE.

   An interactive program has the same responsibility as a batch
program for testing its input for errors, but the interactive
program can respond to errors in a very different way. Since
the batch program cannot communicate with the user until after
execution is completed it has only two options when an error is
encountered: either abort execution, or effect some form of
repair so execution can continue. The interactive program has
the additional possibility of going back to the user and asking
him to try again. This is so much more effective than either of
the batch strategies that it is almost always used. The
interactive program should persistently return to the user until
it elicits the required input. For example, in Section 2.6.1
there was a subtask concerning instructions. This should
actually be programmed as follows:

```
/* OPTIONAL INSTRUCTIONS */
    PUT SKIP LIST('DO YOU WANT INSTRUCTIONS?');
    ANSWER = ' ';
    ANSWER_LOOP: DO WHILE((ANSWER ¬= 'YES') |
                          (ANSWER ¬= 'NO'));
        PUT LIST('ANSWER ''YES'' OR ''NO''');
        GET LIST(ANSWER);
        END ANSWER_LOOP;
    IF ANSWER = 'YES' THEN DO;
        /* RULES OF CHECKERS */
            PUT SKIP LIST(...
```

This segment simply will not terminate until a valid datum -- in
this case either 'YES' or 'NO' -- is obtained from the terminal.

A segment such as this should be the standard technique for every request for input in an interactive system -- that is, a prompting message followed by a persistent loop that will not terminate until an acceptable response has been obtained.

A more sophisticated version of this approach would be to produce more detailed information as the user shows less ability to provide reasonable answers. A very short prompting message would be used initially, with provision for additional and more detailed information to be printed if the user does not respond successfully on his first try. Some interactive programs are written so they will accept some word such as "help" as input to any request -- and the program responds by describing what the user's options are at that point.

2.6.3 A Game-Playing Program

We will illustrate a complete program for an interactive system using a simple variation of a venerable game called NIM. This variation is just complex enough to be interesting, yet is simple enough to describe and program.

We call the game "Match-Snatch". There are two players. Our program will represent one player and the user at the terminal will be the other player, but we will initially describe the game as it would be played by two people.

Some number of matchsticks are placed in a pile between the two players. A "move" is for a player to remove some number of matches from those remaining in the pile. To be a valid move, he must take at least one match, and not more than some number agreed upon as a move-limit before the game begins. The players alternate moves and the object of the game is to avoid being the player who has to take the last match. (Obviously, without the move-limit the game would be trivial since faced with a pile of n matches the first player would immediately take n-1 and the second player would lose on his first move.) A typical game might start with a pile of fifteen matches and have a move-limit of three. In the computer version of Match-Snatch there will, of course, not actually be any physical pile of matches. A variable, say MATCHES, will represent the number of matches in the imagined pile. The removal of matches from the pile will be simulated by announcing an integer representing the number to be removed. This number will be subtracted from MATCHES and the game will terminate when the value of MATCHES becomes zero.

There is an algorithm for playing this game which will allow the first player to assure himself victory if he unfailingly follows the algorithm. If he lapses on even one move, then this same algorithm becomes available to his opponent and allows him to guarantee victory -- if he is more careful. It is not difficult to discover what this algorithm is. Suppose the move-limit is k matches. If you can take enough matches to leave just one in the pile your opponent will lose on his next move. So obviously, if the pile presented to you on some move contains n matches, where 2 <= n <= k+1, you will simply take n-1 matches and leave your opponent with 1. But if n > k+1 it is not that simple since you cannot take enough matches to leave only 1. However, if you manage to leave k+2 matches in the pile after your move, no matter how many matches your opponent takes in his next move he cannot leave you with 1, and you will be able to leave him with 1 on your next move. By repeating this reasoning, you will discover that if you leave 2k+3 matches after some move you will surely be able to leave k+2 after the next move and leave 1 on the move after that. In general, if you can arrange to leave m(k+1)+1 matches in the pile after your move, for m=0,1,2,..., you will be able to win the game in m more moves. But if you ever fail to leave m(k+1)+1 matches after your move then your opponent can move to leave you m(k+1)+1 and he is in the driver's seat unless he gets careless (or unless he doesn't understand the game).

Our Match-Snatch program uses this algorithm for the computer's moves, so that if the user grants the computer the first move the user will always lose (unless the user has been clever and chosen initial values for the number of matches and the move-limit so that the number of matches is m(k+1)+1 when the program makes its first move.) If the user claims the first move he <u>can</u> win, but if he slips up just once the computer will seize the opportunity and win.

In addition to acting as one player the Match-Snatch program also operates the game. It negotiates the initial conditions with the user, keeps track of the number of matches and announces the outcome. A high-level comment outline would look very much like that of the Checker program in Section 2.6.1:

```
/* MATCH-SNATCH GAME */
    /* INITIALIZATION */
        /* GET GAME PARAMETERS */
        /* DETERMINE WHO MOVES FIRST */
    /* ALTERNATE MOVES -- USER & PROGRAM */
    /* REPORT OUTCOME */
```

A complete program to play Match-Snatch on an interactive system is given below.

```
*PL/C ID='CHARLES MOORE'
 /* MATCH-SNATCH GAME */
 MATCH_SNATCH: PROCEDURE OPTIONS(MAIN);
     DCL MATCHES FIXED DEC, /* NUMBER OF MATCHES LEFT */
         MOVE_LIMIT FIXED DEC, /* LIMIT ON EACH MOVE */
         WHOSE_MOVE CHAR(3), /* 'YOU'=PROG; 'ME'=USER */
         MOVE FIXED DEC; /* CURRENT MOVE */
     /* INITIALIZATION */
         /* GET GAME PARAMETERS */
             PUT SKIP LIST('WELCOME TO MATCH-SNATCH');
             PUT SKIP;
             MATCHES = 0;
             PILE_LOOP: DO WHILE(MATCHES < 1);
                 PUT SKIP LIST
                     ('HOW MANY MATCHES TO START?');
                 GET LIST(MATCHES);
                 IF MATCHES < 1 THEN PUT SKIP LIST
                     ('MUST BE AT LEAST 1');
                 END PILE_LOOP;
             MOVE_LIMIT = 0;
             LIMIT_LOOP: DO WHILE((MOVE_LIMIT < 2) |
                                    (MOVE_LIMIT > MATCHES));
                 PUT SKIP LIST
                     ('HOW MANY IN 1 MOVE?');
                 GET LIST(MOVE_LIMIT);
                 IF MOVE_LIMIT < 1 THEN PUT SKIP LIST
                     ('MUST BE AT LEAST 1');
                 IF MOVE_LIMIT > MATCHES THEN PUT SKIP
                     LIST('NOT THAT MANY MATCHES');
                 END LIMIT_LOOP;
         /* DETERMINE WHO MOVES FIRST */
             WHOSE_MOVE = ' ';
             FIRST_LOOP: DO WHILE((WHOSE_MOVE ¬= 'ME') &
                                    (WHOSE_MOVE ¬= 'YOU'));
                 PUT SKIP LIST
                     ('WHO MOVES FIRST?',
                     '''YOU'' OR ''ME''');
                 GET LIST(WHOSE_MOVE);
                 END FIRST_LOOP;
             PUT SKIP;
```

```
      /* ALTERNATE MOVES -- USER & PROGRAM */
          MOVE_LOOP: DO WHILE(MATCHES > 0);
            IF WHOSE_MOVE = 'ME'
             THEN DO; /* USER'S MOVE */
               MOVE = 0;
               USER_LOOP: DO WHILE((MOVE < 1) |
                                   (MOVE > MATCHES) |
                                   ((MOVE > MOVE_LIMIT));
                  PUT SKIP LIST
                     ('HOW MANY DO YOU TAKE?');
                  GET LIST(MOVE);
                  IF MOVE < 1 THEN PUT SKIP LIST
                     ('MUST TAKE AT LEAST 1');
                  IF MOVE > MOVE_LIMIT THEN PUT SKIP LIST
                     ('THAT''S MORE THAN WE AGREED ON');
                  IF MOVE > MATCHES THEN PUT SKIP LIST
                     ('THERE AREN''T THAT MANY');
                  END USER_LOOP;
               MATCHES = MATCHES - MOVE;
               PUT SKIP LIST('THERE ARE', MATCHES, 'LEFT');
               WHOSE_MOVE = 'YOU'; END;
             ELSE DO; /* PROGRAM'S MOVE */
               MOVE = MOD(MATCHES -1, MOVE_LIMIT + 1);
               IF MOVE = 0 THEN MOVE = 1;
               PUT SKIP LIST('I TAKE', MOVE, 'MATCHES');
               MATCHES = MATCHES - MOVE;
               PUT SKIP LIST('THERE ARE', MATCHES, 'LEFT');
               WHOSE_MOVE = 'ME'; END;
            END MOVE_LOOP;
   /* REPORT OUTCOME */
            /* PLAYER WHO MADE LAST MOVE LOST */
        IF WHOSE_MOVE = 'ME'
            THEN PUT SKIP(2) LIST
                 ('YOU WON, NICE GOING.');
            ELSE PUT SKIP(2) LIST
                 ('I WON, TOUGH LUCK.');
   END MATCH_SNATCH;
*DATA
```

If a game of Match-Snatch were played by executing this program on an interactive system the output would look roughly like the lines shown below. We have indented the lines that represent input from the terminal to distinguish them from lines of output printed by the program. We have also slightly modified the format of some of the output lines relative to what would actually be produced by the program as given above.

```
WELCOME TO MATCH-SNATCH

HOW MANY MATCHES TO START?
    10
HOW MANY IN 1 MOVE?
    0
MUST BE AT LEAST 1
HOW MANY IN 1 MOVE?
    15
NOT THAT MANY MATCHES
HOW MANY IN 1 MOVE?
    4
WHO MOVES FIRST?   'YOU' OR 'ME'
    'I DO'
WHO MOVES FIRST?   'YOU' OR 'ME'
    'ME'

HOW MANY DO YOU TAKE?
    9
THAT'S MORE THAN WE AGREED ON
HOW MANY DO YOU TAKE?
    2
THERE ARE 8 LEFT
I TAKE 2 MATCHES
THERE ARE 6 LEFT
HOW MANY DO YOU TAKE?
    2
THERE ARE 4 LEFT
I TAKE 3 MATCHES
THERE ARE 1 LEFT
HOW MANY DO YOU TAKE?
    0
MUST TAKE AT LEAST 1
HOW MANY DO YOU TAKE?
    2
THERE AREN'T THAT MANY
HOW MANY DO YOU TAKE?
    1

I WON, TOUGH LUCK.
```

Section 2 Exercises

Exercises 1 to 8 refer to the accounting problem of Section 2.4.

1. Why is ACCT declared as ACCT(0:201) instead of ACCT(0:200)?

2. For each of the 6 errors discussed in the first part of
Section 2.4, indicate whether the program should stop or whether
it may be reasonable to continue.

3. Change the program to consider these 6 errors. These changes
should not be made by trying to revise the final program.
Instead, go back to the proper step (3, 4, or 5) and perform the
complete analysis and program creation once more, this time with
the view of checking and documenting possible input errors.

4. Suppose the signal ending the accounts is a single 0 instead
of two 0's. Change the program to reflect this. In making the
changes, repeat the program analysis and development from the
beginning; don't attempt to just change the final program.
Which signal is better and why?

5. Suppose we wish to change the end-of-transaction signal to a
single 0 instead of three. Change the program to reflect this.

6. Below are several problem statements. For each, develop an
algorithm in English to solve it. This algorithm should contain
no details about arrays used, variables used, etc. It should be
only the first step toward a final program -- on the same level
of detail as algorithm (2.4a). Note that the problem statements
do not in fact give you exact details about the input. Compare
your algorithms with each other and with (2.4a).   Relate your
algorithms to the program schemata of Section II.2.

   a) The input consists of two lists X and Y of numbers.
   Print out the number of times each number in list Y occurs
   in the first list X.

   b) The input consists of a list of bank accounts and
   transactions concerning these accounts.   Print out the
   number of transactions for each account.

   c) The input consists of the text of a book, punched on
   cards, followed by a list of words. Print out the number
   of times each word on the list is used in the book.

   d) The input consists of a list of student records (name,
   address, grades in each course, etc.), followed by a list
   of a few student names. Find and print out the average,
   highest, and lowest grade point average for the students
   given in the second list.

7. In developing subalgorithm (2.4e), one problem was preventing
the "Process transaction just read" statement from being
executed if the transaction just read was the end-of-list

signal.   Is there another way to write the loop without adding
conditional statements?   If you produce a different version,
with or without conditional statements or GO TOs, is it more
efficient? Easier to understand? Easier to modify?

8. Suppose the account numbers were limited to three digits.
Can you think of a way to sort the accounts efficiently? What
modifications would you have to make in the program?   What are
the relative merits of your solution and the one developed here
in terms of time and space?

9. Below are several problem statements. For each, develop an
algorithm, which shows the overall structure of the final
program. Your algorithm should probably be along the lines of
algorithm (2.4e).
    a) The input consists of a list of integers. Print out all
    those integers which are even.
    b) The input consists of a list of integers.   Print out
    those integers which are prime. (An integer is prime if it
    is greater than 1 and evenly divisible only by 1 and
    itself.   The integers 2, 3, 5, 7, 11, 59 are prime; the
    integers -2, 0, 1, 4, 9, 100 are not.)
    c) The input consists of a list of names of people.   Print
    out all the names that contain the letter A.

10.   "Comment outlines" for the top level of development of
several programs are given below.   Complete the programs by
adding the actual PL/I statements that will perform what is
specified by the heading comments. The problem requirements
given in these comments are sketchy; assume whatever detail is
necessary to write the programs. Document all such assumptions.

10a.   /* DETERMINE POSITIVE ROW AVERAGES, AND NBR ZEROS */
      POSROW: PROCEDURE OPTIONS(MAIN);
          DCL TAB(10,10) FLOAT DEC, /* GIVEN ARRAY IS */
              (NR, NC) FIXED DEC; /* TAB(1:NR,1:NC) */
          DCL (SUM(10),AVG(10)) FLOAT DEC;
                /* SUM(1:NR) ARE ROW SUMS OF TAB */
                /* AVG(1:NR) ARE ROW AVERAGES OF TAB */
          DCL ZEROS(10) FIXED DEC;
                /* ZEROS(1:NR) ARE NBR OF ZEROS IN ROWS */
          DCL (I,J) FIXED DEC;

          /* READ AND TEST: NR AND NC */

          /* LOAD TAB IN ROW MAJOR ORDER */

          /* REPLACE NEGATIVE ENTRIES WITH 0, AND */
          /* COUNT ALL ZEROS IN EACH ROW */

          /* COMPUTE ROW AVERAGES FOR NON-ZERO ENTRIES */

          /* DISPLAY AVG AND NBR ZEROS FOR EACH ROW */

          END POSROW;

10b. /* READ 7X9 ARRAY, INVERT ODD ROWS, */
      /* FIND COLUMN MAXIMA, AND DISPLAY */
      INVMAX: PROCEDURE OPTIONS(MAIN);
          DCL TAB(7,9) FLOAT DEC;
          DCL COLMAX(9) FLOAT DEC; /* COLUMN MAXIMA */
          DCL (I,J) FIXED DEC;

          /* LOAD ARRAY (ROW MAJOR ORDER) */

          /* REVERSE ORDER OF ELEMENTS IN ODD-NUMBERED ROWS */

          /* FIND MAXIMUM VALUE IN EACH COLUMN */

          /* DISPLAY COLUMN MAXIMA */

          END INVMAX;

10c. /* REVERSE STRINGS AND TEST FOR "A" BEFORE "B" */
      REVTEST: PROCEDURE OPTIONS(MAIN);
          DCL STR(50) CHAR(20), /* TABLE OF STRINGS IS: */
              N FIXED DEC, /* STR(1:N) */
              L FIXED DEC; /* L CHARS IN EACH STR */
          DCL (I,J) FIXED DEC;

          /* READ NBR AND LENGTH OF STRINGS FROM INITIAL DATA */

          /* LOAD ARRAY OF STRINGS */

          /* INVERT EACH STRING, */
          /* CHARACTER BY CHARACTER, END FOR END */

          /* PRINT A LIST OF INVERTED STRINGS IN WHICH AN "A" */
          /* APPEARS TO THE LEFT OF THE FIRST "B" */

          END REVTEST;

10d. /* ROTATE SQUARE ARRAY QUARTER-TURN CLOCKWISE */
      ROTATE: PROCEDURE OPTIONS(MAIN);
          DCL (AR(40,40),AR2(40,40)) FLOAT DEC, /* ARRAYS ARE */
              N FIXED DEC; /* AR(N,N), AR2(N,N) */
          DCL (I,J) FIXED DEC;

          /* READ NBR OF ROWS, AND LOAD AR BY ROWS */

          /* COPY EACH COLUMN OF AR, LEFT TO RIGHT, */
          /* INTO ROW OF AR2, TOP TO BOTTOM */

          /* DISPLAY ROTATED ARRAY AR2 BY ROWS, TOP TO BOTTOM*/

          END ROTATE;

11. For each of the following problems, develop a program to
the point of having a "comment outline", such as those
illustrated in Exercise 10.

11a. Given a list of non-zero numbers (with zero added to the
end as a stopping flag) determine which numbers in the list are
not unique (that is, which appear more than once).   The list may
be long but it will not contain more than 40 different numbers.

11b. Given a list of not more than 100 non-negative numbers
(with -1 added as a stopping flag) either:

> 1. print a list of the numbers which are greater than the
> final value on the list and which are not repeated in the
> list, or
> 2. print a list of the numbers which are greater than the
> average of all the numbers on the original list.

Do 1 if there are more numbers on the list greater than the
first value, than there are numbers less than the first value;
otherwise do 2.   There will be at least one value given.   That
is, the -1 stopping flag will not be the first value given.

11c. Given three lists of numbers, each n numbers long, produce
another list called the "merged list" with the following
properties:

> 1.   It contains all the non-zero values from the 3 lists.
> 2. Values on the merged list are in the same order they
> appeared in the given lists.
> 3.   If a value was in position i in one of the given lists,
> it will appear in the merged list before any number that
> was in a position later than i in any one of the given
> lists.

The 3 given lists are preceded by an integer n (less than 50)
specifying the length of each of the 3 given lists.   Print the
merged list first, 3 values per line.   Then print the given
lists in 3 column format.   For example, if the data are:

    4,   7,0,3,9,   0,4,5,0,   1,2,0,0

the output would be:

    MERGED LIST
        7   1   4
        2   3   5
        9

    GIVEN LISTS
        7   0   1
        0   4   2
        3   5   0
        9   0   0

12. Rewrite the following program so that it has the same
function but is properly structured and well-presented with
appropriate labels, comments and indentation.

```
TEST: PROCEDURE OPTIONS(MAIN);
DCL (J,N,K) FIXED DEC;
DCL LIM FLOAT DEC;
GET LIST(J,N,K,LIM);
J = 1;
LOOP: IF J = N+1 THEN GO TO BODY;
J = 1;
LOOP2: IF J = K THEN GO TO OUT;
IF X(J) < LIM THEN PUT SKIP LIST(J, X(J));
J = J+1;
GO TO LOOP2;
DCL X(50) FLOAT DEC;
BODY: GET LIST(X(J));
X(J) = X(J) + J;
J = J+1;
GO TO LOOP;
OUT: END TEST;
```

13. The game of NIM is similar to the Match-Snatch game
described in Section 2.6.3. The differences are that there are
several piles of matches in NIM instead of one, and in each move
a player may take as many matches as he wishes (but at least
one) but only from one pile. The object of NIM may be either to
take the last match, or to avoid having to take the last match,
at the option of the players and decided upon in advance.

Write an interactive program to play NIM. The parameters of
the game are

1. How many piles there are;
2. How many matches there are in each pile;
3. Whether the winner takes the last match, or avoids
   doing so;
4. Who plays first.

As for Match-Snatch there is an algorithm for playing NIM
such that the player to go first can win under all but some very
special conditions. However it is not a trivial exercise to
determine this algorithm. But even without an "optimal"
algorithm you should be able to write a program that will be a
"good" NIM player. In fact, if several students write NIM-
playing programs, you could have a "NIM tournament"! This is
actually done with programs that play Chess. Every year there
is a tournament among the World's Chess-playing programs. Some
of the programs play good Chess but so far they can all be
beaten by any really excellent human Chess player.

Section 3   General Design Considerations

The preceding sections have described the basic idea of program development in several different ways:

1. Break a problem into a sequence of sub-problems.

2. Refine a statement into several finer statements with increasing detail.

3. Expand a statement of <u>what</u> has to be done into a specification of <u>how</u> it is to be done.

4. Expand "high-level" commands such as "solve", "find" or "compute" into lower-level statements of a programming language.

5. Translate a problem description from English to PL/I.

These are different aspects of the same general process: the systematic transformation of a <u>statement of requirements in English</u> to a <u>detailed specification of actions in PL/I</u>.

We outlined the phases of the process in Section 1 and gave examples in Section 2. In Section 3 we review the process and describe several of the key issues in more detail.

3.1 <u>Top-Down Development</u>

In general, development decisions should be made in "outside-in", "top-down" order -- in order of increasing detail. In the accounting problem of 2.4, initially there were a number of questions that could have been raised and answered -- how accounts should be stored, how the transactions should be processed, how the transactions should be stored, etc. Out of all these, we chose the one which helped determine the overall structure and which led to a correct program with just more detail: what were the main subproblems and in which order should they be executed?

This is not to say that your thoughts shouldn't skip to various parts of the program in varying amounts of detail. (They will whether you want them to or not.) There is nothing wrong in beginning by looking at various possibilities for the representation of data and subalgorithms to process them.

Sometimes this is necessary in order to obtain a better
understanding of the problem and possible solutions. Sometimes
this is necessary in order to come up with any idea at all. But
this should just be considered a side trip. Any ideas
discovered on it should <u>not</u> be accepted as final, and the main
program development should then proceed <u>top-down</u>. It may be
necessary to develop several alternatives to some depth before
it is clear which one is best.

   This top-down process is not as easy and straightforward as
it may seem from the examples given in Section 2. Programming,
like any problem solving, is a trial and error process.
Mistakes will be made, or just the wrong avenue explored, which
will cause the programmer to undo several levels of refinements
(discarding several parts of the tree) and to repeat the process
in a different manner. This "backing up" is discussed in more
detail in Section 3.1.3.

   Programming in top-down fashion may seem foreign and
difficult, especially to beginners. Yet for most problems it is
the best approach, because it will lead to efficient,
understandable, and correct programs. Attempt right from the
beginning to develop programs in a top-down, outside-in, general
statement to fine detail, manner.

   In programming in this fashion we attempt to make <u>one</u> clear
decision at a time. A decision leads to a refinement of part of
the program. The two types of refinement are:

   1. A statement is refined.

   2. The method of storing data is refined, by describing
       the variables used to store the data.

We discuss these separately in the next two subsections.

3.1.1 <u>Refining a Statement</u>

<u>Concentrating on "What" rather than "How"</u>

   One of the advantages of top-down programming is that it
helps us concentrate initially on <u>what</u> is to be done, and then
systematically becomes concerned with <u>how</u>. For example, in
developing the overall structure of the accounting problem in
2.4, we refined "Solve the problem" into algorithm (2.4a):

              Read in and set up the accounts;
              Read in and process the transactions;
              Print the results;

Here, we were not <u>primarily</u> interested in <u>how</u> the accounts and
transactions were to be stored or processed, but only in <u>what</u>
was to be done, so that we could concentrate on the order in

which the various functions were to be performed.

   As another example, consider the sorting problem of 2.3.
Sorting is refined in terms of

        "move the maximum element to the end of the list".

This states what is to be done, but not how.   There are   several
methods that could be used.   "Move..." is refined into

        "find the position of the maximum"
        "interchange maximum and last".

This suggests what could be done to accomplish "move..." without
specifying   how   either   "find..." or   "interchange..." will   be
performed.

Limiting Ourselves to Understandable Refinements

   When refining a statement we replace a statement of what to
do by an algorithm which indicates how to do it.   In making such
a refinement it is important to limit ourselves to refinements
we can easily understand, and which we can easily communicate to
others.

   Given a statement, what possibilities exist?   The most
general possibility is a sequence of statements to be executed
in order.   Thus we should attempt to break the original
statement into successive parts to be executed in order.   Other
possibilities for a refinement are:

   1.   Use a conditional statement to break the problem into
        two subcases.

   2.   Break it into several (instead of two) subcases.

   3.   Replace it by a loop (perhaps with initialization
        statements).

Faced with these limited possibilities for refining a statement,
we can focus attention on the following questions:

   1.   How can it be broken up into successive parts?

   2.   Does it break up easily into two or more subcases?

   3.   Is it an iteration problem -- can a loop be used?

These methods of refinement lead naturally to the program units
described in Section II.1.

   The symbol scanning problem of Section 2.5 is a good example.
Given an "unprocessed" string in CARD, we wanted to "process"
the left-most "symbol" of that string into SYMBOL.   We refined

this into a sequence of four steps:

    S1: Delete blanks preceding the first nonblank in CARD
        and the rest of the input;
    S2: Find the first blank in CARD and the input;
    S3: Put the symbol into SYMBOL;
    S4: Delete the symbol from CARD.

We now have four simpler problems to refine. The problems of no
word on a card or a word split onto two cards have been
postponed -- in fact, we didn't even have to mention them.

Using Suitable Notation for Statements

    Whatever language and notation suit the problem at hand
should be used in order to aid in an orderly development and to
make the final program as lucid as possible. Usually the
initial notation consists of English commands like "Sort the
list", "Process the transactions" and "Generate a value to ...".
Any imperative statement can be used, provided its meaning is
sufficiently clear.

    In particular, it is often convenient to invent control
mechanisms that do not exist in PL/I (and perhaps not in any
real programming language). One control mechanism we have been
using all the time is the "exit statement", which we have had to
write as a GO TO statement. As other examples, the meaning of
the following two algorithms should be clear without any formal
definition of how the "for each" statement is to be executed:

    For each account in the list
        IF the account balance $<$ 0 THEN Print a message.

    For each position of the chessboard
        IF the position is occupied by a white piece THEN DO;
                IF the white piece can capture the black king
                    THEN Print "check".
                IF the white piece can capture the black queen
                    THEN Print "watch out!".   END;

Using such statements helps postpone decisions about the order
in which the accounts or positions on the chessboard should be
processed. These can wait, and will probably depend on how the
list and chessboard are stored as variables. Once we decide on
an order, translating the "for each" loops into WHILE loops will
not be difficult.

    As another example, consider a program to simulate a baseball
game. We have variables which keep track of the inning, number
of outs, men on base, etc., and we have a way of generating an
integer PITCH to represent what happens next. A partial list of
the values of PITCH and the corresponding actions are given
below:

value of PITCH	action after pitch
1	ball
2	strike
3	foul ball
4	single
5	double
etc.	

We need a program section that will select one of these alternatives depending on the value of PITCH. This is the multiple alternative situation discussed in Section II.1.3.3 and it needs the "case statement" which, unfortunately, is lacking in PL/I. But this doesn't mean that we can't use some form of case statement as a convenient notation in our development. For example:

```
Do one of following, depending on value of PITCH:
    1: Process ball;
    2: Process strike;
    3: Process foul ball;
    4: Process single;
    5: Process double;
     etc.
```

Eventually this will have to be expressed in the statements actually available in the programming language being used (see (II.1.3.3a) and (II.1.3.3b)), but during development it is clearer to have it in the form shown here.

3.1.2 Refining a Data Description

Data refinements are just as important as statement refinements, but decisions about how to store the data should be postponed as long as possible, until no further statement refinements can be made without knowing more about the data structures used.

You will gradually learn that there are many different ways of keeping data in variables. For example, the list of accounts in Section 2.4 can be kept in unsorted form in an array, or sorted in ascending or descending order. There are also more sophisticated storage structures such as hash tables, singly linked lists, doubly linked lists, circular lists, dequeues, stacks and trees. Each method has advantages and disadvantages, depending on the nature and form of the operations to be performed. In order to intelligently choose a method for data representation, it is necessary to wait until the operations to be performed on the data are well understood.

The method of storing transactions in the bank problem is a good illustration. We could have initially decided to use an array, since there were many transactions. But waiting and later deciding based on what was to be done with the transactions led to the discovery that only <u>one</u> transaction had to be stored at any time.

Whenever you decide upon variables, <u>write down their names with their exact meanings immediately</u>. Don't wait until you write the declaration for them. Every variable is important (or else it shouldn't be in the program) and you <u>must</u> know exactly why it is there. Don't trust these exact meanings to your memory; write them down.

A recent incident will illustrate the importance of this. A student came in with a two-page program, the relevant parts of which are given in (3.1.2a). The program was a simplified "text editor"; it read text -- a sequence of words interspersed with symbols for commands like "begin a new line" and "begin a new paragraph" -- and printed out the text as formatted by the commands. Each output line was "right justified", which means that not only were the left margins lined up, but also the right margins. (Right justification is performed by inserting extra blanks between words, as in the lines you are now reading.)

There was obviously an error, since occasionally a blank at the end of a word was missing -- "the big black fox" might come out as "thebig black fox". The problem was found by <u>examining the exact role of the variables</u>. Looking at the program, it was surmised that OUTLINE would contain the current line to be written out and LENGTHLINE would contain its length. The student was asked what N meant, since its meaning was not written down. After some uncertainty he said "Oh, it's just the length of the word being added to the current line OUTLINE." ("It's just" is used often when one doesn't really know. It seems to belittle the variable, making it all right not to know exactly why it is there.)

The program was then examined to find if N was <u>always</u> assigned and used in this way. The error was exposed when it was discovered that in one place, N was the length of the word, while in the other it was the length plus one, to take into account the blank character following it.

```
         ...
         IF ...
                THEN DO; ...   WORD = SUBSTR(LINE,M,N);
                               WORD = WORD || " ';
                      ...             END;
(3.1.2a)        ELSE DO; ...   WORD = WORD || ' ';
                               N = LENGTH(WORD);
                      ...             END;
         ...
         LENGTHLINE = LENGTH(OUTLINE) + N;
         OUTLINE = ...
         ...
```

The importance of clearly understanding and having an exact written description of each variable cannot be overemphasized.

Using Suitable Notation for Data

We used notation outside PL/I in Section 2.4 during development of the accounting program, programming in terms of a "table of accounts" and a "transaction" as long as possible before describing how these quantities were to be represented in the PL/I program. In effect, we talked as if the whole table of accounts were contained as a value in a variable. Data can often be represented using variables in many ways, and it is important to talk in general terms about the "list" or the "records" until more is known about the operations to be performed on them.

Using high-level notation for data structures is just as important as for processing actions. However it is difficult to give good examples of this until you have more programming experience and are familiar with a variety of different data structures. We leave this discussion to another book.

3.1.3 Backing Up

Program development is a trial and error process. We make refinements and try some subalgorithms, and if they don't serve our purpose we redo them. Redoing one subalgorithm may require us to change other parts of the algorithm, both in data structures and in statements, and it is important that all these changes be made in a systematic way. This should usually be done by "backing up" to a previous level of the algorithm which the changes don't affect, and then proceeding to redo all the top-down refinements taking the changes into account.

For example, suppose a top-down analysis has produced the tree of refinements (3.1.3a), where each Si is a statement and the lines leading down from a statement represent a sequence of statements to be executed from left to right, to replace that statement. Now suppose while attempting to refine statement S19 that we discover a mistake, or recognize that a change in data structures designed earlier will make S19 more efficient. In order to make the change, we must back up to a point where the change has no effect. Suppose this is S2 (see tree (3.1.3b)). Then we must proceed downward again, redoing all refinements (in the example, S4-S7, S11-S15, S18 and S19) to make sure that every refinement leads to a correct program.

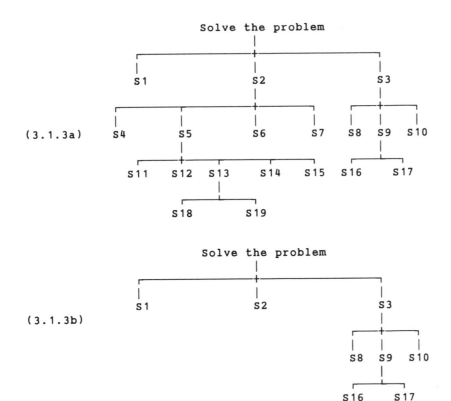

(3.1.3a)

(3.1.3b)

Backing up in this manner is extremely important if a correct program is desired. There is a limit to how much we can keep in our heads, and the only way to extend this limit is to keep things well organized on paper. The more complicated the program, the more important it is to back up systematically.

If instead of using such a systematic procedure, we just "looked around" and tried to figure out what to change, the chances are that we would miss at least one place to change or would change some segment incorrectly. Backing up with a tree as a guide indicates not only what has to be changed, but also what doesn't have to be changed. For example, in the above illustration, once we decide that the change affects only S2 and its refinements, we need not worry about changing anything else in the tree.

To illustrate this process on a real problem, consider again the sorting problem of 2.3. The algorithm used in (2.3e) is:

```
        /* SORT L(1:N) */
            SUBLIST_LOOP: DO M = N TO 2 BY -1;
(3.1.3c)            Find position of maximum in L(1:M);
                Interchange maximum and L(M);
                END SUBLIST_LOOP;
```

Now consider a different way of performing the same task. Instead of finding the largest value and then making one interchange at the end, compare successive values and interchange immediately if out of order:

```
          /* SWAP VALUES OF L(1:M) TO PUT LARGEST IN L(M)*/
               SWAP_LOOP: DO I = 2 TO M BY 1;
(3.1.3d)          IF L(I-1) > L(I) THEN Swap L(I-1) and L(I);
               END SWAP_LOOP;
```

This refinement has a property which may be of some use. Note that it looks at successive adjacent pairs of L(1:M) and swaps any pair that is out of order. If no swaps occur during an execution of this subalgorithm, then no adjacent pair is out of order and the array is already sorted. Hence, if no swaps occur the algorithm can be terminated.

How will we stop execution? We have a new idea now, but we must fit it in at the right program level. Part of the change must occur not only in (3.1.3d), but also in the higher level algorithm (3.1.3c) since it must terminate. Thus we should back up to the statement "Sort L(1:N)" and refine anew. This new refinement will be a modification of (3.1.3c).

Looking at (3.1.3c) we see that we now have _two_ stopping conditions:

1.   (M < 2), and

2.   "no swaps performed during one execution of the loop body".

We introduce a new variable SORTED which has the following meaning:

Whenever the condition of the main loop is evaluated, SORTED = 1 means the array is definitely known to be sorted, while SORTED = 0 means we aren't sure.

Now modify (3.1.3c) into (3.1.3e):

```
          /* SORT L(1:N) */
               SORTED = 0;
               M = N;
               BUBBLE_LOOP: DO WHILE ((SORTED = 0) & (M >= 2));
(3.1.3e)          Swap values of L(1:M) to put largest in L(M),
                    and also set SORTED as necessary;
               M = M - 1;
               END BUBBLE_LOOP;
```

Now proceed down again to the next level, redoing the English substatement:

```
    /* SWAP L(1:M) TO PUT LARGEST IN L(M) AND SET SORTED*/
       SORTED = 1;              /* ASSUME L(1:M) IS SORTED */
       SWAP_LOOP: DO I = 2 TO M BY 1;
          IF L(I-1) > L(I) THEN DO;
             Swap L(I-1) and L(I);
             SORTED = 0; END;
          END SWAP_LOOP;
```

This yields the final program known as bubble sort (presumably because it "bubbles" the largest value to the top of the list):

```
    /* SORT L(1:N) USING BUBBLE SORT ALGORITHM */
       SORTED = 0;
       M = N;
       BUBBLE_LOOP: DO WHILE ((SORTED = 0) & (M >= 2));
          /* SWAP L(1:M) TO PUT LARGEST IN L(M) AND SET SORTED*/
             SORTED = 1;              /* ASSUME IT IS SORTED*/
             SWAP_LOOP: DO I = 2 TO M BY 1;
                IF L(I-1) > L(I) THEN DO;
(3.1.3f)              T = L(I-1); L(I-1) = L(I); L(I) = T;
                   SORTED = 0;    END;
             END SWAP_LOOP;
       M = M - 1;
       END BUBBLE_LOOP;
```

The important point in the example is to note how we backed up to a higher program level in order to incorporate changes in a systematic manner. One can just look around and try to find all necessary places to change in a haphazard manner, but doing it in a systematic manner is actually easier and more reliable.

This systematic backing up process is particularly useful during testing. If an error is located during testing, it should be corrected by backing up as we have described here, and then proceeding down again, taking into account whatever changes are necessary. The discovery of an error during testing may well occur several days after that section of the program is written and your recollection may be less than perfect. Unless you proceed very systematically in the repair process there is a good chance you will introduce new errors while trying to eliminate old ones.

3.2 Sources of Ideas for Refinements

"How to invent something" is difficult to describe, and it is not clear that creativity can be effectively taught. Fortunately, the typical programmer is rarely asked to develop something radically different, and the type of creativity required is modest. Greater amounts of determination, logical thinking, hard work, attention to detail, and patience are involved. We attempt in this section to give some insight into how and where program ideas originate.

3.2.1 <u>Sources of Ideas for Algorithms</u>

A programmer has two main sources of ideas:

1. Programs previously written or studied;

2. Familiar algorithms from everyday life.

For the beginner, the first source is practically non-existent. One obvious way to expand this source is to read and study <u>good</u> programs written by others. Besides expanding the set of algorithms one has at his disposal, it helps teach and emphasize good style and programming practices. Surprisingly, studying other people's programs is not a common practice, even among professional programmers.

The second source of ideas is almost unlimited. Every day we use algorithms or see others use them. Often, of course, they are informal and not too well defined, and describing them precisely may be difficult. But the ideas are there.

The accounting problem is a good example of this. How did we know what to do? Perhaps we imagined what a clerk would do to manually perform this task. In order to write a program for it, we needed only to be able to write down an exact description of the process the clerk performs, taking into account the format of the input (which the clerk need not worry about) and the fact that all data must be stored in variables. The top-down method of development was used only to aid us in writing the algorithm correctly and precisely.

As a second example, suppose we have an array B(1:N) whose values are in ascending order. We want to find the position J of another variable X in the list. That is, search B for X and store in variable J an integer such that B(J) = X. If no such integer exists, store 0 in J. If the list were not sorted we would use a simple search as in 2.2:

```
        SEARCH_LOOP: DO J = 1 TO N BY 1;
            IF B(J) = X THEN GO TO TERM_SEARCH;
            END SEARCH_LOOP;
        J = 0;
        TERM_SEARCH:;
```

However, the additional information that B is sorted may permit a more efficient algorithm.

Everyday situations in which something is sought in an ordered list are numerous, and in general a more efficient search method is used. A good example is looking for a name in the telephone book. To find a name, say "Smith", we look at some entry in the book rather randomly, but as near to the S's as we can get. The entry serves to divide the book into two parts -- "before" the entry and "after" the entry. If this entry is less than Smith (alphabetically), then Smith is located in the second part, after the entry. So we "discard" the first part and repeat the process using only the last part. If the entry is greater than Smith, we discard the second part and repeat the process using the first part.

Thus we can repeat a process over and over until we find the desired entry or until we have discarded the whole list (in which case the desired value is not in the list). This repetition suggests the use of a WHILE loop, and after some work we arrive at the following algorithm:

```
Let the list to be searched be B(1:N);
SEARCH_LOOP: DO WHILE (list to be search is not empty);
   K = index of some entry B(K) still in list, near X;
   IF B(K) = X THEN DO;
      J = K;
      GO TO TERM_SEARCH; END;
   IF B(K) < X
      THEN discard first  half of list, including B(K);
      ELSE discard second half of list, including B(K);
   END SEARCH_LOOP;
J = 0; /* MEANS X IS NOT IN THE LIST */
TERM_SEARCH:;
```

The statement

        "K = index of some entry B(K) still in list, near X;"

is not precise enough. How do we compute "near"? To simplify this, let us just use

        K = index of middle entry of the list;

which is easier to compute. It may not be as good an algorithm as we use with the telephone book, but this change does make it easier to program. When searching the telephone book, we have common sense information which is not ordinarily available to the program. For example, we know there are lots of S's and T's, but few W's and X's. This certainly affects the way we perform the search. The main problem in developing a program based on our experiences is to be able to formalize how we do something, to ferret out the essential details.

This is the beginning of the development of a well-known algorithm called binary search. It is a vast improvement over the algorithm used in 2.2. For example, if there are 32,768 entries, the 2.2 algorithm may have to look at all the entries, while binary search will never have to look at more than 16 of them! The key point here is that the idea for this algorithm comes from the prosaic task of using a directory.

3.2.2 Solving Simpler Problems

Since we have not previously seen every problem we are asked to solve and program, somehow we must be able to find connections between the problems at hand and problems whose solutions we already know (or at least whose solutions are easier). Two obvious methods are to simplify the problem and to find related problems.

It is often useful to explore a problem similar in structure to the one assigned, but is simpler in detail. One can explore alternative strategies and algorithms in this simpler context, and chose which strategy to pursue for the real problem.

To illustrate consider the sorting problem again. We have all done this -- sorted mailing lists, books on shelves, and so on. The problem and its solution are not unfamiliar, but explaining precisely how to sort is not easy if we haven't seen an algorithm for it before. Let us attack the problem as if we had not seen it earlier, and look for simpler problems within the sort.

What must happen for the list $L(1:N)$ to be sorted? For one thing, the largest value must eventually appear in $L(N)$. This is a simpler problem which we know how to handle (Section I.5, Exercise 4f).

```
          N1_LOOP: DO I = 1 TO N-1 BY 1;
(3.2.2a)      IF L(I) > L(N) THEN Swap L(I) and L(N);
          END N1_LOOP;
```

What else must be done? The second largest value must appear in $L(N-1)$. If the largest has already been put into $L(N)$ by the above algorithm, then this means we want to put the largest of $L(1:N-1)$ into $L(N-1)$. This is roughly the same as (3.2.2a):

```
          N2_LOOP: DO I = 1 TO N-2 BY 1;
              IF L(I) > L(N-1) THEN Swap L(I) and L(N-1);
          END N2_LOOP;
```

Continuing, we should recognize that we are performing essentially the same process a number of times. Getting back to the original problem, we can write it as

```
          Swap values of L(1:N)    to put largest in L(N);
          Swap values of L(1:N-1) to put largest in L(N-1);
          Swap values of L(1:N-2) to put largest in L(N-2);
                            ...
          Swap values of L(1:2)    to put larger  in L(2);
```

or

```
              /* SORT L(1:N) BY SUCCESSIVE MAXIMA */
              SMAX_LOOP: DO M = N TO 2 BY-1;
(3.2.2b)         Swap values of L(1:M) to put largest in L(M);
              END SMAX_LOOP;
```

One way of refining the English substatement of (3.2.2b) is

```
              /* SWAP VALUES OF L(1:M) TO PUT LARGEST IN L(M) */
              SWAP_LOOP: DO I = 1 TO M-1 BY 1;
(3.2.2c)         IF L(I) > L(M) THEN Swap L(I) and L(M);
              END SWAP_LOOP;
```

Note that we got the idea for the program by tackling smaller simpler ones and noticing that we had to repeat essentially the same process many times. We then returned to the original level and wrote the program (3.2.2b). At this point, we knew how to write the segment for "Swap values of L(1:M) to put largest in L(M)", and yet we still wrote this statement in English in (3.2.2b). This was because we wanted to make one decision at a time, the decision turning out to be the order in which the values were placed in their final positions (first L(N), then L(N-1), and so on). How the values get in their positions is not a problem of (3.2.2b), but the order in which they get there is. We can even design different algorithms for swapping the values, different from the one in (3.2.2a) which helped us find the solution. Sometimes tackling a simpler problem or a subproblem is the only way we can proceed. But once the process of solving the simpler problem has led to an idea, set the solution to the simpler problem aside, at least temporarily, and concentrate again on the top-down analysis.

One way to find a simpler problem is to temporarily make the problem definition simpler. Set aside all inessential details (perhaps even some of the essential ones), until a simple, understandable problem emerges. Once this has been solved, the original problem can be attacked with more understanding. This deletion of material must of course be done with care to make sure that the remaining problem is instructive and not trivial.

To illustrate this, consider the following problem:

(3.2.2d) A Text Editor. Input to the program is to consist of normal words, on cards, each adjacent pair being separated by one or more blanks. A word may be split onto two cards (the end of one and the beginning of the next). The words are to be read in and written out in 60-character lines. Each line is to be both right and left justified (as are the lines of this book). A word may not be split onto two lines, unless it is more than 60 characters long or unless otherwise there will be only one word on a line (these are probably errors, but the program must handle them).

Interspersed between words (and separated from them by one or more blanks) may be commands to be executed by the program, at the time they are read. These are:

command	meaning
)L	Begin a new output line;
)P	Begin a new paragraph (indent 3 spaces);
)E	End of input.

When processing a command, if a partially filled line must be written out, do not right-justify that line. For example, the last line of a paragraph is never right-justified. Commands may not appear as words in the input; only as commands.

Below is some sample input, with the corresponding output shown at the right, using 14-character instead of 60-character lines to save space:

Sample input	Sample output
)P One way to find a simpler	| One way to
problem is to make the)L)L	|find a simpler
problem	|problem is to
definition simpler.	|make the
Throw out all	|
inessential details.)E	|problem defini
	|tion simpler.
	|Throw out all
	|inessential de
	|tails.

This description is full of details, and it is difficult to know where to start, so begin by temporarily setting details aside to make it simpler:

1. Any number of blanks may separate a pair of words, and a word can be split on two cards. This may be difficult, so initially consider the input to be just a series of words and commands. That seems to be the essential point.

2. Why are lines 60 characters, and not 61 or 62? Perhaps the line length should be part of the input to the program. For now, since we need some length, use 60.

3. Justifying a line looks relatively complicated, but does not seem important relative to the overall structure of the program. Set it aside.

4. The problem of words of 60 characters or more and the problem of only one word on the line do not seem essential. Set them aside.

5. The commands are essential, and yet probably difficult to work with. Try setting them aside, and if that doesn't work out, bring them back.

This leads to the following problem description:

(3.2.2e) <u>Simplified Text Editor</u>. Read in a sequence of "words"
and print them out on 60-character lines. Put as many as
possible on one line, but separate each pair by a blank.
Don't split words across two lines.

This simpler problem is much easier to understand and work with.
A variable L (say) will hold the line currently being built.   It
will be written out when the next word to be inserted causes it
to be longer than 60 characters.   The following algorithm could
be designed fairly quickly:

```
          L = '';           /* NOTHING IS IN THE CURRENT LINE */
          WORD_LOOP: DO WHILE (there is another input word);
             Read the next word into WORD;
(3.2.2f)     IF LENGTH(L) + LENGTH(WORD) > 60 THEN DO;
               Print L;
               L = ''; END;
             Add WORD onto L;
             IF LENGTH(L) < 60 THEN Add 'b' onto L;
             END WORD_LOOP;
          Remove blank from end of L, if it has one;
          Print L;
```

The most important part of the original problem left out of
(3.2.2e) is the commands, so now reinsert them. This will
complicate the algorithm (3.2.2f), so we first should hide some
of its details. (3.2.2f) can be rewritten as

```
          L = '';           /* NOTHING IS IN THE CURRENT LINE */
          WORD_LOOP: DO WHILE (there is more input);
(3.2.2g)     Read the next word into WORD;
             Process the word in WORD;
             END WORD_LOOP;
          Remove blank from end of L, if it has one;
          Print L;
```

In adding commands, we see we must process either a word or
command. We also know when to stop the loop -- when the command
)E is read. Rewriting (3.2.2g) with this information yields

```
          L = '';           /* NOTHING IS IN THE CURRENT LINE */
          WORD = '';   /* NO WORD OR COMMAND READ YET */
          WORD_LOOP: DO WHILE (WORD ¬= ')E');
             Read the next word or command into WORD;
(3.2.2h)     IF WORD is a command
               THEN Process WORD as a command;
               ELSE Process WORD as text;
             END WORD_LOOP;
          Remove blank from end of L, if it has one;
          Print L;
```

where "process WORD as text" is

```
/* PROCESS WORD AS TEXT */
    IF LENGTH(L) + LENGTH(WORD) > 60 THEN DO;
        Print L;
        L = ''; END;
    Add WORD onto L;
    IF LENGTH(L) < 60 THEN Add 'b' onto L;
```

We now have a reasonable solution to the simpler problem (3.2.2e) plus commands. At this point the original problem should be reread and programmed in top-down fashion, using (3.2.2h) as a model.

On the text editor problem just described, the most common "mistake" is to write the main part of the program as a loop:

```
CARD_LOOP: DO WHILE (there exists a card);
    Read a card;
    Process the card;
    END CARD_LOOP;
```

This then requires a second loop in processing the card, and the whole program is unnecessarily complicated because a word could be split across card boundaries. If the problem is first simplified, we realize that the card boundary problem is just a detail to be handled at a later time, and is not an essential point in understanding the general flow of the program.

3.2.3 <u>Solving Related Problems</u>

Consider writing a program segment to sort an array C(1:N) in descending order: C(1) ≥ C(2) ≥ ... ≥ C(N). You might recall having developed an <u>ascending</u> sort in the previous section (program (3.2.2b)). The new sorting program could just be a modification of the previous one.

Related problems, both in programming and in the everyday world, are a rich source of ideas. If we can find something related which we know how to handle, then the problem becomes much simpler.

In the previous section, we discussed solving simpler problems, which are of course related to the original problem. By a "related problem" in this section we mean one which is roughly the same order of magnitude in size or complexity. One which, with some work, can be <u>transformed</u> into the desired one. Everybody uses related problems all the time, and in effect we are just saying the obvious here. The point is that you should become <u>aware</u> of the fact that you are using related problems; this will increase your ability to find solutions and design programs. Learning consists not only of doing something, but also of learning why and how one does it.

In programming, related problems occur more often   than   one
might think. For example, consider the four parts of Exercise 6
of Section 2. Although these look quite different, at the
highest level they all have the same algorithmic solution:

        Read in a list of values;
        Read and process a second list of values;
        Print results.

In fact, they are equivalent at this level to algorithm (2.4a)
of the accounting problem of Section 2.4 and differ only in the
meaning of "values", "read", "process", and "results".
Similarly, all the problems of Exercise 9 of Section 2 have the
solution

        Read a value;
        INPUT_LOOP: DO WHILE (there exists input);
            Process the value read;
            Read the next value;
            END INPUT_LOOP;

Each of these is an interpretation of schema (II.2b). In order
to see that problems are related, we must be able to recognize
the important elements of a problem.   All four problems in
Exercise 6 of Section 2 look different on first inspection,
until we state them in a more general manner.

Most programs include a number of simple subalgorithms, many
of which seem to occur over and over again (with perhaps slight
variations). Examples are algorithms to:

    Search a list.
    Search a sorted list.
    Find the position of a particular value on a list.
    Find the maximum or the average of a set of values.
    Delete duplicate values from a list.
    Read in a list of values which ends with some signal.

Many of these will become part of your "repertoire of
algorithms" and you will find that programming consists in part
in determining how these standard subalgorithms should be
combined into a larger program. In order to do this, however,
you must be able to recognize familiar problems in the mass of
detail of the overall problem, and work on modifying them to fit
the current problem.

3.3 Handling Input Errors

Programs are written to be used in the real world -- which means that they must not assume that input data will always conform exactly to the problem specifications. In general, programs must check all input for errors, and when errors are detected provide informative output that will help the user to find and correct the mistake. When a data error is not detected, the best that can happen is that the program will "blow up" -- an infinite loop will be executed, in PL/C an array subscript will be out of range, or some similar indication will be given. The worst that can happen is that the program processes the erroneous input as if it were correct, giving no indication that anything is wrong. If and when the error is eventually detected, it can be embarrassing and costly to correct.

Once you recognize the possibility that data errors can exist -- and in most situations are in fact likely to exist, you must decide what is the most reasonable response. For example, six alternative program segments are given in (3.3a) to (3.3f) below. Each is an interpretation of schema (II.2d); each is designed to perform the same task -- compute the sum of a set of integer data values. They differ only in the manner in which they react to a non-integer datum. In each case assume these segments are run in a program with the following declarations:

```
DECLARE SUM FLOAT DECIMAL;
DECLARE INTG FIXED DECIMAL;
DECLARE N FIXED DECIMAL;
DECLARE NBR FLOAT DECIMAL;
```

To understand these segments, recall that the FLOOR built-in function yields the greatest integer not greater than its argument. That is, FLOOR(3.5) is 3; FLOOR(-4.5) is -5.

```
(3.3a)   /* SUM N INTEGER DATA VALUES */
             SUM = 0;
             GET LIST(N);
             SUM_LOOP: DO WHILE ( N > 0 );
                 GET LIST(INTG);
                 SUM = SUM + INTG;
                 N = N - 1;
                 END SUM_LOOP;

(3.3b)   /* SUM N INTEGER DATA VALUES */
             SUM = 0;
             GET LIST(N);
             SUM_LOOP: DO WHILE ( N > 0 );
                 GET LIST(NBR);
                 SUM = SUM + NBR;
                 N = N - 1;
                 END SUM_LOOP;
```

```
(3.3c)   /* SUM N INTEGER DATA VALUES */
            SUM = 0;
            GET LIST(N);
            SUM_LOOP: DO WHILE ( N > 0 );
                GET LIST(NBR);
                IF NBR = FLOOR(NBR) THEN SUM = SUM + NBR;
                N = N - 1;
                END SUM_LOOP;


(3.3d)   /* SUM N INTEGER DATA VALUES */
            SUM = 0;
            GET LIST(N);
            SUM_LOOP: DO WHILE ( N > 0 );
                GET LIST(NBR);
                IF NBR ¬= FLOOR(NBR) THEN
                    PUT SKIP(2) LIST
                        ('NON-INTEGER VALUE:', NBR);
                SUM = SUM + NBR;
                N = N - 1;
                END SUM_LOOP;


(3.3e)   /* SUM N INTEGER DATA VALUES */
            SUM = 0;
            GET LIST(N);
            SUM_LOOP: DO WHILE ( N > 0 );
                GET LIST(NBR);
                IF NBR = FLOOR(NBR)
                    THEN SUM = SUM + NBR;
                    ELSE PUT SKIP(2) LIST
                        ('NON-INTEGER VALUE:', NBR);
                N = N - 1;
                END SUM_LOOP;


(3.3f)   /* SUM N INTEGER DATA VALUES */
            SUM = 0;
            GET LIST(N);
            SUM_LOOP: DO WHILE ( N > 0 );
                GET LIST(NBR);
                IF NBR ¬= FLOOR(NBR) THEN GO TO TERM_SUM;
                SUM = SUM + NBR;
                N = N - 1;
                END SUM_LOOP;
            TERM_SUM:;
```

If the data happen to be perfect -- that is, N integers -- these
six segments are equivalent. If one or more non-integers are
present the segments behave quite differently:

> (3.3a) quietly "repairs" non-integers by dropping any
> fractional part. No indication of their presence is given.

> (3.3b) is not restricted to integers at all. It includes
> fractional portions of values in the sum. No indication of
> the presence of non-integers is given.

(3.3c) only includes integers in the sum. It rejects non-integers, not including them, but not reporting their presence.

(3.3d) reports the presence of non-integers, but includes them in the sum.

(3.3e) reports the presence of non-integers and does not include them in the sum.

(3.3f) terminates the process on encountering the first non-integer value, without including this value in the sum, and without reporting the premature termination. All subsequent values are left unread.

There are several other possibilities but these should serve to illustrate the point. One cannot say, in general, which of these responses is best. That depends upon the requirements of the particular problem. But one can say that it is generally necessary to admit the possibility of different types of errors, determine what response is appropriate, and write the program accordingly.

With some errors the program should stop and print a message. For example, in the accounting problem of Section 2.4 if the end-of-account signal is missing, then all transactions have been read as accounts, and there is no hope of proceeding usefully. With other errors the program should just print a message and continue. For example, if a transaction gives a non-existent account number, that transaction can be rejected and a message can be printed.

Many programs process data that actually consists of sections that are quite independent. For example, in Section 2.4 the data pertaining to each account is independent of the data preceding and following. An error in a particular item of data may well make processing for that account meaningless until the error is corrected, but it does not affect processing of the other accounts. This suggests that a well-designed program would reject the erroneous data with an informative error message, skip over that account, but resume processing with the next account. Error rates of several percent in hand-prepared data are not unusual and programs that have to process thousands of data cards are commonplace. If these programs were to stop as soon as any error is encountered and insist that it be repaired before proceeding they would be impractical to use. On the other hand there are cases where the data are all logically related and the effects of errors are cumulative. In such cases it is pointless to continue processing. It requires both knowledge of the problem and good judgement to decide whether an error should terminate processing or whether there is some action that will permit continuation to be useful.

One could conceivably overdo error checking. The programmer must weigh each type of input error and the damage its

occurrence , might cause against the amount of programming
necessary to detect it.   But at least the programmer should
think of all the possible errors and come to a rational decision
on each one.   If necessary the manager should be questioned
about them. Very often the person in charge may not have
thought about all the possibilities and will be delighted to
hear they can be detected. On the other hand, he may be able to
tell the programmer that a particular error will never occur
because, for example, the data is produced by another program of
known reliability.

In some cases error processing is so important that it
dominates the program.   For example, there are programs whose
sole purpose is to screen data for errors so that these can be
corrected prior to submitting the data for actual processing.
In general, error processing should be considered an important
and integral part of the problem. Error processing is usually
more successful when it is developed along with other
requirements rather than being added on after the program is
otherwise finished.

Part II and Part III References

Aho, A. V., J. E. Hopcroft and J. D. Ullman, <u>The Design and Analysis of Computer Algorithms</u>, Addison-Wesley, 1974

Dahl, O. J., E. W. Dijkstra and C. A. R. Hoare, <u>Structured Programming</u>, Academic Press, 1972

Dijkstra, E. W., "GO TO Statement Considered Harmful", <u>Communications of the ACM</u>, March 1968

Dijkstra, E. W., <u>A Short Introduction to the Art of Programming</u>, Eindhoven University, 1971

Kernighan, B. W. and P. J. Plauger, <u>Elements of Programming Style</u>, McGraw-Hill, 1974

Kernighan, B. W. and P. J. Plauger, "Programming Style: Examples and Counterexamples", <u>ACM Computing Surveys</u>, December 1974

Knuth, D. E., "Structured Programming with GO TO Statement", <u>ACM Computing Surveys</u>, December 1974

McGowan, C. L. and J. R. Kelly, <u>Top-Down Structured Programming Techniques</u>, Petrocelli/Charter 1975

Mills, H., "Top Down Programming in Large Systems", in Rustin (ed.), <u>Debugging Techniques in Large Systems</u>, Prentice-Hall, 1971

Polya, G., <u>How to Solve It</u>, Princeton, 1945 (also excerpted in Newman, <u>The World of Mathematics</u>, <u>Vol. 3</u>, Simon & Schuster, 1956)

Van Tassel, D., <u>Program Style, Design, Efficiency, Debugging and Testing</u>, Prentice-Hall, 1974

Weinberg, G. M., <u>The Psychology of Computer Programming</u>, Van Nostrand, 1971

Wirth, N., "Program Development by Stepwise Refinement", Communications of the ACM, April 1971

Wirth, N., Systematic Programming: An Introduction, Prentice-Hall, 1973

Wirth, N., "On the Composition of Well-Structured Programs", ACM Computing Surveys, December 1974

Yohe, J. M., "An Overview of Programming Practices", ACM Computing Surveys, December 1974

PART IV   INDEPENDENT SUBPROGRAMS

Section 1   External Procedures

The language features presented in Part I are adequate to write small programs, but something more is required if we are to effectively write and test significant programs. We need some means of organizing things so that

1. different sections of the program can be made relatively independent, so they can be written and tested separately;

2. program segments can be written in one place and executed "remotely" from some other point in the program;

3. program segments can be written so that they can be reused in different contexts without having to be rewritten; and

4. large programs can be easily constructed from smaller ones already written and checked out.

These capabilities are provided by "procedures" in PL/I. One defines a procedure in one place in a program. This procedure can then be "called" or "invoked" into action from other places within the program. In executing the procedure, it behaves as if it were copied into each position from which it is invoked.

This technique is not peculiar to programming. For instance, when baking a cake we might be instructed to "make chocolate icing, page 56". The icing recipe is a separate procedure, with its own set of instructions. To execute this command, we postpone further action on the cake, turn to the icing recipe, and execute it. When finished, we return to the cake recipe and continue where we left off.

The following program is a simple example of the use of PL/I procedures. Its execution prints the following three lines:

```
FIRST LINE
SECOND LINE
FIRST LINE
```

The program is given below:

```
*PL/C ID='ALAN DEMERS'
/* PRINT 3 LINES */                                    ¬
P3LINES: PROCEDURE OPTIONS(MAIN);          |main
    C1: CALL FIRST;                        |procedure
    C2: CALL SECOND;                       | P3LINES
    C3: CALL FIRST;                        |
    END P3LINES;                                       ⌋
*PROCESS
/* PRINT FIRST LINE */                                 ¬
FIRST: PROCEDURE;                          |
    F1: PUT SKIP LIST('FIRST LINE');       |procedure
    F2: RETURN;                            | FIRST
    END FIRST;                                         ⌋
*PROCESS
/* PRINT SECOND LINE */                                ¬
SECOND: PROCEDURE;                         |
    S1: PUT SKIP LIST('SECOND LINE');      |procedure
    S2: RETURN;                            | SECOND
    END SECOND;                                        ⌋
*DATA
```

While all of our previous programs have consisted of a single procedure, this program consists of three separate procedures:

P3LINES is the main procedure because "OPTIONS(MAIN)" is given in its heading. A program must have exactly one main procedure.

FIRST is an external procedure. It is essentially an independent program that is executed by being "called" from the main procedure. When executed it causes the literal 'FIRST LINE' to be printed.

SECOND is another external procedure.   When executed it causes the literal 'SECOND LINE' to be printed.

The *PROCESS cards are control cards (which must start in column 1) that denote the start of an external procedure much as the *PL/C card denotes the start of the main procedure.

The execution of any PL/C program always starts at the first statement of the main procedure, and continues until the main procedure is completed. In this case the first statement in P3LINES is

```
C1: CALL FIRST;
```

The execution of a CALL statement is accomplished by executing the procedure that it references -- in this case, the procedure named FIRST. You may think of the execution of the main procedure as having been suspended temporarily while FIRST is being executed, and resumed when FIRST is completed. It is probably better to think of the execution of FIRST as being the execution of the CALL FIRST statement.

P3LINES consists of three statements C1, C2 and C3. Since there is no loop or condition its execution consists simply of the execution of C1, C2 and C3 in order. But effectively, this means execute procedure FIRST, then execute procedure SECOND, and then execute procedure FIRST again. It doesn't matter that C3 requires the execution of a procedure that has already been executed once -- the same external procedure can be executed any number of times in the course of executing a program.

Now consider what it means to execute procedure FIRST in more detail. The first statment in FIRST is

        F1: PUT SKIP LIST('FIRST LINE');

which causes the literal 'FIRST LINE' to be printed. The next statement is

        F2: RETURN;

which asserts that the execution of FIRST, and hence the execution of CALL FIRST, has been completed. So, in effect, the result of executing

        C1: CALL FIRST;

is to execute the statement

        F1: PUT SKIP LIST('FIRST LINE');

since that is the only executable statement in FIRST. Overall, the result of executing P3LINES would be to produce the same printed output as the following program:

```
*PL/C ID='ALAN DEMERS'
/* PROGRAM TO PRINT 3 SIMPLE LINES */
PRINT3: PROCEDURE OPTIONS(MAIN);
    PUT SKIP LIST('FIRST LINE');
    PUT SKIP LIST('SECOND LINE');
    PUT SKIP LIST('FIRST LINE');
    END PRINT3;
*DATA
```

This second form is obviously simpler and no one would actually use the first form -- but then no one would use a computer to write these three lines anyway. However, if the body of FIRST were a substantial program segment, it would be useful to be able to execute this segment from different points in the program (C1 and C3) without having to rewrite the segment.

We will illustrate the idea of procedures by another example in Section 1.1, and then explore the definition and use of procedures in more detail in the following sections.

1.1 A Procedure to Interchange Values

Consider the task of exchanging the values of two variables X and Y. We can do this with the three assignment statements shown in (1.1a). These statements use a third variable T, in addition to X and Y.

```
(1.1a)    T = X;
          X = Y;
          Y = T;
```

Alternatively, we can write a procedure to do this:

```
          *PROCESS
          /* SWAP VALUES OF X AND Y */
          SWAP: PROCEDURE(X, Y);
              DECLARE (X, Y) FIXED DECIMAL;
(1.1b)        DECLARE T FIXED DECIMAL;
              T = X;
              X = Y;
              Y = T;
              RETURN;
              END SWAP;
```

This procedure definition would be placed at the end of the program, out of the way. Then, wherever we wanted to swap the values of X and Y, instead of writing the three statements of (1.1a) we would instead write the single statement

```
          CALL SWAP(X, Y);
```

Executing this statement is equivalent to executing all of the statements in the body of the procedure SWAP.

For example, a complete program using the procedure SWAP of (1.1b) is given in (1.1c). During each repetition of the body of SWAP_LOOP in (1.1c) the GET statement obtains the next two values from the data list and assigns them to X and Y. Then if those values are out of order the CALL statement "passes" X and Y to the procedure SWAP. The next statement to be executed is the first assignment statement in SWAP, that is T = X. That and the two following assignment statements interchange the values. The execution of the RETURN statement terminates the procedure SWAP and hence completes the execution of the CALL SWAP(X, Y) statement. The next statement executed is the PUT. This cycle is repeated N times, which completes the execution of SWAP_LOOP. A final PUT statement completes the execution of the main

procedure ORDER2 so the execution of the program is finished.
Execution does <u>not</u> continue on into the SWAP procedure; SWAP is
not a main procedure and is executed only by means of a CALL.

```
            *PL/C ID='CHARLES MOORE'
            /* ORDER N DATA PAIRS */
            ORDER2: PROCEDURE OPTIONS(MAIN);
                DCL (X, Y, I, N) FIXED DECIMAL;
                PUT LIST('ORDERED PAIRS:');
                PUT SKIP;
                GET LIST(N);
                SWAP_LOOP: DO I = 1 TO N BY 1;
                    GET LIST(X, Y);
                    IF X > Y THEN CALL SWAP(X, Y);
(1.1c)              PUT SKIP LIST(X, Y);
                    END SWAP_LOOP;
                PUT SKIP(2) LIST('END OF LIST');
                END ORDER2;
            *PROCESS
            /* SWAP VALUES OF X AND Y */
            SWAP: PROCEDURE(X, Y);
                DECLARE (X, Y) FIXED DECIMAL;
                DECLARE T FIXED DECIMAL;
                T = X;
                X = Y;
                Y = T;
                RETURN;
                END SWAP;
            *DATA
                3,
                9, 8,    5, 0,    1, 15
```

Execution of (1.1c) with the data shown would print the
following lines:

```
            ORDERED PAIRS:

                8           9
                0           5
                1           15


            END OF LIST
```

Now let's go one step further. Suppose we wanted to swap the
values of some pair of variables whose names were <u>not</u> X and Y.
More generally, suppose we wanted to swap the value of one pair
of variables at some point in the program and swap the values of
a <u>different</u> pair of variables at some other point. It would be
convenient not to have to have two different swap routines just
because the variables to be swapped happened to have different
names. For example, suppose there is a data list consisting of
values in groups of three, and each group is to be rearranged so
that its values are in non-decreasing order -- that is, a sort
on lists of length 3. Each group could be assigned as values to
a set of three variables, say A, B and C. Then by comparing A

and B and swapping their values if they are out of order;
comparing B and C and swapping their values if out of order; and
finally comparing A and B again and swapping their values if out
of order, the three values would be put in non-decreasing order.
(This is, of course, just a special case of the sorting
algorithm of Section III.2.3.) The point is that we would need
to swap A and B, then B and C, and then A and B again. It may
surprise you to learn that the SWAP procedure of (1.1b) is
capable of doing this, without any change whatever. This is
illustrated in (1.1d).

```
          *PL/C ID='WILLIAM MAXWELL'
           /* ORDER N DATA TRIPLES */
           ORDER3: PROCEDURE OPTIONS(MAIN);
               DCL (A, B, C, I, N) FIXED DECIMAL;
               PUT LIST('ORDERED TRIPLES:');
               PUT SKIP;
               GET LIST(N);
               SWAP_LOOP: DO I = 1 TO N BY 1;
                   GET LIST(A, B, C);
                   IF A > B THEN CALL SWAP(A, B);
                   IF B > C THEN CALL SWAP(C, B);
                   IF A > B THEN CALL SWAP(A, B);
(1.1d)             PUT SKIP LIST(A, B, C);
                   END SWAP_LOOP;
               PUT SKIP(2) LIST('END OF LIST');
               END ORDER3;
          *PROCESS
           /* SWAP VALUES OF X AND Y */
           SWAP: PROCEDURE(X, Y);
               DECLARE (X, Y) FIXED DECIMAL;
               DECLARE T FIXED DECIMAL;
               T = X;
               X = Y;
               Y = T;
               RETURN;
               END SWAP;
          *DATA
           4,
           17, 23, 15,
           9, 56, 1,
           105, 0, -2,
           42, 43, 44
```

Execution of (1.1d) with the data shown would print the
following lines:

          ORDERED TRIPLES:

              15   17   23
               1   9   56
              -2   0   105
              42   43   44

          END OF LIST

In each repetition of the body of SWAP_LOOP in (1.1d) the GET obtains the next three values from the data list and assigns them to A, B and C, respectively. If the values of A and B are out of order they need to be swapped. The statement

        CALL SWAP(A, B);

calls the procedure SWAP and directs it to swap the values of A and B. The variable A takes the place of X in SWAP; the variable B takes the place of Y. The execution of this CALL statement is equivalent to executing SWAP as if its assignment statements had been written as

        T = A;
        A = B;
        B = T;

After the execution of SWAP is completed, the next statement to be executed is another conditional CALL of SWAP. This time if the values of B and C are out of order SWAP is called to interchange their values. This time B takes the place of X in SWAP and C takes the place of Y. SWAP is now executed as if its assignment statements had been written as

        T = B;
        B = C;
        C = T;

After completion of this execution of SWAP the next statement is a third conditional CALL of SWAP. This again checks the ordering of A and B (which may have been upset by the interchange of B and C). After execution of these three conditional calls the values of A, B and C will be in non-decreasing order.

    The point is that each particular execution of SWAP will interchange the values of whatever variables are specified in the CALL statement that causes that execution. The fact that SWAP is written in terms of X and Y is immaterial. In fact, X and Y in SWAP are not variables at all -- they are _parameters_. A parameter is used _in place of a variable_ in writing a procedure because it is not known until the procedure is called what particular variable it will be. The specific variables to be used by the procedure are given in the call, and are known as the _arguments of the call_. A and B are the arguments of the first call of SWAP in (1.1d); B and C are the arguments of the second call; and A and B are the arguments of the third call. Before executing a procedure the _parameters are replaced by the corresponding arguments_ of that particular call.

    The replacement of parameters with arguments is exactly the same in (1.1c), but in that case the arguments happened to have the same names as the parameters -- which allowed us to postpone explaining what really happened until (1.1d). But actually, even in (1.1c) the parameter X in SWAP and the argument X in the

call are different -- they just happen to have the same name.
The execution of CALL SWAP(X, Y) passes arguments X and Y to
SWAP to have their values interchanged. The first parameter X
of SWAP is replaced by the first argument X of the call; the
second parameter Y by the second argument Y. It is just a
coincidence that the names happen to be the same. Any pair of
variables could be passed as arguments to SWAP to have their
values interchanged.

However, the attributes of the arguments must exactly match
those of the corresponding parameter. For example, if the
variables A, B and C in (1.1d) had been declared to be FLOAT
DECIMAL this program would not work properly, simply because the
attributes of the arguments would not match the FIXED DECIMAL
attributes of the parameters of SWAP.

Note that exactly the same procedure SWAP is used in both
(1.1c) and (1.1d). This reuse of a procedure is a common
occurrence in programming. It means that after you have been
programming awhile and have accumulated a repertoire of commonly
used program segments you will not have to write each new
program entirely from scratch. A procedure is a particularly
convenient way to package a program segment so that it can be
moved from one program to another.

1.2 Definition of a Procedure

We are only considering "external" procedures -- that is,
procedures whose definitions are positioned so that they are not
within the body of any other procedure. (There are other kinds
of procedures in PL/I, but they are beyond the scope of this
book.) Programs (1.1c) and (1.1d) show the proper position for
a procedure definition. The general form of the definition of
an external procedure is

```
*PROCESS
/* Comment summarizing what the procedure does */
procedure-name: PROCEDURE(list of parameters);
     Declarations to specify parameters;
     Declarations to create variables;
     Statements;
     END procedure-name;
```

The *PROCESS card is a control card, similar to the *PL/C or
*DATA card. Like all control cards it must begin in column 1,
whereas all other program cards should leave column 1 blank. On
most systems *PROCESS will cause the source listing to skip to a
new page so that the listing of each external procedure begins
at the top of a new page. (At some installations PL/C is
modified so that only a few lines are skipped rather than
skipping to a new page.) Any number of external procedures may
be included in a program.

The procedure-name is any PL/I identifier. (If the procedure name is longer than seven characters a warning message will be given, but this is irrelevant for our purposes and may be ignored.) This is the name by which the procedure will be called to be executed. Procedure names should be chosen to suggest the action that the procedure performs, like SWAP in (1.1c). All procedure-names must be different. That is, you cannot have two procedures with the same name, and procedure-names must not be the same as the name of any variable or label in the program.

The list of parameters is a sequence of identifiers, separated by commas. These identifiers are the parameters of the procedure and are not names of variables. The parameter names have absolutely no connection with names used in other procedures.

1.2.1 Parameter Declarations

There are now two different sets of declarations -- for parameters and for variables. The first set specifies the type attributes of the parameters. The form of parameter declarations is almost like that of variable declarations. For example

```
*PROCESS
/* SET Z TO SOL'N TO HEAT EQN IN (X,Y) */
HEAT: PROCEDURE(X, Y, Z);
     DECLARE (X, Y) FLOAT DECIMAL;
     DECLARE Z FIXED DECIMAL;
     ...
```

The INITIAL attribute must not be given in a parameter declaration. Since a parameter is not a variable, it does not have a value -- hence cannot have an initial value. (A parameter is replaced by a variable when the procedure is called.)

The form of the declaration of parameters also differs for character-string parameters and for array parameters. The length of a string parameter must be left unspecified. This is indicated by giving "*" for the length -- that is, by writing CHARACTER(*) or CHAR(*). For example

```
          *PROCESS
          /* DELETE OCCURRENCES OF STR2 IN STR1 */
          DEL_STRG: PROCEDURE(STR1, STR2);
(1.2.1a)      DECLARE STR1 CHARACTER(*);
              DECLARE STR2 CHARACTER(*) VARYING;
              ...
```

When executing the procedure, the length of a string parameter is always the length of the argument associated with it. If the

arguments that will be associated with a string parameter have
the VARYING attribute, then the string parameter declaration
should also include VARYING. But note that this just means that
the string parameter will be associated with VARYING arguments;
not that the parameter's length will vary from one execution to
the next because of association with arguments of different
length.

The declaration of array parameters is discussed in Section
1.3.3.

Except for this use of the "*" you cannot tell from the
declaration alone whether a parameter or a variable is being
declared. The distinction depends entirely upon whether or not
the name appears in the parameter list in the procedure heading.
If the name is on that list it is the name of a parameter; if
the name is not on that list it is the name of a variable.

All parameters should be declared and their type attributes
given explicitly. PL/I does not absolutely insist on this, but
if you do not give a complete declaration of each parameter PL/I
will supply default attributes and these usually will not match
the attributes of the corresponding arguments. If this happens,
the result of unmatched attributes will surely surprise and
mystify you. Without complete declarations your program will
sometimes work, and sometimes not. The explanation is quite
complicated and it is far simpler to always provide explicit
declarations.

Some procedures do not need any parameters. In such cases
there are no parameter lists, and no declarations of parameters.
Examples of such parameterless procedures are given in (1.2.4a)
and (1.2.4b).

We sometimes speak of an "input parameter" or an "output
parameter", depending upon whether the parameter is used to
receive or return a value. However, this just describes the way
in which the parameter is used in the body of the procedure and
has no effect on the way it should be declared.

For example, in (1.1b) the parameters X and Y of SWAP are
both input and output parameters, since the argument associated
with each of these parameters both supplies a value to SWAP and
is assigned a value by SWAP. In (1.2.1a) the parameter STR1 of
DEL_STRG is similarly both input and output, but the parameter
STR2 is input only.

1.2.2 Local Variables

The second set of declarations creates variables, just as we
have been doing since our first example in Section I.1.1. You
can recognize that these declarations create variables rather
than parameters simply because they declare names that did not
appear on the parameter list. For example

```
*PROCESS
/* SET MAXFN TO MAX FUNCTION VALUE */
SAVEMAX: PROCEDURE(MAXFN, NEWVAL);
    DECLARE (MAXFN, NEWVAL) FLOAT DECIMAL;
    DECLARE (TEMP, SQVAL) FLOAT DECIMAL;
    ...
```

TEMP and SQVAL are variables and not parameters because they do
not appear in the parameter list with MAXFN and NEWVAL. PL/I
allows both parameters and variables to be given in the same
declaration, but this makes it less clear to a human reader so
we suggest that you use separate declarations for parameters and
local variables.

Now that we are concerned with more than one procedure we
must note that variables are "local" to the procedure in which
they are declared. This means that they can be used by name
only in that procedure. Their names are not known outside that
procedure. Each procedure has its own set of variables,
independent of those of every other procedure, and it is
immaterial if some of the names happen to coincide. For example

```
*PL/C ID='S. WORONA'
/* EDIT TEXT BY SKIPPING LINES WITH DUPLICATES */
CONTROL: PROCEDURE OPTIONS(MAIN);
    DECLARE FLAG FIXED DECIMAL;
    ...
    END CONTROL;
*PROCESS
/* SET F TO 0|1 IF LINE HAS|HAS-NO DUPLICATES */
SETF: PROCEDURE(F, LINE);
    DECLARE F FIXED DECIMAL;
    DECLARE LINE CHAR(*);
    DECLARE FLAG FLOAT DECIMAL;
    ...
    END SETF;
```

The two variables FLAG in CONTROL and FLAG in SETF are entirely
different objects that just happen to have the same name. In
this case they happen to have different attributes, but that is
immaterial. They could both be FIXED DECIMAL or one could be a
character string and the other an array. Also note that the
variables of a procedure are created as the procedure is
entered, and then destroyed when that execution of the procedure
is completed. This is discussed further in Sections 1.3 and
1.5.

1.2.3 Labels in a Procedure

Labels are also "local" to the procedure in which they are declared. (The declaration or definition of a label is just its use as a prefix to a statement.) The label names in one external procedure have nothing to do with names in any other procedure. The label given in a GO TO statement must be inside the same external procedure as the GO TO itself. For example

```
*PL/C ID='PAUL HARTER'
/* TEST INPUT AND OUTPUT FORMATS */
TEST: PROCEDURE OPTIONS(MAIN);
    ...
    /* TEST INPUT FORMATS */
        ...
        DATA_LOOP: DO WHILE(ITEM ¬= -1);
            ...
            END DATA_LOOP;
        TERM_DATA:;
    ...
    END TEST;
*PROCESS
/* CONVERT EDIT FORMAT */
CONVERT: PROCEDURE(X, D);
    ...
    CONV_LOOP: DO WHILE( D > 0 );
        ...
        IF X = 0 THEN GO TO TERM_CONV;
        ...
        END CONV_LOOP;
    TERM_CONV:;
    ...
    RETURN;
    END CONVERT;
*DATA
```

The GO TO in CONVERT branches to TERM_CONV which is a label in CONVERT. It would not be legal for a GO TO in CONVERT to branch to TERM_DATA, which is a label in TEST. This means that you cannot escape from an external procedure by means of a GO TO statement.

It is permissible for the same label to be used in two different procedures. In the example above TERM_CONV could be used as a label in TEST even though it is already used as a label in CONVERT. There is no ambiguity -- a GO TO always refers to the label in the same procedure. This means that in choosing labels in one procedure you need not be concerned with whether the same identifier has been used in another procedure. It also means that a particular identifier can be used as a label in one procedure and a variable in another procedure without any conflict.

1.2.4 <u>Statements in the Procedure Body</u>

   The procedure body consists of a sequence of statements which
are executed whenever the procedure is called. Any statement
may appear within the procedure body -- an assignment,
conditional, GET, PUT, compound statement, a loop, or a call on
another procedure (as explained in Section 1.4). Note however
that these statements may contain parameters as well as
variables. This means that the body cannot be executed unless
it is properly called, with variables as arguments to replace
the parameters. We write the procedure as if <u>the parameters</u>
<u>were variables or arrays</u>, knowing that they will be replaced by
actual variables or arrays when the procedure is called. In
effect, the procedure is a way of describing a <u>specified action</u>
on <u>unspecified variables</u>.

   The procedure body should include a RETURN statement to
indicate when execution of the procedure is to be terminated
(and hence when execution of the calling statement is
completed). If RETURN is omitted, it is implied when execution
reaches the END of the procedure. It is good practice to put
the RETURN in explicitly to emphasize (for the human reader)
what happens at the end of a procedure.

   Execution of a PL/I program consists of <u>one execution of the</u>
<u>main procedure</u>. In effect, PL/I executes a single implied call
(without arguments) of the main procedure. Execution of the
program is finished whenever that single execution of the main
procedure is completed -- regardless of whether or not other
external procedures happen to follow the main procedure.
Procedures are executed only if they are called; you cannot "run
into" a procedure and execute it as you might with a DO loop.
For example, the execution output of (1.2.4a) would be

              LINE 1
              LINE 3

Note that "LINE 2" will <u>never be printed</u> because L2 is never
called.

```
           *PL/C ID='D. SEVERANCE'
           /* PRINT 2 LINES */
           PRT2: PROCEDURE OPTIONS(MAIN);
               PUT LIST('LINE 1');
(1.2.4a)       PUT SKIP LIST('LINE 3');
               END PRT2;
          *PROCESS
           /* PRINT 'LINE 2' */
           L2: PROCEDURE;
               PUT SKIP LIST('LINE 2');
               RETURN;
               END L2;
          *DATA
```

As another example, the execution output of (1.2.4b) is

```
        LINE 1
        LINE 2
        LINE 2
        LINE 2
        LINE 3
```

Note that "LINE 2" is printed three times <u>before</u> "LINE 3" as a result of three calls of L2, but "LINE 2" does not appear after "LINE 3".

```
           *PL/C ID='JOHN DENNIS'
            /* PRINT 2 IDENTIFICATION LINES */
            PPL: PROCEDURE OPTIONS(MAIN);
               DCL I FIXED DECIMAL;
               PUT LIST('LINE 1');
               PRINT_LOOP: DO I = 1 TO 3 BY 1;
(1.2.4b)          CALL L2;
                  END PRINT_LOOP;
               PUT SKIP LIST('LINE 3');
               END PPL;
           *PROCESS
            /* PRINT 'LINE 2' */
            L2: PROCEDURE;
               PUT SKIP LIST('LINE 2');
               RETURN;
               END L2;
           *DATA
```

Note that neither (1.2.4a) nor (1.2.4b) involves parameters and arguments since procedure L2 does not require any input information and does not return any information to the calling procedure. These examples are unrealistically simple, and one would not actually write procedures that are this short and simple. But some procedures need no parameters.

1.3 <u>Procedure Calls</u>

1.3.1 <u>Calls and Arguments</u>

There are two forms of procedure call. The second form (without arguments) is used for procedures that have been defined without parameters, as in (1.2.4a) and (1.2.4b).

```
   CALL procedure-name(list of arguments);
```

```
   CALL procedure-name;
```

The procedure-name given in the CALL must be the name of a procedure whose definition is included in this program.

The arguments in the list are separated by commas. Each argument may be a reference to a variable or the name of an array (see Section 1.3.3). The first argument corresponds to (replaces) the first parameter of the procedure, the second argument corresponds to the second parameter, and so on. The number of arguments given in the call of a procedure must exactly match the number of parameters given in the definition of that procedure. Even if one of the arguments will not be used in a particular call, some harmless argument must be given so that the proper number of arguments will be present.

A procedure call is a PL/I statement and can be placed anywhere in a program that an assignment statement or a GET or PUT could appear. For example, it can be executed conditionally:

```
        IF B < 0 THEN CALL FIX(B);
```

It can be in the body of a DO loop:

```
        NEXT_LOOP: DO WHILE (X > 10**-5);
            CALL NEXT(X);
            END NEXT_LOOP;
```

Note that in NEXT_LOOP, unless the procedure NEXT eventually makes the value of X small enough this will be an infinite, never-ending loop.

A procedure call can even appear within the body of another procedure, as will be explained in Section 1.4.

Execution of a procedure call includes replacing parameters by arguments. We have described this replacement as a sort of "textual" substitution of one name for another. However, this replacement can be interpreted in several different ways, and we must therefore define more carefully what we mean by replacement, or parameter-argument correspondence. In order to do this, we must adopt a notation for describing which variables can be referenced at each point in a program.

Suppose we have a program with the procedures and declarations shown in (1.3.1a). We can show the variables and parameters of this program in boxes associated with their procedures as in (1.3.1b). This shows the variables that belong to each of the procedures, at some point during the execution of AXES. The array A and the variables I, J, X and T are declared in the main procedure, so they are shown in the box for that procedure. There is another variable T declared in SWAP and shown in the box for SWAP, but this variable has not yet been assigned a value. X and Y are declared as the parameters of SWAP and are shown in the box for SWAP, but note that they do not have lines for their values. When SWAP is called these parameters will be associated with some variables in the main procedure that are given as arguments of the call. This process is described in detail in Section 1.3.2.

```
        *PL/C ID='JOHN HOPCROFT'
        /* PROGRAM TO ROTATE AXES */
        AXES: PROCEDURE OPTIONS(MAIN);
             DCL A(2) FIXED DECIMAL;
             DCL (I, J, X, T) FIXED DECIMAL;
             ...
             CALL SWAP(I, J);
(1.3.1a)     ...
             END AXES;
        *PROCESS
        /* SWAP VALUES OF X AND Y */
        SWAP: PROCEDURE(X, Y);
             DCL (X, Y) FIXED DECIMAL;
             DCL T FIXED DECIMAL;
             T = X;
             X = Y;
             Y = T;
             RETURN;
             END SWAP;
        *DATA
```

```
            ┌───────────┐   ┌───────────┐
            |A(1)->3    |   |           |
            |A(2)->8    |   |           |
            |I---->2    |   |X          |
(1.3.1b)    |J---->1    |   |Y          |
            |X---->6    |   |T->?       |
            |T---->4    |   |           |
            └───────────┘   └───────────┘

               AXES            SWAP
```

    Note that we have drawn an arrow from each variable name to
the line to which it is attached. Recall from Section I.2 that
a name is attached by means of an arrow to a line; we omit the
arrows only when the two are close enough. We will see that
parameters are also attached to lines at the time parameter-
argument correspondence is made. But in (1.3.1b) no arrows are
attached to parameters X and Y because SWAP has not been called
yet.

    When executing a statement, to determine which variable a
name references, we look only in the box of variables for the
procedure in which that statement occurs.   Although both the
main procedure AXES and external procedure SWAP have a variable
T, these two variables are completely separate and distinct.
Names used in one external procedure have absolutely no effect
on the names used in another.

1.3.2 <u>Associating Arguments with Parameters</u>

Let us examine in detail how the execution of the statement CALL SWAP(I, J); in the main procedure of (1.3.1a) actually works. Execution of a procedure call takes place as follows:

1. Draw a box to contain the variables and parameters of the procedure (Fig. 1b).

2. Within the box write the parameters (Fig. 1c).

3. Make the parameter-argument correspondence as follows: Each argument name has an arrow leading from it. For each parameter, draw an arrow from it to the same line to which the corresponding argument points (Fig. 1d). The first parameter corresponds to the first argument; the second parameter to the second argument, etc.

4. Within the box, write the variables declared locally within the procedure, using "?" to indicate where a value has not yet been assigned (Fig. 1e).

5. Execute the procedure body. Whenever a parameter is referenced, use the line to which it is attached. (The results of executing statements T=X; X=Y; Y=T; are shown in Figs. 1f, 1g, and 1h.)

6. Erase the procedure's box and any arrows leading from it; execution of the procedure call is now finished (Fig. 1i).

Study these steps carefully. Understanding this simple case of parameter-argument correspondence is necessary for understanding the more complicated situations that will arise later.

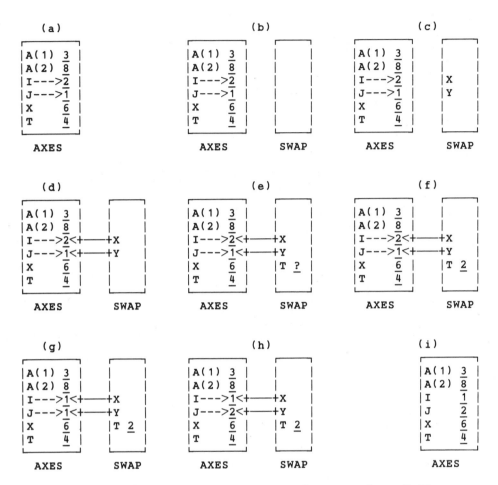

Figure 1. Example of Execution of a Procedure Call

During execution of a program, the equivalent of these boxes and arrows are actually "drawn" as we have depicted. Storage locations are set aside to hold the variables and the "parameter arrows" of a procedure. The parameter arrow locations contain references to the locations where the arguments reside.

Figure 1 illustrates several important points. First, the names used in one external procedure have nothing to do with names used in others. Both AXES and SWAP happen to have a variable named T, but these are two different variables which, by coincidence, happen to have the same name. Any reference to T in AXES is assumed to mean the variable T declared in AXES; any reference to T in SWAP refers to the T declared in SWAP. You should not go out of your way to use common names like this, but on the other hand, there is no reason to avoid it. If T is the natural and suggestive name for the variable in both cases, then it should be used in both cases. PL/I gives you the freedom of choosing the best name for a variable in each procedure without worrying about whether that name happens to be used in another procedure.

Secondly, this fact that the names in each procedure are independent means that the names of parameters have nothing to do with the names of arguments. Arguments and parameters are matched strictly <u>according to the order</u> in which they appear in their respective lists -- their names are irrelevant in this matching. Figure 1 is drawn for the particular call shown in (1.3.1a), matching parameter X with argument I and parameter Y with argument J. Matching for various other possible calls is shown in Figure 2. (In Figures 2g, 2i and 2j the values for the subscripts I and J are taken from Figure 1a.)

```
                                 Argument<----Parameter
    (a) CALL SWAP(J,I);          J<----X,     I<----Y

    (b) CALL SWAP(X,J);          X<----X,     J<----Y

    (c) CALL SWAP(J,X);          J<----X,     X<----Y

    (d) CALL SWAP(T,X);          T<----X,     X<----Y

    (e) CALL SWAP(A(1),J);       A(1)<----X, J<----Y

    (f) CALL SWAP(A(1),A(2));    A(1)<----X, A(2)<----Y

    (g) CALL SWAP(A(J),A(I));    A(1)<----X, A(2)<----Y

    (h) CALL SWAP(J,J);          J<----X,     J<----Y

    (i) CALL SWAP(A(2),A(I));    A(2)<----X, A(2)<----Y

    (j) CALL SWAP(I,A(I));       I<----X,     A(2)<----Y
```

Figure 2. Matching Arguments and Parameters for (1.3.1a)

The correspondence between parameters and arguments is determined <u>before</u> execution of the body of the procedure begins, and <u>is not changed</u> throughout the particular execution. This means that if a subscripted variable is given as an argument, the subscript is evaluated before the execution of the procedure begins, and the correspondence between parameter and argument is based on this initial value. Although the value of the subscript may change during execution of the procedure the argument-parameter correspondence is <u>not</u> revised. For example in Figure 2j, A(I) is given as the second argument. The value of I (from Figure 1a) is 2 so A(2) is associated with the second parameter Y. The value of I will be changed by SWAP, but this will not alter the association of Y with A(2). Thus, according to the values in Figure 1a, after execution of CALL SWAP(I,A(I)), I will be 8 and A(2) will be 2.

Finally, and most importantly, execution of a call statement
works as described above <u>only if the attributes of each argument
exactly match those of the parameter</u> with which it is
associated. That is, if a parameter is declared to be FIXED
DECIMAL then it must be associated with an argument that has
also been declared FIXED DECIMAL. If the parameter is FLOAT
DECIMAL then the associated argument must also be FLOAT DECIMAL.
If the parameter is CHARACTER then the argument must also be
CHARACTER; if CHARACTER VARYING, then the argument must also be
CHARACTER VARYING. The following is <u>not correct</u>:

```
            ...
            DECLARE WORD1 CHAR( 10 );
            DECLARE WORD2 CHAR( 50 ) VARYING;
            ...
            CALL FOLD( WORD1, WORD2 );
            ...
        *PROCESS
         /* FOLD STG2 INTO STG1 */
         FOLD: PROCEDURE( STG1, STG2 );
            DECLARE ( STG1, STG2 ) CHAR( * );
            ...
```

The first argument WORD1 matches the type of the first parameter
STG1, but WORD2 <u>does not match</u> STG2 since WORD2 is a VARYING
string and STG2 is not. If the attributes do not exactly match,
PL/C will print a warning message and then proceed to execute
the procedure anyway. The results can be confusing since the
program will sometimes appear to work properly and sometimes
not. The explanation is more than we want to get into here --
just make sure that the attributes match.

The only exception to this type matching requirement is that
an <u>argument</u> may or may not have the INITIAL or STATIC
attributes. (STATIC variables will be explained in Section
1.5.) A <u>parameter</u> <u>cannot</u> have either of these attributes, so
they are not considered in the matching of argument and
parameter attributes.

1.3.3 <u>Array Names as Arguments and Parameters</u>

Individual elements of an array may be passed as arguments to
a procedure that is expecting to receive a simple variable, as
for example in Figure 2. But it is often convenient to pass an
entire array as a single argument. This can be done if

1. both the parameter and the argument are declared as
   arrays,

2. both have the same number of dimensions and

3. both have the same type attributes (FIXED DECIMAL, FLOAT
   DECIMAL, CHARACTER or CHARACTER VARYING).

The parameter is declared to be an array, but only the number of dimensions and not the size is given in the declaration. This is done by giving an asterisk where the size would normally be given:

```
DECLARE ROW(*) FLOAT DECIMAL;
DECLARE TABLE(*,*) FIXED DECIMAL;
DECLARE WORDS(*) CHARACTER(*);
```

The size of a parameter array is the size of the argument array with which it is associated. This may vary from one call to the next, but the number of dimensions must be the same. That is, a parameter array of one dimension (a column array) cannot be associated with an argument array of two dimensions (a table array). As with simple variables, the <u>type attributes of the parameter array must exactly match those of the argument array</u>. A simple example is shown in (1.3.3a).

```
          *PL/C ID='JOHN WILLIAMS'
          /* PROGRAM TO SUM ITEMS OF A DATA LIST */
          SUMER: PROCEDURE OPTIONS(MAIN);
              DCL ITEM(50) FLOAT DECIMAL;
              DCL N FIXED DECIMAL; /* DATA LIST IS ITEM(1:N) */
              DCL SUM FLOAT DECIMAL;
              DCL I FIXED DECIMAL;
              GET LIST(N);
              IF (N<1)|(N>50)
                  THEN PUT LIST('IMPROPER DATA LENGTH',N);
              READ_LOOP: DO I = 1 TO N BY 1;
                  GET LIST(ITEM(I));
                  END READ_LOOP;
              CALL COMPSUM(ITEM, N, SUM);
(1.3.3a)      PUT SKIP LIST('SUM OF', N, 'ITEMS IS:', SUM);
              END SUMER;
          *PROCESS
          /* SET SUM TO SUM OF VECT(1:M) */
          COMPSUM: PROCEDURE(VECT, M, SUM);
              DCL VECT(*) FLOAT DECIMAL;
              DCL M FIXED DECIMAL;
              DCL SUM FLOAT DECIMAL;
              DCL J FIXED DECIMAL;
              SUM = 0;
              SUM_LOOP: DO J = 1 TO M BY 1;
                  SUM = SUM + VECT(J);
                  END SUM_LOOP;
              RETURN;
              END COMPSUM;
          *DATA
          5
          49.3, 4E2, -42, 17, 263.15
```

Another example is the procedure SEARCH in (1.3.3b).   SEARCH has four parameters:

Parameter 1: the array to be searched
Parameter 2: the index of the last element to be searched
Parameter 3: the value being searched for
Parameter 4: the index of the element found (or 0).

Figure 3 illustrates execution of

CALL SEARCH(B, M, X, K);

where the arguments in the calling procedure CALP have been declared:

DECLARE B(0:4) FIXED DECIMAL;
DECLARE (M, X, K) FIXED DECIMAL;

The values of the arguments before the call are shown in Figure 3a. The parameter-argument correspondence is depicted in Figure 3b. Note that parameter A refers to the whole array B(0:4), even though the procedure does not reference every element. Since M is 2, only B(1:2) is searched and the result of execution is a 0 in K.

```
         *PROCESS
         /* SEARCH A(1:N) FOR VALUE X, SET J SO THAT A(J)=X */
         /* STORE 0 IN J IF NO SUCH INTEGER EXISTS */
         SEARCH: PROCEDURE(A, N, X, J);
              DECLARE (A(*), X) FIXED DECIMAL;
              DECLARE (N, J)    FIXED DECIMAL;
(1.3.3b)      S_LOOP: DO J = 1 TO N BY 1;
                   IF A(J) = X THEN GO TO TERM_SEARCH;
                   END S_LOOP;
              J = 0;    /* INDICATES VALUE NOT FOUND */
         TERM_SEARCH: RETURN;
         END SEARCH;
```

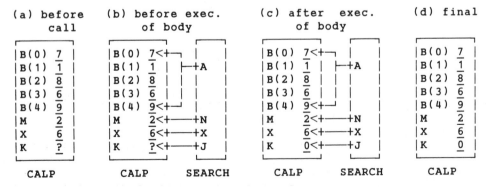

Figure 3. Execution of CALL SEARCH(B, M, X, K);

The program in (1.3.3b) uses a GO TO to escape from the DO
loop. Although this is the technique we have used since Section
I.4.3.2, there is a better solution to the exit problem in this
special   case   where   exit   from   the   DO loop also implies
termination of the procedure. This is shown in (1.3.3c).   The
action of (1.3.3c) is clearer and RETURN should always be used
in place of a terminating GO TO whenever possible. A procedure
may have any number of RETURN statements.

```
             *PROCESS
             /* SEARCH A(1:N) FOR VALUE X, SET J SO THAT A(J)=X */
             /* STORE 0 IN J IF NO SUCH INTEGER EXISTS */
             SEARCH: PROCEDURE(A, N, X, J);
                     DECLARE (A(*), X) FIXED DECIMAL;
                     DECLARE (N, J)    FIXED DECIMAL;
(1.3.3c)     S_LOOP: DO J = 1 TO N BY 1;
                     IF A(J) = X THEN RETURN;
                     END S_LOOP;
             J = 0;      /* INDICATES VALUE NOT FOUND */
             RETURN;
             END SEARCH;
```

1.4 Nested Procedure Calls

Thus far we have been considering only procedure calls in the
main procedure.   Actually, since a procedure call may appear
anywhere that a statement may appear, this includes the body of
any procedure.   A call is simply placed wherever the action of
the procedure is required, with the call designating the
particular arguments upon which the procedure is to be executed.

(1.4a) illustrates a complete program consisting of a main
procedure and three external procedures. The main procedure
SRTG reads in a list of integers, calls procedure SORT to sort
the   list,   and   then   prints   the list.   This SORT uses a
successive-minima algorithm, a fairly obvious variation of the
one used in Section III.2.3. It calls two other procedures:
FINDMIN to determine the array element with minimum value, and
SWAP to interchange the values of two variables. The ordering
of the four procedure definitions in (1.4a) is not significant;
any ordering could have been used. (Although it is customary to
give the main procedure first it is not necessary to do so.)

The program consists of four separate sections, each of which
performs some logically independent task, each written as a
separate procedure. Each can be understood by itself, without
having to understand how the others work. In actual practice
one would rarely write such short procedures as are shown here;
this program would have been just as readable had we written
just a main program and a SORT procedure, performing the FINDMIN
and SWAP commands within the sort procedure itself. We have
written (1.4a) this way just to illustrate the use of nested
calls.

```
*PL/C ID='J. HARTMANIS'
/* READ IN 3 INTEGERS, PRINT IN SORTED ORDER */
SRTG: PROCEDURE OPTIONS(MAIN);
    DECLARE (A(3), I, M) FIXED DECIMAL;
    READ_LOOP: DO I = 1 TO 3 BY 1;
        GET LIST(A(I));
        END READ_LOOP;
    M = 3;
    ST: CALL SORT(A, M);
    PRINT_LOOP: DO I = 1 TO 3 BY 1;
        PUT LIST(A(I));
        END PRINT_LOOP;
    END SRTG;
*PROCESS
/* SORT ARRAY X(1:N) USING SUCCESSIVE MINIMA */
SORT: PROCEDURE(X, N);
    DECLARE (X(*), N) FIXED DECIMAL;
    DECLARE (I, J) FIXED DECIMAL;
    MIN_LOOP: DO I = 1 TO N-1 BY 1;
        /* PUT MINIMUM OF X(I:N) IN X(I) */
            FI: CALL FINDMIN(X, I, N, J);
            SW: CALL SWAP(X(I), X(J));
        END MIN_LOOP;
    RETURN;
    END SORT;
*PROCESS
/* SET J TO INDEX OF MINIMUM OF X(I:N) */
FINDMIN: PROCEDURE(X, I, N, J);
    DECLARE (X(*), I, N, J) FIXED DECIMAL;
    DECLARE K FIXED DECIMAL;
    J = I;
    FIND_LOOP: DO K = I+1 TO N BY 1;
        IF X(K) < X(J) THEN J = K;
        END FIND_LOOP;
    RETURN;
    END FINDMIN;
*PROCESS
/* SWAP VALUES OF X AND Y */
SWAP: PROCEDURE(X, Y);
    DECLARE (X, Y) FIXED DECIMAL;
    DECLARE T FIXED DECIMAL;
    T = X;   X = Y;   Y = T;
    RETURN;
    END SWAP;
*DATA
    2, 8, 1
```

(1.4a)

When a program has several procedure calls, it becomes
difficult to remember where to return to when execution of a
procedure is finished. To make this easier, we extend our box
convention. First, label each procedure call with a unique
name. Then, when a box is drawn for a procedure, put the label
of the procedure call at the bottom of the box. For example,
when we first execute ST: CALL SORT(A, M); of (1.4a), we place
the name ST at the bottom of SORT's box as in Fig. 4b. Upon
termination of SORT we can then see that we were executing ST.

Let us now execute program (1.4a). Fig. 4a shows the
variables after the list of values has been read, and just
before execution of the statement labeled ST. Note that I is 4
because of the way the preceding loop is executed. Fig. 4b
shows the state of affairs after the SORT procedure body
execution has begun, and just before the call labeled FI is
executed for the first time. Thus I (within SORT) has the value
1. J still has no value.

Statement FI is now executed. A box for procedure FINDMIN is
drawn, the parameter correspondences are made, and the local
variable K is created. Fig. 4c shows the boxes at this stage,
just before execution of the procedure body. Note that the
arrow for argument X of SORT has been copied over to parameter X
of FINDMIN. Similarly parameter N of FINDMIN points where
parameter N of SORT does.

Now procedure body FINDMIN executes and terminates. We show
the boxes just after the completion of the call on FINDMIN and
before execution of statement SW in Fig. 4d. J is now 3 since
A(3) contains the minimum value of A(1:3). We now execute the
call SW. Fig. 4e shows the state of affairs just before
execution of the body of SWAP. Note carefully where parameters
X and Y point. The parameter X corresponds to the argument X(I)
in SORT. Since X in SORT is A and I has the value 1, this is
A(1). Similarly, Y refers to A(3). Thus SWAP will exchange the
values of A(1) and A(3).

When SWAP finishes, its box will be deleted and we will
return to the point following the call labelled SW in SORT. The
values of A(1) and A(3) will be interchanged.

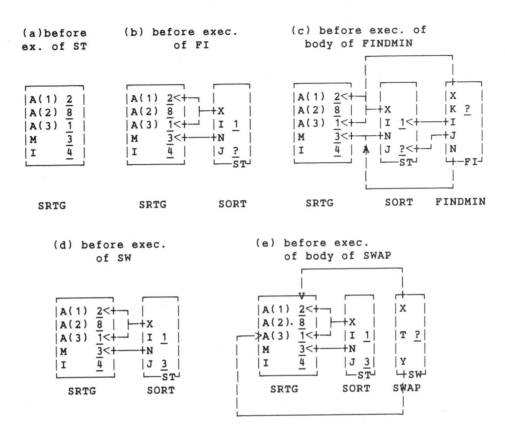

Figure 4.   Partial Execution of Program (1.4a)

It might occur to you to wonder what would happen if a procedure "called itself". That is, what if CALL P(...) is located in the body of procedure P? In many programming languages this would be a serious error, but it is permitted in PL/I, and in fact is very useful. The process is called "recursion", or "recursive execution". However, it is somewhat complicated to explain and we are not going to use this facility in this Primer. If you are interested in recursion read Section VI.4 of our Introduction to Programming.

1.5 <u>STATIC Variables</u>

Section 1.3.2 described the execution of a procedure call. The creation and erasure of the boxes in Figure 1 accurately reflect what actually takes place during each execution of a call. In particular the local variables, such as T in Figure 1, are <u>created</u> <u>as</u> <u>the</u> <u>procedure</u> <u>is</u> <u>entered</u> and <u>destroyed</u> <u>on</u> <u>return</u> <u>from</u> <u>the</u> <u>procedure</u>. This happens each time that the procedure is executed; during the intervals between executions the local variables simply do not exist. This process is called "dynamic storage management" and in PL/I variables that are treated in this way are said to be "automatic". The AUTOMATIC attribute can be explicitly specified in their declaration but this is not necessary since AUTOMATIC is the default assumption.

Dynamic storage management permits efficient use of storage space. Since variables are assigned storage space only when their procedures are being executed, the same space can be used at different times for different variables. However, it also means that information about AUTOMATIC variables is not preserved from one execution of a procedure to the next. For example, a procedure could not even keep a cumulative count of the number of times it had been called.

To permit retention of information a variable can be declared STATIC. A static variable is created just before execution of the <u>main procedure</u> begins, and it remains around during all of execution. It is not destroyed on return from a procedure; it retains whatever value exists at the time of return. If the procedure is executed again the static variables already exist and need not be created at entry. If a static variable is declared with the INITIAL attribute the initial value is assigned only once as the variable is created and not each time the procedure is entered. Note, however, that a <u>static variable</u> <u>is still local</u> to the procedure in which it is declared. Although it exists throughout execution of the program (and not just when its procedure is being executed) it cannot be accessed from any other procedure.

For example, the values of J printed by repeated calls of
INCR in (1.5a) are always 1 because J is recreated with initial
value 0 on each call. By contrast the values of K are 1, 2 and
3 since this static variable retains its value from one call to
the next. It is created and assigned initial value zero only
once, just before execution of the main program begins.

```
              ...
              CALLCOUNT = 0;
              COUNT_LOOP: DO WHILE (CALLCOUNT < 3);
                  CALLCOUNT = CALLCOUNT + 1;
                  CALL INCR;
                  END COUNT_LOOP;
              ...
(1.5a)
        *PROCESS
         /* INCREASE J & K BY 1, AND PRINT */
         INCR: PROCEDURE;
             DCL J FIXED DEC INIT(0);
             DCL K FIXED DEC INIT(0) STATIC;
             J = J + 1;
             K = K + 1;
             PUT SKIP LIST(J, K);
             RETURN;
             END INCR;
```

As another example, COUNT in (1.5b) has the simple task of
counting the number of times that it has been called and
reporting this count to the calling procedure. This could be
used to count the occurrences of some particular event in
various places in a program -- say, the occurrences of negative
numbers in a set of data arrays.

```
        *PROCESS
         /* SET N TO CUMULATIVE NUMBER OF CALLS */
         COUNT: PROCEDURE(N);
             DECLARE N FIXED DECIMAL;
(1.5b)       DECLARE CT FIXED DECIMAL STATIC INIT(0);
             CT = CT + 1;
             N = CT;
             RETURN;
             END COUNT;
```

As a third example, NEXTLET in (1.5c) serves to divide input words of ten characters each into individual letters. Each time NEXTLET is called it returns the next letter of the input data stream to the calling procedure. On the first call, and every tenth call thereafter, NEXTLET obtains a new word from the external data list.

```
          *PROCESS
          /* SET L TO NEXT LETTER OF 10 LETTER WORD */
          NEXTLET: PROCEDURE(L);
              DECLARE L CHAR(*);
              DECLARE WORD CHAR(10) STATIC;
              DECLARE COUNT FIXED DEC STATIC INIT(10);
              /* GET NEW WORD (EVERY TENTH CALL) */
                  IF COUNT = 10 THEN DO;
(1.5c)                    GET LIST(WORD);
                          COUNT = 0; END;
              /* PICK OUT NEXT LETTER */
                  COUNT = COUNT + 1;
                  L = SUBSTR(WORD, COUNT, 1);
              RETURN;
              END NEXTLET;
```

The local variable WORD in NEXTLET must be static because it must get a value from the data list on the first call and retain this value for nine more calls. If it were not declared to be static the value would be lost on return from the first call. COUNT is similarly declared static so that NEXTLET can keep track of the position in WORD of the "next" letter, and so it will know when the data word is exhausted and a new value must be obtained from the data list.

Note that STATIC applies only to variables. A parameter in a procedure cannot be declared STATIC. It would not make any sense to do so since parameters are associated with arguments each time a procedure is called.

Section 1 <u>Summary</u>

1. An external procedure is a sub-program that performs some distinct, clearly specified task.

2. The definition (or declaration) of an external procedure (excluding the main procedure) has the form:

```
*PROCESS
/* Comment describing function of procedure */
procedure-name: PROCEDURE(list of parameters);
    Declarations of parameters;
    Declarations of local variables;
    Statements; (including RETURN)
    END procedure-name;
```

3. External procedures are placed (in any order) after the main procedure and before the *DATA card.

4. External procedures are executed by CALLing them by name. There can be many calls of a particular procedure, located anywhere in the main procedure or in any external procedure.

5. Execution of an external procedure is terminated by executing a RETURN statement. This completes execution of the particular CALL statement that caused this particular execution of the procedure.

6. An external procedure has its own local variables, independent of the variables of any other procedure. Normally these local variables are created each time execution of the procedure begins and are destroyed when that execution terminates. However, local variables can be made "permanent" by declaring them to be STATIC.

7. An external procedure has its own local statement labels, accessible only to GO TOs within that procedure. It is not possible to exit from an external procedure by means of a GO TO.

8. Communication between external procedures is by means of the parameters of the procedure declaration and the arguments of the CALL. Parameters and arguments are matched in the order listed (independent of their names). The attributes of parameters should exactly match those of the corresponding arguments.

Section 1 Exercises

1. For each sequence of statements below, write a procedure
with that sequence as the body, complete with declarations. The
parameters are those variables and arrays described in the
comment. Other variables should be local to the procedure. All
variables are fixed decimal.

```
a) /* STORE THE MAXIMUM OF A AND B IN C*/
     IF A >= B
          THEN C = A;
          ELSE C = B;

b) /* STORE THE SUM OF THE ELEMENTS OF A(1:N) IN SUM*/
     SUM = 0;
     SUM_LOOP: DO I = 1 TO N BY 1;
          SUM = SUM + A(I);
          END SUM_LOOP;

c) /* REVERSE THE ELEMENTS OF ARRAY X(1:N)*/
     FIRST = 1; LAST = N;
     REV_LOOP: DO WHILE (FIRST < LAST);
          T = X(FIRST);
          X(FIRST = X(LAST);
          X(LAST) = T;
          FIRST = FIRST + 1;
          LAST = LAST - 1;
          END REV_LOOP;
```

2. Make the program segments of Exercise 2, Section I.5, into
procedures. Only the variables described in the comment of each
program segment should be parameters.

3. Execute the following procedure calls by hand, drawing all
necessary boxes. Procedure SWAP is given in (1.1b). Assume all
variables are fixed decimal.

```
a) CALL SWAP(A,B); where     A 5     B 6
b) CALL SWAP(T,X); where     T 3     X 4
c) CALL SWAP(Y,X); where     Y 1     X 8
d) CALL SWAP(V,V); where     V 3
```

4. Write procedures for the program segments of Exercises 4, 5
and 6 of Section I.5.

5. Write a procedure MEAN which, given an array segment X(1:N)
calculates the mean of the values. The mean is the sum of the
elements divided by N.

6. Execute the following procedure calls by hand, drawing all the boxes. Procedure SEARCH is given in (1.3.3c). The variables used are given below.

T(0) 6	N0 0	F 8
T(1) 8	N1 1	G 5
T(2) 4	N2 2	H 6
T(3) 9	N3 3	I 3

    a) CALL SEARCH(T, N0, H, I);
    b) CALL SEARCH(T, N1, H, I);
    c) CALL SEARCH(T, N3, H, I);
    d) CALL SEARCH(T, N3, G, I);
    e) CALL SEARCH(T, N3, F, I);

7. Write a procedure with five parameters that will set the fifth parameter equal to the sum of the first four.

8. Write a procedure MEDIAN which, given an array segment $X(1:N)$ calculates the median of the values. The median is the value such that half the numbers are greater than that value and half are less. One way to do this is to first sort the array and then pick the middle value. If you use this method, use a previously written sort procedure to do the sorting. But be careful; MEDIAN should not change the order of the values in its argument array -- a procedure should never modify the arguments unless its specific task is to modify them.

9. Write a program to read a list of values and to print out the mean and the median. Your program should use the procedures written in Exercises 5 and 8.

10. Write a procedure which calculates sin(x) using the formula

$$\sin(x) = x/1! \ - \ x^3/3! \ + \ x^5/5! \ - \ x^7/7! \ + \ ...$$

The number of terms of the series to be used should be a parameter of the procedure. Next, write a program to compare the values of sin(x) calculated using the built-in SIN function against those values calculated by your procedure. Run the program with various values of x and various values of the number of terms used in the series.

11. Write a procedure to calculate the product of two n by n matrices $A(1:N,1:N)$ and $B(1:N,1:N)$. Each element $C(i,k)$ of the resulting matrix $C(1:N,1:N)$ is defined as the sum of the values

$$A(i,j) * B(j,k) \quad \text{for } j = 1, ..., N.$$

12. Assume you are given the subroutine FLP shown below and told only that IN is an input parameter, OUT is an output parameter, and that the routine neither reads any data nor prints any lines. Write a program that will allow FLP to be tested by repeatedly calling it with different input values and displaying the results. Your program will include FLP but not change it in any way.

```
*PROCESS
/* SET OUT TO ...  */
FLP: PROCEDURE(IN, OUT);
    DCL IN CHAR(*) VARYING, OUT FIXED DEC;
    ...
    RETURN;
    END FLP;
```

13. What is the <u>execution</u> output from the program shown below:

```
*PL/C ID='T. TEITELBAUM'
/* SQUARE-DUPLICATE AND PRINT EACH OF J DATA PAIRS */
LST: PROCEDURE OPTIONS(MAIN);
    DCL L CHARACTER(8) VARYING;
    DCL (N, J, K) FIXED DECIMAL;
    GET LIST(J);
    EDIT_LOOP: DO K = 1 TO J BY 1;
        GET LIST(L, N);
        CALL EDITOR(N, L);
        PUT SKIP LIST(L, N);
        END EDIT_LOOP;
    END LST;
*PROCESS
/* SQUARE NBR; DUPLICATE FIRST CHAR OF CHR */
EDITOR: PROCEDURE(NBR,CHR);
    DCL NBR FIXED DECIMAL;
    DCL CHR CHARACTER(*) VARYING;
    IF NBR ¬= 0 THEN CALL SQUARE(NBR);
    IF CHR ¬= ' ' THEN CALL DUP(CHR);
    RETURN;
    END EDITOR;
*PROCESS
/* DUPLICATE FIRST CHARACTER OF STR */
DUP: PROCEDURE(STR);
    DCL STR CHARACTER(*) VARYING;
    STR = SUBSTR(STR,1,1) || STR;
    RETURN;
    END DUP;
```

(exercise 13 continued on next page)

```
*PROCESS
/* SET VALUE = SQUARE OF VALUE */
SQUARE: PROCEDURE(VALUE);
    DCL VALUE FIXED DECIMAL;
    VALUE = VALUE * VALUE;
    RETURN;
    END SQUARE;
*DATA
4, 'X', 4, 'YY', -3, 'XYX', 0, '4',
4, 'ABC', 567.9032
```

14. Write a procedure that will read a list of words (quoted strings of characters) whose lengths may be anywhere from 1 to 15 characters, and will print a list of any words that occur more than once in this data list. The end of the data list is indicated by the string '<*>', which is not itself considered an item on the list. Title the output appropriately.

15. Write a body for the procedure REPTEST, started below, so it will perform the task described in the heading comment. That is, it should check for repetitions of each character in the argument word. Any repetition of a character should be replaced by an asterisk. For example, 'AAABCDDBE' would become 'A**BCD**E'.

```
*PROCESS
/* REPLACE ALL REPEATED OCCURRENCES (EXCEPT THE FIRST)*/
/* OF ANY CHARACTERS IN WORD BY '*' */
REPTEST: PROCEDURE(WORD);
    DCL WORD CHAR(*) VARYING;
    ...
    END REPTEST;
```

16.   What is the <u>execution</u> output from the following program?

```
*PL/C ID='R. BECHHOFER'
 /* PROBLEM IV.1.16, PRIMER */
 PROB: PROCEDURE OPTIONS(MAIN);
      DCL M FIXED DEC,
          N FIXED DEC INIT(4);
      CALL_LOOP: DO M = 1 TO 3 BY 1;
           CALL SUB(M);
           PUT SKIP LIST('RESULT IS:', M, N);
           END CALL_LOOP;
      PUT SKIP LIST('AFTER LAST CALL',M,N);
      END PROB;
*PROCESS
 /* PRINT N AND M+2 */
 SUB: PROCEDURE(N);
      DCL N FIXED DECIMAL;
      DCL M FIXED DECIMAL INIT(5);
      M = M + 2;
      PUT SKIP LIST('INSIDE',M,N); RETURN;
      PUT SKIP LIST('STILL INSIDE',M,N);
      RETURN;
      END SUB;
*DATA
```

17.   Write a procedure DEBLANK to serve as a subroutine to eliminate all blanks from a varying character string given as argument.

18.   Modify the subroutine DEBLANK of Exercise 17 so that it has a second parameter, which is fixed decimal. If the second argument has a non-zero value then DEBLANK is to return as the value of the second argument the <u>cumulative</u> number of blanks that have been eliminated in all calls so far (including the current call). If the value of the second argument is zero then it is to remain unchanged by DEBLANK.

19. Complete the procedure FINDMAX started below. This is a
procedure to receive positive numbers and report the greatest of
the numbers received. Its action when called is the following:

-if ACT=1 the value given in VAL is to be saved -- that is,
it is to be stored in some available slot in the array
VALS. If this can be done indicate success by returning
with RES=1; if no space is available indicate failure by
returning with RES=0.
-if ACT=2 then the maximum of the values currently in VALS
is to be returned in VAL. This maximum value is to be
removed from VALS and the space it occupied made available
for a new arrival. Indicate success by returning with
RES=1 and failure (if VALS is empty) by returning with
RES=0.

```
*PROCESS
/* SAVE VAL IF ACT=1; RETURN MAX VAL IF ACT=2; */
/* RES = 1,0 FOR SUCCESS,FAILURE */
FINDMAX: PROCEDURE(VAL,ACT,RES);
     DCL VAL FLOAT DEC;
     DCL (ACT, RES) FIXED DEC;
     DCL VALS(5) FLOAT DEC STATIC INIT(-1,-1,-1,-1,-1);
     ...
     END FINDMAX;
```

20. Write a procedure GETMAX: PROCEDURE(VAL,ACT,RES); that has
exactly the same action from the caller's point-of-view as
FINDMAX of Exercise 19. GETMAX is to work by calling FINDMAX,
except that by keeping track of the kinds of calls GETMAX knows
when FINDMAX would fail (return with RES=0) so in these cases
GETMAX doesn't bother to call FINDMAX. It simulates FINDMAX's
action and returns directly. Do not change FINDMAX.

21. Write a procedure that can be used to sum all the elements
in a set of adjacent rows in a two-dimensional array. The
parameters (all fixed decimal) are to be the following (in the
order listed below):
    Parameter 1: the array
    Parameter 2: the number of columns in the array
    Parameter 3: the first row to be included
    Parameter 4: the last row to be included
    Parameter 5: the sum of the required elements (the result).

22. Write a main procedure that can be used to test the summing
procedure of Exercise 21. That is, this main procedure should
    a) read a set of values that will serve as arguments
    b) print the argument values (appropriately titled)
    c) call the summing procedure
    d) print the sum value returned.

Section 2   The Uses of Procedures

Procedures provide three different capabilities:

1. The ability to write a section of program in one place and have it executed as if it were written in another.

2. The ability to write a section in terms of parameters so that it can be used for different variables at different times. This is effectively defining a new <u>operation</u> to be used in a program, like SORT(A,N) or SWAP(X,Y).

3. The ability to create an independent environment whose names are distinct from those of the rest of the program, and for which the total communication is clearly and completely specified.

2.1 <u>Subroutines</u>

The term "subroutine" is often used in programming to identify some sequence of statements that is needed in more than one place in a program. It is convenient to be able to write the common statements only once and use them as often as and wherever necessary. If a subroutine is written in a general way, without commitment to particular variable names, its opportunity for use is clearly increased. This obvious use of procedures in PL/I was suggested by the examples of the preceding sections.

There is generally a sense of both <u>permanence</u> and <u>portability</u> in subroutines. That is, they are written so that they can be used in more than one program. There are various "libraries" of subroutines that are quite permanent and widely used. In effect, the built-in functions of PL/I -- SQRT, MAX, MIN, MOD, etc. -- constitute such a library.

Subroutines can be considered a means of <u>extending</u> a programming language; of adding whatever operators or statements the user needs that the language doesn't happen to offer. For example, in (1.1b) we developed a procedure to interchange the values of two variables. With this procedure appended to any program the "swap" operation is effectively added to the language. The procedure SEARCH in (1.3.3c) is another, more complex, example.

In Part III we often used a statement at a "higher level" than PL/I, and then translated or expanded it into PL/I. By writing a subroutine to perform that task we effectively add that high-level statement to the language (at least temporarily). For example, in Section III.2.3 we developed a program to order the elements of an array. If this were written as an external procedure with the array as argument then one could regard

     CALL SORT(A);

as part of the language. Moreover, the procedure could be saved and reused in future programs whenever we had need of that particular function. For all practical purposes we could now think of "sort" as an operation available in our private augmented-PL/I. In the development of future programs, once we reached a point where the algorithm required "sort" we would not have to refine that particular branch of the tree any further.

Subroutines exploit all three capabilities of external procedures. The first two are obvious, but it is the third -- the independent environment -- that allows a subroutine to be moved freely from one program to another without any concern for whether the variables in the subroutine happen to coincide with names in the host program.

2.2 Control Sections

Procedures can be used simply to improve the clarity and readability of programs. The techniques described in Part II, which make small programs clear and understandable, don't always work well when applied directly to large programs. For example, if the units at the highest level are so long that it is impossible to comprehend them as a single unit, then their role and relationship to other units is less clear. The indentation convention which makes vertical left-alignment significant in understanding a program clearly works best if successive statements with the same alignment appear on the same page. If the successor to a particular unit is several pages away vertical alignment is much less effective as a way of emphasizing the structure of a program.

Procedures can be used to alleviate all these problems by reducing the apparent size of programs. Simply take some convenient section of program, write it in some remote position as an external procedure, and provide a CALL in its original location. For example, suppose one has to perform some task on each element of a 3-dimensional array:

```
                /* GRIMBLE THE ARRAY AR */
                  PLANE: DO I = 1 TO R BY 1;
                    ROW: DO J = 1 TO S BY 1;
                      COL: DO K = 1 TO T BY 1;
                            /* GRIMBLE AN ELEMENT */
                               ...
                           END COL;
                       END ROW;
                   END PLANE;
```

This unit is reasonably clear as long as the body of the "grimble an element" task is not too large. If it is large, or if it involves many levels of nesting, it is worthwhile writing it as a separate procedure:

```
                ...
                /* GRIMBLE THE ARRAY AR */
                  PLANE: DO I = 1 TO R BY 1;
                    ROW: DO J = 1 TO S BY 1;
                      COL: DO K = 1 TO T BY 1;
                            CALL GRIMBLE(AR(I,J,K));
                           END COL;
                       END ROW;
                   END PLANE;
                ...
           *PROCESS
            /* PERFORM GRIMBLE PROCESS UPON G */
            GRIMBLE: PROCEDURE(G);
                DECLARE G FLOAT DECIMAL;
                ...
                RETURN;
                END GRIMBLE;
```

Some reasonable rules-of-thumb for the size of individual units are:

1. The body of a unit should be no more than 50 lines (1 page) in length.

2. Nesting should not exceed 3 or at most 4 levels.

To maintain these limits, use procedures so that a CALL can replace some section of program, thereby reducing the size or apparent nesting level of the main program.

Procedures should be routinely used in this way. In fact, any program of more than one or two pages should be entirely written in this manner. At the highest level the program should consist of little more than CALL statements. The main procedure, doing nothing but calling other procedures, serves as a control section of the program. It is short and shows clearly how the program is organized and the major steps in its action.

The sorting program in (1.4a) is written in this manner. The actual sorting is done by a procedure SORT called from the main

procedure. This allows the main procedure to be very short and
clear: it simply reads the data, calls SORT, and prints the
sorted results. The details of how the sorting is actually done
do not obscure the simple sequence of tasks in the main
procedure.

The accounting problem of Section III.2.4 provides an even
better example. This program has three sections:

```
/* READ AND SET UP THE ACCOUNTS.*/
/* READ AND PROCESS THE TRANSACTIONS.*/
/* PRINT THE RESULTS.*/
```

In the abbreviated form given in III.2.4 this all fits on one
page and is not difficult to follow. A useful program for a
realistic version of this problem, including adequate error
checking, would be many pages long. It might still consist of
three sections, but if each section were long and complicated
the overall structure would not be clear to the reader. To
preserve clarity of structure the main procedure of this program
should be a control section, with each of the sub-tasks written
as a separate procedure:

```
/* READ AND SET UP THE ACCOUNTS.*/
    CALL ACCTRD(N, ACCT, WITH, DEP, IBAL, CBAL);
/* READ AND PROCESS THE TRANSACTIONS.*/
    CALL PTRAN(N, ACCT, WITH, DEP, IBAL, CBAL);
/* PRINT THE RESULTS.*/
    CALL PRINT(N, ACCT, WITH, DEP, IBAL, CBAL);
```

With this organization the accounts are declared in the main
procedure and passed as arguments to each of the processing
procedures. The extra variables needed to process the
transactions -- TACCT, DEPWITH, AMT -- are needed only by PTRAN
so they are declared in PTRAN rather than the main procedure.

As another example, the index for this book was produced by a
sizable program. Nevertheless, its high level structure is
clear from its control section:

```
/* PRIMER INDEX */
INDEX: PROCEDURE OPTIONS(MAIN);
    DCL LN(3000) CHAR(50); /* TABLE OF LINES */
    DCL TOPLINE FIXED DEC INIT(0); /* TOP LINE IN LN */
    /* READ TOPIC/PG-NBR PAIRS INTO LN */
        CALL LOAD(LN,TOPLINE);
    /* SORT REFERENCES INTO ALPHABETICAL ORDER */
        CALL SORT(LN,TOPLINE);
    /* CONDENSE MULTIPLE REFERENCES TO A SINGLE LINE */
        CALL CONDENSE(LN,TOPLINE);
    /* CONVERT LINES TO FORMAT REQ'D BY TEXT-EDITOR */
        CALL CONVERT(LN,TOPLINE);
    /* PUNCH CARD FOR EACH LINE */
        CALL PUNCH(LN,TOPLINE);
    END INDEX;
```

These examples apparently violate the suggestion of Section II.1.6.1 that comments should not duplicate the program statements. In these cases the task of the procedure is sufficiently complex that it is not adequately implied by the procedure-name. Hence these comments give a more complete idea of the task performed by each CALL and are worth the extra trouble.

In general, a good way to organize and present a large program is to have four sections:

1. A block of comments that fully and precisely describe the function of the program.

2. A control section of not more than one page that calls various procedures to do the work.

3. A block of comments serving as a "table of contents" for the following procedures.

4. A set of external procedures, called by the control section.

Of course, some of the individual procedures may be so large that they would also benefit from the same treatment. Entry to such a procedure would encounter another control section, which would call other procedures. There is really no limit to how large a program can become, and still be understandable, if procedures are used to keep the apparent size down to where the techniques of Part II are effective.

2.3 Sectional Independence

An external procedure is a totally independent section of a program, and this independence is very useful. Communication between external procedures is solely through parameters and arguments. Separate procedures have no other effects on each other. When reading a program you can analyze each external procedure separately, with complete confidence that no action (or mistake) elsewhere in the program will have the slightest effect on this procedure, except possibly in the way that it affects the values of arguments. The modularity sought in the discussion of "program units" in Part II is provided automatically by external procedures.

When writing a program section, if you write it as an external procedure you have less to worry about. You are entirely concerned with how to perform the required action. You have no concern that other sections of program will interfere with this one, or that this section may have unexpected side-effects elsewhere. You need not remember what variable names have been used elsewhere in the program; you can use whatever names are most natural for this local use. For example, you can use I as a subscript without wondering whether I is the index of some outer loop, and hence must not be disturbed. You can use SUM for a local variable without having to check to see whether that particular identifier is already in use. For example, compare the program segments given in (2.3a) and (2.3b).

(2.3a)

```
            ...
        OUT_LOOP: DO I = 1 TO R BY 1;
            ...
            SUM = TOTAL + NEWVAL(I);
            ...
            MID_LOOP: DO J = 1 TO S BY 1;
                ...
                /* SET TRIAL(J) TO SUM OF X(1:T) */
                    SUM = 0;
                    SUM_LOOP: DO I = 1 TO T BY 1;
                        SUM = SUM + X(I);
                        END SUM_LOOP;
                    TRIAL(J) = SUM;
                ...
                END MID_LOOP;
            ...
            END OUT_LOOP;
        ...
```

(2.3b)

```
            ...
        OUT_LOOP: DO I = 1 TO R BY 1;
            ...
            SUM = TOTAL + NEWVAL(I);
            ...
            MID_LOOP: DO J = 1 TO S BY 1;
                ...
                CALL INSUM(X, T, TRIAL(J));
                ...
                END MID_LOOP;
            ...
            END OUT_LOOP;
        ...
    *PROCESS
    /* SET RESULT = SUM OF Y(1:N) */
    INSUM: PROCEDURE(Y, N, RESULT);
        DECLARE (RESULT, Y(*)) FLOAT DECIMAL;
        DECLARE N FIXED DECIMAL;
        DECLARE I FIXED DECIMAL;
        DECLARE SUM FLOAT DECIMAL INITIAL(0);
        SUM_LOOP: DO I = 1 TO N BY 1;
            SUM = SUM + Y(I);
            END SUM_LOOP;
        RESULT = SUM;
        RETURN;
        END INSUM;
```

(2.3a) is incorrect because both the loop index I and the
variable SUM are accidentally re-used. The error is obvious in
this case because (2.3a) is short and most of the details have
been omitted. However, if (2.3a) were several pages long so
that the beginning of OUT_LOOP was several pages away from
SUM_LOOP, and if the first part had been written several days
earlier so that the details had been forgotten, then it would be
very easy for such an error to occur. The risk would be reduced
if the innermost summing task were written as a separate
procedure, as in (2.3b). Then it is no longer necessary to
check the rest of the program before choosing variable names for
this task.

This independence of sections is particularly useful when a
program is to be produced by a team of programmers. If each
programmer (or group) is assigned a separate external procedure
the communication problems are minimized. Joint planning will
concern only the function of each procedure, and its parameter
communication. Given this "problem specification" the design
and development of the procedure can proceed as described in
Part III, just as if this were an independent problem. It
should also be tested as if it were an independent problem. The
procedures should be integrated into a final program only after
there is great confidence in their individual performance.

For example, suppose a program is required to perform some
task upon an array of words that are in alphabetical order.
Suppose that the input consists of lines in which the words are
not in alphabetical order. Obviously the program will be
required to scan lines and break them up into individual words,
and then sort the resulting list of words into alphabetical
order. It is useful to design a program with these "scan" and
"sort" tasks as separate procedures. As far as the principal
program is concerned all that has to be specified for these
tasks is the action to be performed and the manner in which
arguments are to be given. This specification is called the
"interface" between the procedures. Once the interfaces have
been specified the design, writing and testing of the scan
procedure, the sort procedure and the rest of the program could
proceed independently. All three could be done by one person
(working in any order), by three separate programmers, or parts
could be drawn from a library of existing subroutines. The
programmers of the different procedures do not have to discuss
with each other what local variables and labels they plan to use
in their particular procedure.

One particularly important aspect of interface specification
is the identification of each parameter as input, output , or
both input and output. The independence of procedures protects
the variables of one procedure from the actions of other
procedures -- except for those variables that are given as
arguments in the call of another procedure. Since PL/I does not
protect argument variables the calling and called procedures must
have a clear understanding as to how each is to be treated. For
example, if the calling procedure regards a particular argument

as providing only input to another procedure, the called
procedure must not change the value of that argument. A
procedure should change the value of the argument associated
with a particular parameter <u>only if it is explicitly agreed that
it is an output parameter</u>.

2.3.1 <u>Separation of Action and Control</u>

Recall the discussion in Section II.2 about the separation of
action and control. Schema (2a) was used as an example:

```
/* Comment describing action of the unit */
    i = 0;
    loop-name: DO WHILE ( i < n );
        i = i + 1;
        Body
        END loop-name;
```

We wanted to be able to state that this schema would repeat the
body n times regardless of what the action of the body was.
However, this statement is true only if the body is restricted:

1. it may not alter the values of i or n,

2. and it may not execute a GO TO or a RETURN.

Suppose the body is written as a separate external procedure
named TASK:

```
        ...
    /* Comment describing action of the unit */
        i = 0;
        loop-name: DO WHILE ( i < n );
            i = i + 1;
            CALL TASK(...);
            END loop-name;
(2.3.1a)     ...
    *PROCESS
    /* Comment describing function of TASK */
    TASK: PROCEDURE(...);
        ...
        RETURN;
        END TASK;
```

Now the body does not have access to the variables i and n of
the calling procedure (assuming that they are not given as
arguments of the call) so it is not necessary to further
restrict the body in this regard. The RETURN statement is now
harmless in the body, since its execution will only terminate
one execution of TASK. A GO TO cannot be used to escape from an
external procedure. This means that <u>any program</u> can be given as
this external procedure body with <u>confidence that it will be
repeated n times</u>.

However, there is one other aspect of the question that was
neglected in II.2 but should be mentioned here. For example,
suppose the following were given as the body of TASK:

```
ENDLESS_LOOP: DO WHILE ('1'B);
     END ENDLESS_LOOP;
```

This condition is initially true, and remains true, so this DO
loop will be repeatedly endlessly. The procedure will never
terminate so the execution of its first call will never be
completed. Therefore, it obviously will not be repeated n
times. Hence we must modify our statement so that the guarantee
of n repetitions only holds if the <u>program is finite</u> -- that is,
if it will eventually terminate. For practical purposes, the
guarantee only holds if the program will terminate in less than
the time limit imposed. The DO WHILE loop shown here is obvious
trouble, but unfortunately there are many less obvious ways to
make an error in a program and have the same effect on
execution. For example

```
ENDLESS_LOOP: DO I = 1 TO N BY 1;
     SUM = SUM + X(I);
     I = I - 1;
     END ENDLESS_LOOP;
```

This loop never terminates because the body of the loop
interferes with the loop index I so that its value never reaches
the terminating value N.

There might also be an error that terminates execution, which
would also cause the procedure to fail to be executed n times.
For example

```
SUM_LOOP: DO WHILE ('1'B);
     SUM = SUM + X(I);
     I = I + 1;
     END SUM_LOOP;
```

No matter how many elements X has, the subscript I will
eventually exceed the maximum permissible value. This will
result in an error in each iteration of the loop, which will
eventually exceed the error limit under which the program is run
and cause execution to be terminated. That is, the execution of
the <u>entire program</u> is terminated and not just the execution of
the faulty procedure.

Nevertheless these are local problems. They cannot affect
what is done elsewhere in the program. If the procedure TASK in
(2.3.1a) is <u>finite</u> and <u>executable</u>, then it is repeated n times.

Section 2 <u>Examples</u>

*PL/C ID='RALPH CONWAY' CMPRS NOOPLIST

```
/* CALCULATCR PROGRAM */                                    PL/C-R7.1--66 10/20/75 10:58 PAGE   1

STMT LEVEL NEST BLOCK MLVL  SOURCE TEXT

                           /* CALCULATOR PROGRAM */
                           /* DATA IS '+' OR '*', FOLLOWED BY 2 NUMBERS */
                           /* REPEAT UNTIL 'F' */
      1                    CALC: PROCEDURE OPTIONS(MAIN);
      2    1          1       DCL (X, Y) FLOAT DEC; /* OPERANDS */
      3    1          1       DCL OPERATION CHAR(1);

      4    1          1       GET LIST(OPERATION);
      5    1    1     1       OP_LOOP: DO WHILE(OPERATION ¬= 'F');
      6    1    1     1          GET LIST(X, Y);
                                 /* PERFORM OPERATION */
      7    1    1     1          IF OPERATION = '+'  THEN DO;
      9    1    2     1             CALL ADDR(X, Y);
     10    1    2     1             GO TO FIN_OPN; END;
     12    1    1     1          IF OPERATION = '*' THEN DO;
     14    1    2     1             CALL MULT(X, Y);
     15    1    2     1             GO TO FIN_OPN; END;
     17    1    1     1          PUT SKIP(2) LIST('UNKNOWN OPERATION');
     18    1    1     1          FIN_OPN:;
     19    1    1     1          GET LIST(OPERATION);
     20    1    1     1          END OP_LOOP;
     21    1          1       RETURN;
     22    1          1    END CALC;
```

*PROCESS

```
                           /* ADDITION SUBROUTINE */
     23                    ADDR: PROCEDURE(VAL1, VAL2);
     24    1          2       DCL (VAL1, VAL2) FLOAT DEC;
     25    1          2       DCL SUM FLOAT DEC;
     26    1          2       DCL MESSAGE CHAR(3) INIT('ADD');
     27    1          2       SUM = VAL1 + VAL2;
     28    1          2       CALL RESULT(MESSAGE, VAL1, VAL2, SUM);
     29    1          2       RETURN;
     30    1          2    END ADDR;
```

*PROCESS

```
                           /* MULTIPLICATION SUBROUTINE */
     31                    MULT: PROCEDURE(VAL1, VAL2);
     32    1          3       DCL (VAL1, VAL2) FLOAT DEC;
     33    1          3       DCL PRODUCT FLOAT DEC;
     34    1          3       DCL MESSAGE CHAR(8) INIT('MULTIPLY');
     35    1          3       PRODUCT = VAL1 * VAL2;
     36    1          3       CALL RESULT(MESSAGE, VAL1, VAL2, PRODUCT);
     37    1          3       RETURN;
     38    1          3    END MULT;
```

```
  STMT LEVEL NEST BLOCK MLVL  SOURCE TEXT
*PROCESS

                              /* PRINTING ROUTINE */
    39                        RESULT: PROCEDURE(OPERN, FIRST, SECOND, ANS);
    40    1        4              DCL OPERN CHAR(*);
    41    1        4              DCL (FIRST, SECOND, ANS) FLOAT DEC;
    42    1        4              DCL OPNBR FIXED DEC STATIC INIT(0);
    43    1        4              OPNBR = OPNBR + 1;
    44    1        4              PUT SKIP(2) LIST('OPERATION NUMBER', OPNBR);
    45    1        4              PUT SKIP LIST(OPERN, FIRST, 'AND', SECOND);
    46    1        4              PUT SKIP LIST('RESULT IS', ANS);
    47    1        4              RETURN;
    48    1        4              END RESULT;
```

ERRORS/WARNINGS DETECTED DURING CODE GENERATION:

      WARNING: NO FILE SPECIFIED. SYSIN/SYSPRINT ASSUMED. (CGOC)

```
OPERATION NUMBER          1
MULTIPLY                  2.00000E+00            AND                 3.00000E+00
RESULT IS                 6.00000E+00

UNKNOWN OPERATION

OPERATION NUMBER          2
MULTIPLY                  5.30000E+01            AND                 6.56999E+01
RESULT IS                 3.48209E+03

OPERATION NUMBER          3
ADD                       4.00000E+00            AND                 7.00000E+00
RESULT IS                 1.10000E+01
```

IN STMT   21 PROGRAM RETURNS FROM MAIN PROCEDURE.
IN STMT   21 SCALARS AND BLOCK-TRACE:

***** MAIN PROCEDURE CALC

```
OPERATION='F'           Y= 7.00000E+00        X= 4.00000E+00
NON-0 PROCEDURE EXECUTION COUNTS:
NAME       STMT COUNT  NAME       STMT COUNT  NAME       STMT COUNT  NAME       STMT COUNT
ADDR       0023 00001  RESULT     0039 00003  MULT       0031 00002  CALC       0001 00001

LABEL EXECUTION COUNTS:
NAME       STMT COUNT  NAME       STMT COUNT  NAME       STMT COUNT  NAME       STMT COUNT
FIN_OPN    0018 00004  OP_LOOP    0005 00001
```

```
      COMPILATION STATISTICS  (0048 STATEMENTS)       |                 EXECUTION STATISTICS
SECONDS  ERRORS  WARNINGS  PAGES  LINES  CARDS  INCL'S | SECONDS  ERRORS  WARNINGS  PAGES  LINES  CARDS  INCL'S  AUX I/O
  .10      0        1        2      83     56     0    |  .04      0        0        1     19      5      0       0
--------------------------------------------------------+--------------------------------------------------------
BYTES   SYMBOL TABLE   INTERMEDIATE CODE   OBJECT CODE |  STATIC CORE   AUTOMATIC CORE   DYNAMIC CORE   TOTAL STORAGE
USED    2413(  3K)     1068(  2K)          1080(  2K)  |  358(  1K)     674(  1K)        0(  0K)        4378(  5K)
UNUSED  7715(  7K)     8740(  8K)         17044( 16K)  | 16106( 15K)  16106( 15K)       8740(  8K)     16106( 15K)
```

THIS PROGRAM MAY BE RERUN WITHOUT CHANGE IN A REGION 15K BYTES SMALLER USING TABLESIZE=   604

Section 2 <u>Exercises</u>

1. Suppose there were no ABS built-in function in PL/I to find
the absolute value of an argument. Design and write a procedure
that would provide this "extension" to the language. (Note: The
ABS built-in function does not change the value of its argument,
so neither should your procedure. Use one parameter for input
and a second parameter for output.)

2. Write a procedure to add two matrices, producing a third
matrix.   A matrix C is the sum of two matrices A and B if each
element of C is the sum of the elements in the corresponding
positions in A and B. That is

        c(i,j) = a(i,j) + b(i,j)

All three matrices must have the same number of rows and
columns. The procedure should have five parameters:
    Parameter 1: first input matrix
    Parameter 2: second input matrix
    Parameter 3: output matrix
    Parameter 4: number of rows in each matrix
    Parameter 5: number of columns in each matrix.

3. Write a procedure to "rotate" a square matrix (one with the
same number of rows as columns) 90^0 clockwise. That is, the
element initially in the upper left corner will become the
element in the upper right corner, etc. The procedure should
have two parameters:
    Parameter 1: matrix to be rotated
    Parameter 2: number of rows (or columns).

4. Write a procedure to format print lines from individual
words supplied as arguments. The procedure should have a single
parameter which is a varying length character string.   On each
call the procedure is presented with a "word". It builds a
print line with these words, adding each new word to the right
end of the line (with an intervening blank between words).   The
line length is at most 60 positions. When a new word cannot be
added to the line without exceeding this length, the old line is
printed and a new line is begun starting with the word that
wouldn't fit on the old line.

5. Convert the final symbol-scanning program of Section III.2.5
into a procedure to deliver individual symbols when the input
consists of test lines.

6. Write the programs described in Exercise 10 of Section III.2
in the form described in IV.2.2. That is, write them with a
short control section calling external procedures to perform the
actual subtasks.

PART V   PROGRAM TESTING

Section 1   Errors, Testing and Correctness

Programming almost never results in an error-free program; it is just too complicated and detailed a process. If conducted by a careful and competent person the probability of each possible error is very small -- but there are so many opportunities that the probability of avoiding all errors is also very small. Prudence demands that we assume each new program is incorrect until we can demonstrate otherwise. We must accept the fact that testing is an integral part of the programming process -- and that a program is not really "finished" until we have demonstrated its correctness.

The magnitude of the testing effort required for large problems might surprise you. Often at least half of the manpower, cost and elapsed time of the total programming process is consumed in testing. In spite of this the results are often not always satisfactory. Computers are not publically regarded as reliable, when in fact they are exceedingly reliable machines -- handicapped by inadequately tested programs. However when the programming process is highly disciplined and when testing is planned as the program is being created rather than afterwards, testing is easier and the resulting programs are significantly more reliable.

Very few beginning programmers take the trouble to learn to test their programs efficiently. To plan testing in advance seems to be admitting failure in writing the program, so most beginners assume an ostrich-like, head-in-the-sand attitude, until the evidence that errors are present is unmistakable. Then testing proceeds in a manner that can charitably be called "random". This attitude winds up wasting a great deal of time, yet it is still the usual approach. Testing does not have to be nearly as time-consuming or as unpleasant as many beginners make it seem, but it must be taken seriously -- it is an art that must be studied and learned.

Before describing some techniques and tools that can be used to demonstrate that a program is correct, let us discuss the meaning of "correctness".

1.1 <u>The Meaning of Correctness</u>

"Program correctness" is not easily defined. The programmer and user of a program may discover they use quite different meanings of the word "correctness", and hence have quite different expectations of program performance. Consider the following possible interpretations of correctness -- listed in order of increasing difficulty of achievement:

1. The program contains no syntax errors that can be detected during translation by the language processor.

2. The program contains no errors, either of syntax or invalid operation, that can be automatically detected during translation or execution of the program.

3. There exists some set of test data for which the program will yield the correct answer.

4. For a typical (reasonable or random) set of test data the program will yield the correct answer.

5. For deliberately difficult sets of test data the program will yield the correct answers.

6. For all possible sets of data which are valid with respect to the problem specification, the program yields the correct answers.

7. For all possible sets of valid test data, and for all likely conditions of erroneous input, the program gives a correct (or at least reasonable) answer.

8. For all possible input, the program gives correct or reasonable answers.

In the early stages of your programming experience you will feel harassed by error messages during translation, and feel a sense of achievement when you have attained level 1 correctness. However, the absence of error messages is only a necessary and not a sufficient condition for reasonable correctness. You will eventually regard the detection of such errors as a helpful service, which unfortunately detects only the easiest of errors.

Some students never mature beyond level 3 for an interpretation of correctness. We are regularly involved in arguments challenging the grade assigned to a problem on grounds that it "worked" on the student's own data, hence must be correct. In effect, the student is arguing that level 3 is adequate. Considering higher levels (say 4, 5 or 6) it is clear that satisfactory performance on any single set of test data is not sufficient grounds for an assertion of correctness, but failure on a single test is sufficient to demonstrate that the program is not correct. <u>No matter how many tests the program may have passed successfully, just one test on which it fails is</u>

<u>enough to show that it is not correct</u>. This is not inherently a
democratic process, and a program that works "most of the time"
is a dangerous tool.

From the "customer's" point of view a reasonable definition
of correctness is certainly not less than level 6. Level 7 is
better and level 8 is what he would really like. The programmer
may   maintain   that   a   literal   interpretation of problem
specifications cannot demand more than level 6, while the
customer will maintain that certain implied requirements do not
have to be explicitly stated. In effect, this corresponds to
the "implied warranty of merchantability" that accompanies a
manufactured product. A consumer is entitled to assume that a
product is "suitable for the purpose for which it is intended".
A car buyer, for example, can rightfully assume that all the
wheels will remain firmly attached to the car, without having to
obtain a written guarantee from the dealer. In the same way,
much is assumed about a computer program, without its having
been explicitly detailed in the problem requirements. The user
of a program is entitled to consider it incorrect if it fails to
satisfy implicit as well as explicit requirements.

Unfortunately this often leads to heated discussions between
programmer and user, the object being to assign blame for a
program belatedly found to be incorrect. The programmer takes
the   position   that   there   is no such thing as implicit
requirements; the user maintains that, in retrospect, anything
he neglected to specify is covered by implicit commonsense
requirements.   Both parties should realize that implicit
requirements are an inherent part of most problem descriptions,
and that it is a <u>mutual</u> responsibility to explore this subject
to ensure mutual understanding of context of use, nature of
errors, appropriate reactions and communications.

The <u>primary responsibility rests with the programmer</u>.   A
program is <u>incorrect if it does not serve the user's purposes</u>.
This may occur because the programmer failed to elicit an
adequate description, because he failed to recognize implicit
requirements, or because he made mistakes in designing or
translating the algorithm into a programming language. Most
programmers admit responsibility for only the last two sources
of error, but the distinction between different types of failure
is not interesting to a user with an unsolved problem.

In summary, the situation is the following. The user would
like to have level 8 correctness -- but this is usually
impossible, and he might as well get used to that fact. Level 7
is a reasonable compromise, which is obviously going to lead to
arguments since it leaves critical questions open to varying
interpretations.   The programmer's dilemma is that level 5 is
the highest that can be achieved by purely empirical means -- by
running the program on test cases -- so he must thoughtfully
design test cases while writing the program that will permit a
plausible assertion that level 6 has been achieved. To achieve
level 7 the programmer must know enough about the intended use

of the program to estimate what errors are likely to be encountered, and what response is appropriate.

1.2 Types of Errors

There are four distinct types of errors:

1. Errors in understanding the problem requirements.

2. Errors in understanding the programming language. For example, errors could result from not understanding PL/I's assignment of default attributes in implicit declarations.

3. Failure of the algorithm underlying the program.

4. Accidents. Errors where you knew better but simply slipped up.

Errors in understanding the problem description will no doubt increase as the problems you work on become larger, more varied, and less precisely stated. Although one can learn from experience, human communication is difficult at best; English is surprisingly ambiguous; and programming demands an unfailing precision. Some errors of this type seem inevitable. Caution and more and more communication with the user will tend to keep these errors to a minimum.

Errors in understanding the programming language will diminish in frequency with experience, but unfortunately PL/I is a large and rich language with many curious and unexpected properties, so the opportunities for this type of error are numerous. The best antidote is to stick to the simple, well-thought-out language features, and to leave the vague, tricky ones alone.

The third type of error is greatly reduced in frequency by systematic development and careful structuring of programs. Errors that remain are in fairly predictable places -- often just entry and exit problems -- and can be systematically sought using the diagnostic tools described in the following sections. These kinds of errors must be kept to a minimum if you want to be known as a good programmer. They are the hardest to correct later on. One main purpose of a programming course is to get you to think carefully, methodically, completely, and in a structured manner so that these kinds of errors don't often occur.

Accidents occur everywhere in the process, to experienced as well as beginning programmers. They range from syntax errors detected by the translator to subtle errors with intermittent effect that elude competent and persistent testing. The only general defense is a skeptical attitude that regards every program segment as a potential haven for accidental errors.

It somehow can be very difficult to spot our own mistakes. We will go over a troublesome section of program many times and be unable to spot an obvious error. Often a fresh view will help to find an error quickly. A colleague or programming consultant can spot an error not because he knows more, but because he has no preconceptions about what the program is supposed to do. He reads what _is_ there, and not what he wants to be there. Quite often we ourselves will see the error while explaining the program to a friend or consultant. Programming _should_ be more of a group process, with at least two people reading and understanding each program segment.

You _must_ accept the fact that _all_ errors in the program are your responsibility. Too much time is wasted trying to blame the _computer_, the _programming language_, or the _problem description_. In Section 1.1 we asserted that the programmer must accept responsibility for clarification of problem requirements; now we exonerate the computer and the language.

True machine errors are exceedingly rare, so every time you become convinced a machine error has happened, you are just postponing the eventual necessity of discovering what really happened. Blaming errors on the programming language is a similar delusion. Every programming language has its surprises -- things that are done in an unexpected way. (PL/I is especially culpable in this regard.) While the language may be unreasonable, it is _not wrong_. For example, what is the value of I printed by the following program segment?

```
        ...
    SUM_LOOP: DO I = 1 TO 45 BY 1;
        ...
        END SUM_LOOP;
    PUT SKIP LIST(I);
        ...
```

Whether or not it seems reasonable to you, the value 46 is printed. It is your responsibility to learn what the language actually means, and what execution will actually do, rather than assume it means whatever you think is reasonable.

In this connection you might as well learn to distrust every source of assistance in the programming process, except the computer. Both programming language reference manuals and textbooks (including this one) contain errors. Each teacher, and each programming consultant at your computing center has his own misconceptions about certain programming language features. Again, the best way to guard against such misunderstandings is to use only the simple, well-used features of the language. When learning a new programming language feature, _always_ use it in several small examples, to learn how it really works, before using it in a large program.

Section 2   The Design of Test Cases

It is reasonable to initially test a new program on easy test cases. However, satisfactory execution for such test cases only demonstrates "level 3 correctness" (see Section 1.1) and this is not sufficient. Further test cases must be used to attain levels 4 or 5. You must not be satisfied that your program is correct as soon as it will successfully run some single set of test data.

Contriving difficult test cases is an art that has to be learned. It draws upon your knowledge of programming and experience with the kinds of errors likely to occur. For example, having experienced difficulty before with declarations, conditions, and entry and exit from repetitions, you should contrive test cases that exhibit the following properties:

a. Extremes of volume: the legal minimum and maximum, as well as too little and too much.

b. Extreme values: the legal minimum and maximum as well as excessive values -- too big, too small, too negative.

c. Special values: zero, blank, one, etc., depending on the problem.

d. Non-integer values, where allowed.

e. Values falling on and near stated limits.

f. Repeated values and ties of various sorts.

Unfortunately, even the most persistent, perceptive and malicious testing campaign cannot demonstrate more than level 5 correctness, and yet level 6 is the minimum reasonable standard. We cannot ever (well, hardly ever) demonstrate level 6 experimentally, since we cannot run a program for all possible sets of input. We can try difficult cases, and infer from success on these that many other cases, somehow "bracketed" by the hard ones, will be handled properly. But the precise meaning of "bracket" and the rules of inference are not clear. No matter how many tests have been run successfully we cannot absolutely state that level 6 has been achieved -- that the program would yield the correct answer for all possible valid input. On the other hand, to disprove correctness we only have to find <u>one</u> test case on which the program fails.

The situation can be summarized as follows. Testing a program can never prove its correctness (at level 6 or higher); it can only fail to disprove its correctness. Based on the effort and ingenuity expended in failing to disprove correctness we can acquire increasing confidence in a program's reliability, but this can never reach the level of absolute proof.

Testing in which one examines only the input and output of a program without studying its internal construction is sometimes called "black-box testing". It is not a bad way to start testing, but at some point an examination of the internal construction must be used to contrive adequately difficult test cases. Furthermore, any hope of asserting correctness beyond level 5 is beyond the ability of experimental testing, and will have to depend upon the examination of the program itself and not just its external actions.

2.1 Testing the Program of I.1.1e

To illustrate the limits of experimental, black-box testing, suppose that example (2.1a) is submitted as a solution to the "find maximum" problem of Section I.1.1. (2.1a) is absurd, but the point is to see what prospects there are of discovering all its absurdities solely by running it with various sets of test data.

```
     *PL/C ID='G. SALTON'
      /* COMPUTE THE MAXIMUM OF NON-NEGATIVE NUMBERS */
      /* DUMMY -1 ADDED FOR STOPPING TEST */
      FINDMAX: PROCEDURE OPTIONS(MAIN);
         DCL (NUMBER,      /* THE CURRENT NUMBER */
              MAXNBR,      /* MAXIMUM NUMBER SO FAR */
              COUNT)       /* NBR OF NUMBERS SO FAR */
                    FIXED DECIMAL;
(2.1a)
         MAXNBR = 2; /* INITIAL VALUE < POSSIBLE DATA VALUES */
         COUNT = 1;
         GET LIST(NUMBER, NUMBER);
         MAX_LOOP: DO WHILE (NUMBER ¬= -1);
           COUNT = COUNT + 1;
           IF NUMBER = 63 THEN NUMBER = -3;
           IF NUMBER = MAXNBR THEN MAXNBR = MAXNBR +1;
           IF NUMBER > MAXNBR THEN MAXNBR = NUMBER;
           GET LIST(NUMBER);
           END MAX_LOOP;
         MAXNBR = 12;
         PUT LIST('NUMBER OF VALUES =', COUNT);
         PUT SKIP LIST('MAXIMUM VALUE =', MAXNBR);
         END FINDMAX;
      *DATA
         3, 7, 12, 2, 6, -1
```

(2.1a) actually provides the correct answer <u>for the data given</u>, so it is "correct" at level 3 (according to Section 1.1). If the ever-optimistic programmer accepts this as confirmation of correctness, he will have declared an incredibly bad program "correct".

This program actually produces correct answers for many sets of data: any set for which the maximum value is 12. Only if data with a maximum other than 12 is used will an error be discovered.

Assuming the strange preference for 12 is detected, and "MAXNBR = 12;" is removed, the program will give correct answers for even more sets of test data. But it will still have difficulty in the situations below. Good test cases would detect a, b, c, f and g, and might detect d, but discovering e is just a matter of luck.

   a. The maximum value happens to be the first value.
   b. The maximum value appears two or more times in the set.
   c. The maximum value is not an integer (it has significant digits to the right of the decimal point).
   d. The maximum value is less than 2.
   e. The maximum value happens to be 63.
   f. No input is provided.
   g. No -1 stopping value is supplied.

2.2 <u>Multiple Test Cases</u>

To allow running several tests in one computer run, we must be able to repeat execution of a program with different sets of data. This is easily done in PL/I just by changing the "main" procedure to an ordinary external procedure and adding a new main procedure to control the repetition. For example, suppose (2.2a) is some program that processes data until a stopping flag of -1 is encountered. (2.2b) illustrates a simple "test control" procedure that will cause (2.2a) to be repeated N times, where N is given as the first item of data. When testing is complete the program must of course be restored to its original form by removing the test control procedure and replacing the original "main" procedure card. Note also that the main procedure TSC can be used to test <u>any</u> such program, as long as its name is EPD. We need not write a different test control main procedure for each different program. (A RETURN has been added to EPD in (2.2b) since this has been our practice in external procedures. It is not really necessary, since EPD will return when it reaches the END anyway. If the RETURN is given explicitly, as in (2.2b), it would not have to be removed when EPD is run as a separate program. RETURN can be used in main procedures, although we have not done so in our examples.)

(2.2a)   *PL/C ID='GREG ANDREWS'
           /* EDIT POSITIVE DATA; STOP ON -1 */
           EPD: PROCEDURE OPTIONS(MAIN);
               ...
               END EPD;
           *DATA
           23, 74, 56.1, 423.19, -1

(2.2b)   *PL/C ID='GREG ANDREWS'
           /* TEST CONTROL FOR EPD ROUTINE */
           TSC: PROCEDURE OPTIONS(MAIN);
               DCL N FIXED DEC;   /* TOTAL NUMBER OF TESTS */
               DCL NSOFAR FIXED DEC; /* NUMBER PERFORMED SO FAR*/
               GET LIST(N);
               PUT SKIP(3) LIST(N, 'CONSECUTIVE TESTS OF EPD');
               /* REPEAT EPD N TIMES */
                 NSOFAR = 0;
                 TEST_LOOP: DO WHILE (NSOFAR < N);
                     NSOFAR = NSOFAR + 1;
                     PUT SKIP(2) LIST('EPD TEST NUMBER', NSOFAR);
                     CALL EPD;
                     END TEST_LOOP;
               END TSC;
           *PROCESS
           /* EDIT POSITIVE DATA; STOP ON -1 */
           EPD: PROCEDURE;
               ...
               RETURN;
               END EPD;
           *DATA
            3
            23, 74, 56.1, 423.19, -1
            0, 1, 1, 0, -1
            9999, 0.01, 0.001, 0, 0, -1

Section 2 __Examples__

```
*PL/C ID='J. ROGERS', CMPRS, NOOPLIST

/* TEST MEAN-MAX-MIN PROGRAM */                                    PL/C-R7.1--66 10/20/75 10:58 PAGE   1

STMT LEVEL NEST BLOCK MLVL  SOURCE TEXT


                            /* TEST MEAN-MAX-MIN PROGRAM */
     1                      TESTM: PROCEDURE OPTIONS(MAIN);
     2    1           1         DCL NBRTESTS FIXED DEC; /* NUMBER OF SEPARATE TESTS */
     3    1           1         DCL TESTNBR FIXED DEC INIT(0);
     4    1           1         GET LIST(NBRTESTS);
     5    1           1         TEST_LOOP: DO WHILE(NBRTESTS > 0);
     6    1    1      1             TESTNBR = TESTNBR + 1;
     7    1    1      1             PUT SKIP(3) LIST('TEST NUMBER', TESTNBR);
     8    1    1      1             PUT SKIP(2);
     9    1    1      1             CALL MMM;
    10    1    1      1             NBRTESTS = NBRTESTS - 1;
    11    1    1      1             END TEST_LOOP;
    12    1           1         PUT SKIP(3) LIST('END OF TESTS');
    13    1           1         END TESTM;


*PROCESS


                            /* COMPUTE MEAN, MAX AND MIN OF DATA */
                            /* STOP WHENEVER A VALUE OCCURS TWICE IN SUCCESSION */
    14                      MMM: PROCEDURE;
    15    1           2         DCL (LAST, CURRENT) FLOAT DEC; /* VALUES READ FROM DATA */
    16    1           2         DCL (MAXVAL, MINVAL) FLOAT DEC;
    17    1           2         DCL (SUM, MEAN) FLOAT DEC;
    18    1           2         DCL COUNT FIXED DEC; /* NUMBER OF VALUES READ */
                                /* INITIALIZE */
    19    1           2         GET LIST(LAST);
    20    1           2         COUNT = 1;
    21    1           2         MAXVAL = LAST;
    22    1           2         MINVAL = LAST;
    23    1           2         SUM = LAST;
    24    1           2         GET LIST(CURRENT);
    25    1           2         DATA_LOOP: DO WHILE (CURRENT ¬= LAST);
    26    1    1      2             COUNT = COUNT + 1;
    27    1    1      2             SUM = SUM + CURRENT;
    28    1    1      2             MAXVAL = MAX(MAXVAL, CURRENT);
    29    1    1      2             MINVAL = MIN(MINVAL, CURRENT);
    30    1    1      2             LAST = CURRENT;
    31    1    1      2             GET LIST(CURRENT);
    32    1    1      2             END DATA_LOOP;
                                /* PRINT RESULTS */
    33    1           2         PUT LIST('RESULTS OF MEAN-MAX-MIN PROGRAM');
    34    1           2         PUT SKIP(2) LIST(COUNT, 'VALUES READ');
    35    1           2         MEAN = SUM/COUNT;
    36    1           2         PUT SKIP LIST('MEAN IS', MEAN);
    37    1           2         PUT SKIP LIST('MAXIMUM IS', MAXVAL);
    38    1           2         PUT SKIP LIST('MINIMUM IS', MINVAL);
    39    1           2         END MMM;

ERRORS/WARNINGS DETECTED DURING CODE GENERATION:

    WARNING: NO FILE SPECIFIED. SYSIN/SYSPRINT ASSUMED. (CGOC)
```

```
*PL/C ID='R. PERRY', CMPRS

*OPTICNS IN EFFECT*      TIME=(0,15),PAGES=30,LINES=2000,NOATR,NOXREF,FLAGW,BNDRY,NOCMNTS,SORMGIN=(2,72,1),
*OPTIONS IN EFFECT*      ERRORS=(50,50),TABSIZE=2532,UDEF,SOURCE,OPLIST,CMPRS,HDRPG,AUXIO=10000,LINECT=60,NOALIST,MCALL,
*CPTICNS IN EFFECT*      MTEXT,DUMP=(S,F,L,E,U,R),DUMPE=(S,F,L,E,U,R),DUMPT=(S,F,L,E,U,R)

/* TEST "A" COUNTING PROGRAM */                                         PL/C-R7.1--66 10/20/75 10:58 PAGE   1

    STMT LEVEL NEST BLOCK MLVL  SOURCE TEXT

                                    /* TEST "A" COUNTING PROGRAM */
     1                              TESTA: PROCEDURE OPTIONS(MAIN);
     2    1              1              DCL TEST CHAR(4);
     3    1              1              DCL TESTNBR FIXED DEC;
     4    1              1              GET LIST(TEST);
     5    1              1              TEST_LOOP: DO WHILE(TEST = 'TEST');
     6    1    1         1                  GET LIST(TESTNBR);
     7    1    1         1                  PUT SKIP(3) LIST('TEST NUMBER', TESTNBR);
     8    1    1         1                  PUT SKIP(2);
     9    1    1         1                  CALL COUNTA;
    10    1    1         1                  GET LIST(TEST);
    11    1    1         1                  END TEST_LOOP;
    12    1              1              PUT SKIP(3) LIST('END OF TESTS');
    13    1              1              END TESTA;


*PROCESS NOOPLIST


                                    /* COUNT A'S IN INPUT WORDS. STOP ON 'ENDDATA' */
    14                              COUNTA: PROCEDURE;
    15    1              2              DCL (WORDCOUNT, ACOUNT) FIXED DEC INIT(0);
    16    1              2              DCL WORD CHAR(80) VARYING;
    17    1              2              DCL POSN FIXED DEC; /* POSITION IN WORD */
    18    1              2              GET LIST(WORD);
    19    1              2              WORD_LOOP: DO WHILE(WORD ¬= 'ENDDATA');
    20    1    1         2                  WORDCOUNT = WORDCOUNT + 1;
                                           /* COUNT A'S IN WORD */
    21    1    1         2                  COUNT_LOOP: DO POSN = 1 TO LENGTH(WORD) BY 1;
    22    1    2         2                      IF SUBSTR(WORD,POSN,1) = 'A'
    23    1    2         2                          THEN ACOUNT = ACOUNT + 1;
    24    1    2         2                      END COUNT_LOOP;
    25    1    1         2                  GET LIST(WORD);
    26    1    1         2                  END WORD_LOOP;
                                           /* PRINT RESULTS */
    27    1              2              PUT LIST('RESULTS OF "A" COUNTING PROGRAM ');
    28    1              2              PUT SKIP(2) LIST('IN', WORDCOUNT, 'WORDS');
    29    1              2              PUT SKIP LIST('THERE WERE', ACOUNT, 'A''S');
    30    1              2              END COUNTA;

ERRORS/WARNINGS DETECTED DURING CODE GENERATION:

    WARNING: NO FILE SPECIFIED. SYSIN/SYSPRINT ASSUMED. (CGOC)
```

Section 2 <u>Exercises</u>

1. Consider the "list-inquiry" program developed in Section III.2.2.

    a. Make a list of the potential problems, special cases, extreme values, etc. that ought to be tested before this program is pronounced "correct".

    b. Devise a set of test data that will reveal a flaw (if one exists) for each of the problems listed in 1.a.

    c. Devise a test procedure for "list-inquiry", such as the one shown in (2.2b), so that several of the test cases produced in 1.b can be combined in a single run.

2. Repeat exercise 1 for the sorting program developed in Section III.2.3.

3. Repeat exercise 1 for the symbol-scanning program developed in Section III.2.5.

Section 3   Automatic Diagnostic Services

A limited amount of diagnostic information is provided automatically for the programmer, as syntactic mistakes are detected or when invalid actions are to be performed. This information is especially helpful to beginners, since they tend to make many errors of this type. But as programmers gain experience, such errors become relatively less frequent and significant, and their elimination is only a prelude to serious testing. These syntactic slips and keypunch mistakes must be eliminated before the demonstration of correctness can begin.

These automatic services help reveal some "accidents" (see Section 1.2) and occasionally a language or algorithm error. When a program runs without any diagnostic messages, correctness only at level 2 (as defined in Section 1.1) has been achieved.

3.1 Detection of Errors

Only two types of errors are automatically detected: syntax errors are detected during loading and reported on the source listing, and requests to perform invalid actions are detected during execution and reported in the execution output. These are discussed in Sections 3.1.1 and 3.1.2.

3.1.1 Syntax Errors

Regardless of what programming language is used, every violation of the syntax rules of the language should be detected by the computer during loading of the program. The manner in which detection is announced and the amount of explanation provided depends upon the language used. In many cases the flaw is obvious and the correction is straightforward. However, in some situations the actual error may be far removed from the statement where its presence was detected. In these cases the messages provided are not always helpful. For example

        Y = X(I);

might be flagged as erroneous not because it is improperly formed, but because a missing or faulty declaration has failed to declare X as an array. However mystifying the error messages

may be, they are neither spontaneous nor random. There is
something in your program that is wrong, or at least suspicious,
and you must find out what it is. However elusive the cause,
every syntax error must be tracked down.

Unfortunately, many mistakes are not recognizable as such by
PL/I. For example, suppose an assignment statement should be
given as

        COUNT = COUNT + 1;

Each of the following variations might somehow appear in place
of the correct statement:

        a.   COUNT = COUNT +.1;
        b.   COUNT = COUNT - 1;
        c.   CONUT = COUNT + 1;
        d.   COUNT = CONUT + 1;
        e.   COUNT = COUNT + 1

None of these alternatives is correct, but only the missing
semi-colon in e will be recognized as a syntax error. Each of
the others is syntactically but not functionally correct in this
program. (Alternative d will be detected as an execution error
since it tries to use a variable CONUT to which, presumably, no
value has been assigned.)

Comparable mistakes in a declaration are often more
mystifying. For example, if you mistakenly put a comma between
a variable and its attributes in a declaration:

    DCL J, FIXED DEC;   instead of   DCL J FIXED DEC;

no syntax error is reported, but the variables created are quite
different from what you intended. There is a variable J with
attributes FIXED BINARY (the default attributes for a variable
beginning with "J"), and another variable FIXED with attributes
FLOAT DECIMAL. If you write

        DCL J, FIX DEC;

no error is reported -- and you may think that you have
discovered a valid abbreviation for FIXED, but actually you have
just declared two variables J and FIX. (See Section I.8.1.)

To detect and correct this type of error it is important that
you be able to see exactly what variables are created and what
attributes they are given. This information is provided by an
automatic "cross-reference and attribute listing". If this
listing is not produced automatically as the default option at
your computer installation then you should specify XREF and ATR
on the *PL/C card on at least the early runs of each program.
For example, suppose a program begins

```
          *PL/C ID='CHARLES MOORE', XREF, ATR
          /* CALCULATE MEAN QUEUE LENGTH */
STMT 1    QMN: PROCEDURE OPTIONS(MAIN);
STMT 2        DECLARE QUEUE FLOAT DECIMAL;
STMT 3        DECLARE J FIXED DECIMAL;
STMT 4        DECLARE STATE FIXED DECIMAL INITIAL(0);
STMT 5        DECLARE SIZE(50) FLOAT DECIMAL;
              ...
```

The numbers shown at the left of the lines are the statement
numbers assigned by PL/I. They are given on the source listing,
and referred to by the cross-reference and attribute listing.
The cross-reference and attribute listing would be printed after
the source listing. It would look like the following:


```
/* CALCULATE MEAN QUEUE LENGTH */

DCL NO.     IDENTIFIER     ATTRIBUTES AND REFERENCES

   3        J              AUTOMATIC,ALIGNED,DECIMAL,FIXED(5,0)
                           9,13,22

   1        QMN            ENTRY,DECIMAL,FLOAT(6)

   2        QUEUE          AUTOMATIC,ALIGNED,DECIMAL,FLOAT(6)
                           11,13,27

   5        SIZE           (*)AUTOMATIC,ALIGNED,DECIMAL,FLOAT(6)
                           15,32

   4        STATE          AUTOMATIC,INITIAL,ALIGNED,DECIMAL,
                           FIXED(5,0)
                           8,11
```

The first line of the program (not counting the *PL/C card) is
used as a title for this listing. The identifiers are arranged
alphabetically in the listing. The first in this case is J,
declared in line 3. It is a fixed decimal number of five
digits, with zero digits to the right of the decimal point. It
has also been given the default attributes AUTOMATIC (the
opposite of STATIC), and ALIGNED (having to do with the way the
number is stored internally). This is the "attribute" part of
the listing. Don't be misled because the attributes are
separated by commas in this listing -- they must not be
separated by commas in a declaration. The next line is the
"cross-reference" part. Under the attributes it lists the
numbers of all the statements in which this identifier is used
-- 9, 13 and 22 in this case, although that part of the program
has not been shown. The next identifier is QMN, the procedure-
name. This was declared in statement 1 just by giving it as a
prefix to the main procedure. PL/I calls a procedure-name an
"ENTRY". It also has the type attributes DECIMAL,FLOAT(6) but
the attributes of procedure-names are irrelevant for the portion

of PL/I we are using. The third identifier is QUEUE, declared
in line 2 with explicit DECIMAL and FLOAT, and default AUTOMATIC
and ALIGNED.   QUEUE is used (referenced) in statements 11, 13
and 27. The symbol (*) in the attribute list for SIZE shows
that it is an array of one dimension. (A two-dimensional array
would be denoted (*,*) in the listing.) The actual number of
elements in the array does not appear on the attribute listing.
The attribute list for STATE includes INITIAL, which shows that
it has been assigned an initial value -- but the attribute
listing does not show what the initial value was.

If line 3 of the program had accidentally been given as

        DECLARE J, FIXED DECIMAL;

there would be no syntax error message, but the problem would be
apparent in the attribute listing since J would not be
DECIMAL,FIXED as expected, and there would be an extra line for
identifier FIXED, declared in line 3. You should always <u>check
the attribute listing, line by line, against your declarations</u>
to make sure that each variable and parameter was created
exacted as you intended. Make sure the INITIAL attribute
appears for those variables that need to be initialized. Except
for procedure-names (called ENTRYs) and labels (called STATEMENT
LABEL CONSTANTs), which are declared by use, every identifier on
the list should be the result of one of your declarations.

If you use a variable without declaring it, PL/I assumes you
are making an "implicit declaration" and creates the variable
assigning it certain "default attributes". It is not a good
idea to rely on this feature of PL/I, since the default rules
are complicated and confusing. By checking for a blank in the
"DCL NO." column you can determine which variables you forgot to
declare explicitly.

In many cases a blank in the "DCL NO." column will indicate a
keypunch (or spelling) mistake in the name of a variable. For
example, if there is a variable named SUM but in one instance
you keypunched this as SMU, PL/I will take this as the implicit
declaration of a new variable SMU. Fortunately, this "kindness"
is revealed by a line in the attribute listing for the new
variable SMU, with the number of the statement in which it is
"used".   When the spelling mistake is corrected in that
statement the unintended new variable will disappear from the
attribute listing. <u>Check every line with a blank under "DCL
NO."</u> to see whether you omitted a declaration of an intended
variable, or unintentionally created a variable by a
misspelling.

3.1.2 Invalid Operations

Just what constitutes an invalid operation depends on the language and computer being used. Generally these include such operations as:

    a. dividing by zero,
    b. taking the square root of a negative number, or
    c. adding two numbers whose sum exceeds the largest number the computer can handle

Usually invalid operations are caused by an action in some statement other than the one accused in the error message. That is, if STMT 69 attempts to take the square root of X which is negative, the problem lies not in 69 but in the statement that assigned the negative value to X. Execution error messages simply announce the point at which the result of an error causes an invalid operation to be requested, and unfortunately they rarely can give much hint as to what actually caused the error.

Some languages are more helpful than others in this regard. For example, if an array has been declared AMT(1:5), PL/C will automatically object to executing the statement

        SUM = SUM + AMT(6);

but PL/I will not. PL/I will execute this statement, obtain some extraneous value for AMT(6), and provide no warning at all that anything unusual has occurred. PL/C will also not permit a variable to be used until it has been assigned a value. For example, the failure to initialize a variable is a very common error:

        /* SET TOTAL TO SUM OF A(1:N) */
            TOTAL_LOOP: DO I = 1 TO N BY 1;
                TOTAL = TOTAL + A(I);
                END TOTAL_LOOP;

If TOTAL has not been used earlier in the execution of the program PL/C will report an error in that TOTAL is being used before it has been assigned any value. (It will set the value to 0 and continue execution.) Unfortunately, if TOTAL has been assigned a value anywhere previously PL/C will not recognize that there is an error. The program will just be wrong in that whatever previous value has been assigned to TOTAL will be the starting point for the sum of A(1:N).

3.2 <u>Automatic Repair of Errors</u>

In most programming languages the detection of a syntax error
during translation of a program will prevent the program's
execution. If there are no translation errors and execution
begins, the detection of an error during execution will cause
execution to be terminated. However, PL/C does not operate this
way.   After reporting an error to the user, PL/C makes some
repair and continues.   It would be nice to make a <u>correction</u>,
but all PL/C provides is a <u>repair</u>. Sometimes a repair happens
to be a correction; it achieves what the programmer intended.
While this occurs fairly often, the real purpose of the repair
is simply to permit continuation of execution.   The objective is
to <u>obtain</u> <u>as</u> <u>much</u> <u>information</u> <u>as</u> <u>possible</u> <u>from</u> <u>each</u> <u>attempt</u> <u>to</u>
<u>process</u> <u>a</u> <u>program</u>. PL/C seeks to execute <u>any</u> program, no matter
how wrong it might be, in hopes of obtaining maximum information
for its author.

Every syntax error is repaired in PL/C.   After the error
messages are given the repaired statement is displayed. For
example:

```
      . . .
  8     1           1          X=Y*(X+Z;
    ERROR IN STMT    8  MISSING ) IN COLUMN 10 (SY04)
         FOR STMT    8  PL/C USES  X=Y*(X+Z);
      . . .
```

In simple cases involving commas, parentheses and semi-colons
the repair is often a successful correction.   But be careful and
study each repair closely; the likelihood is that the repair was
<u>not</u> what you intended.   In order to interpret the results of
execution properly, you must know how each statement was
repaired.

Sometimes PL/C works hard to make an executable program out
of strange input.   For example, suppose the following single
card were presented as if it were a complete program:

        PTU FILE(OUTPUT A+1 'CORRECTION.

PL/C changes it to the following:

        $L001$: PROCEDURE OPTIONS(MAIN);
                PUT FILE(OUTPUT) LIST(A+1,'CORRECTION.');
                END;

To see how PL/C effects these changes, try it.   Punch the
erroneous single card and run it as a PL/C program. Another
interesting one-card program you might try is:

        THIS IS A LOT OF NONSENSE

As a last resort, when PL/C is thoroughly confused, a faulty
statement is replaced with a null statement (that is, just a

semi-colon). This preserves syntactic correctness and permits
the program to be executed, but the prospects of useful output
are much diminished. PL/C does issue a warning message during
execution of a program whenever one of these null statements is
executed.

   Error repair also takes place during execution of a PL/C
program.   For example, suppose an array X is declared X(1:5),
and in statement 45 an element of the array is referenced by
X(I).   Suppose at some point statement 45 is executed when the
value of I is 12. PL/C will produce the following message:

   ***** ERROR IN STMT 45 SUBSCRIPT 0001 OF X IS OUT OF
           BOUNDS (0012).   0005 IS USED. (EX19)

As indicated in the message the repair is to use the closest
valid subscript -- 5 in this case.   (EX19) is the "error
number", referring to a complete list of errors and explanations
in the PL/C User's Guide. With the subscript repaired to refer
to an existing element of X the execution of the program can
continue.   (Note, however, that the value of I is not changed.)

   As another example, suppose statement 55   includes   an
expression using the square root built-in function -- SQRT(P).
Suppose statement 55 is executed when the value of P is
negative. PL/C will produce the following message:

   ***** ERROR IN STMT 55 SQRT ARGUMENT IS NEGATIVE.
           RESULT IS SET TO SQRT(ABS(ARG)). (EX62)

By taking the absolute value of the argument the square root
function can be executed, and execution of the program can
continue. In this case it is very unlikely that this repair is
a reasonable correction, so it is unlikely that the results of
the program will be meaningful, but continued execution may
yield information about other errors so that more than one error
can be corrected on the next submission.

   PL/C is significantly different from PL/I in this regard.   In
fact, PL/C is unique among programming languages in the extent
to which it attempts to repair user errors to   continue
execution.   Although sometimes particular repairs turn out not
to be helpful, and may be confusing, we believe that overall the
result is generally useful, but we acknowledge that our
preference for this "error-repairing" philosophy is   not
universally shared.   If you would rather not have this kind of
help, give the option ERRORS=(1,1) on your *PL/C card.

3.3 PL/C Post-Mortem Dump

After execution of a program, PL/C automatically prints a "post-mortem dump". The nature and form of this information is described in Section I.7.2.4. If printing the dump is not the default option at your computer installation you should specify DUMP on the *PL/C card. Alternatively, you can specify DUMPE, in which case the dump will be printed only if at least one error is detected during execution of the program.

The dump provides a considerable amount of useful information. The display of final values of variables often helps by showing values of variables that you did not expect to be interested in, and hence did not bother to display. It also reveals variables created but never used -- often due to a keypunch spelling error, or a faulty declaration (although the XREF/ATR listing is better for this purpose).

A particularly helpful type of information provided in the post-mortem dump is the frequency count for labels and entry-names. PL/C automatically counts the number of times each label and entry-name is encountered during execution of a program and these values are reported in the dump. For example, suppose a program includes the following segment:

```
                    . . .
     STMT 23        ROW_LOOP: DO I = 1 TO N BY 1;
                        . . .
     STMT 31            COL_LOOP: DO J = 1 TO M BY 1;
                           . . .
     STMT 39                END COL_LOOP;
     STMT 40            END ROW_LOOP;
                    . . .
```

The dump might include the following counts:

```
        NAME         STMT  COUNT
        COL_LOOP     0031  00052
        ROW_LOOP     0023  00001
```

These values indicate that ROW_LOOP was executed only once, and that when it was executed the value of N must have been 52 since COL_LOOP, nested inside ROW_LOOP, was executed 52 times.

Although the dump is produced automatically there are some actions on your part that will increase the usefulness of the information it provides. For example, avoid the reuse of variables -- even temporary utility variables, such as subscripts. Since the dump reports only the final value of each variable, each time you reuse a variable you are throwing away potentially useful information about the early portions of the program. (The examples in the Primer do not generally follow this suggestion, but it is nevertheless a good idea.) For example, suppose a program contains the following segment:

```
      ...
      TEST_LOOP: DO ITEST = 1 TO N BY 1;
          ...
          IF X < Y THEN GO TO TERM_TEST;
          ...
          END TEST_LOOP;
      TERM_TEST: ;
      ...
```

In analyzing the results of test execution of this program you
may need to know whether TEST_LOOP ran to normal completion (N
iterations), or whether it was terminated prematurely by the
GO TO exit.   If neither N nor ITEST was used subsequently in
execution their final values, as displayed in the dump, will
indicate how TEST_LOOP terminated. On the other hand, if you
routinely use I for the index of TEST_LOOP and most other loops
in your program the value of I will have been changed by some
later loop and the dump will not tell you how TEST_LOOP
terminated.   You would have to rerun the program with a
temporary output statement such as

        PUT SKIP(2) LIST('FINAL I & N AFTER TEST_LOOP:',I,N);

placed after TERM_TEST.

    Another helpful practice is to <u>include extra labels</u> in your
program.   A label can be given on any statement, and since PL/C
will automatically count the number of times it is encountered
this can be used to provide very helpful information about how
execution proceeded. For example, we have followed the practice
of providing a label on every loop. This is not really required
but it helps to identify the END of each loop and it permits the
dump to tell you how many times each loop was executed.
Similarly, other labels -- not required by execution -- can be
added to other types of statements just so the dump will tell
you how often they are executed.

Section 3 **Examples**

```
*PL/C ID='T. BISHOP', XREF, ATR, CMPRS
*OPTIONS IN EFFECT*    TIME=(0,15),PAGES=30,LINES=2000,ATR,XREF,FLAGW,BNDRY,NOCMNTS,SORMGIN=(2,72,1),ERRORS=(50,50),
*OPTIONS IN EFFECT*    TABSIZE=2532,UDEF,SOURCE,OPLIST,CMPRS,HDRPG,AUXIO=10000,LINECT=60,NOALIST,MCALL,MTEXT,DUMP=(S,
*OPTIONS IN EFFECT*    F,L,E,U,R),DUMPE=(S,F,L,E,U,R),DUMPT=(S,F,L,E,U,R)
/* PRINT LIST OF WORDS WITHOUT DUPLICATES */                                   PL/C-R7.1--66 10/20/75 10:58 PAGE   1

   STMT LEVEL NEST BLOCK MLVL   SOURCE TEXT
                               /* PRINT LIST OF WORDS WITHOUT DUPLICATES */
                               NODUP: PROCEDURE OPTIONS(MAIN);
    1    1          1            DCL DIFWORD(1:100) CHAR(20) INIT((100)' '); /* LIST OF WORDS */
    2    1          1            DCL NEWWORD CHAR(20);
    3    1          1            DCL (WCOUNT, DWCOUNT) FIXED DEC INIT(0);
    4    1          1            /* TITLE OUTPUT LIST */
    5    1          1            PUT 'LIST OF WORDS WITH DUPLICATES DELETED
      ERROR IN STMT     5  STRING CONSTANT RUNS ACROSS CARD BOUNDARY IN COLUMN 16 (SY50)
      ERROR IN STMT     5  IMPROPER I/O PHRASE (SY22)
      ERROR IN STMT     5  MISSING ( IN COLUMN 16 (SY02)
      ERROR IN STMT     5  MISSING ) IN COLUMN 12 (SY04)
      ERROR IN STMT     5  MISSING SEMI-COLON (OR MISUSE OF RESERVED WORD) (SY08)
            FOR STMT    5  PL/C USES  PUT LIST ('LIST OF WORDS WITH DUPLICATES DELETED');

    6    1          1                PUT SKIP(2);
                               /* PROCESS DATA TO 'ENDDATA' */
    7    1          1                GET LIST(NEWWORD);
    8    1          1            DATA_LOOP: DO WHILE(NEWWORD ¬= 'ENDDATA');
    9    1    1     1                WCOUNT = WCOUNT + 1;
                               /* TEST FOR PREVIOUS OCCURRENCE */
   10    1    1     1                IF WCOUNT ¬= 1 THEN
   11    1    1     1                    TP_LOOP: DO WD = 1 TO DWCOUNT BY 1;
   12    1    2     1                        IF DIFWORD(WD) = NEWWORD
   13    1    2     1                            THEN GO TO SKIPPRT;
   14    1    2     1                        END TP_LOOP;
                               /* ENTER INTO WORD LIST, AND PRINT */
   15    1    1     1                DWCOUNT = DWCOUNT + 1;
   16    1    1     1                DIFWORD(DWCOUNT) = NEWWORD;
   17    1    1     1                PUT SKIP LIST(NEWWORD);
   18    1    1     1            SKIPPRT:
      ERROR IN STMT    18  IMPROPER ELEMENT IN COLUMN 24 (SY16)
      ERROR IN STMT    18  MISSING : (SY09)
                                    GET LIST(NEWWORD);
            FOR STMT   18  PL/C USES  SKIPPRT: GET LIST (NEWWORD);

   19    1    1     1            END DATA_LOOP;
                               /* PRINT SUMMARY LINE */
   20    1          1                PUT SKIP(2) LIST('AMONG', WCOUNT, 'WORDS THERE WERE');
   21    1          1                PUT SKIP LIST(DWCOUNT, 'DIFFERENT WORDS');
   22    1          1            END NODUP;

DCL NO.         IDENTIFIER                ATTRIBUTES AND REFERENCES

    8          DATA_LOOP                 STATEMENT LABEL CONSTANT

    2          DIFWORD                   (*)AUTOMATIC,INITIAL,UNALIGNED,CHARACTER,STRING
                                         12,16

    4          DWCOUNT                   AUTOMATIC,INITIAL,ALIGNED,DECIMAL,FIXED(5,0)
                                         11,15,15,16,21

    3          NEWWORD                   AUTOMATIC,UNALIGNED,CHARACTER,STRING
                                         7,8,12,16,17,18
```

```
/* PRINT LIST OF WORDS WITHOUT DUPLICATES */                       PL/C-R7.1--66 10/20/75 10:58 PAGE   2
DCL NO.       IDENTIFIER                        ATTRIBUTES AND REFERENCES


   1          NODUP                             ENTRY,BINARY,FIXED(15,0)

  18          SKIPPRT                           STATEMENT LABEL CONSTANT
                                                13

  11          TP_LOOP                           STATEMENT LABEL CONSTANT

   4          WCOUNT                            AUTOMATIC,INITIAL,ALIGNED,DECIMAL,FIXED(5,0)
                                                9,9,10,20

              WD                                AUTOMATIC,ALIGNED,DECIMAL,FLOAT(6)
                                                11,12
```

ERRORS/WARNINGS DETECTED DURING CODE GENERATION:

        WARNING: NO FILE SPECIFIED. SYSIN/SYSPRINT ASSUMED. (CGOC)

LIST OF WORDS WITH DUPLICATES DELETED

AB
BA
AA

AMONG   5   WORDS THERE WERE
        3   DIFFERENT WORDS

IN STMT   22   PROGRAM RETURNS FROM MAIN PROCEDURE.

IN STMT   22   SCALARS AND BLOCK-TRACE:

***** MAIN PROCEDURE NODUP

```
WD= 3.00000E+00        DWCOUNT=        3       WCOUNT=        5       NEWWORD='ENDDATA
NCN-O PROCEDURE EXECUTION COUNTS:
NAME        STMT COUNT  NAME        STMT COUNT  NAME        STMT COUNT  NAME        STMT COUNT  NAME        STMT COUNT
NODUP       0001 00001

LABEL EXECUTION COUNTS:
NAME        STMT COUNT  NAME        STMT COUNT  NAME        STMT COUNT  NAME        STMT COUNT  NAME        STMT COUNT
SKIPPRT     0018 00005  TP_LOOP     0011 00004  DATA_LOOP   0008 00001
```

```
        COMPILATION STATISTICS  (0022 STATEMENTS)    |                EXECUTION STATISTICS
  SECONDS  ERRORS  WARNINGS  PAGES  LINES  CARDS  INCL'S | SECONDS  ERRORS  WARNINGS  PAGES  LINES  CARDS  INCL'S  AUX I/O
    .10       7       1       2     91     30      0 |    .02       0       0       1     13     1      0       0
----------------------------------------------------------+----------------------------------------------------------------
  BYTES     SYMBOL TABLE    INTERMEDIATE CODE    OBJECT CODE |  STATIC CORE    AUTOMATIC CORE    DYNAMIC CORE    TOTAL STORAGE
  USED      1273(  2K)       666(  1K)          818(  1K) |   340(  1K)       3113(  4K)        0(  0K)        5513(  6K)
  UNUSED    8855(  8K)      9359(  9K)        18382( 17K) | 14971( 14K)      14971( 14K)     9359(  9K)       14971( 14K)
```

THIS PROGRAM MAY BE RERUN WITHOUT CHANGE IN A REGION 14K BYTES SMALLER USING TABLESIZE=   319

Section 4   Explicit Diagnostic Facilities

It is generally difficult to ascertain correctness by using only results displayed as part of the problem requirements. Some temporary provision must be made to <u>obtain</u> <u>additional printed</u> <u>output</u> <u>during</u> <u>testing</u>.

The additional information needed to establish the correctness of a section of program is most easily identified while that section is being written; hence the temporary testing facilities should be designed and included as the program is being written. Unfortunately, many programmers will not admit that extra output is <u>always</u> required, and make no provision to obtain it until after the program has been completed and test runs show something to be wrong.

The <u>basic</u> <u>diagnostic</u> <u>tool</u> in any programming language is the <u>ordinary</u> <u>output</u> <u>statement</u>. If you learn where to position temporary output statements and what information to display, you can test any program. Some languages include special facilities for printing diagnostic information. These facilities are only a convenience, since nothing is provided that could not be obtained with other elements of the language, but they are nevertheless important. Testing is a non-trivial task, often as costly and difficult as writing the program in the first place. Powerful specialized facilities increase the likelihood that testing is properly done, and at the same time reduce its cost.

4.1 <u>Flow Tracing</u>

In Sections I.4.1.2 and I.4.4 we referred to the hand execution of programs as "tracing". The same word is used to describe computer execution when detailed information about the flow of execution is obtained. This can be done by placing output statements at strategic points in the program, but PL/I provides a more convenient way. In order to "check" all values that are assigned to certain key variables, one can list these variables in a "CHECK prefix" given before a procedure:

```
(CHECK( list )):
procedure-name: PROCEDURE ...
```

This CHECK prefix should be given on a separate card so that it can be conveniently removed when testing is completed. Note

that the list of variables is enclosed in one set of
parentheses, and the entire prefix is enclosed in another set.
Like a label prefix the CHECK prefix is followed by a colon.

   Each time a variable on the CHECK list is assigned a value, a
message is automatically printed. For example, consider

```
          *PL/C ID='TOM WILCOX'
          /* PROCEDURE TO COMPUTE THE QUADRATIC SUM OF DATA */
          (CHECK(POINT,IQSUM,QUADSUM)):
          QUADSUMMER: PROCEDURE OPTIONS(MAIN);
              ...
          GET LIST(POINT);
          QUADSUM = 0;
          QSUM_LOOP: DO IQSUM = 1 TO POINT BY 1;
              ...
              END QSUM_LOOP;
          ...
          END QUADSUMMER;
```

(4.1a)

The CHECK output from (4.1a) is similar to what would be
produced by (4.1b):

```
          *PL/C ID='TOM WILCOX'
          /* PROCEDURE TO COMPUTE THE QUADRATIC SUM OF DATA */
          QUADSUMMER: PROCEDURE OPTIONS(MAIN);
              ...
          GET LIST(POINT);
          PUT SKIP DATA(POINT);
          QUADSUM = 0;
          PUT SKIP DATA(QUADSUM);
          QSUM_LOOP: DO IQSUM = 1 TO POINT BY 1;
              PUT SKIP DATA(IQSUM);
              ...
              END QSUM_LOOP;
          PUT SKIP DATA(IQSUM);
          ...
          END QUADSUMMER;
```

(4.1b)

Labels can also be checked. For example

```
          (CHECK(MAIN_LOOP)):
          SOLVE: PROCEDURE OPTIONS(MAIN);
              ...
              MAIN_LOOP: DO WHILE ...
```

is equivalent to writing

```
          SOLVE: PROCEDURE OPTIONS(MAIN);
              ...
              PUT SKIP LIST('MAIN_LOOP;');
              MAIN_LOOP: DO WHILE ...
```

(4.1c) illustrates checking both labels and variables:

```
    *PL/C ID='G. HILLENBRAND'
     /* SUM INTEGERS FROM 1 TO ABSOLUTE VALUE OF DATUM */
     /* STOP ON FIRST ZERO DATUM */
     (CHECK(VALUE, INVERT, SUM)):
     ABS_SUM: PROCEDURE OPTIONS(MAIN);
          DCL (VALUE,    /* NEW VALUE READ IN */
               SUM,      /* SUM OF INTEGERS */
               I)   FIXED DECIMAL;
(4.1c)    GET LIST(VALUE);
          VALUE_LOOP: DO WHILE(VALUE ¬= 0);
               IF VALUE < 0 THEN INVERT: VALUE = -VALUE;
               /* SUM INTEGERS FROM 1 TO VALUE */
                 SUM = 0;
                 SUM_LOOP: DO I = 1 TO VALUE BY 1;
                     SUM = SUM + I;
                     END SUM_LOOP;
             PUT SKIP LIST('VALUE IS:',VALUE,'SUM IS:',SUM);
             GET LIST(VALUE);
             END VALUE_LOOP;
          END ABS_SUM;
    *DATA
     2, -3, 0
```

Without the CHECK prefix, execution output is:

VALUE IS:	2	SUM IS:	3
VALUE IS:	3	SUM IS:	6

With the CHECK prefix, PL/C execution of (4.1c) will produce the following output (PL/I output is slightly different):

```
    CHECK IN STMT 0003:    VALUE=        2;
    CHECK IN STMT 0007:    SUM=      0;
    CHECK IN STMT 0009:    SUM=      1;
    CHECK IN STMT 0009:    SUM=      3;
    VALUE IS:     2      SUM IS:      3
    CHECK IN STMT 0012:    VALUE=       -3;
    CHECK IN STMT 0006:    INVERT;
    CHECK IN STMT 0006:    VALUE=        3;
    CHECK IN STMT 0007:    SUM=      0;
    CHECK IN STMT 0009:    SUM=      1;
    CHECK IN STMT 0009:    SUM=      3;
    CHECK IN STMT 0009:    SUM=      6;
    VALUE IS:     3      SUM IS:      6
    CHECK IN STMT 0012:    VALUE=        0;
```

To CHECK an array the array-name is given in the CHECK prefix and not a subscripted variable referencing a particular element of the array. For example, if an array is declared AR(10), (CHECK(AR)) could be given as a prefix, but <u>not</u> (CHECK(AR(I))) or (CHECK(AR(7))). PL/I and PL/C differ somewhat in the CHECK printing for an array. If an array is CHECKed, PL/I prints the <u>entire</u> array upon completion of execution of any statement that

causes one or more elements of the array to receive a value.
PL/C prints only the particular element receiving the value.

The CHECK prefix applies only to the statements written
within the particular procedure -- not statements in other
external procedures that may be called. For example, in (4.1d)
WORD and TALLY will be CHECKed in ENCODE, but CHECKing will not
occur during the execution of SCRAM, which is called from
ENCODE. Checking will occur, however, immediately after
executing CALL SCRAM(WORD) since WORD <u>might have changed</u> value
during execution of the call.

```
        *PL/C ID='MARK BODENSTEIN'
        /* ENCODE AND DISPLAY LIST OF WORDS */
        (CHECK(WORD, TALLY)):
        ENCODE: PROCEDURE OPTIONS(MAIN);
            ...
            CALL SCRAM(WORD);
(4.1d)      ...
            END ENCODE;
        *PROCESS
        /* SCRAMBLE CHARACTERS OF A */
        SCRAM: PROCEDURE(A);
            ...
            END SCRAM;
```

CHECKing could be invoked in SCRAM by giving SCRAM its own CHECK
prefix -- regardless of whether or not ENCODE has a CHECK
prefix. In PL/C (but not in PL/I) the parameters of a procedure
can also be CHECKed, as shown below:

```
        *PROCESS
        /* SCRAMBLE CHARACTERS OF A */
        (CHECK(A, K)):
        SCRAM: PROCEDURE(A);
            ...
            END SCRAM;
```

The point is that CHECKing is <u>local to the procedure to which
the CHECK prefix is applied</u>, and does not affect the entire
program just because a CHECK prefix is applied to the main
procedure.

4.1.1 <u>Limiting the Scope of CHECK</u>

The CHECK feature is a convenient means of producing
diagnostic output. In fact, the problem is that it can easily
produce more printed output than you can reasonably use. For
example, suppose you CHECKed TEMP so that an announcement was
printed each time an interchange took place in a sorting
program:

```
*PROCESS
/* SORT A(1:N) INTO INCREASING ORDER */
(CHECK(TEMP)):
SORT: PROCEDURE(A, N);
    DECLARE A(*) FLOAT DECIMAL;
    DECLARE N FIXED DECIMAL;
    DECLARE TEMP FLOAT DECIMAL;
    DECLARE (I,J) FIXED DECIMAL;
    /* MAKE N-1 SELECTING PASSES OVER A(1:J) */
        SELECT_LOOP: DO J = N TO 2 BY -1;
            /* SET A(J) TO MAX OF A(1:J) */
                MAX_LOOP: DO I = 1 TO J-1 BY 1;
                    IF A(I) > A(I+1) THEN DO;
                        TEMP = A(I);
                        A(I) = A(I+1);
                        A(I+1) = TEMP; END;
                END MAX_LOOP;
        END SELECT_LOOP;
    END SORT;
```

In SORT the statement assigning a value to TEMP, which will cause a CHECK line to be printed each time it is executed, is inside a 2-level nested loop. It could be executed a great many times, depending upon the value of N and the initial order of the values of A. It could be executed as many as $N^2/2$ times. For example, this means that for N = 100, as many as 5000 lines of CHECK output could be printed. Most student programs are run under fairly severe line limits, so execution would be terminated before this many lines were actually printed. But even if this many lines could be printed it would be wasteful -- of paper, computer time, and reading time -- to print them. Virtually all of the useful information would be given in the lines produced by the first few passes over the array and the last few passes. If the process gets started properly and terminates properly it is very likely to perform properly in between times. Hence what is needed is some means of turning the CHECKing mechanism on and off, selectively. This can be done in PL/C with the CHECK and NOCHECK statements. When NOCHECK is executed, all printing generated by the CHECK prefix is suppressed. When CHECK is executed, CHECK printing is resumed (if it has been suppressed). These statements can be positioned arbitrarily in a procedure to make the action of the CHECK prefix effective in only a small section of the procedure.

The CHECK and NOCHECK statements can be used in several different ways. For example, two conditional statements could be inserted in the SORT procedure shown above:

```
        ...
    /* MAKE N-1 SELECTING PASSES OVER A(1:J) */
        SELECT_LOOP: DO J = N TO 2 BY -1;
            IF J = N - 2 THEN DO;
                PUT SKIP LIST
                    ('SELECT_LOOP, END OF PASS 2');
                NOCHECK; END;
            IF J = 3 THEN CHECK;
            /* SET A(J) TO MAX OF A(1:J) */
                ...
```

The conditional NOCHECK statement will turn the CHECKing off on the third pass over the array, and print a message announcing the end of the second pass. The conditional CHECK statement will turn the printing back on again for the second last and last passes. With these controls, when N = 100 the CHECK output would not exceed 200 lines, and this would contain as much useful information as the output from an unrestricted CHECK.

Alternatively, you can specify a limit on the number of CHECK lines that can be printed. This is done by giving the limit as an expression in a CHECK statement:

```
    CHECK(expression);
```

To execute this statement, the expression is evaluated to provide an integer which specifies the number of CHECK actions to be printed. After this quantity of messages the NOCHECK suppression is automatically invoked. Printing can be resumed by execution of another CHECK statement. For example, CHECK(10) permits up to ten CHECK messages to be printed, and then no more until another CHECK statement is executed. This could be used in the SORT procedure as follows:

```
        ...
    /* MAKE N-1 SELECTING PASSES OVER A(1:J) */
        CHECK(2*N);
        SELECT_LOOP: DO J = N TO 2 BY -1;
            IF J = 3 THEN DO;
                PUT SKIP LIST
                    ('SELECT_LOOP, RESUME CHECK');
                CHECK; END;
            /* SET A(J) TO MAX OF A(1:J) */
                ...
```

Note that while these two alternatives both limit the CHECK output to a reasonable volume, they are basically different strategies. The first limits CHECKing to a certain portion of the execution -- regardless of how much output that might yield. The second strategy simply puts a limit on the volume of CHECK output -- without considering the number of passes over the list that might be involved in producing that much output. Either seems reasonable in this case, but sometimes one or the other will be preferable and you should be aware that both are available.

Note that CHECK and NOCHECK <u>statements</u> <u>control</u> the action of
the CHECK   <u>prefix</u> -- they do not take the place of the prefix.
CHECK and NOCHECK statements in a procedure without a CHECK
prefix are completely ineffective -- they act as a null
statement during execution. This means that when you have
finished testing a procedure you can remove the CHECK prefix,
but leave any CHECK and NOCHECK statements in place. Eventually
you will want to take them out, but it is a good idea to leave
them in place until it is absolutely certain that you will not
have to do further testing of this procedure.

4.2 <u>The Memory Dump</u>

An alternative to tracing is to periodically display the
values of key variables. This is called "dumping memory". It
does not provide as complete information, but for just that
reason it is useful in a preliminary search to determine the
neighborhood of an error. By displaying values at different key
points (usually section interfaces) during execution, one can
determine which intervals need to be traced in detail.

PL/I has no special facilities for dumping, but the normal
PUT statement is generally adequate.

It is important that each dump display contain enough
identification to relate it to the proper point in the program.
For example, statements like the following should be used:

            PUT SKIP(2) LIST('TEST DUMP POINT AL3');
            PUT SKIP DATA(I, X(I), TOTAL);
            PUT SKIP;

This dump output is separated by blank lines from other
execution output, and is given an identifying title. The
PUT DATA statement is useful in dumping so the names as well as
the values will be displayed, but since a literal cannot be
given in a PUT DATA statement a separate PUT LIST statement must
be used for the title.

PL/C provides two special PUT options that are useful for
dumping:

            PUT ALL;

            PUT ARRAY;

PUT ALL displays the current values of all simple variables in
the active procedures, while PUT ARRAY displays arrays as well
as simple variables. This automatically gives the name as well
as the value of each variable, plus an indication of which
procedures are currently active, and the STMT number of the
statement which causes the dump.

4.2.1 <u>Data Display</u>

In analyzing test output it is essential that you be able to know with absolute certainty just what data values were obtained by each execution of a GET statement. The only sure way of knowing is to <u>print the values out immediately after they are read in</u>. The CHECK feature will, of course, do this for you automatically if you CHECK every variable that is assigned a value from external data. However, this will report the results of assignment statements as well as GET statements, and this may cause more printing than you need. In PL/C you can use the CHECK and NOCHECK statements to limit the CHECK action to GET statements only. That is, list the variables in the CHECK prefix, but execute a NOCHECK at the beginning of the procedure. Then bracket each GET with CHECK and NOCHECK statements. For example:

```
(CHECK(X, Y, A, N)):
ROTATE: PROCEDURE ...
    DECLARE ...
    NOCHECK;
    ...
    CHECK;
    GET LIST(X, Y);
    NOCHECK;
    ...
    CHECK;
    GET LIST(A, N);
    NOCHECK;
    ...
    END ROTATE;
```

Alternatively, you can insert temporary PUT statements immediately after each GET. As in the case of the dump, these statements must adequately identify their output. For example, suppose a program contained the following segment to load an array:

```
/* LOAD A(1:N) FROM DATA */
    GET LIST(N);
    LOAD_LOOP: DO I = 1 TO N BY 1;
        GET LIST(A(I));
        END LOAD_LOOP;
```

In testing form, this segment might look like the following:

```
/* LOAD A(1:N) FROM DATA */
    GET LIST(N);
    PUT SKIP(2) LIST('LOAD_LOOP.  N=', N);
    PUT SKIP LIST('VALUES OF A(1:N):');
    LOAD_LOOP: DO I = 1 TO N BY 1;
        GET LIST(A(I));
        PUT LIST(A(I));
        END LOAD_LOOP;
    PUT SKIP(2);
```

Section 4 <u>Summary</u>

Actions that can be taken by the programmer to increase the amount of diagnostic information produced during execution of a program are:

1. Specify the XREF, ATR and DUMP options on the *PL/C card (if these are not produced automatically at your installation).

2. Give a CHECK prefix on a procedure to have PL/I automatically report each time a value is assigned to one of the variables listed in the prefix:

```
(CHECK(list of variables)):
procedure-name: PROCEDURE...
```

In PL/C the list can include parameters as well as variables.

3. Include labels on the list in the CHECK prefix to have PL/I automatically report each time the label is encountered during execution.

4. In PL/C use the CHECK and NOCHECK statements in a procedure that has a CHECK prefix to limit the quantity of CHECK printing.

5. Insert extra PUT statements at key points in the program to report the values of significant variables:

```
PUT SKIP(2) LIST('identifying title');
PUT SKIP DATA(list of variables);
PUT SKIP;
```

In PL/C, PUT ALL or PUT ARRAY can be used to give a complete dump of the values of variables at that point in execution.

6. In PL/C increase the information provided by the post-mortem dump by not re-using variables at different points in the program, and by providing extra labels to take advantage of the automatic frequency counting.

7. Use the CHECK feature or PUT statements to print the value of each data item immediately afer it is read.

Section 4 **Examples**


```
*PL/C ID='T. BISHOP', CMPRS

*OPTIONS IN EFFECT*    TIME=(0,15),PAGES=30,LINES=2000,NOATR,NOXREF,FLAGW,BNDRY,NOCMNTS,SORMGIN=(2,72,1),
*OPTIONS IN EFFECT*    ERRORS=(50,50),TABSIZE=2532,UDEF,SOURCE,OPLIST,CMPRS,HDRPG,AUXIO=10000,LINECT=60,NOALIST,MCALL,
*OPTIONS IN EFFECT*    MTEXT,DUMP=(S,F,L,E,U,R),DUMPE=(S,F,L,E,U,R),DUMPT=(S,F,L,E,U,R)
```

```
/* PRINT LIST OF WORDS WITHOUT DUPLICATES */                              PL/C-R7.1--66 10/20/75 10:58 PAGE   1

STMT LEVEL NEST BLOCK MLVL  SOURCE TEXT

                                  /* PRINT LIST OF WORDS WITHOUT DUPLICATES */
    1                             (CHECK(NEWWORD, TP_LOOP, DWCOUNT)):
                                  NODUP: PROCEDURE OPTIONS(MAIN);
    2    1              1             DCL DIFWORD(1:30) CHAR(20) INIT((30)' '); /* LIST OF WORDS */
    3    1              1             DCL NEWWORD CHAR(20);
    4    1              1             DCL (WCOUNT, DWCOUNT) FIXED DEC INIT(0);
    5    1              1             CHECK(24);
                                      /* TITLE OUTPUT LIST */
    6    1              1             PUT LIST('LIST OF WORDS WITH DUPLICATES DELETED');
    7    1              1             PUT SKIP(2);
                                      /* PROCESS DATA TO 'ENDDATA' */
    8    1              1             GET LIST(NEWWORD);
    9    1              1             DATA_LOOP: DO WHILE(NEWWORD ¬= 'ENDDATA');
   10    1    1         1                WCOUNT = WCOUNT + 1;
                                         /* TEST FOR PREVIOUS OCCURRENCE */
   11    1    1         1                IF WCOUNT ¬= 1 THEN
   12    1    1         1                   TP_LOOP: DO WD = 1 TO DWCOUNT BY 1;
   13    1    2         1                      IF DIFWORD(WD) = NEWWORD
   14    1    2         1                         THEN GO TO SKIPPRT;
   15    1    2         1                      END TP_LOOP;
                                         /* ENTER INTO WORD LIST, AND PRINT */
   16    1    1         1                DWCOUNT = DWCOUNT + 1;
   17    1    1         1                DIFWORD(DWCOUNT) = NEWWORD;
   18    1    1         1                PUT SKIP LIST(NEWWORD);
   19    1    1         1             SKIPPRT:;
   20    1    1         1             GET LIST(NEWWORD);
   21    1    1         1             END DATA_LOOP;
   22    1              1             PUT ARRAY;
                                      /* PRINT SUMMARY LINE */
   23    1              1             PUT SKIP(2) LIST('AMONG', WCOUNT, 'WORDS THERE WERE');
   24    1              1             PUT SKIP LIST(DWCOUNT, 'DIFFERENT WORDS');
   25    1              1             END NODUP;
         WARNING: FEATURES INCOMPATIBLE WITH PL/I-F HAVE BEEN USED (SY40)

ERRORS/WARNINGS DETECTED DURING CODE GENERATION:

    WARNING: NO FILE SPECIFIED. SYSIN/SYSPRINT ASSUMED. (CGOC)
```

```
LIST CF WORDS WITH DUPLICATES DELETED

CHECK IN STMT 0008:     NEWWORD='ABCDEFG          ';
CHECK IN STMT 0016:     DWCOUNT=        1;
ABCDEFG
CHECK IN STMT 0020:     NEWWORD='ABCDEFH          ';
CHECK IN STMT 0012:     TP_LOOP;
CHECK IN STMT 0016:     DWCOUNT=        2;
ABCDEFH
CHECK IN STMT 0020:     NEWWORD='ABCDEFG          ';
CHECK IN STMT 0012:     TP_LOOP;
CHECK IN STMT 0020:     NEWWORD='XBCDEFG          ';
CHECK IN STMT 0012:     TP_LOOP;
CHECK IN STMT 0016:     DWCOUNT=        3;
XBCDEFG
CHECK IN STMT 0020:     NEWWORD='ABCDEF           ';
CHECK IN STMT 0012:     TP_LOOP;
CHECK IN STMT 0016:     DWCOUNT=        4;
ABCDEF
CHECK IN STMT 0020:     NEWWORD='ABCDEFG          ';
CHECK IN STMT 0012:     TP_LOOP;
CHECK IN STMT 0020:     NEWWORD='XBCDEFG          ';
CHECK IN STMT 0012:     TP_LOOP;
CHECK IN STMT 0020:     NEWWORD='A                ';
CHECK IN STMT 0012:     TP_LOOP;
CHECK IN STMT 0016:     DWCOUNT=        5;
A
CHECK IN STMT 0020:     NEWWORD='B                ';
CHECK IN STMT 0012:     TP_LOOP;
CHECK IN STMT 0016:     DWCOUNT=        6;
B
CHECK IN STMT 0020:     NEWWORD='B                ';
XNDDATA

12345678901234567890
IN STMT   22  ARRAYS, SCALARS AND BLOCK-TRACE:

***** MAIN PROCEDURE NODUP

WD= 9.00000E+00      WCOUNT=       14    DIFWORD(1)='ABCDEFG          '    DIFWORD(2)='ABCDEFH
                     DIFWORD(3)='XBCDEFG          '    DIFWORD(4)='ABCDEF           '    DIFWORD(5)='A
DIFWORD(5)='A                '    DIFWORD(6)='B                '    DIFWORD(7)='XNDDATA
                     DIFWORD(8)='                 '    DIFWORD(9)='12345678901234567890'
DIFWORD(10)='                 '    DIFWORD(11)='                 '    DIFWORD(12)='
                     DIFWORD(13)='                 '    DIFWORD(14)='                 '
DIFWORD(15)='                 '    DIFWORD(16)='                 '    DIFWORD(17)='
                     DIFWORD(18)='                 '    DIFWORD(19)='
DIFWORD(20)='                 '    DIFWORD(21)='                 '    DIFWORD(22)='
                     DIFWORD(23)='                 '    DIFWORD(24)='                 '    DIFWORD(27)='
DIFWORD(25)='                 '    DIFWORD(26)='                 '    DIFWORD(27)='
                     DIFWORD(28)='                 '    DIFWORD(29)='
DIFWORD(30)='                 '    DWCOUNT=         9    NEWWORD='ENDDATA          '


END OF DIAGNOSTIC OUTPUT

AMONG                    14         WORDS THERE WERE
         9           DIFFERENT WORDS


IN STMT   25  PROGRAM RETURNS FROM MAIN PROCEDURE.
```

/* PRINT LIST OF WORDS WITHOUT DUPLICATES */   PL/C-R7   POST-MORTEM DUMP   PAGE   1

IN STMT   25 SCALARS AND BLOCK-TRACE:

***** MAIN PROCEDURE NODUP

WD= 9.00000E+00   WCOUNT=   14   DWCOUNT=   9   NEWWORD='ENDDATA   '

NON-0 PROCEDURE EXECUTION COUNTS:
NAME	STMT COUNT	NAME	STMT COUNT	NAME	STMT COUNT	NAME	STMT COUNT	NAME	STMT COUNT
NODUP	0001 00001								

LABEL EXECUTION COUNTS:
NAME	STMT COUNT	NAME	STMT COUNT	NAME	STMT COUNT	NAME	STMT COUNT	NAME	STMT COUNT
SKIPPRT	0019 00014	TP_LOOP	0012 00013	DATA_LOOP	0009 00001				

	COMPILATION STATISTICS (0025 STATEMENTS)						EXECUTION STATISTICS						
SECONDS	ERRORS	WARNINGS	PAGES	LINES	CARDS	INCL'S	SECONDS	ERRORS	WARNINGS	PAGES	LINES	CARDS	INCL'S	AUX I/O
.08	0	2	1	50	33	0	.09	0	0	1	62	4	0	0

BYTES	SYMBOL TABLE	INTERMEDIATE CODE	OBJECT CODE	STATIC CORE	AUTOMATIC CORE	DYNAMIC CORE	TOTAL STORAGE
USED	1325(2K)	736(1K)	902(1K)	340(1K)	1437(2K)	0(0K)	3973(4K)
UNUSED	8803(8K)	9289(9K)	18252(17K)	16511(16K)	16511(16K)	9289(9K)	16511(16K)

THIS PROGRAM MAY BE RERUN WITHOUT CHANGE IN A REGION 16K BYTES SMALLER USING TABLESIZE=   332

Section 4 Exercises

1. Rewrite the program given in (I.1.1e) as it should be for an initial testing run

    a) using additional PUT statements,

    b) using the PL/I CHECK feature,

    c) using the PL/C CHECK prefix,   CHECK   and   NOCHECK statements,

    d) with a test control procedure similar to (V.2.2b) that permits the program to be repeated with several data sets.

2. What execution output is produced by the program shown below?

```
*PL/C ID='J. DENNIS'
/* MOVE MINIMUM TO HEAD OF LIST */
(CHECK(MINPOS)):
MINMOVE: PROCEDURE OPTIONS(MAIN);
     DCL L(50) FLOAT DECIMAL;
     DCL MINVAL FLOAT DEC; /* MIN VALUE SO FAR */
     DCL MINPOS FIXED DEC; /* POSITION OF MINVAL IN LIST */
     DCL N FIXED DEC;      /* EFFECTIVE LENGTH OF LIST */
     DCL I FIXED DEC;
     /* LOAD L(1:N) FROM DATA */
         GET LIST(N);
         IF (N<1)|(N>50) THEN DO;
             PUT SKIP(4) LIST('IMPROPER LENGTH');
             GO TO TERM_MINMOVE; END;
         LOAD_LOOP: DO I = 1 TO N BY 1;
             GET LIST(L(I));
             END LOAD_LOOP;
     /* SET MINVAL TO MINIMUM OF L(1:N), */
             /* AND SET MINPOS TO INDEX OF MINVAL IN L */
         MINVAL = L(1);
         MINPOS = 1;
         LOC_LOOP: DO I = 2 TO N BY 1;
             IF L(I) < MINVAL THEN DO;
                 MINVAL=L(I); MINPOS=I; END;
             IF I = 4 THEN NOCHECK;
             END LOC_LOOP;
         CHECK;
     /* SWAP MIN L(I) WITH L(1) AND REPORT */
         L(MINPOS) = L(1);
         L(1) = MINVAL;
         PUT SKIP LIST('MIN VALUE IS', L(1));
         PUT SKIP LIST('ORIG INDEX OF MIN IS', MINPOS);
     TERM_MINMOVE:;
     END MINMOVE;

 *DATA
     8, 7, 6, 9, 8, 5, 4, 6, 4, 3
```

<u>3</u>. Rewrite the following program to give essentially the same
diagnostic output, but without using the CHECK facility.

```
*PL/C ID='EDYTHE DAVIES'
 /* COMPUTE BOUNDED INTEGER SUMS */
 (CHECK(LOW, HIGH, INT, SUM)):
 SUMER: PROCEDURE OPTIONS(MAIN);
      DCL (LOW, HIGH) FIXED DEC; /* RANGE LIMITS */
      DCL INT FIXED DEC;         /* CURRENT INTEGER */
      DCL SUM FIXED DEC;         /* SUM OF INTEGERS */

      GET LIST(LOW, HIGH);
      IF LOW > HIGH THEN PUT SKIP LIST('IMPROPER BOUNDS');

      /* SET SUM TO SUM OF INTEGERS FROM LOW TO HIGH */
          SUM = 0;
          SUM_LOOP: DO INT = LOW TO HIGH BY 1;
               SUM = SUM + INT;
               END SUM_LOOP;

      PUT SKIP LIST(LOW, HIGH, SUM);
      END SUMER;
 *DATA
```

<u>4</u>. Rewrite the following program segment to give essentially the
same diagnostic output, but without using the CHECK facility.

```
 (CHECK(L1, L2, L3)):
 X: PROCEDURE ...;
     ...
     L1: IF X + Y < Z
          THEN L2: Y = 2*Z;
          ELSE L3: Y = 0;
     ...
```

5. How many lines of <u>execution</u> output would be produced by the
following program:

```
*PL/C ID='DOROTHY DAVIES'
 /* COUNT OCCURRENCES OF SPECIFIED CHARACTER */
 (CHECK(WORDNUM, CHARNUM)):
 CTCHAR: PROCEDURE OPTIONS(MAIN);
      DCL WORD CHAR(30) VARYING; /* WORD TO BE TESTED */
      DCL TESTCHAR CHAR(1);      /* CHAR TO BE COUNTED */
      DCL NBR FIXED DEC INIT(0); /* NO. OF OCCURRENCES */
      DCL (WORDNUM, CHARNUM) FIXED DEC;
      GET LIST(TESTCHAR);
```

(exercise 5 continued on next page)

```
/* PROCESS EACH INPUT WORD UNTIL 'END' */
    GET LIST(WORD);
    WORDNUM = 1;
    WORD_LOOP: DO WHILE(WORD ¬= 'END');
        /* COUNT OCCUR. OF TESTCHAR IN WORD.  */
        CT_LOOP: DO CHARNUM=1 TO LENGTH(WORD) BY 1;
            IF SUBSTR(WORD,CHARNUM,1)=TESTCHAR
                THEN COUNT: NBR = NBR + 1;
            END CT_LOOP;
        GET LIST(WORD);
        WORDNUM = WORDNUM + 1;
        END WORD_LOOP;
    WORDNUM = WORDNUM-1; /* DON'T COUNT END MARKER*/

/* DISPLAY RESULTS */
    PUT SKIP LIST('TEST CHAR IS:',TESTCHAR);
    PUT SKIP LIST('TOTAL OCCURENCES:',NBR);
    PUT SKIP LIST('NBR WORDS TESTED:',WORDNUM);

END CTCHAR;

*DATA
'P',
'1P2P3P4P5P6P7P', '123P123P123P',
'PPPPPPP', 'M', 'MP', '12345678P', 'END'
```

6. Rewrite the program given below so that its action is
unchanged except that it will print additional diagnostic
information. This information should include
   a) an announcement of the beginning of each pass,

   b) the details of each interchange.

```
*PL/C ID='EV DAVIES'
/* SORT LIST INTO ASCENDING ORDER */
SORT: PROCEDURE OPTIONS(MAIN);
    DCL L(50) FLOAT DEC; /* LIST TO BE SORTED */
    DCL N FIXED DEC;      /* EFFECTIVE LENGTH */
    DCL TEMP FLOAT DEC;
    DCL (I,J) FIXED DEC;

    /* LOAD L(1:N) FROM DATA */
        GET LIST(N);
        IF N>50 THEN PUT SKIP LIST('LIST TOO LONG');
        LOAD_LOOP: DO I = 1 TO N BY 1;
            GET LIST(L(I));
            END LOAD_LOOP;
```

(exercise 6 continued on next page)

```
     /* SORT L(1:N) BY "BUBBLE SORT", */
     /* BRINGING LARGEST TO TOP ON EACH PASS */
         BUBBLE_LOOP: DO J = N TO 2 BY -1;
           /* CARRY MAX VALUE TO END OF L(1:J) */
             MAX_LOOP: DO I = 1 TO J-1 BY 1;
                 /* INTERCHANGE IF OUT OF ORDER */
                   IF L(I)>L(I+1) THEN DO;
                     TEMP = L(I);
                     L(I) = L(I+1);
                     L(I+1) = TEMP; END;
               END MAX_LOOP;
           END BUBBLE_LOOP;

     /* DISPLAY L(1:N) IN SORTED ORDER */
         PUT SKIP(2) LIST('SORTED LIST');
         PUT SKIP(2);
         PRINT_LOOP: DO I = 1 TO N BY 1;
             PUT SKIP LIST(L(I));
             END PRINT_LOOP;

     END SORT;
   *DATA
```

<u>7</u>. Rewrite the program given below adding suitable diagnostic
facilities.

```
   *PL/C ID='GEN DAVIES'
    /* CHANGE DUPLICATE CHARACTERS IN INPUT WORDS TO '*'.  */
    /* END OF WORD LIST IS INDICATED BY WORD 'END'.  */
   DELDUP: PROCEDURE OPTIONS(MAIN);
       DCL WORD CHAR(78) VARYING;
       DCL (CHR,TEST) FIXED DEC;

     /* READ AND PROCESS EACH WORD UNTIL 'END' IS READ */
         GET LIST(WORD);
         WORD_LOOP: DO WHILE (WORD ¬= 'END');
           PUT SKIP LIST(WORD,'IS CHANGED TO');
           /* REPLACE DUPLICATE CHARACTERS IN WORD BY * */
             CHR_LOOP: DO CHR=1 TO LENGTH(WORD)-1 BY 1;
               TEST_LOOP: DO TEST = CHR+1 TO LENGTH(WORD)
                           BY 1;
                 IF SUBSTR(WORD,TEST,1) =
                         SUBSTR(WORD,CHR,1)
                       THEN SUBSTR(WORD,TEST,1) = '*';
               END TEST_LOOP;
             END CHR_LOOP;
           PUT LIST(WORD);
           GET LIST(WORD);
           END WORD_LOOP;

     END DELDUP;
   *DATA
```

Section 5   Modular Testing

5.1 Bottom-Up Testing

It is essentially impossible to test large programs -- there are just too many combinations of things to be tested. Really all we can do is thoroughly test small segments of programs and then construct a large program from these components. The testing of a program should be based on the tree that was constructed during the development of the program. During development the tree is constructed in a generally top-down direction, as the problem statement is successively refined into program units. Testing can follow the tree from the bottom-up, as the correctness of components is used to assert the correctness of a compound unit. At any point, the development tree illustrates how a particular task is decomposed into a sequence of subtasks. Equivalently, it shows the sequence of subtasks, each of whose correctness is necessary to assert the correctness of the task.

The lowest level of the tree should be program units whose structure and function are sufficiently simple that they can be clearly understood and exhaustively tested. One can then understand and test at the next level up, in terms of these proven components.

5.2 Independent Test of Procedures

Testing should take advantage of the procedural structure of a program. Each major subroutine should be tested separately. This requires the construction of a "driver routine" -- a program whose sole purpose is to call the procedure to be tested, supply it with arguments and display its results. The idea is essentially the same as the control procedure in Section 2.2 except that the procedure being tested usually has parameters. There is undeniably some extra effort required to write such drivers but it is comparatively modest once you have written one or two of them and the effort is generously rewarded by a reduction of test time when you put the program together.

For example, suppose a program must be protected against a number of special conditions that might occur in its data. The testing provisions might usefully be isolated as a separate procedure:

```
*PROCESS
/* DETECT AND CORRECT EACH CATACHRESIS IN A(1:N) */
DATATEST: PROCEDURE(A, N);
    DCL A(*) FLOAT DEC;
    DCL N FIXED DEC;
        ...
    END DATATEST;
```

This subroutine can be tested by the following type of driving routine:

```
*PL/C ID='J. MORE'
/* TESTING DRIVER FOR DATATEST */
DTDRIVER: PROCEDURE OPTIONS(MAIN);
    DCL X(10) FLOAT DEC;
    DCL N FIXED DEC INIT(10);
    DCL I FIXED DEC;
    /* LOAD AND PRINT X(1:N) */
        PUT SKIP LIST('ARRAY SIZE IS', N);
        LP_LOOP: DO I = 1 TO N BY 1;
            GET LIST(X(I));
            PUT SKIP LIST(X(I));
            END LP_LOOP;
    CALL DATATEST(X, N);
    PUT SKIP(2) LIST('CORRECTED ARRAY AFTER DATATEST');
    RESULT_LOOP: DO I = 1 TO N BY 1;
        PUT SKIP LIST(X(I));
        END RESULT_LOOP;
    END DTDRIVER;
*PROCESS
/* DETECT AND CORRECT EACH CATACHRESIS IN A(1:N) */
(CHECK(T, V, L6)):
DATATEST: PROCEDURE(A, N);
    ...
    END DATATEST;
*DATA
```

5.2.1 Testing with Dummy Procedures

It is often useful to replace actual procedures with highly simplified versions during program development and testing. The simplest replacement is just a dummy procedure that returns immediately upon entry without doing anything at all. This strategy can allow the testing of the calling procedure before the called procedure has been written, or before the called procedure has been thoroughly tested. It can also be used to shortcut the action of a fully-tested procedure just to reduce the cost (or printing volume) of testing the calling procedure.

For example, in Section 5.2 certain error-checking provisions of a program are isolated in a procedure DATATEST. For initial testing of the main program, using carefully prepared, error-free data, these provisions are not needed and the program could be run with the following version of DATATEST:

```
*PROCESS
/* DUMMY VERSION OF INPUT ERROR-CHECKING ROUTINE */
DATATEST: PROCEDURE(A, N);
    DCL A(*) FLOAT DEC;
    DCL N FIXED DEC;
    RETURN;
    END DATATEST;
```

This dummy version of DATATEST looks like the real DATATEST to the calling procedure. As far as the calling procedure knows, the real DATATEST is present performing the required checking -- but never discovering anything wrong. The dummy and real versions of DATATEST can be interchanged repeatedly as program testing proceeds.

Sometimes it is desirable to have the dummy procedure report each time it is called and display the values of the arguments given in the call. A dummy version of DATATEST that would report in this way is shown below.

```
*PROCESS
/* DUMMY VERSION OF INPUT ERROR-CHECKING ROUTINE */
DATATEST: PROCEDURE(A, N);
    DCL A(*) FLOAT DEC;
    DCL N FIXED DEC;
    DCL I FIXED DEC;
    PUT SKIP(2) LIST('DATATEST CALLED.',
        'VALUES OF A(1:N) ARE:');
    PRINT_LOOP: DO I = 1 TO N BY 1;
        PUT SKIP LIST(A(I));
        END PRINT_LOOP;
    PUT SKIP;
    RETURN;
    END DATATEST;
```

Section 5 <u>Examples</u>

```
*PL/C ID='RALPH CONWAY', CMPRS, NOOPLIST

/* CALCULATOR PROGRAM */                                              PL/C-R7.1--66 10/20/75 14:21 PAGE  1

  STMT LEVEL NEST BLOCK MLVL  SOURCE TEXT


                        /* CALCULATOR PROGRAM */
                        /* DATA IS '+' OR '*', FOLLOWED BY 2 NUMBERS */
                        /* REPEAT UNTIL 'F' */
                        /* TEST OF MAIN CONTROL SECTION */
     1                  CALC: PROCEDURE OPTIONS(MAIN);
     2    1         1       DCL (X, Y) FLOAT DEC; /* OPERANDS */
     3    1         1       DCL OPERATION CHAR(1);

     4    1         1       GET LIST(OPERATION);
     5    1         1       OP_LOOP: DO WHILE(OPERATION ¬= 'F');
     6    1    1    1           GET LIST(X, Y);
                                /* PERFORM OPERATION */
     7    1    1    1               IF OPERATION = '+'  THEN DO;
     9    1    2    1                   CALL ADDR(X, Y);
    10    1    2    1                   GO TO FIN_OPN; END;
    12    1    1    1               IF OPERATION = '*' THEN DO;
    14    1    2    1                   CALL MULT(X, Y);
    15    1    2    1                   GO TO FIN_OPN; END;
    17    1    1    1               PUT SKIP(2) LIST('UNKNOWN OPERATION');
    18    1    1    1           FIN_OPN: ;
    19    1    1    1           GET LIST(OPERATION);
    20    1    1    1           END OP_LOOP;
    21    1         1       RETURN;
    22    1         1       END CALC;

*PROCESS


                        /* ADDITION SUBROUTINE */
    23                  ADDR: PROCEDURE(VAL1, VAL2);
    24    1         2       DCL (VAL1, VAL2) FLOAT DEC;
    25    1         2       PUT SKIP(2) LIST('ADDR CALLED WITH', VAL1, VAL2);
    26    1         2       RETURN;
    27    1         2       END ADDR;

*PROCESS


                        /* MULTIPLICATION SUBROUTINE */
    28                  MULT: PROCEDURE(VAL1, VAL2);
    29    1         3       DCL (VAL1, VAL2) FLOAT DEC;
    30    1         3       PUT SKIP(2) LIST('MULT CALLED WITH', VAL1, VAL2);
    31    1         3       RETURN;
    32    1         3       END MULT;

ERRORS/WARNINGS DETECTED DURING CODE GENERATION:

     WARNING: NO FILE SPECIFIED. SYSIN/SYSPRINT ASSUMED. (CGOC)
```

```
*PL/C ID='RALPH CONWAY', CMPRS, NOOPLIST
```

PL/C-R7.1--66 10/20/75 14:21 PAGE   1

```
/* CALCULATOR PROGRAM */

STMT LEVEL NEST BLOCK MLVL  SOURCE TEXT

                              /* CALCULATOR PROGRAM */
                              /* TEST OF ADDITION SUBROUTINE */
                              TESTAD: PROCEDURE OPTIONS(MAIN);
    1                            DCL (T1, T2) FLOAT DEC;
    2    1          1           DCL NBRTESTS FIXED DEC;
    3    1          1           GET LIST(NBRTESTS);
    4    1          1           TEST_LOOP: DO WHILE(NBRTESTS > 0);
    5    1    1     1              GET LIST(T1, T2);
    6    1    1     1              PUT SKIP(3) LIST('NEW TEST');
    7    1    1     1              PUT SKIP LIST(T1, T2);
    8    1    1     1              PUT SKIP;
    9    1    1     1              CALL ADDR(T1, T2);
   10    1    1     1              NBRTESTS = NBRTESTS - 1;
   11    1    1     1              END TEST_LOOP;
   12    1    1     1           PUT SKIP(3) LIST('END OF TESTS');
   13    1          1           END TESTAD;
   14    1          1
```

```
*PROCESS

                              /* ADDITION SUBROUTINE */
                              ADDR: PROCEDURE(VAL1, VAL2);
   15                            DCL (VAL1, VAL2) FLOAT DEC;
   16    1          2           DCL SUM FLOAT DEC;
   17    1          2           DCL MESSAGE CHAR(3) INIT('ADD');
   18    1          2           SUM = VAL1 + VAL2;
   19    1          2           CALL RESULT(MESSAGE, VAL1, VAL2, SUM);
   20    1          2           RETURN;
   21    1          2           END ADDR;
   22    1          2
```

```
*PROCESS

                              /* PRINTING ROUTINE */
                              RESULT: PROCEDURE(OPERN, FIRST, SECOND, ANS);
   23                            DCL OPERN CHAR(*);
   24    1          3           DCL (FIRST, SECOND, ANS) FLOAT DEC;
   25    1          3           PUT SKIP(2) LIST('RESULT CALLED WITH');
   26    1          3           PUT SKIP LIST(OPERN, FIRST, SECOND, ANS);
   27    1          3           RETURN;
   28    1          3           END RESULT;
   29    1          3
```

ERRORS/WARNINGS DETECTED DURING CODE GENERATION:

    WARNING: NO FILE SPECIFIED. SYSIN/SYSPRINT ASSUMED. (CGOC)

```
*PL/C ID='RALPH CONWAY', CMPRS, NOOPLIST
 /* CALCULATOR PROGRAM */                                PL/C-R7.1--66 10/20/75 14:21 PAGE   1

   STMT LEVEL NEST BLOCK MLVL  SOURCE TEXT
                              /* CALCULATOR PROGRAM */
                                 /* DATA IS '+' OR '*', FOLLOWED BY 2 NUMBERS */
                                 /* REPEAT UNTIL 'F' */
                              CALC: PROCEDURE OPTIONS(MAIN);
    1                            DCL (X, Y) FLOAT DEC; /* OPERANDS */
    2    1        1               DCL OPERATION CHAR(1);
    3    1        1               GET LIST(OPERATION);
    4    1        1               OP_LOOP: DO WHILE(OPERATION ¬= 'F');
    5    1        1                 GET LIST(X, Y);
    6    1    1   1                 /* PERFORM OPERATION */
                                       IF OPERATION = '+'  THEN DO;
    7    1    1   1                         CALL ADDR(X, Y);
    9    1    2   1                         GO TO FIN_OPN; END;
   10    1    2   1                     IF OPERATION = '*' THEN DO;
   12    1    1   1                         CALL MULT(X, Y);
   14    1    2   1                         GO TO FIN_OPN; END;
   15    1    2   1                 PUT SKIP(2) LIST('UNKNOWN OPERATION');
   17    1    1   1                 FIN_OPN:;
   18    1    1   1                 GET LIST(OPERATION);
   19    1    1   1                 END OP_LOOP;
   20    1    1   1               RETURN;
   21    1        1             END CALC;
   22    1        1
 *PROCESS

                              /* ADDITION SUBROUTINE */
   23                         ADDR: PROCEDURE(VAL1, VAL2);
   24    1        2             DCL (VAL1, VAL2) FLOAT DEC;
   25    1        2             DCL SUM FLOAT DEC;
   26    1        2             DCL MESSAGE CHAR(3) INIT('ADD');
   27    1        2             SUM = VAL1 + VAL2;
   28    1        2             CALL RESULT(MESSAGE, VAL1, VAL2, SUM);
   29    1        2             RETURN;
   30    1        2             END ADDR;
 *PROCESS

                              /* MULTIPLICATION SUBROUTINE */
   31                         MULT: PROCEDURE(VAL1, VAL2);
   32    1        3             DCL (VAL1, VAL2) FLOAT DEC;
   33    1        3             DCL PRODUCT FLOAT DEC;
   34    1        3             DCL MESSAGE CHAR(8) INIT('MULTIPLY');
   35    1        3             PRODUCT = VAL1 * VAL2;
   36    1        3             CALL RESULT(MESSAGE, VAL1, VAL2, PRODUCT);
   37    1        3             RETURN;
   38    1        3             END MULT;
 *PROCESS

                              /* PRINTING ROUTINE */
   39                         RESULT: PROCEDURE(OPERN, FIRST, SECOND, ANS);
   40    1        4             DCL OPERN CHAR(*);
   41    1        4             DCL (FIRST, SECOND, ANS) FLOAT DEC;
   42    1        4             DCL OPNBR FIXED DEC STATIC INIT(0);
   43    1        4             OPNBR = OPNBR + 1;
   44    1        4             PUT SKIP(2) LIST('OPERATION NUMBER', OPNBR);
   45    1        4             PUT SKIP LIST(OPERN, FIRST, 'AND', SECOND);
   46    1        4             PUT SKIP LIST('RESULT IS', ANS);
   47    1        4             RETURN;
   48    1        4             END RESULT;
 ERRORS/WARNINGS DETECTED DURING CODE GENERATION:

      WARNING: NO FILE SPECIFIED. SYSIN/SYSPRINT ASSUMED. (CGOC)
```

Section 5 Exercises

1.   Write a dummy version of the "list-inquiry" program developed in Section III.2.2 that could be used to test a larger program of which list-inquiry was to be a part.

2.   Repeat exercise 1 for the sorting program developed in Section III.2.3.

3.   Consider the procedure SORT in (IV.1.4a).

   a.   Make a list of the potential problems, special cases, extreme values, etc. that ought to be tested before this procedure is pronounced "correct".

   b.   Devise a set of test data that will reveal a flaw (if one exists) for each of the problems listed in 1.a.

   c.   Devise a "test driver" that will allow the SORT procedure to be tested independently of the rest of (IV.1.4a). The driver should permit several of the test cases developed in 3.b to be combined in a single run.

   d.   Devise a dummy version of SORT that will allow the main procedure SRTG of (IV.1.4a) to be tested without using the actual SORT procedure.

Section 6   Testing Habits and Error Patterns

Testing a non-trivial program is a difficult task, probably requiring as much time, effort and knowledge as the construction of the program in the first place. In testing you are effectively looking for an unknown number of needles in a haystack. Yet too often this search is not conducted in a systematic and intelligent manner. Consequently testing takes longer than it should, and is less likely to reveal all of the errors present. The preceding sections of Part V have described the particular tools available in PL/C and have given suggestions and examples of their use. But it will require both thought and practice to learn to use these tools effectively.

It is helpful to critically analyze your own testing habits by reviewing the course of the battle after testing is completed. For example, how many times have you written a program that ran perfectly on the first try? How many times have you submitted a new program for its first run just to see if it might happen to "work", before giving serious thought to the information you will need to find out why it doesn't work? Once in a great while you may be lucky, but the odds are that you consistently waste the first few computer runs just discovering that something is wrong.

After you have finally tracked down an error, review the strategy of your attack. Knowing what the error is, and where it is, determine what sort of attack would have been most effective. Evaluate each test run to see which runs actually provided useful information. The next error will, of course, be different, but in the long run a pattern will emerge. You will learn what sort of information is generally useful, at what points in a program to seek information, and how to systematically eliminate possibilities. It is good practice to save every output until testing is completed. Then go back and see which runs were wasted and why, and see which errors should have been detected several runs earlier.

Admittedly it is very difficult to force yourself to do this. By the time you finish testing a program you are usually thoroughly sick of looking at it and thinking about it. But unless you learn from this experience you are doomed to repeat it -- and as your assignments become more complex the burden of testing will become overwhelming.

6.1 The Complete Development and Testing Process

The development process described in Part III and the testing process of Part V should be closely interwoven. The steps that should be followed in the development and testing of a significant program are outlined below. Although the steps occur roughly in the order shown, in practice there is a good deal of overlap and backtracking.

1. Clarify the problem requirements (Section III.1.1).

2. Design a program strategy (Section III.1.2), producing a development tree (III.1.2.2) and a comment outline (III.1.2.3).

3. Specify critical data structures (Section III.1.3).

4. Determine the procedure structure of the program (Section IV.2) to suit the higher level of the development tree.

5. Develop the program and test data for each procedure independently.

   5.1 Clarify the functional requirements of the procedure.

   5.2 Clarify the communications interface for the procedure -- the number and types of parameters.

   5.3 Write a dummy version of the procedure (Section 5.2.1) that will serve in place of this procedure in testing other parts of the program.

   5.4 Design an internal strategy for the procedure, producing a development tree and comment outline. (If the procedure is large, repeat the entire process from step 4 at this level.)

   5.5 Write the program -- that is, write the actual program statements to perform tasks described in the comment outline.

   5.6 Verify the program against the algorithm. In particular, check the role of each variable, and the entry and exit conditions for each loop.

   5.7 Add diagnostic facilities -- temporary statements, prefixes, etc. to provide tracing and intermediate results during testing.

   5.8 Design a sequence of test cases, ranging from trivial to maliciously difficult.

   5.9 Write a driving program (Section 5.2) that will permit the procedure to be run independently of the rest of the program. It should permit multiple tests in a single run (Section 2.2).

6. Perform a sequence of diagnostic runs of each procedure separately. When errors are revealed make the necessary corrections. If the error is superficial you can make a correction and continue the process. If the problem is more deeply rooted it may be necessary to abandon testing and return to the development process. That is, if you find a statement is wrong -- fix it; but if you find that the algorithm is inadequate -- start over. Don't apply band-aids to a procedure that needs major surgery.

6.1 The first run should provide enough information to eliminate all syntax and keypunch errors. Follow up each error message until you understand why it was given. Check every line in the XREF-ATR listing to make sure each variable in the program was explicitly declared and has the proper attributes. It may take more than one run to reveal all errors of this sort, since one error can sometimes mask another -- but don't get in the "one bug per run" habit.

6.2 On each run compare the results produced with what you expected (which implies that you know in advance what the answers should be). This comparison involves

a. tracing messages and statement frequency counts to make sure the flow-of-control in execution was as expected, and

b. intermediate as well as final results.

6.3 When the most difficult test cases have passed examination without any surprises, remove the temporary diagnostic provisions for the procedure. (Save a listing that shows these provisions in place so that if it turns out their removal was premature, they can be restored with a minimum of difficulty.)

7. Replace the dummy procedures with real procedures and make final test runs that concentrate on testing the interfaces and communication between procedures. If the program is a large one this should not happen all at once. Insert real procedures one at a time and test after each insertion.

This seems like a very involved process. It is -- because the production of correct programs for substantial problems is a demanding task. Various shortcuts are obviously appropriate for small problems -- but unfortunately the techniques that are tolerable on small problems are too often extended to larger problems. It is essentially impossible to test a medium-sized program (say, 100 statements or more) all at once without any special diagnostic provisions and carefully designed test data. Yet neophyte programmers regularly attempt this impossible task. They spend seemingly endless hours in the battle, and conclude that programming is something to be avoided if possible and otherwise endured. The brief moment of elation when a program finally "runs" is not adequate compensation for the hours of frustration, and is forgotten altogether when the program subsequently fails on the instructor's set of test data.

Large programs can be written to perform interesting and useful tasks. It is a practical and creative process that can yield considerable satisfaction -- and remunerative employment. But the production of reliable programs is a complex and demanding art, which requires time and effort to learn.

Section 7　　Testing with an Interactive System

Section III.2.6 identified the distinguishing characteristic of an interactive system as the ability to communicate with a program during its execution. This provides the opportunity to defer supplying data until the program is actually being executed, and hence allows you to see output up to that point in execution before having to decide what data to supply. III.2.6 shows how this can be used to write truly interactive programs in which the user and the computer cooperate in the solution of a problem.

An interactive system is also valuable during testing of a program. This ability to see intermediate results before supplying further test data can be very helpful. It allows you to accomplish in a single run what would require several runs in a batch system. Even programs that do not require interactive execution once they are established to be correct, can usefully employ interactive execution during testing. A common mode of operation where both interactive and batch systems are available is to test every new program interactively and then, when testing has been completed, to run the program in the more economical batch mode if it does not really require interactive execution.

This ability to postpone the supply of test data would in itself be sufficient justification for the use of an interactive system during testing, but there are two further advantages of testing on an interactive system that are discussed in the following sections.

7.1 Program Entry and Syntax Checking

When program statements are entered on the terminal of an interactive system the syntax checking described in Section 3.1.1 takes place on a statement-by-statement basis, and any errors detected are reported to the user at the terminal immediately after entry of the offending statement. PL/CT, like PL/C, not only reports the errors but also proposes a repaired form of the statement. In PL/C the repaired statement is what is actually used in execution of the program -- since the user

does not see the repair until after execution has been completed
he has no chance to object to it. However, in PL/CT the user
sees the proposed repair as soon as it is made and has the
alternatives of accepting it (by doing nothing) and allowing it
to be used in execution, or rejecting it and reentering the
program with a proper correction.

Unfortunately, in its present form, PL/CT does not allow the
simple replacement of a single statement -- the altered program
must be reentered from the beginning. However, PL/CT is usually
used in conjunction with some "text-editing" system, so that
this alteration and resubmission is not difficult, but there are
several such editors and you will have to get instructions for
their use from your own computing installation.

7.2 The "Terminal Procedure" of PL/CT

During execution of a program, in addition to its role as an
input and output device for GET and PUT statements, the terminal
(and the user) can also act as if it were part of the program.
That is, the execution of the program can be interrupted and
statements can be entered from the terminal for immediate
execution. When you have finished executing statements from the
terminal the execution of the original program can be resumed.
It is somewhat analogous to the action that occurs when a CALL
statement is encountered in execution of a program. The
execution of the calling procedure is interrupted and the
execution of the called procedure is initiated. When execution
of the called procedure is completed execution of the calling
procedure is resumed. Because of this analogy we refer to this
role of the terminal as the "terminal procedure". There are
several ways in which you can "call" this terminal procedure;
that is, ways in which you can interrupt the execution of the
program so you can execute statements from the terminal. These
are:

1. Striking the "attention key" on the terminal.

2. Encountering an execution error in the program.

3. Encountering a "breakpoint" that you have established
   in the program specifically for this purpose.

4. Completing execution of a specified number of
   statements in the normal program.

Initially we will explain just the first two of these methods,
to give a general idea of what is happening, and then give a
more complete explanation involving all four methods.

7.2.1 Attention and Error Calls of the Terminal Procedure

Imagine that there are two integer-valued variables in your program named ATTN_FLAG and ERROR_FLAG, each with initial value 0. Assume that these are somehow "global" variables that are accessible to every procedure in the program. (There is, in fact, such a type of variable in PL/I, but we don't use it in the **Primer**.) Suppose that the effect of striking the attention key on the terminal is to instantaneously assign the value 1 to ATTN_FLAG and that the "execution error routine" of PL/C has been modified so that on every execution error it assigns the value 1 to ERROR_FLAG (in addition to its chores of issuing messages and making repairs).

Now suppose that a conditional call like the one shown below has been automatically inserted <u>before each statement</u> of your original program:

```
IF (ATTN_FLAG = 1) | (ERROR_FLAG = 1)
    THEN CALL TERMINAL_PROCEDURE;
```

These inserted statements are invisible (so they do not appear on the source listing) and unnumbered (so they do not affect the numbering of the original statements). Suppose also that a procedure is automatically added to your program:

```
TERMINAL_PROCEDURE: PROCEDURE;
    ATTN_FLAG = 0;
    ERROR_FLAG = 0;
    statements to be entered from terminal
    END TERMINAL_PROCEDURE;
```

This would mean that anytime your program encountered an execution error it would complete processing of the statement containing the error, including printing the error message and making the usual PL/C repair, but then before beginning execution of the next statement of the original program it would pause and give you the opportunity to enter statements from the terminal. For example, you might want to display the values of certain variables to see why the error occurred, and you might want to change the values of variables to improve upon the repair provided automatically by PL/C. When you have completed action from the terminal the execution of the original program is resumed.

Similarly, if you strike the attention key on the terminal the program will complete the statement currently being executed and call the terminal procedure before beginning the next statement.

Unlike real procedures, this imaginary terminal procedure does not consist of a fixed sequence of statements. Except for the fixed initial statements that reset the flags the terminal procedure consists of whatever statements you enter from the terminal. These statements are executed immediately, one at a

time, and are not saved. In general, the terminal procedure
will be different each time it is called since you will enter
different statements from the terminal. The particular
statements that can be given on the terminal in this way are
described in Section 7.2.3. These statements are called "debug
commands" since their principal use is in "debugging" (testing)
of a program.

Note that the input-output and procedure roles of the
terminal are completely distinct. During testing of a program
you will generally use the terminal alternately in both roles.
Once testing is completed the procedure role is not needed and
the terminal serves only as an input and output device for GET
and PUT statements in the original program. But during testing
it is important that you understand the two roles and know which
one you are using at each instant.

PL/CT helps make the distinction clear by printing a
distinctive message each time the terminal procedure is called.
For example, if you strike the attention key while the program
happens to be executing statement number 162 PL/CT will enter
terminal procedure mode with the message

        ATTN AT STMT 163. DBC:

If an execution error occurs in statement 513 PL/CT will enter
terminal procedure mode with the message

        AFTER EXEC ERROR; NOW AT STMT 514. DBC:

Every PL/CT message that ends with "DBC:" means that the system
is in terminal procedure mode and the proper response by the
user is to enter a "debug command" from the terminal.

There is no automatic message printed on the terminal when
the system comes to the terminal to get data to satisfy the
execution of a GET statement. As noted in Section III.2.6 it is
a good idea to precede each GET statement in the program with a
PUT that will cause a suitable "prompting message" to be printed
on the terminal before each request for data.

7.2.2 Pause and Step Calls of the Terminal Procedure

It is even more useful to be able to enter terminal procedure
mode at specified places in the program, or after executing some
specified number of statements. With such an ability the
terminal can be used to "trace" execution of a program. At each
point of interrupt you can explore the values of key variables
and assign new values as appropriate, and then resume execution
of the program. This can be done by establishing "breakpoints"
in the program -- called "pauses" in PL/CT -- and by "stepping"
the program through execution. These facilities in PL/CT can be
explained by extending the description of the last section.

Suppose that, in addition to ATTN_FLAG and ERROR_FLAG, there
are four other integer-valued global variables and an integer-
valued global array added to your program:

```
DECLARE
     STEP          FIXED DECIMAL INITIAL(c),
     STEP_RESET    FIXED DECIMAL INITIAL(c),
     IGNORE        FIXED DECIMAL INITIAL(0),
     IGNORE_RESET  FIXED DECIMAL INITIAL(0),
     PAUSE(1:n)    FIXED DECIMAL INITIAL((n)0)
```

Assume c in this declaration is some large integer, like 2^{16},
and n is the number of statements in the program. Now suppose
that each statement i in the original program is preceded and
followed by invisible unnumbered statements as shown below:

```
IF (PAUSE(i) = 1) |
   (STEP = 0) |
   (ATTN_FLAG = 1) |
   (ERROR_FLAG = 1)
          THEN CALL TERMINAL_PROCEDURE;
statement i
STEP = STEP - 1;
```

This is analogous to the conditional call inserted in Section
7.2.1 except that there are now four ways of activating the call
instead of only two, and that a "step-counter" is reduced by 1
after each statement is executed. The idea is essentially the
same. The corresponding version of the terminal procedure would
be:

```
TERMINAL_PROCEDURE: PROCEDURE;
     IF IGNORE ¬= 0 THEN DO;
               IGNORE = IGNORE - 1;
               RETURN; END;
     IGNORE = IGNORE_RESET;
     STEP = STEP_RESET;
     ATTN_FLAG = 0;
     ERROR_FLAG = 0;
     statements to be entered from terminal
     END TERMINAL_PROCEDURE;
```

Now assume that ATTN_FLAG and ERROR_FLAG will be assigned value
1 by the attention key and execution error routine, as before.
Assume that STEP_RESET is assigned a value specifying the number
of program statements to be executed before coming back to
terminal procedure mode. Assume that PAUSE(i) has value 1 if
you want to enter terminal procedure mode before executing
statement i, and is 0 otherwise. Finally, assume IGNORE_RESET
has an integer value specifying the number of pauses to be
ignored before coming back to the terminal. The statements that
make these assignments to STEP_RESET, PAUSE(i), and IGNORE_RESET
are debug commands and are described in the next section.

With these assumptions the program can be interrupted to
enter statements from the terminal in each of the four ways
listed in Section 7.2. You can interrupt at will by striking
the attention key, but it is impossible to time this so as to
have any real control over where you are in the program, so it
is less useful than it might seem. The program will be
interrupted after an execution error is detected, which is
useful, but as noted in earlier sections of Part V, the serious
testing really begins after all of the errors that can be
detected by PL/C have been eliminated. Hence you will primarily
use the pause and step interrupts to trace the program and make
certain it is executing as you intended.

7.2.3 Statements in the Terminal Procedure

The statements that can be entered and executed from the
terminal in PL/CT are called "debug commands" because they are
primarily used for debugging or testing a program. Some of
these commands are normal PL/C statements, while some are new
statements -- not part of PL/C -- that are necessary to control
the pause and step calls to the terminal. In each case the
command is executed immediately upon entry at the terminal. It
is not saved, and it does not become part of the program. If it
is to be executed a second time -- it must be entered again from
the terminal.

The debug commands corresponding to PL/C statements have the
same effect as if that statement had been encountered in the
original program. These statements are the following:

        PUT SKIP LIST(list of variables);

        PUT SKIP DATA(list of variables);

        assignment statement
                The right-side of the assignment must be a constant;
                it cannot be a variable or an expression containing an
                operator.

        RETURN;
                End execution of the terminal procedure and resume
                execution of the original program.

        GO TO label;
                End execution of the terminal procedure and resume
                execution of the original program beginning with the
                statement whose label is given.

        CHECK;

        NOCHECK;

        PUT ALL;

        PUT ARRAY;

    The debug commands that are not PL/C statements are the
following. Their actions are explained in terms of the
hypothetical global variables described in Section 7.2.2.

        STEP m;
                Assign value m to STEP_RESET. This will permit m
                statements of the program to be executed, and then
                will call the terminal procedure. This interval will
                be used until another STEP command is given. That is,
                each time execution of the original program is
                resumed, at most m statements will be executed before
                coming back to the terminal.

        PAUSE AT s;
                Assign value 1 to PAUSE(s), the element of the PAUSE
                array corresponding to statement number s. A
                particular statement is specified by giving either its
                number from the source listing, or a label or
                procedure-name that is given as a prefix to the
                statement. That is, the command can be given as

                        PAUSE AT 45;

                or as

                        PAUSE AT SUM_LOOP;

        NOPAUSE AT s;
                Assign value 0 to PAUSE(s).

        IGNORE m;
                Assign value m to IGNORE_RESET. This will cause the
                program to ignore the next m pauses encountered, and
                call the terminal procedure on the m+1 pause.

        PUT s, m;   or   PUT s;
                This command is to display the contents of one or more
                lines from the source listing (since the original
                source listing may not be available at the terminal).
                PUT s, m; means display m lines beginning with the
                line on which statement number s begins. If m is not
                given, one line is assumed.

    You may have noticed that the terminal procedure is not
exactly like the external procedures described in Part IV. The
terminal procedure has no parameters and no local variables or
labels of its own. You can enter statements from the terminal
(PUT, assignment, GO TO) that refer to variables and labels in
the original program, which could not be done in an external
procedure. The explanation is that the terminal procedure is an
example of a different kind of procedure -- called an "internal
procedure" -- that we have not otherwise used in the Primer.
For an explanation of internal procedures see Part VI of our

Introduction to Programming, but the following rule will suffice
for you to use PL/CT:

> Debug commands (statements in the terminal procedure)
> in PL/CT can refer to exactly those variables, labels
> and procedure-names that could be referred to by the
> original program at the point of interrupt.

For example, suppose you were interactively testing the
program given in (IV.1.4a) and you interrupted execution just
before executing the statement with label SW in the procedure
SORT.   In the terminal procedure called from this point you
could display or change the values of variables I and J, and of
parameters X and N, but not the variables in any other
procedure. Similarly, you could refer to the labels MIN_LOOP,
FI and SW since they are local to SORT, but you could not refer
to READ_LOOP or PRINT_LOOP which are in procedure SRTG and not
in SORT.

7.2.4 An Example of Interactive Testing

Suppose you wanted to test the procedure FINDMIN of (IV.1.4a)
on a PL/CT terminal.   After entering the entire program you
would give a PL/C command to begin execution. By specifying the
PAUSE option on this command you would cause the program to
pause immediately after it begins execution of the main
procedure.   It will enter terminal procedure mode with the
prompting message

>   PAUSED AT STMT   2. DBC:

You can use this opportunity to set a pause at label SW in SORT,
but since you are effectively in procedure SRTG you cannot refer
directly to a label in SORT.   However you can refer to
statements by number anywhere in the program, so give the
command

>   PAUSE AT 17;

PL/CT will indicate that this has been done, and request the
entry of the next command by prompting

>   DBC:

Enter the command

>   RETURN;

Program execution will resume and continue until just before the
first execution of the statement with label SW in SORT. PL/CT
will then enter terminal mode with the prompting message

>   PAUSED AT STMT   17. DBC:

To check and make sure you have the right statement you might
give the command

        PUT 17;

and PL/CT would reply

        SW: CALL SWAP(X(I), X(J));
        DBC:

Now you could assign values to the input arguments of FINDMIN:

        I = 1;
        DBC:
        N = 2;
        DBC:

If no assignment is made to X from the terminal the values will
remain as read in SRTG before the call of SORT. You could check
these values with a PUT command.   Now you could execute the
procedure FINDMIN by giving the command

        GO TO FI;

Since the pause is still in place at SW, PL/CT will execute the
single statement with label FI and then return to the terminal
with the prompt

        PAUSED AT STMT   17. DBC:

To see what FINDMIN found to be the minimum of X(1:2) you could
now enter the command

        PUT SKIP LIST(J);

You could then supply new values of I and J, and new values of
X, and repeat the execution of FINDMIN until you are satisfied
that it is correct. Then remove the pause at SW by giving

        NOPAUSE AT SW;   or   NOPAUSE AT 17;

and proceed to test another section of the program.

APPENDIX A   Summary of PL/C Subset Used in PRIMER

The following is a summary of the subset of the PL/C language that is used in the _Primer_. For a description of the full PL/C and PL/I languages see Appendix A of our _Introduction to Programming_.

This Appendix simply indicates what elements of the language are included in the subset. It shows the general form of each construction included, but does not explain what it does or how it should be used. To find the appropriate explanation in the body of the text, look up the keywords of these constructions in the Index.

Program

```
    *PL/C ID='programmer-name' options
    /* Comment describing function of program */
    procedure-name: PROCEDURE OPTIONS(MAIN);
        Declaration of variables;
        Statements;
        END procedure-name;
   *PROCESS options
    /* Comment describing function of procedure */
    procedure-name: PROCEDURE(parameters);
        Declarations of parameters;
        Declarations of local variables;
        Statements;
        END procedure-name;
    ...
   *DATA
        Data list
```

In addition to the program structure shown above, most installations require one or more control cards before the *PL/C card, and one or more control cards after the data list. These cards vary from one installation to another -- get local instructions.

Declarations

```
DECLARE ident1 attributes, ident2 attributes, ... ;
DECLARE (ident1, ident2, ... ) attributes;
DECLARE ident(lb1:ub1,lb2:ub2,... ) attributes;
```

Attributes

```
FIXED DECIMAL
FLOAT DECIMAL
CHARACTER(length)
CHARACTER(length) VARYING
STATIC
INITIAL(constant)
INITIAL(c1, c2, ... )
INITIAL(c1,(r1)c2,(r2)(c3,c4,... ),... )
```

Statements

```
variable = expression;

SUBSTR(s,f,l) = string-expression;

IF condition THEN statement;

IF condition
    THEN statement₁;
    ELSE statement₂;

IF condition
    THEN DO; ... ; END;
    ELSE DO; ... ; END;

loop-name: DO WHILE(condition);
    statement₁; statement₂; ... ;
    END loop-name;

loop-name: DO index-var = expr₁ TO expr₂ BY expr₃;
    statement₁; statement₂; ... ;
    END loop-name;

GO TO statement-label;
    ...
Statement-label:;

null;

CALL procedure-name;

CALL procedure-name(argument variables);

RETURN;
```

```
GET LIST(variables);

GET EDIT(string-variable)(COL(1),A(80));

PUT LIST(variables and literals);

PUT SKIP(n) LIST(variables and literals);

PUT DATA(variables);

PUT SKIP(n) DATA(variables);

PUT ALL;

PUT ARRAY;

CHECK;

CHECK(expression);

NOCHECK;
```

Condition Prefix

```
(CHECK(variables, labels and parameters)):
procedure-name: PROCEDURE...
```

Operators

```
+       -       *       /       **       ||
```

Relations

```
=       ¬=      >       ¬>      >=      <       ¬<      <=
```

Boolean Operators

```
&       |       ¬
```

Comments

```
/* text */
```

Constants

integers (fixed-point)

decimal and exponential (floating-point)

character strings

'1'B, '0'B ("true" and "false" in conditions)

Built-in Functions

```
ABS(x)
ATAN(x)
COS(x)
COSD(x)
EXP(x)
FLOOR(x)
LENGTH(s)
LOG(x)
LOG10(x)
MAX(x1,x2,...,xn)
MIN(x1,x2,...,xn)
MOD(x,y)
SIN(x)
SIND(x)
SQRT(x)
SUBSTR(s,f,l)   and   SUBSTR(s,f)
TAN(x)
TAND(x)
```

Pseudo-variable

SUBSTR(s,f,l)   and   SUBSTR(s,f)

Abbreviations

```
DCL for DECLARE
DEC for DECIMAL
INIT for INITIAL
CHAR for CHARACTER
VAR for VARYING
```

APPENDIX B   Operating Procedures for PL/C

Appendix B.1 <u>Program Deck Structure</u>

1. The control cards described below are only those for PL/C.
Other cards may be required in front of these to invoke PL/C, or
after the program to end the "job", depending on your computer
system.   Get local instructions for those cards. PL/C control
cards have * in column 1 and a keyword starting in column 2 (see
B.3.1):

>   *PL/C or *PLC
>   *PROCESS
>   *OPTIONS
>   *DATA

2. *PL/C precedes each separate program (several programs may
be run together as a single job). If a program has more than
one external procedure the procedures are separated by *PROCESS.

3. If data cards are needed, a *DATA card follows the program
and the data follows *DATA (but not on the same card as *DATA).
If no data is present, *DATA is optional.

4. PL/C uses whatever space or "region" is assigned to it by
the operating system.   A minimum of about 100K is required.
Methods of specifying region size vary; get local instructions.

B.1.1 <u>Examples of PL/C Card Decks</u>

These examples are to illustrate the placement of control cards to separate program cards and data cards, and to illustrate batching of several programs as a single job. For more detail on the internal structure of a program deck see the beginning of Appendix A.

1. Single program without data:
    *PL/C options
        source program cards

2. Single program with data:
    *PL/C options
        source program cards
    *DATA
        data cards

3. Program with main and external procedures
    *PL/C options
        source program cards for main procedure
    *PROCESS options
        source program cards for external procedure
    *DATA
        data cards

4. Three independent programs run as one job:
    *PL/C options
        source program cards for program 1
    *DATA
        data cards for program 1
    *PL/C options
        source program cards for program 2 (main proc)
    *PROCESS options
        source program cards for program 2 (ext. proc)
    *DATA
        data cards for program 2
    *PL/C options
        source program cards for program 3

B.2 <u>Program Options</u>

Two (equivalent) samples are:

    *PL/C ID='KATHY CONWAY', XREF, ATR, TIME=(0,30)
    *PL/C I='KATHY CONWAY' X A T=(,30)

Options may be specified on *PL/C, *PROCESS or *OPTIONS cards. Options may be given in any combination, in any order, separated by blanks and/or commas. They may be continued onto a card with * in column 1 and columns 2-3 blank. But an individual option may not be split over a card boundary. Options may be abbreviated or misspelled; only a few key letters are significant, as indicated in the listing of options below.

The prefix letters N or NO designate negated options. Certain
options can only be given on the *PL/C card, as noted.

    Options on the *PL/C card, and the default values for options
not specified, are in effect throughout the program, except as
temporarily overridden on *PROCESS and *OPTIONS cards. *PROCESS
options apply only to the one external procedure following that
card. *OPTIONS options apply only to the remainder of the
external procedure in which the card appears. After each
external procedure, options are reset to the "global" *PL/C and
default values.

    In the listing below the normal default value of each option
is underlined, but these choices are easily changed by each
installation, and yours may be different from what is shown
here. In addition, each installation can override options so
that user specification of such options is ineffective. This
listing does not include all PL/C options -- see the PL/C User's
Guide.

ATR, NOATR, A
    Produce attribute listing.

BNDRY, NOBNDRY, B
    Strings and comments limited by card boundary.

DUMP, DUMP=(d1,d2,...), NODUMP, D (on *PL/C only)
    Produce post-mortem dump.
    Dump options are:
        BLOCKS, B
            Traceback of blocks active at termination.
        SCALARS, S
            Final values of scalar variables in active
            blocks. (Implies B.)
        ARRAYS, A
            Final values of arrays in active blocks.
            (Implies S and B.)
        FLOW, F
            History of last 18 transfers of control.
        LABELS, L
            List of labels with frequency of encounter.
        ENTRIES, E
            List of entry-names with frequency of call.
        REPORT, R
            Statistics on run (time, core usage,
            auxiliary I/O operations, etc.)
        UNREAD, U
            List of first 5 or fewer unread data cards.
        Depth
            An integer giving limit on number of active
            blocks for B, S and A dump options. If 0 is
            given, depth is unlimited.
    Supplied default DUMP options are (B,S,F,L,E,R,U,0).

DUMPE, <u>DUMPE</u>=(d1,d2,...), NODUMPE, DE (on *PL/C only)
    Produce post-mortem dump only if error was encountered
    during execution.
    Supplied default DUMPE options are (B,S,F,L,E,R,U,0).

DUMPT, <u>DUMPT</u>=(d1,d2,...), NODUMPT, DT (on *PL/C only)
    Produce post-mortem dump only if execution was terminated
    by an error.
    Supplied default DUMPT options are (B,S,F,L,E,R,U,0).

ERRORS=(c,r), E (on *PL/C only)
    Suppress execution if c or more compile errors.
        If c=0 suppress execution unconditionally.
    Terminate execution after r runtime errors.
        If r=0 there is no limit on runtime errors.
    Supplied default c=50, r=50.

FLAGE, <u>FLAGW</u>, FE, FW
    FLAGW prints both warnings and error messages.
    FLAGE suppresses warnings.

ID='name', I (on *PL/C only)
    Program identification name (20 characters maximum).
    Supplied default name = '*** NO ID ***'

LINES=n, L (on *PL/C only)
    Maximum number of lines to be printed.
    Supplied default n=2000.

PAGES=n, P (on *PL/C only)
    Maximum number of pages to be printed.
    Supplied default n=30.

SORMGIN=(s,e), SORMGIN=(s,e,c), SM
    Establish source card margins:
        s is first column scanned; supplied default s=2.
        e is last column scanned; supplied default e=72.
        c is carriage control column; supplied default c=1.
           (See item 2 in B.3.2.)

<u>SOURCE</u>, NOSOURCE, S
    Print source program listing.

TIME=(m,s), T (on *PL/C only)
    Time limit (compilation + execution).
        m is minutes; blank is equivalent to 0;
           supplied default m=0.
        s is seconds; blank is equivalent to 0;
           supplied default s=15.

<u>UDEF</u>, NOUDEF, U (on *PL/C only)
    Monitor use of uninitialized variables.

XREF, <u>NOXREF</u>, X
    Produce cross-reference listing.

B.3 Card Formats

For all types of cards the contents of columns 1 and 2 may be significant to the "operating system" and cause a card to be intercepted and never reach PL/C. The characters // in columns 1 and 2 are significant to most IBM systems, and the characters /* are significant to some. Both combinations should be avoided in 1-2 of all cards (data cards as well as program). A common error is to begin a comment in column 1. If a card with // in 1-2 reaches PL/C:

  1. If 3-80 are blank it is treated as an end-of-file and it terminates the program. PL/C expects either a *PL/C card to begin a new program or to have the job ended by the operating system. Any number of consecutive // cards with 3-80 blank are equivalent to one.

  2. If 3-80 are not blank the entire card is ignored.

B.3.1 Control Cards

Control cards have * in column 1. (Some installations may use another character instead of *.) The control keyword -- PL/C, PROCESS, OPTIONS or DATA -- begins in 2. The continuation of a control card has * in 1 and 2-3 blank. Control cards are not affected by SORMGIN. Options on control cards can be in any order, separated by blanks and/or commas, but not split over a card boundary.

B.3.2 Program Cards

1. The default card field for source statements is 2-72. The contents of 73-80 are ignored, but appear on the source listing.

1a. Columns to the right of the right margin (default 73-80) can be used for identification and numbering. A four-character abbreviation of the program name can be punched in 73-76, and automatically duplicated from one card to the next (see Appendix B.3.4). Cards should be serially numbered in 77-80 with initial numbers in intervals of ten or more to leave room for later insertions. For example, a sorting program might be identified and initially numbered:

                    SORT0010
                    SORT0020
                    SORT0030
                      ...

Card numbering seems unnecessary until you or the computer operator drops one of your decks.

2. The default position for the specification of carriage control for the listing of the source program is column 1. Carriage control characters do not appear on the source listing. Only 5 of the USASI codes are recognized for this purpose:

<blank>   space 1 line before printing (normal mode)
0   space 2 lines before printing
-          space 3 lines before printing
+   do not space before printing (overprint)
1   skip to channel 1 (page eject)

2a. If any character other than these five appears in column 1 PL/C assumes that text accidentally began in 1 instead of 2.

3. The default source card format can be altered by specifying SORMGIN on the *PL/C, *PROCESS or *OPTIONS card. The form is:

    SORMGIN = (s,e,c)
        where: s is the leftmost column to be included
                 e is the rightmost column to be included
                 c is the column for carriage control

The maximum column specification is 100, and the carriage control column must be outside of the s,e field. If SORMGIN is used paragraphs 1 and 2 above must be altered accordingly. The correction in 2a only applies when s=2 and c=1.

4. When the BNDRY option is in effect (usually the default), PL/C does not permit any element to be split over a card boundary. That is, keywords, identifiers, constants and comments cannot start on one card and continue on the next. This limits the length of literals, and means that for long comments each card must be a separate comment.

When NOBNDRY is specified, literals and comments may be continued over a card boundary (as in PL/I). The maximum length of a literal is then 256 characters. There is no limit on the length of a comment. Note that the card boundary is as defined by the SORMGIN option and not the physical card boundary. For example, with the default SORMGIN of (2,72,1) column 2 directly follows 72 of the previous card -- no blank is supplied. Note also that NOBNDRY applies only to literals and comments. In PL/C one still cannot continue a keyword, an identifier or an arithmetic constant over a card boundary.

B.3.3 Data Cards

The card field for data cards is always 1 to 80. Data cards are not affected by the SORMGIN or BNDRY options. Data cards are considered to be a continuous stream of characters and the card boundary is of no significance. That is, column 1 of a card directly follows 80 of the previous card, and any element may be continued over a card boundary.

B.3.4 Format Control on the Keypunch

The use of program format to emphasize the structure of a program requires a convenient means of indenting. The keypunch offers a facility comparable to the "tab stops" on a typewriter for this purpose. The "stops" are set by a control card which is placed around a drum in the upper center of the IBM 029 keypunch. When the "star wheels" are lowered onto the face of this drum (by depressing the left side of the toggle switch just below the drum), pushing the SKIP key on the keyboard will cause the card to advance to the next "stop" position, specified by a field-starting punch as shown below.

The drum control card also controls automatic skipping, automatic duplication (copying from one card to the next), and the alpha/numeric shift of the keyboard. Consider the control card to be divided into sets of adjacent columns called "fields". One character is used to start a field (in the left-most column), and another to continue the field:

Type of field:	To start:	To continue:
alpha shift	1	A
numeric shift	blank	&
automatic skip	-	&
automatic duplicate	/	A

The alpha/numeric shift in the control card can be overridden by the ALPHA and NUMERIC keys on the keyboard. For the automatic skip and automatic duplicate to be effective the AUTO SKIP DUP switch at the left top of the keyboard must be ON (in the up position).

The following is a generally useful drum control card:
    1; automatic skip
    2-5, 6-9, 10-13, 14-17, ...; alpha fields with
                    stops every four columns
    73-76; automatic duplicate (for program identification)
    77-80; numeric (for card serial number)

The control card would be punched as follows:

```
                 1         2         3         4
columns    12345678901234567890123456789012345678 90
cont.char  -1AAA1AAA1AAA1AAA1AAA1AAA1AAA1AAA1AAA1AA

                 4         5         6         7         8
columns    12345678901234567890123456789012345678 90
cont.char  AAAAAAAAAAAAAAAAAAAAAAAAAAAAAAAAAA/AA &&&&
```

With this drum card, to punch a PL/C control card with a * in column 1 you have to momentarily turn off the AUTO SKIP DUP switch to suppress the skip over column 1.

   If you do not want to use columns   73-80   for   card
identification, columns 73-80 of the control card would be
punched as follows, to automatically release the card as soon as
column 72 is punched, and feed a new card:

                                            7   8
        columns   34567890
        cont.character   -&&&&&&

   Without an automatic skip or duplicate in column 73 it is
easy to accidentally continue punching program text beyond
column 72 and the result can be mystifying. Characters in 73-80
are not scanned by PL/C (unless directed to by the SORMGIN
option), but since they are printed it is not obvious that they
have been ignored. This often produces errors for a statement
that looks correct on the listing.

APPENDIX C   The PL/CT Interactive System

Appendix C is taken directly from the PL/CT User's Guide, distributed by the Department of Computer Science and the Office of Computer Services of Cornell University.

PL/CT - A Terminal Version of PL/C
Release 2

User's Guide to the Cornell-CMS Version

C. G. Moore III, S. L. Worona and R. W. Conway

PL/CT is a special version of PL/C designed to permit programs to be run interactively from a typewriter terminal. It is completely compatible with normal PL/C -- that is, the source languages accepted by PL/C and PL/CT are identical and the results of execution are exactly the same. Hence a program can be developed and tested under PL/CT and subsequently run under normal PL/C (or vice-versa).

PL/CT permits the user to interact with the program during its execution. Output will be printed on the terminal and input data may be requested from the terminal. The course and rate of execution can be controlled from the terminal. It is also possible to interrupt execution and display and alter the values of variables. However, the source program itself cannot be changed under PL/CT. PL/CT receives a complete program, compiles it, and then executes it in interactive mode. But to make any change in the program it is necessary to leave PL/CT, make the change under the CMS editor, and then present the modified program to PL/CT for complete recompilation.

This Guide provides only minimal information about CMS, perhaps sufficient for very straightforward programming tasks. For additional information see the following publications: IBM VM/370: Command Language Guide for General Users (GC20-1804); IBM VM/370: EDIT Guide (GC20-1805); IBM VM/370: Terminal User's Guide (GC20-1810).

Levels and Modes

The most complicated aspect of using CMS-PL/CT is understanding that you are communicating with the system at several different levels. Sometimes you are entering commands telling the command processor what to do, sometimes you are entering lines that are PL/I source statements, and sometimes you are entering data required for the execution of your PL/I program. It is essential that you understand the difference between these levels, and that you understand the means by which you indicate the proper level to the system.

CMS handles this problem of levels by establishing different "modes" of communication. The highest level is called command mode. When the system is in command mode it assumes that anything entered is a command (and not a program line or data). Two of these commands change the mode of the system: the EDIT command causes the system to enter EDIT mode; the PLC command causes it to enter PL/CT mode. When the system is in EDIT mode it assumes that anything entered is an EDIT sub-command. One of these sub-commands causes the system to shift to INPUT mode in which it assumes that everything entered is a line to be stored in a dataset. Similarly there are modes within PL/CT that determine whether input from the terminal is considered to be source program lines, execution data, or execution debugging sub-commands. It is difficult to describe, but it works fairly naturally in practice. The relationship between levels, modes, commands and sub-commands can be summarized in the following table:

CMS Command Mode
    Input:
        EDIT to enter EDIT mode
        ERASE to delete a dataset
        LISTFILE to list the names of datasets
        LOGOFF to end the terminal session
        PLC to enter PL/CT mode

    ## EDIT Mode
        Input: (sub-commands)
            INPUT to enter INPUT mode
            DELETE to delete 1 or more lines
            LOCATE to locate a certain line
            CHANGE to change part of a line
            TYPE to display 1 or more lines
            TOP, BOTTOM, UP, DOWN to move the line pointer
            SAVE to save a copy of a dataset
            QUIT to return to command mode

        ## INPUT Mode
            Input:
                Lines to be inserted in dataset
                Null line to return to EDIT mode

<u>PL/CT Mode</u>
>   Input:
>   Source program lines
>   Execution data
>   Debug commands
>   Returns to CMS command mode when program execution
>   is completed, or STOPped, or two
>   consecutive ATTNs occur.

Command Mode

The system indicates that it is in command mode with the prompting message 'R; T=runtime time-of-day'.

<u>Commands</u> (optional abbreviation below full form)

EDIT dataset-name PLC
E

>   "Dataset-name" is a string of not more than 8 characters, beginning with a letter.

>   If "dataset-name" is the name of an existing dataset, then EDIT will retrieve that dataset and <u>EDIT mode</u> is entered to allow you to make modifications to that dataset. If "dataset-name" is not the name of any existing dataset, then EDIT will create a new dataset with that name. In this case, when you enter <u>EDIT mode</u>, EDIT will type "NEW FILE", to indicate it has created a new, empty dataset. You should then use the INPUT sub-command to enter lines into the new dataset.

ERASE dataset-name
>   Delete the indicated dataset.

LISTFILE * * A
L

>   List the contents of your dataset catalog -- the names of all your datasets. (The names will appear in "full" form, rather than the simple form that is sufficient for the purposes described here.)

LOGOFF
>   End the terminal session. The system will reply with a line giving the cost of the session. The system leaves command mode and will accept no further commands. Turn off the terminal and the coupler and replace the telephone handset.

PLC sp-list DATA(d-list) OPTIONS(op-list) PAUSE SAVE n
>   Cause the system to enter <u>PL/CT mode</u> to compile and execute a PL/C program. "Sp-list" specifies the source program; "d-list" specifies the input data for execution of the program; "op-list" specifies PL/C options; PAUSE causes a

return to the terminal before beginning execution of the
program; "SAVE n" saves n lines of the source listing for
display during execution. All of the phrases after PLC are
optional; their order is immaterial except that sp-list (if
given) must come first.

Because of CMS restrictions a PLC command must not contain
a sequence of more than 8 characters without a blank
character appearing. This will not be a problem if you use
the following rules in typing a PLC command:
     (1) always type a blank after a comma
     (2) always type a blank before or after a
          parenthesis (left or right)
     (3) use dataset-names of 6 characters or less

     The source-program dataset (specified by sp-list)
contains lines equivalent to the source program cards
submitted to batch-PL/C -- including PL/C control cards
(*PL/C, *PROCESS, etc.) Sp-list should be given in one of
the following forms:
     1. a dataset name
     2. an asterisk, indicating program will be entered
     from the terminal. This is the default assumption if
     no source-program-list is given.
     3. a list of dataset names, separated by commas and
     enclosed in parentheses. The datasets listed are
     "concatenated" -- the first line of one dataset
     follows the last line of the predecessor dataset on
     the list -- and presented as a single dataset to
     PL/CT.

     Data for the execution of the program is obtained in one
of the following ways:
     1. If the concatenated source-program dataset
     contains a *DATA line, input data will be drawn from
     that dataset. The DATA option on the PLC command
     should be omitted.
     2. If there is no *DATA line in the source-program
     dataset <u>and</u> the DATA option is omitted, then DATA(*)
     is assumed and PL/CT will return to the terminal for
     input data.
     3. If there is no *DATA line in the source-program
     dataset and the DATA option is given on the PLC
     command then input data will be drawn from the dataset
     concatenated from the items given in d-list. Items
     may be datasets or asterisks, as in sp-list.

When a dataset is entered from the terminal, its end must
be indicated by entering a null line consisting of simply a
carriage return.

     Op-list specifies PL/C options to be applied <u>after</u> any
options that may be given on a *PL/C card in the source-
program dataset. (This may be used to override the *PL/C
options. A *PL/C card need not be present.) Remember when

typing in this list that CMS will not accept more than 8
characters without a blank.

    PAUSE is given if you want your program to enter debug
mode   just   before   program execution begins.   It is
equivalent to pressing "ATTN" just as program execution
begins (which is hard to do).   This will give you the
opportunity to set PAUSEs in the program before it begins
to execute.

    PL/CT will save a copy of the source listing for display
during execution unless the NOSAVE option is given. SAVE n
saves the <u>first n lines</u> of the listing.   The default is
SAVE 200.   This feature uses a lot of memory, so if you
don't need it, specify NOSAVE; if you have a small program,
specify an n < 200.

    Examples:
      PLC
            Both source program and input data are to come
            from the terminal. The source program lines must
            conclude with a *DATA line to initiate execution,
            just as in batch-PL/C.
      PLC PROB1
            Source program is to come from dataset PROB1. If
            this includes a *DATA card it will also supply
            data, otherwise data will come from the terminal.
      PLC * DATA (P1DATA) SAVE 50
            Source program is to come from the terminal;
            input data from P1DATA. Save only 50 lines of
            the source listing.
      PLC PROX4 DATA (XDATA) OPTIONS (ATR, XREF)
            Source program is to come from PROX4, data from
            XDATA. The cross-reference and attribute listing
            is to be printed.
      PLC (*, PRG1) PAUSE NOSAVE
            Source program is to come first from the terminal
            (perhaps to supply a *PL/C card) and then from
            PRG1; input data is to come from the terminal
            (unless PRG1 includes a *DATA line). Return to
            the terminal before beginning execution. Do not
            save the source listing.
      PLC (CS104, LIBR) DATA (INIT, *)
            Source program is to come from CS104 followed by
            LIBR, data is initially to come from INIT and
            from the terminal when that is exhausted.

Special note: There is a difference between the two
commands PLC * and PLC * DATA (*). The first command
expects the input from the terminal to consist of the
source program, followed by a *DATA card, followed by the
program data. The second form expects the input to consist
of the source program, followed by an end-of-file (carriage
return), followed by the program data.

EDIT Mode

The EDIT facility permits the creation and modification of datasets. The following describes a portion of the full EDIT, assuming you are working with a relatively small dataset and that you have a listing of that dataset available. The full EDIT is much more powerful and flexible than what is described here -- see the IBM VM/370 EDIT Guide (GC20-1805).

The editor keeps track of a "current-line-pointer", which always points to the "current line" in your dataset. Most EDIT sub-commands use the current-line-pointer to determine where editing is to be done, and most alter the current-line-pointer as part of their action. For example, the DELETE command deletes lines beginning with the line pointed to by the current-line-pointer, and then sets the current-line-pointer to point to the next line after those deleted.

EDIT Sub-commands (optional abbreviation below full form)

INPUT
I

> Enter the input sub-mode of EDIT. Subsequent lines are inserted into the dataset after the current line. To terminate this sub-mode enter a "null line" (carriage return only).

DELETE n
DEL

> Delete n lines, beginning with the current line. If n is omitted, delete only the current line. The new current line is the first line after those deleted.

LOCATE /string/ or LOCATE 'string'
L

> Beginning with the current line, search the dataset for the first line containing the sequence of characters given by "string", and make that line the new current line. Use the first form (delimited by slashes) if the string you are searching for contains no /; use the second form (delimited by quotes) if it contains a / but no quotes. If the search is unsuccessful (the string is not found in the portion of the dataset searched) the current-line-pointer is set to point to the last line of the dataset. For example: LOCATE /QQSV/ searches the dataset from the current line to the end of the dataset for the first occurrence of the string of characters "QQSV".

CHANGE /string1/string2/ or CHANGE 'string1'string2'
C

    Replace the leftmost occurrence of "string1" in the current
line with "string2". "String1" and "string2" do not need
to be of the same length. For example, if the current line
is: "THIS IS A LINE" the sub-command: CHANGE /IS/WAS/ would
change the line to: "THWAS IS A LINE".

TYPE n
T

    Print n lines of the dataset, beginning with the current
line. The last line printed becomes the current line.

TOP

    Set the current-line-pointer to an imaginary line before
the first line of the dataset (so that INPUT can be used to
insert lines at the beginning).

BOTTOM
B

    Set the current-line-pointer to the last line of the
dataset.

UP n
U

    Move the current-line-pointer up n lines (1 line if n is
omitted).

DOWN n
DO

    Move the current-line-pointer down n lines (1 line if n is
omitted).

SAVE or SAVE dataset-name PLC
    First form: copy the current version of the dataset into
the file whose name was given in the EDIT command,
replacing the old version. Second form: copy the current
version of the dataset into the file whose name is given in
the SAVE sub-command. EDIT makes a <u>temporary copy</u> of the
specified dataset when you give the EDIT command, and all
<u>changes are performed on this copy</u>. Therefore, if you do
not specify SAVE before QUITing, your changes will be lost.

QUIT

    Terminates the EDIT command. Normally this will be given
just after a SAVE sub-command.

PL/CT Mode

The PL/CT source language is identical to PL/C, but the following default options are different (to reduce the amount of printing):

CMPRS	NOHDRPG
NODUMP, NODUMPE, NODUMPT	NOOPLIST
FLAGE	NOSOURCE

PL/CT Source Program Entry

Programs can be entered in one of two ways:

1. directly to PL/CT from the terminal, or

2. by preparing a dataset which is then
   presented to PL/CT.

For all but trivial programs the second method should be used, since it provides a means of saving the source program for subsequent reuse and/or modification. If a program is presented directly to PL/CT it is not saved in the system and must be reentered to be re-run.

Note that once a source line has been presented to PL/CT (either from the terminal or from a dataset) there is no way within PL/CT to change that line. You must leave PL/CT, change the program, and then re-invoke PL/CT.

Terminal Use During Execution

During execution of a program the PL/CT terminal has two distinct roles:

1. It serves as the normal (that is, SYSIN/SYSPRINT) input/output device for the program. The printed output from PUT statements will appear on the terminal; GET statements will request input data from the terminal (assuming the d-list of the PLC command specifies the terminal). There is <u>no automatic prompt</u> when the program is requesting input data -- hence it is generally good programming practice to place a PUT statement with a prompting message <u>immediately before</u> each terminal GET.

2. In "debug mode" the terminal is used to enter PL/CT "debug commands" -- statements for immediate execution. Debug mode can be entered in the following ways:

   a. Give the <u>PAUSE option</u> on the PLC command that invokes PL/CT. This simulates an "attention interrupt" during the first statement of the program, and enters debug mode before the second statement. This gives you an opportunity to set PAUSEs in the program before its execution begins.

b. Strike the "<u>attention</u>" ("ATTN") key at any time during
program execution. The program will complete execution of
whatever statement is being executed and enter debug mode
before beginning the next statement. If the statement
being executed is a PUT causing printing on the terminal,
the statement will be completed, but actual printing of the
final lines will be suppressed. Moreover, because of the
buffering of printed output both in PL/C and in the
operating system, the handling of printed output on an
attention interrupt is sometimes rather difficult to
understand. <u>Be careful</u> that you hit attention only once,
and then give the system a chance to respond. Hitting two
consecutive attentions (without any intervening action)
will cause the system to leave PL/CT and return to command
mode, losing all trace of the program's execution.

c. After each non-fatal <u>execution error</u>, PL/CT will
automatically enter debug mode. PL/CT prints the usual
error message, makes the usual PL/C error repair, and then
enters debug mode before beginning the next statement.

d. When a <u>PAUSE</u>, or "breakpoint" is encountered in the
source program, PL/CT enters debug mode. PAUSEs may be set
and removed by the debug commands, described below.

e. When a specified number of statements of the original
program have been executed, PL/CT will enter debug mode.
This "STEP interval" can be set by debug commands,
described below.

In each case, PL/CT will print a message indicating the reason
for entering debug mode, and the statement number of the <u>next</u>
<u>statement</u> to be executed. This message will end with the
prompting symbol "DBC:", indicating that PL/CT is in debug mode,
waiting for a debug command to be entered on the terminal.
After each debug command line the prompt "DBC:" will be repeated
to indicate that the system is still in debug mode and is ready
to receive another debug command.

The "debug mode" and the "input data mode" are completely
distinct -- you cannot enter data when PL/CT expects a debug
command, and you cannot enter a debug command when it expects
data.

PL/CT Debug Commands

When the system is in debug mode any of the following commands may be given. Each command is executed immediately; it is not saved, and does not become part of the source program. The format for commands is free-field -- essentially the same as for statements in PL/C, except:
1. Comments are not allowed.
2. Commands may begin in position 1 of the line.
3. Commands cannot be continued onto a second line.

PUT SKIP LIST(variable, ...);
PUT SKIP DATA(variable, ...);
    A restricted form of the PL/C PUT statement. The variable specified can be a scalar, an array, a structure or a subscripted variable with a constant subscript. Variables must be accessible at the point of interrupt under normal PL/C scope rules. Neither expressions nor literals can be given.

    SKIP is assumed and need not be given.

    If neither LIST nor DATA is specified the default output format will be used. If either LIST or DATA is specified, either in a PUT or as a separate command (see below), this sets the default output format. Initially the default is LIST.

    This command may be abbreviated as just "PUT variable;" or just as the variable name alone. That is, assuming that LIST is the default output format, "X;" and "PUT X;" are equivalent to PUT SKIP LIST(X);".

LIST;
    Set the default output format (for debug commands only) to be LIST.

DATA;
    Set the default output format (for debug commands only) to be DATA.

PUT m, n;
    m is a statement number from the source listing, and n is an integer. Display n source lines beginning with the line on which statement m started. If n is omitted from the command, 1 is assumed.

    m can also be given as a label or entry-name, accessible from the point of interrupt under the normal PL/C scope rules.

Variable = constant;
    A restricted form of the PL/C assignment statement. The target variable must be a scalar or a subscripted variable with constant subscript(s). It cannot be a label variable,

an array or a structure. Structure elements must be fully-qualified. Multiple left sides and BY NAME assignment are not allowed.   The right side can only be an arithmetic or string constant -- neither a variable nor an expression is allowed.

STEP n;
    n is an integer. Reset the STEP interval to n, so that PL/CT will re-enter debug mode after execution of n statements of the source program. If n is omitted, 1 is assumed. This STEP interval remains in effect until changed -- it does not just apply to the first RETURN. Note that statements are counted in a manner comparable to PL/C numbering -- that is, END, PROCEDURE, DO are also counted as statements.

NOSTEP;
    Reset the STEP interval to the default value: STEP 2^{16}.

PAUSE AT s;
    Establish a PAUSE before statement(s) s.   s can be given in several forms:

        -a statement number, as given on the PL/C source listing

        -a label or entry-name, which is accessible at the point of interrupt under normal PL/C scope rules

        -an accessible label or entry-name modified by an integer. For example:
            PAUSE AT ERRORPROC+6;
            PAUSE AT TERMLOOP-3;

        -an inclusive range of statements: "s^1 TO s^2" where s^1 and s^2 are any of the forms listed above. s^2 can also be the word END, implying the last statement of the program. For example:
            PAUSE AT 14 TO TERM_LOOP;
            PAUSE AT EVALPROC+3 TO EVALPROC+14;
            PAUSE AT PRINT+6 TO END;

        -ALL, which means "1 TO END".

The PAUSE command may be abbreviated by giving s (or s^1 TO s^2) alone. That is, if a command consists of any of the valid forms for s, "PAUSE AT s;" is assumed.   For example, "36;" is equivalent to "PAUSE AT 36;".

PAUSEs are maintained in a list of fixed length within PL/CT. When this list is full, further PAUSE commands will be rejected. You will have to remove some PAUSEs before new ones can be added.

NOPAUSE AT s;
    Remove the PAUSE (if any) before statement(s) s.   s is
    given in the same forms as for the PAUSE command. Note
    that NOPAUSE can have a range but not a list of arguments.
    That is, "NOPAUSE AT s^1, s^2;" is not valid.   (s2 will be
    considered a separate command -- an abbreviation of
    "PAUSE AT s^2;".)   Also note that since removing the middle
    of a PAUSE range actually creates two ranges, it is
    possible for NOPAUSE to cause overflow of the PAUSE list.

IGNORE n;
    n is an integer. During program execution ignore the first
    n PAUSEs encountered; re-enter debug mode on the n+1st
    PAUSE. If n is omitted, 2^{16} is assumed. This IGNORE count
    remains in effect until changed -- it does not just apply
    to the first RETURN. Initially, the IGNORE count is 0 --
    that is, PL/CT will stop on every PAUSE unless you set the
    PAUSE count to some non-zero value.

NOCHECK;
    Suppress the printing of CHECK output, exactly as in PL/C.

CHECK;
    Resume the printing of CHECK output, as in PL/C except that
    no parameters are allowed on the command.

NOFLOW;
    Suppress the printing of FLOW output, exactly as in PL/C.

FLOW;
    Resume the printing of FLOW output, as in PL/C except that
    no parameters are allowed on the command.

PUT OFF;
    Suppress printing of SYSPRINT output, exactly as in PL/C.

PUT ON;
    Resume printing of SYSPRINT output, exactly as in PL/C.

PUT ALL;
    Display the current values of all automatic, scalar
    variables in the blocks active at the point of interrupt,
    as well as the current values of all static and external
    scalar variables, exactly as in PL/C.

PUT ARRAY;
    Same as PUT ALL but also includes arrays, exactly as in
    PL/C.

PUT FLOW;
    Display recent FLOW history, exactly as in PL/C.

PUT SNAP;
    Display recent calling history, exactly as in PL/C.

RETURN;
>   Leave debug mode and resume execution of the source
>   program. RETURN can be indicated by a null line. That is,
>   after the "DBC:" prompt a carriage return with an empty
>   line is equivalent to a RETURN command.

GO TO label;
>   Leave debug mode and resume execution of the source program
>   starting with the statement whose label is given. This
>   label must be accessible from the point of interrupt under
>   the normal PL/C scope rules.

STOP;
>   Terminate execution of the PL/CT program, exactly as in
>   PL/C.

PL/CT Errors

When errors are detected during <u>compilation</u> of a program the
usual PL/C action is taken. That is, a message is printed, some
repair is automatically effected, compilation continues and
execution will be attempted. (There are a few cases in which
these errors are "fatal" and execution is suppressed.) If the
repair is not satisfactory you must leave PL/CT mode, alter the
source program, and then re-submit it to PL/CT.

Similarly, during <u>execution</u> of the program PL/CT gives the
standard PL/C response -- message and repair -- but then returns
control to the terminal (before executing the next statement of
the program) and requests a debug sub-command.

An error in a debug command will cause a message to be
printed, followed by a prompt "DBC:" for re-entry of the
command. The complete command must be re-entered -- not just
from the point of error. However, if several debug commands
were given on the line containing the error, commands to the
left of the erroneous command will have already been executed
and should not be re-entered.

PL/I and PL/C References

IBM System 360 PL/I Reference Manual, Form C28-8201

IBM System 360 OS PL/I-F Programmer's Guide, Form C28-6594

IBM System 360 DOS/TOS PL/I Programmer's Guide, Form GC24-9005

IBM PL/I Language Specifications, Form C28-6571

PL/C User's Guide, Release 7.5, Department of Computer Science, Cornell University, 1975

PL/CT User's Guide, Release 2/7.5, Department of Computer Science, Cornell University, 1975

PL/C and PL/CT Installation Instructions, Release 7.5, Department of Computer Science, Cornell University, 1975

Conway, R. and D. Gries, *Introduction to Programming, 2nd Edition*, Winthrop, 1975

Conway, R. W. and T. R. Wilcox, "Design and Implementation of a Diagnostic Compiler for PL/I", *Communications of the ACM*, March 1973

Germain, Clarence B., *PL/I for the IBM 360*, Prentice-Hall, 1972

Hughes, Joan K., *PL/I Programming*, Wiley, 1973

Pollack, S. V. and T. D. Sterling, *A Guide to PL/I*, Holt Rinehart Winston, 1969

Weinberg, G. M., *PL/I Programming: A Manual of Style*, McGraw-Hill, 1970

Weinberg, G. M. et al, *Structured Programming Using PL/C*, Wiley, 1973

INDEX

A option, see ATR and ARRAYS options
Abbreviations, 112, 115, 120, 360, 362, 374
ABS function, see Functions
Addition, see Operations
ALGOL, see Programming languages
Algorithm, 179
    source of ideas for, 233
ALL option, see PUT ALL
ALIGNED attribute, see Attributes
ALPHA key, 367
Alphabetic shift, 367
Alternate selection unit, 141
    indentation conventions for, see Indentation
Analysis of a problem, see Problem
And, 48
APL, see Programming languages
Argument,
    array, see Parameter
    matching, see Parameter
Arithmetic expressions, see Expressions
Arithmetic operators, see Operators
ARRAY option, see PUT ARRAY
Arrays, 76
    as arguments, see Parameters
    as parameters, see Parameters
    declaration of, see Declarations
    referring to, 76, 77
ARRAYS dump option, 363
Assignment, 26, 33, 50, 121, 127
    from external data, see Statement, GET
    to strings, 121, 127
Assignment command, 352, 378
Assignment statement, see Statement
ATAN function, see Functions
ATR option, 101, 106, 108, 115, 311, 363
Attention, 348, 349, 377
Attribute listing, see ATR option
Attributes, 22, 358
    ALIGNED, 109, 311
    AUTOMATIC, 108, 275, 311
    BINARY, 114
    CHAR, see CHARACTER
    CHARACTER, 120, 358
    DECIMAL, 18, 22, 358
    DEC, see DECIMAL

        default, 114, 258
        ENTRY, 311
        FIXED, 18, 22, 311, 358
        FIXED BINARY, 114
        FIXED DECIMAL, 18, 22, 108, 311, 358
        FLOAT, 22, 311, 358
        FLOAT DECIMAL, 22, 108, 311, 358
        INITIAL, 115, 121, 257, 311, 358
        INIT, see INITIAL
        length, 120
        precision, 311
        scale, 311
        STATIC, 275, 358
        type, 22
        UNALIGNED, 109
        VARYING, 120, 358
        VAR, see VARYING
AUTOMATIC attribute, see Attributes
Automatic diagnostic services, 309
Automatic repair of errors, see Errors
Automatic storage, see Storage
Automatic variable, see Variable

B option, see BNDRY and BLOCKS options
Backing up, 230
BASIC, see Programming languages
BINARY attribute, see Attributes
Binary search, 191, 235
Blank character,
        use of, 95, 96, 119, 122, 125, 128
BLOCK numbers, 106
BLOCKS dump option, 363
BNDRY option, 363, 366
Body,
        of a compound statement, 56
        of a loop, 45, 50
        of a procedure, 40
Boolean operations, see Operations
BOTTOM sub-command, 375
Bottom-up testing, see Testing
Boundaries, see Card boundaries
Bounds, see Declarations, arrays
Brackets, 22
Branching, see Statement, exit
Breakpoint, 348, 350, 377, 379
Bubble sort, see Sorting
Built-in functions, see Functions

CALL statement, see Statement
        argument of, see Argument
        nesting of, see Nesting
Card boundaries, see SORMGIN option
Card formats, 101, 365
        control cards, 101, 365
        data cards, 101, 366

drum card, see Drum card
    field, 367
    numbering, 365, 368
    program cards, 101, 365
Card reader, 33
Carraige control characters, 366
Case statement, see Statement
CHANGE sub-command, 375
CHAR attribute, see Attributes
CHAR VARYING attributes, see Attributes
CHARACTER attribute, see Attributes
Characters,
    collating sequence of, 119, 125
    legal, 119
    ordering of, 122, 125
Character-valued variables, see Variables, string
CHECK command, 352, 380
CHECK condition, see Conditions
CHECK prefix, see Prefix
CHECK statement, see Statement
Checker-playing program, 211
Checking,
    arrays, 322
    labels, 321
    parameters, 323
    variables, 320
Chess-playing program, 2, 8, 223
Classification of programs, 169
COBOL, see Programming languages
Collating sequence, see Characters
Commands,
    PL/CT debug, 348, 378
    CMS, 370
Comment outline, 181, 220
Comments, 3, 18, 28, 139, 141, 155, 180, 359
Comparison of characters, see Characters
Comparison of PL/I and PL/C, see PL/I
Compiler, 14
Compound condition, 48
Compound statement, 56, 138
    indentation conventions for, see Indentation
Concatenation, 123
Condition, 46, 48, 54, 66, 125, 358
Conditional execution, 53
Conditional statement, 54, 358
    nesting of, see Nesting
Conditions,
    CHECK, 320, 359
    ENDFILE, see End of data,
Confirming correctness, see Correctness
Constant, 359
    integer, see Integer
    string, see Literal
Context limitation, 154
Control cards,

    *DATA, 34, 40, 101, 357, 361
    *OPTIONS, 361
    *PL/C, 3, 101, 105, 357, 361
    *PLC, see *PL/C
    *PROCESS, 256, 361, 357
Control section, see Procedure
Conversion of values, see Values
Correctness,
    confirmation of, 13
    meaning of, 298
    syntactic, 298
    testing for, see Testing
COS function, see Functions
COSD function, see Functions
Cosine function, see Functions
Creation of a variable, see Declaration
Cross reference listing, see XREF option
Current value, see Value

D option, see DUMP option
DATA command, 378
Data, developing notation for, see Notation
*DATA card, see Control cards
Data cards, format of, 36
Data display, 327
DATA format, see GET DATA
Data structure, 182, 188, 197
DBC prompt, 350, 377, 381
DCL, see DECLARE
Debug commands, 378
Debug mode, 376
DEC, see DECIMAL
DECIMAL attribute, see Attributes
DE option, see DUMPE option
Declarations, 18
    bounds, see Declarations, arrays
    default attributes, see Attributes
    factoring in, 22, 116, 120
    form, 111, 358
    grouping of, 112, 183
    implicit, 114
    of arrays, 82, 113
    of character variables, see Declaration, string
    of parameters, see Parameters
    of string variables, 120
    position of, 18, 40, 357
DECLARE, see Declaration
Default attributes, see Attributes
Default options, 105, 363
DELETE sub-command, 374
DEPTH dump option, 363
Design of a program, see Program
Design of test cases, see Test cases
Detection of errors, see Errors
Development, of a program,

Development of a program, see Program
    top-down, see Top-down
Diagnostic PUT options, 360, 380
Diagnostic services, 309
Dimension, see Declarations, arrays
Display, see PUT
Division, see Operations
DO, see compound statement
DO group, see Iterative statement
DO loop, see Iterative statement
DOWN sub-command, 375
Driving routine, 336
Drum card, 367
DT option, see DUMPT option
Dummy procedures, see Procedures
Dump, 106, 109, 316, 326, 363
DUMP option, 316, 363
DUMPE option, 316, 363
DUMPT option, 363
Duplicate on keypunch, 367

E option, see ERRORS and ENTRIES options
EDIT,
    command, 371
    mode, 370, 374
    statement, see GET
    sub-commands, 374
Editor, CMS, 369, 374
ELSE, see conditional statement
Empty string, 120
END,
    see compound statement
    see iterative statement
    see procedure definition
End of data, 7, 10, 34, 68, 86
ENDFILE conditon, see End of data
ENTRIES dump option, 363
Entry-name, see Procedure name
ENTRY attribute, see Attributes
Entry-point, 137, 140
ERASE command, 371
Errors,
    detection of, 15, 108, 309
    during execution, 311, 350, 377, 381
    handling input errors, 85, 176, 196, 242
    keypunch, 101, 109, 114, 115, 311
    repair of, 107, 313, 314
    syntax, 15, 107, 309
    types of, 300
ERRORS option, 315, 364
Escape, see Statement, exit
Execution,
    conditional, see Conditional execution
    errors in, see Errors
    of a program, 14, 105

        output from, see Output
        recursive, see Procedure
        tracing, see Tracing
Execution errors, see Errors
Exit from terminal, see LOGOFF, QUIT, STOP
Exit statement, see Statement
Exit-point, 137, 140
Exp, see Functions
EXP function, see Functions
Exponent, see Operations
Exponential notation, 21, 94
Exponentiation, see Operations
Expressions, 26
        arithmetic, 26, 28
        conversion of value, see Values
        evaluation of, 28
        operators for, see Operations
        string, 121, 123
External data, see Data
External procedure, see Procedures

F option, see FLOW option
False, see Values
FE option, see FLAGE option
Fibonacci numbers, 73, 75
FIXED attribute, see Attributes
FIXED BINARY attribute, see Attributes
FIXED DECIMAL attribute, see Attributes
Fixed-point notation, 360
FLAGE option, 364, 376
FLAGW option, 364, 376
FLOAT attribute, see Attributes
FLOAT BINARY attribute, see Attributes
FLOAT DECIMAL attribute, see Attributes
Floating-point notation, 21, 360
FLOOR function, see Functions
Flow of control, 44, 54, 55, 62, 140, 142, 144, 145
        history of, 110
FLOW command, 380
FLOW dump option, 363
Format,
        of a job, see Job
        of a program, see Program
        of input data, 36, 127
Format control on the keypunch, see Drum card
FORTRAN, see Programming languages
Function,
        argument of, 31
        built-in, see Functions
Functions, 31, 360
        ABS, 31, 90, 296, 360
        ATAN, 31, 360
        COS, 31, 360
        COSD, 32, 360
        cosine, 32, 360

        EXP, 32, 360
        FLOOR, 32, 87, 243, 360
        LENGTH, 32, 124, 360
        LOG, 32, 360
        LOG10, 32, 360
        MAX, 32, 360
        MIN, 32, 360
        MOD, 32, 58, 61, 360
        SIN, 32, 360
        SIND, 32, 360
        sine, 32, 280, 360
        SQRT, 32, 360
        SUBSTR, 32, 123, 127, 129, 360
        TAN, 32, 360
        TAND, 32, 360
FW option, 364, 376

GET statement, 33, 127, 359
        GET EDIT, 127, 359
        GET LIST, 33, 359
GO TO, see Statement, exit
GO TO command, 352, 381
Grouping declarations, see Declarations

Handling input errors, see Errors
Header pages, 106, 376

I option, see ID option
ID option, 364
Identifier, 19
IF, see Conditional statement
IGNORE command, 353, 380
Implicit declaration, see Declarations
Increment of a loop, see Iterative statement
Indefinite repetition, 61, 293
Indentation, 156
        for compound statements, 139
        for conditional statement, 63, 145, 147
        for loops, 53
        for repetition unit, 141
Indentation tab stops, see Drum card
Index variable, 49, 50, 358
INIT, see INITIAL
INITIAL attribute, see Attributes
Initial value, 18
Initialization,
        of repetition, 66, 67
        of variables, 18
Input, see GET
Input data format, see Card formats
Input data mode, 377
Input errors, handling of, see Errors
INPUT mode, 370
INPUT sub-command, 374
Integer,

constants, 360
variables, see Variable
value as subscript, 80
values in data, 85, 242
form in output, 94
Interactive systems, 210, 223, 347, 369
Interchange of values, see Swapping values
Interpreter, 15
Interpretations, 164
Interrupt, 377
Invalid operations, see Operations
Iterative statement, 44, 358
exit problems with, 47, 66
increment, 50, 51, 66
indentation conventions for, see Indentation, loops
initialization problems with, 66, 67
nesting of, see Nesting
termination of, 47, 66

Job, 40, 357, 362
Job format, 40, 357, 362

Keypunch errors, see Errors
Keypunch, format control on, see Drum card
Keypunching, 14, 101, 365
Keyword, 19
Keyword, reserved, see Reserved keywords

L option, see LINES and LABELS options
Label, 57, 358
counts, 110, 317
local, 260
LABELS dump option, 363
Labeling results, 95, 98
Length attribute, see Attributes
LENGTH function, see Functions
Length, of a string, see String length
LEVEL numbers, 106
Levels of a program, 148
Line control, see SKIP
Linear search, 92, 186, 204
LINES option, 364
LISP, see Programming languages
LIST, see GET, see PUT
LIST command, 378
LISTFILE command, 371
Literal, 95
Loading, of a program, 14, 105
Local label, see Label
Local variable, see Variable
LOCATE sub-command, 374
LOG function, see Functions
LOG10 function, see Functions
LOG2 function, see Functions
Logical operators, see Operations

LOGOFF command, 371
Loop, see Iterative statement

Macro level, 106
Main procedure, see Procedure
MAIN in OPTIONS(MAIN), see Procedure
Margins, see Card formats
Match-snatch program, 214
Matrix, 82, 296
MAX function, see Functions
Meaning of correctness, see Correctness
Median, 280
Memory, 14, 22, 110
Memory dump, see Dump
MIN function, see Functions
MLVL numbers, 106
MOD function, see Functions
Modes, 370
Modular testing, see Testing
Multiple subscripts, see Variable
Multiple test cases, see Test cases
Multiplication, see Operations

N-- options, 363
NO-- options, 363
NBNDRY option, 97, 363, 366
Nesting, 51, 62, 271
     conditional, 62
     of iterative loops, 51
     of procedure calls, 271
NEST numbers, 106, 107
NIM-playing program, 223
NOATR option, 363
NOCHECK command, 352, 380
NOCHECK statement, see Statement
NODUMP option, 363
NODUMPE option, 364
NODUMPT option, 364
NOFLOW command, 380
NOPAUSE command, 353, 380
NOSOURCE option, 364
NOSTEP command, 379
Not, 48
Notation,
     floating-point, see Floating-point
     for data, 230
     for statements, 8, 180, 227
     scientific, see Scientific
NOUDEF option, 364
NOXREF option, 364
Null statement, see Statement
Null string, see Empty string
NUMERIC key, 367
Numeric shift, 367

Operating procedures for PL/C, 361
Operations, invalid, 313
Operators, 28, 29, 30, 48, 123, 359
    arithmetic, 28, 30, 359
    Boolean, 48, 359
    logical, 48, 359
    precedence of, 29
    relational, 48
    string, 123
*OPTIONS card, see Control cards
Options, in a job, see Program options
OPTIONS(MAIN), see Procedures
Or, 48
Ordering of characters, see Characters
Outline, comment, see Comment outline
Output, see Statement, PUT
    attribute listing, see ATR option
    cross-reference listing, see XREF option
    post-mortem dump, see Dump
    execution, 42, 93, 106, 109
    source listing, see Source listing

P option, see PAGES option
PAGES option, 364
Parameter, 255, 277
    -argument correspondence, 255, 265
    array, 268
    attribute matching, 256, 263, 268
    character-string, 257
    declaration of, 257
PASCAL, see Programming languages
PAUSE command, 350, 353, 377, 379
PAUSE option, 376
Placement of procedures, see Procedures
PLC command, 371
PL/C, 12
    comparison to PL/I, see PL/I
    examples of card decks for, 362
    operating procedures for, 361
    options in, 362
*PL/C card, see Control card
PL/C symbol, see Symbol
PL/I, 11, 55, 60, 70, 114, 119, 146, 258
    comparison to PL/C, 12, 19, 106, 130, 315, 316, 322, 323
PL/CT, 348, 369
Post-mortem dump, see Dump
Precedence, of operators, see Operations
Precision, 108
Prefix, 57, 320
    CHECK, 320, 359
    label, 57, 358
Print, see PUT
Priority of operators, see Operations
Problem analysis, 9, 176
Problem clarification, 9, 176

Procedure, 249
    body, 261
    call of, 250, 262, 271
    control section, 286
    definition of, 256
    dummy, 338
    entry-name, see Procedure name
    external, 256
    form of, 357
    indentation convention for, 357
    independence of, 289
    internal, 353
    labels in, 260
    local variables in, 259
    main, 40, 105, 357
    nested calls of, 271
    parameter of, 257
    placement of, 256
    procedure-name, 257
    recursive, 274
    RETURN statement, 251
    terminal, 348, 352
    tracing execution of, 266, 270, 274
    use of, 285
*PROCESS card, see Control card
Program,
    design, 179
    development, 175
    execution, see Tracing
    format, 357, 361
    levels, 148
    loading, see Loading
    modification, 160
    predictability, 152
    schema, see Schema
    structure, 133, 357, 361
    translation of, see Translation
    units, 137
    well-structured, 152
Program card, see Drum card
Program options, 106, 357
Programming language, 11
    ALGOL, 11
    BASIC, 11
    COBOL, 11, 12, 31
    FORTRAN, 11, 12, 31, 114
    LISP, 11
    PASCAL, 11, 12
    PL/C, see PL/C
    PL/I, see PL/I
Prompt message, 210, 350
Prompting, see Prompt message
Pseudo-variable, 125, 360
    SUBSTR, 125, 360
PUT ALL, 326, 380

PUT ARRAY, 326, 380
PUT commands, 352, 353, 378
    PUT ALL, 352, 380
    PUT ARRAY, 352, 380
    PUT FLOW, 380
    PUT OFF, 380
    PUT ON, 380
    PUT SNAP, 380
PUT options, 380
PUT statement, see Statement

Question marks, as value, see Undefined value
QUIT sub-command, 375
Quotes, around literals, 95, 127
Quotes, in literals, 97

R option, see REPORT option
Read, see Statement
Real variable, see Variable
Recursive procedure, see Procedure
Refinement,
    ideas for, 233
    limitations for, 226
    of data, 228
    of statements, 225
    suitable notations for, 227
Relations, 48
Repair of errors, see Error
Repetition factor, see Attribute, INITIAL
Repetition unit, 139
Repetitive statement, see Iterative statement
REPORT dump option, 363
Reserved keywords, see Variable
RETURN command, 352, 381
RETURN statement, see Statement

S option, see SOURCE and SCALARS options
SAVE option, 371
SAVE sub-command, 375
SCALARS dump option, 363
Schema, Schemata, 164
Scientific notation, 21
Searching a list, see Linear search and Binary search
Simple statement, 164
Simple variable, see Variable
SIN function, see Functions
SIND function, see Functions
Sine function, see Functions
Skip on keypunch, 367
SKIP option, 94, 359
SM option, see SORMGIN option
SNOBOL, see Programming languages
Solving related problems, 240
Solving simpler problems, 236
SORMGIN option, 364, 366

Sorting, 191, 231, 272
    bubble sort, 233, 335
    successive maxima, 194, 237
Source listing, 42, 106, 371, 376, 378
SOURCE option, 364, 376
SQRT function, see Functions
Square root, see SQRT
Statement, 358
    assignment, 26, 121
    CALL, 262, 358
    case, 146
    CHECK, 323, 327, 359
    compound, see Compound statement
    conditional, see Conditional statement
    developing notation for, see Notation
    exit, 57, 260
    GET, 33, 127
    GO TO, see exit
    input, see GET,
    iterative, see Iterative statement
    label, see Label
    NOCHECK, 324, 327
    null,
    output, see PUT
    PUT, 41, 93, 128
    read, see GET
    repetitive, see Iterative statement
    RETURN, 251, 358
    write, see PUT
STATEMENT LABEL CONSTANT, 312
STATIC attribute, see Attributes
Static storage, see Storage
STATIC variables, see Variable
STEP command, 350, 353, 379
STEP interval, 350, 377, 379
STMT numbers, 106, 107
STOP command, 381
Storage,
    automatic, 275, 311
    static, 275
String,
    assignment, 121
    comparison, 125
    constants, see Literal
    declaration of, see Declarations
    expression, see Expressions
    length, see Attribute, length
    variable, see Variable, string
String operators, see Operations
Structure, of a program, see Program structure
Structured programming, 60, 246
Sub-commands, 370, 374
Subroutine, 285
Subscripted variables, see Variable
SUBSTR function, see Functions

SUBSTR pseudo-variable, see Pseudo-variable
Subtraction, see Operations
Successive maxima, see Sorting
Successive minima, see Sorting
Swappping values, 27, 74, 138, 180, 232, 252
Symbol, in PL/C, 97
Syntax errors, see Errors
SYSIN, 108, 376
SYSPRINT, 108, 376

T option, see TIME option
TAN function, see Functions
TAND function, see Functions
Terminal, 14, 33, 210
Termination, of a unit, 149
TERM_ labels, 59
Test cases, design of, 302
    multiple, 304
    modular testing, 336
Testing correctness, 302
    bottom-up testing, 336
    dummy procedures for, 338
Testing habits, 343
Text-editor problem, 207, 237, 288
THEN, see Conditional statement
TIME option, 364
Titling, 95
TOP sub-command, 375
Top-down programming, 181, 224
Tracing execution, 43, 64
    of procedures, see Procedure
    of nested procedures, see Procedure
Trailer pages, 106
Translation, of a program, 14, 105, 110
Translator, 12, 15
Tree, development, 181, 185, 188, 192, 201, 231
True, see Values
Truncation, 30, see Functions, FLOOR
Type attributes, see Attributes
TYPE sub-command, 375
Types of errors, see Errors

U option, see UDEF and UNREAD options
UDEF option, 364
UNALIGNED attribute, see Attributes
Undefined value ???, see Values
Units, see Program units
UNREAD dump option, 363
UP sub-command, 375
Use of blanks, see Blank
Use of procedures, see Procedure

Values,
    ???, see Value, undefined
    assignment of, see Variable

    Boolean, see Values, true-false
    character, 21
    conversion of, 30
    current, see Variable
    empty string, 120
    initial, see Attribute, INITIAL
    integer, see Integer
    literal, see Literal
    numeric, 21
    real, 21, 22
    true-false, 46, 48, 54, 61, 360
    undefined, 27, 43
Variable, 17
    assignment of value, 17, 25, 115
    attributes, see Attributes
    automatic, see Storage
    character-valued, see Variable, string
    creation of, 17
    current value of, 17
    declaration of, 18, 111
    description of, 17
    identifier, 19, 76
    index, see Index-variable
    initialization of, 21, 115
    integer, 18, 21, 22
    local, 259, 275
    multiply-subscripted, 80
    names, 19, 32
    pseudo-variables, see Pseudo-variable
    real, 21, 22
    reserved keywords, 19
    scalar, 109, 111
    simple, 76, 109, 111
    static, see Storage
    string, 21, 119
    subscripted, 76
Variable-name, see Variable, name
VARYING attribute, see Attributes
VAR, see VARYING
Vector, 82

WHILE loop, 45
Write, see Statement, PUT

X option, see XREF option
XREF option, 101, 106, 108, 115, 311, 364